WAKE UP, PERCY GLOOM!

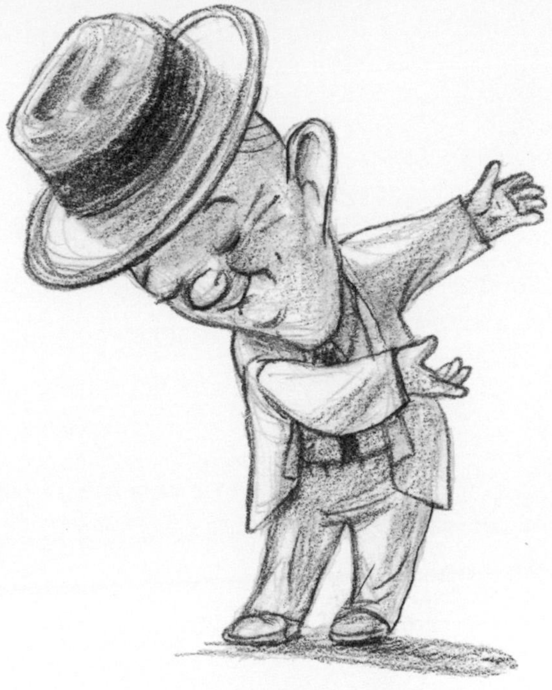

by **CATHY MALKASIAN**

FB

Fantagraphics Books

Other books by Cathy Malkasian:

Percy Gloom (2007)
Temperance (2010)

Fantagraphics Books,
7563 Lake City Way NE
Seattle, Washington 98115

Editor: Gary Groth
Assistant Editor: Jason T. Miles
Design: Emory Liu
Production: Paul Baresh
Associate Publisher: Eric Reynolds
Publishers: Gary Groth and Kim Thompson

To receive a free full-color catalog of comics, graphic novels, prose novels, and other fine
works of artistry, call 1-800-657-1100, or visit www.fantagraphics.com.

ISBN : 978-1-60699-638-6
First Edition: May, 2013
Printed in China

THE FOOL WHO PERSISTS

IN HIS FOLLY

WILL BECOME WISE.

-WILLIAM BLAKE

RECENTLY PERCY GLOOM'S MUM INFORMED HIM THAT
THE TWO OF THEM WERE ALREADY VERY OLD AND WOULD
LIKELY NEVER DIE. THIS NEWS UNSETTLED HIM, BUT IT
RELIEVED SOME CONFUSION, TOO.

THROUGHOUT HIS LIFE PERCY HAD TAKEN LONG NAPS,
ONLY TO WAKE UP YEARS OR SOMETIMES GENERATIONS
LATER.

FLUMMOXED BY ALL THE CHANGE, HE'D ALWAYS
BELIEVED HE'D SLEPT NO MORE THAN A FEW HOURS,
WHILE THE WORLD AROUND HIM HAD GONE MAD
IN A HURRY.

CENTURY AFTER CENTURY HIS MUM WOULD
GUIDE HER SLEEPY SON INTO THE NEW
WORLD'S CUSTOMS AND TABOOS, UNTIL SHE WAS
FINALLY FREE TO TELL HIM THE TRUTH ABOUT
HIS LONGEVITY.

NOT LONG AGO PERCY FOUND HIS IDEAL JOB
AT A FAILING COMPANY. THE FIRST PERSON HE
MET THERE WAS MARGARET. WHEN THEIR JOB
PROSPECTS FIZZLED, PERCY GAVE MARGARET
A TRINKET TO TAKE HER MIND OFF HER
TROUBLES. HIS MUM HAD INVENTED IT AS A
MEANS TO RELIEVE LONELINESS.

THE TRINKET SEEMED TO HAVE AMAZING
PROPERTIES, AND MARGARET LAUNCHED
A NEW LIFE BASED ON WHAT SHE SAW
IN IT. PERCY FEARED THAT HER RECKLESS
OPTIMISM WOULD BRING HER TO HARM.

HE DECIDED TO PROTECT HER, AND FOLLOWED
HER WHEREVER SHE WENT.

NOW HE CAN ONLY DREAM OF
THEIR LIFE TOGETHER...

... BECAUSE HE IS NAPPING AGAIN...

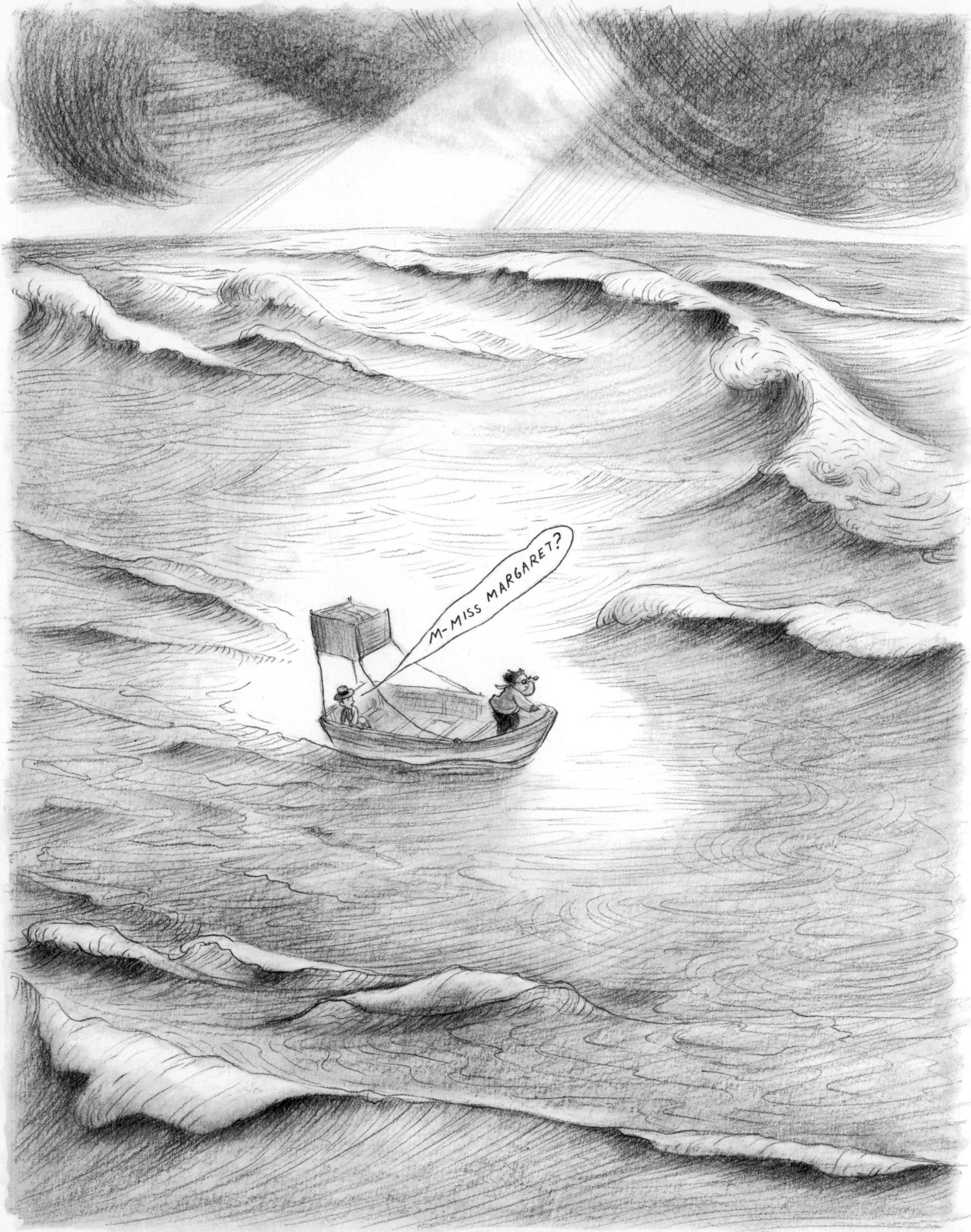
M-MISS MARGARET?

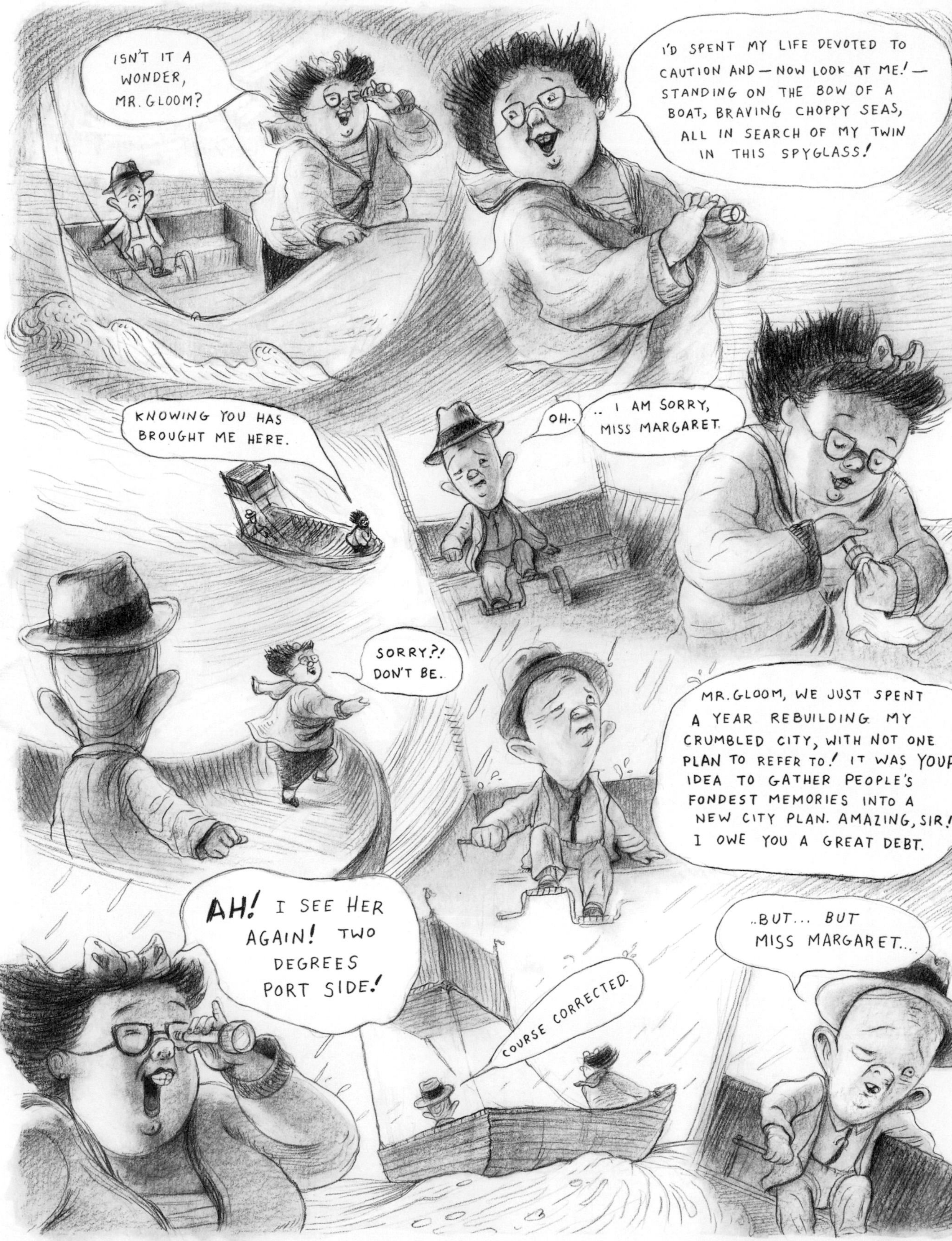
ISN'T IT A WONDER, MR. GLOOM?
I'D SPENT MY LIFE DEVOTED TO CAUTION AND — NOW LOOK AT ME! — STANDING ON THE BOW OF A BOAT, BRAVING CHOPPY SEAS, ALL IN SEARCH OF MY TWIN IN THIS SPYGLASS!
KNOWING YOU HAS BROUGHT ME HERE.
OH..
.. I AM SORRY, MISS MARGARET.
SORRY?! DON'T BE.
MR. GLOOM, WE JUST SPENT A YEAR REBUILDING MY CRUMBLED CITY, WITH NOT ONE PLAN TO REFER TO! IT WAS YOUR IDEA TO GATHER PEOPLE'S FONDEST MEMORIES INTO A NEW CITY PLAN. AMAZING, SIR! I OWE YOU A GREAT DEBT.
AH! I SEE HER AGAIN! TWO DEGREES PORT SIDE!
COURSE CORRECTED.
..BUT... BUT MISS MARGARET...

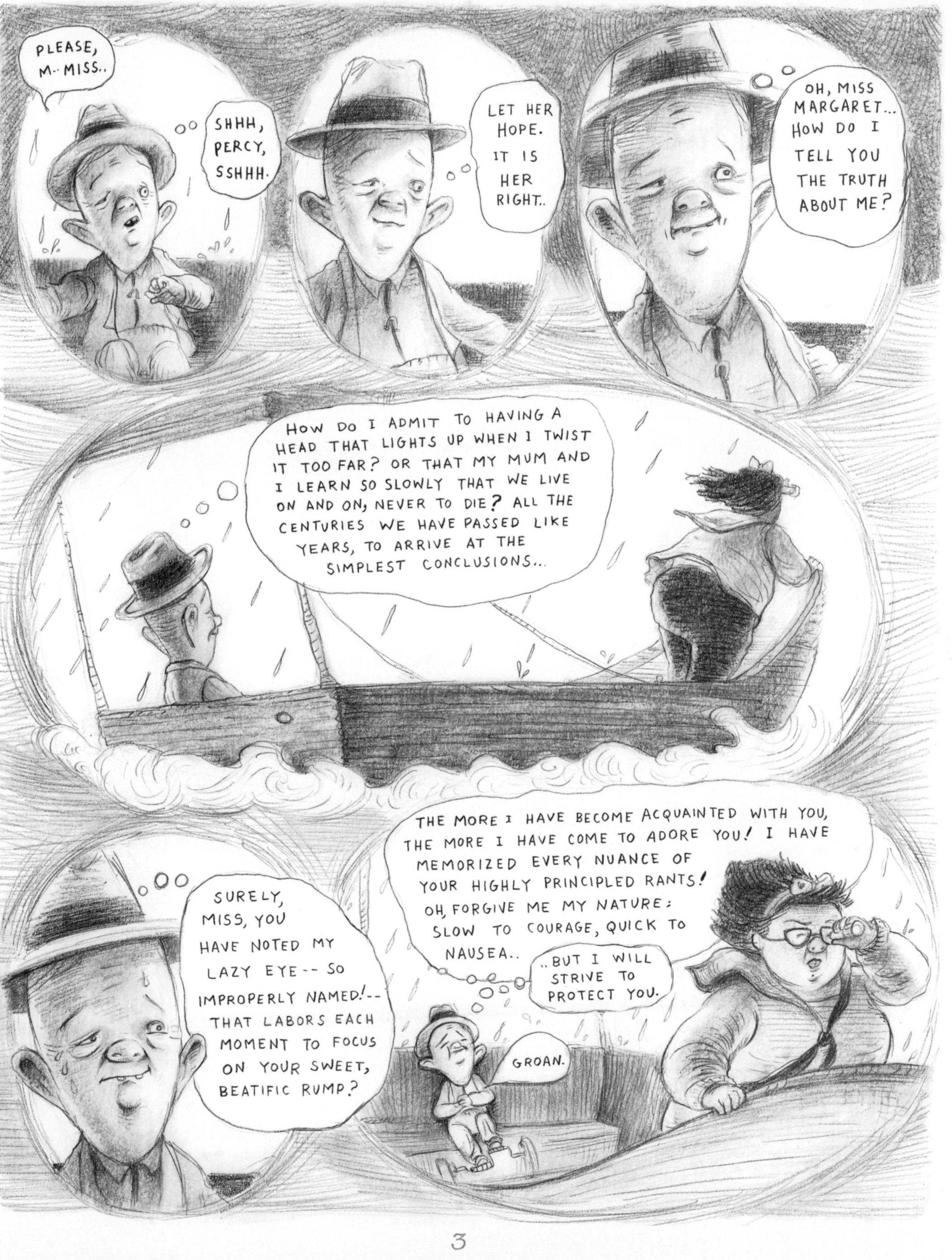
PLEASE, M-- MISS..
SHHH, PERCY, SSHHH.
LET HER HOPE. IT IS HER RIGHT..
OH, MISS MARGARET... HOW DO I TELL YOU THE TRUTH ABOUT ME?
HOW DO I ADMIT TO HAVING A HEAD THAT LIGHTS UP WHEN I TWIST IT TOO FAR? OR THAT MY MUM AND I LEARN SO SLOWLY THAT WE LIVE ON AND ON, NEVER TO DIE? ALL THE CENTURIES WE HAVE PASSED LIKE YEARS, TO ARRIVE AT THE SIMPLEST CONCLUSIONS...
SURELY, MISS, YOU HAVE NOTED MY LAZY EYE -- SO IMPROPERLY NAMED! -- THAT LABORS EACH MOMENT TO FOCUS ON YOUR SWEET, BEATIFIC RUMP?
THE MORE I HAVE BECOME ACQUAINTED WITH YOU, THE MORE I HAVE COME TO ADORE YOU! I HAVE MEMORIZED EVERY NUANCE OF YOUR HIGHLY PRINCIPLED RANTS! OH, FORGIVE ME MY NATURE: SLOW TO COURAGE, QUICK TO NAUSEA..
..BUT I WILL STRIVE TO PROTECT YOU.
GROAN.

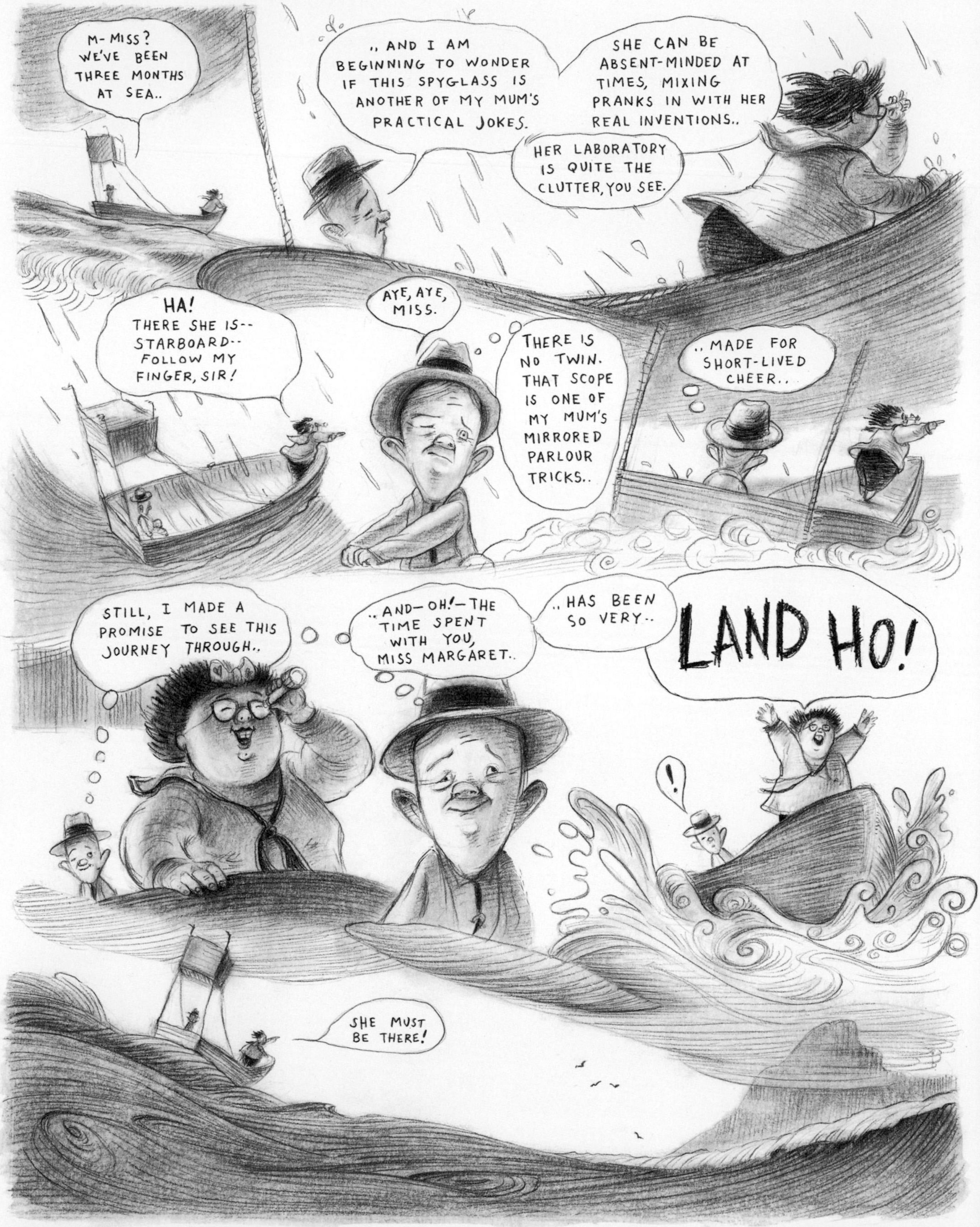
M-MISS? WE'VE BEEN THREE MONTHS AT SEA..
.. AND I AM BEGINNING TO WONDER IF THIS SPYGLASS IS ANOTHER OF MY MUM'S PRACTICAL JOKES.
SHE CAN BE ABSENT-MINDED AT TIMES, MIXING PRANKS IN WITH HER REAL INVENTIONS..
HER LABORATORY IS QUITE THE CLUTTER, YOU SEE.
HA! THERE SHE IS-- STARBOARD-- FOLLOW MY FINGER, SIR!
AYE, AYE, MISS.
THERE IS NO TWIN. THAT SCOPE IS ONE OF MY MUM'S MIRRORED PARLOUR TRICKS..
.. MADE FOR SHORT-LIVED CHEER..
STILL, I MADE A PROMISE TO SEE THIS JOURNEY THROUGH..
.. AND—OH!—THE TIME SPENT WITH YOU, MISS MARGARET..
.. HAS BEEN SO VERY..
LAND HO!
!
SHE MUST BE THERE!

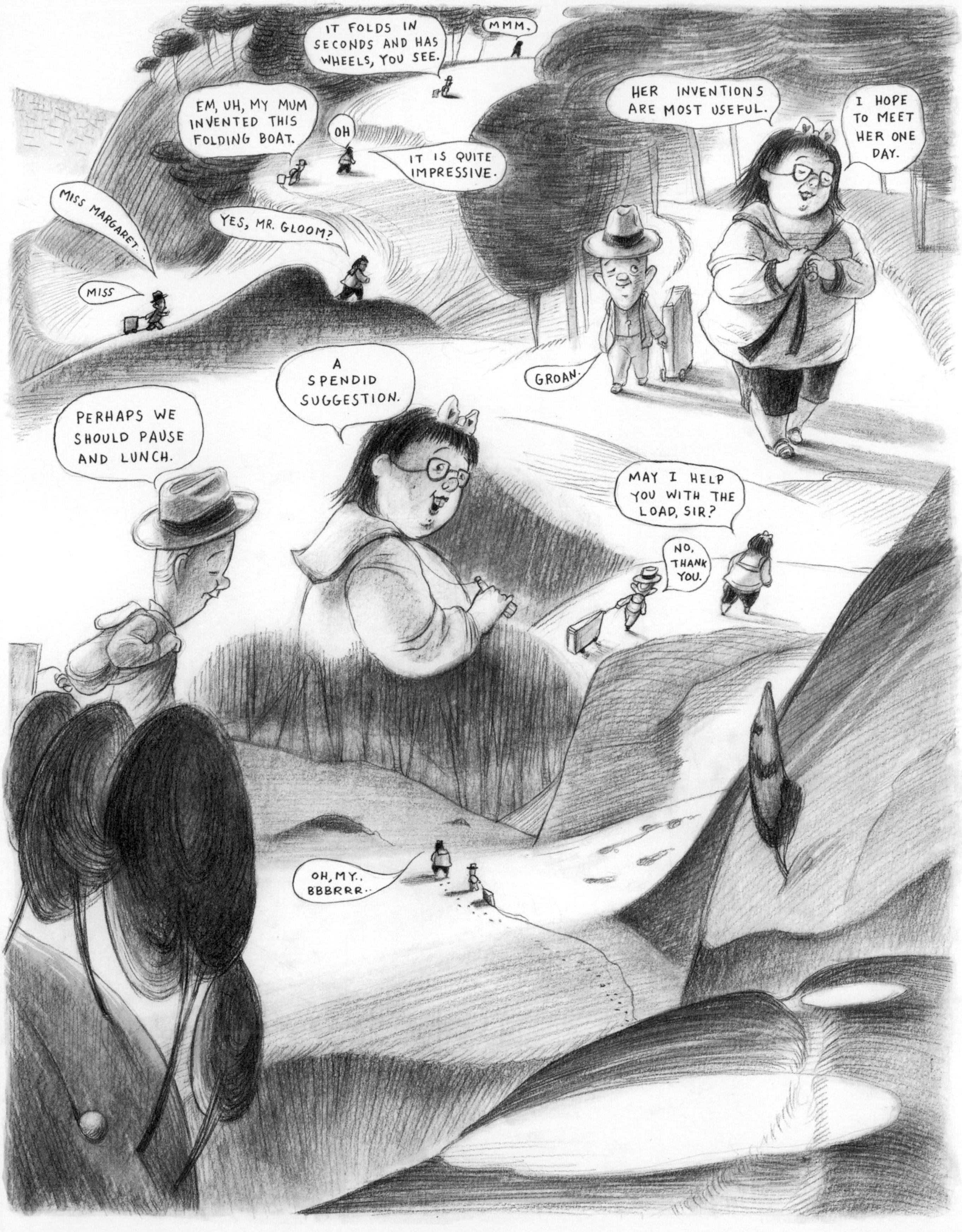
IT FOLDS IN SECONDS AND HAS WHEELS, YOU SEE.
MMM.
EM, UH, MY MUM INVENTED THIS FOLDING BOAT.
OH
IT IS QUITE IMPRESSIVE.
HER INVENTIONS ARE MOST USEFUL.
I HOPE TO MEET HER ONE DAY.
MISS MARGARET...
YES, MR. GLOOM?
MISS
GROAN.
A SPENDID SUGGESTION.
PERHAPS WE SHOULD PAUSE AND LUNCH.
MAY I HELP YOU WITH THE LOAD, SIR?
NO, THANK YOU.
OH, MY.. BBBRRR..

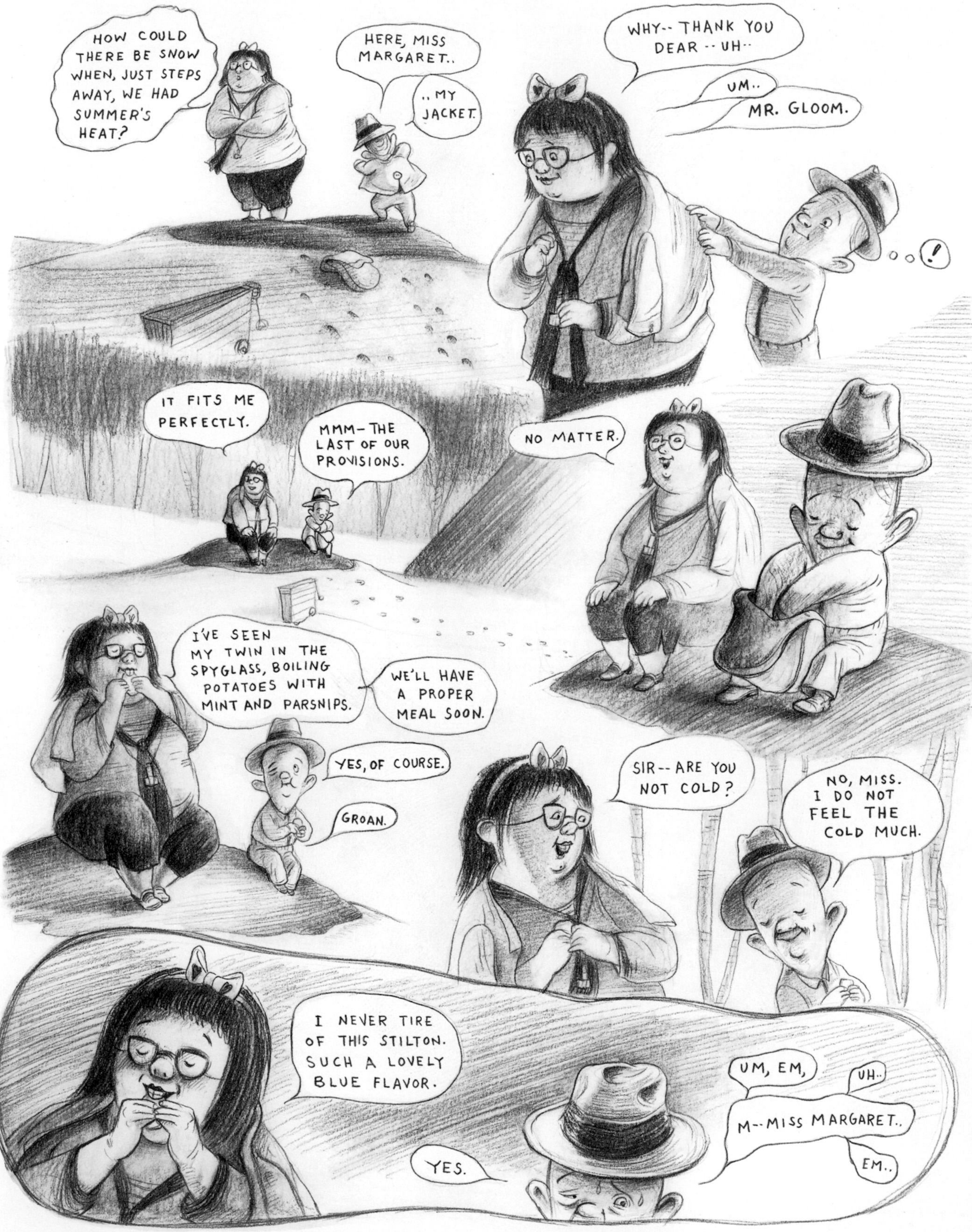
HOW COULD THERE BE SNOW WHEN, JUST STEPS AWAY, WE HAD SUMMER'S HEAT?
HERE, MISS MARGARET..
.. MY JACKET.
WHY-- THANK YOU DEAR -- UH--
UM..
MR. GLOOM.
IT FITS ME PERFECTLY.
MMM- THE LAST OF OUR PROVISIONS.
NO MATTER.
I'VE SEEN MY TWIN IN THE SPYGLASS, BOILING POTATOES WITH MINT AND PARSNIPS.
WE'LL HAVE A PROPER MEAL SOON.
YES, OF COURSE.
GROAN.
SIR-- ARE YOU NOT COLD?
NO, MISS. I DO NOT FEEL THE COLD MUCH.
I NEVER TIRE OF THIS STILTON. SUCH A LOVELY BLUE FLAVOR.
UM, EM,
UH..
M--MISS MARGARET..
EM..
YES.

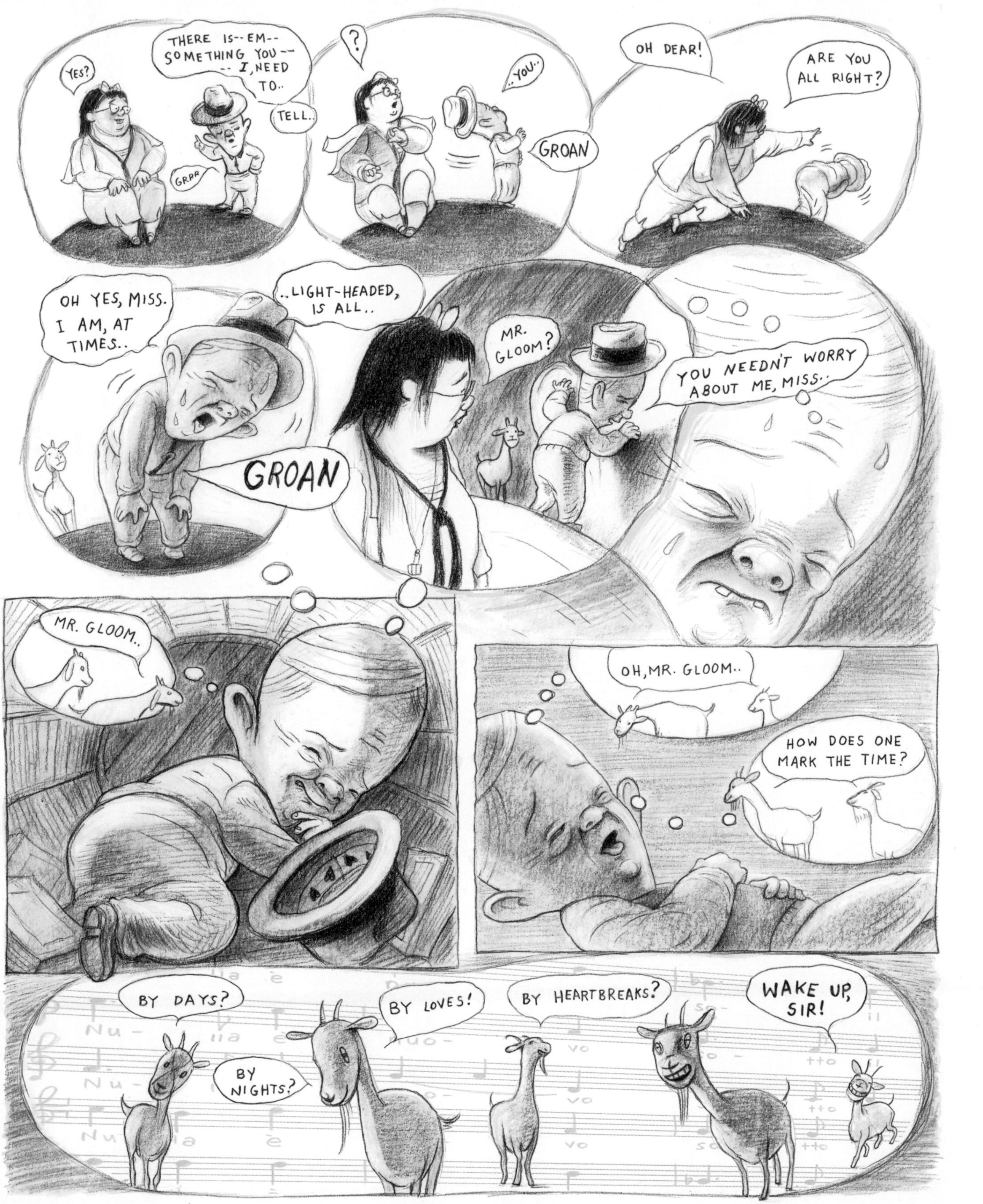
YES?
THERE IS--EM--SOMETHING YOU---- I, NEED TO..
TELL..
GRRR
?
..YOU..
GROAN
OH DEAR!
ARE YOU ALL RIGHT?
OH YES, MISS. I AM, AT TIMES..
..LIGHT-HEADED, IS ALL..
GROAN
MR. GLOOM?
YOU NEEDN'T WORRY ABOUT ME, MISS..
MR. GLOOM..
OH, MR. GLOOM..
HOW DOES ONE MARK THE TIME?
BY DAYS?
BY NIGHTS?
BY LOVES!
BY HEARTBREAKS?
WAKE UP, SIR!

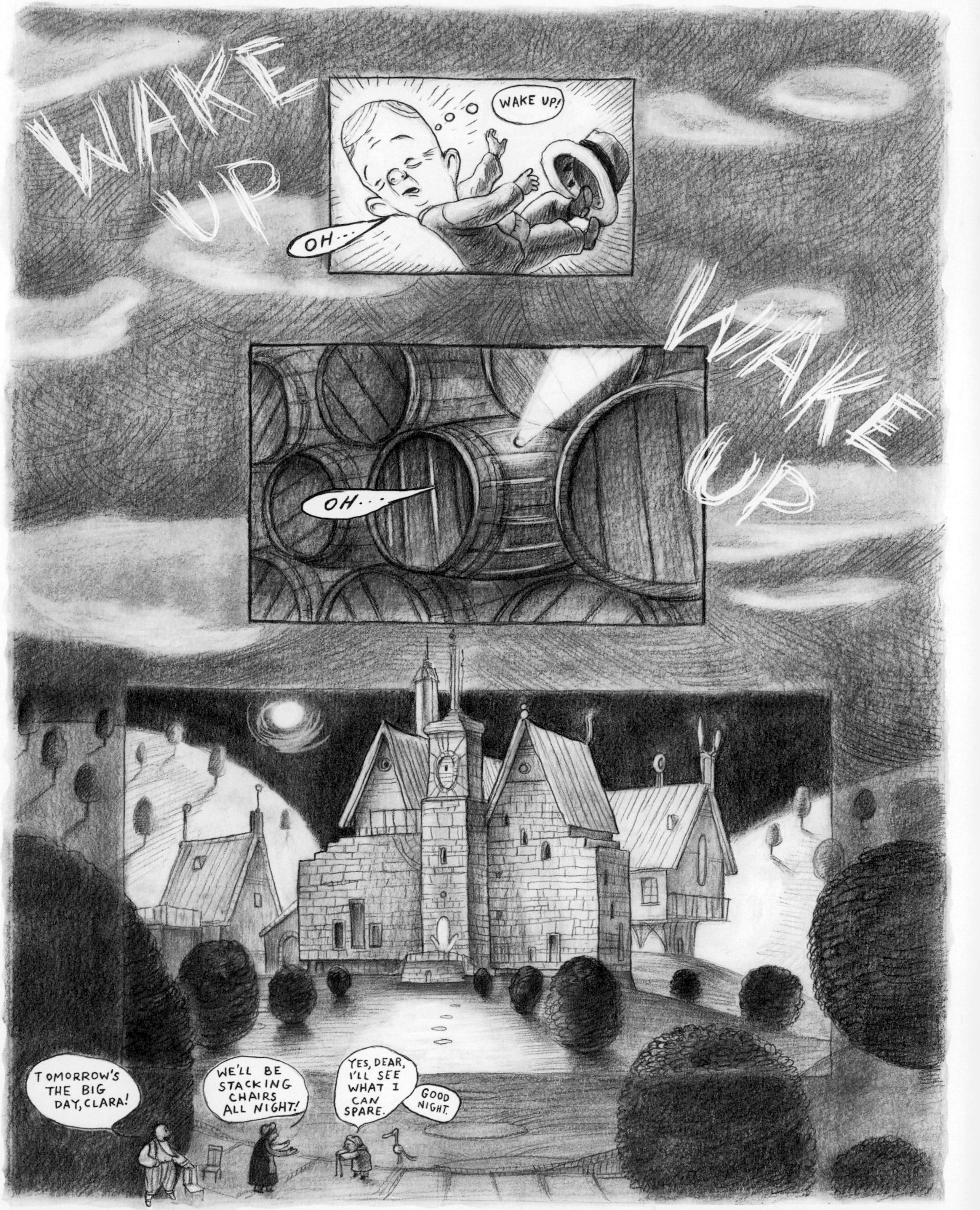
WAKE UP
WAKE UP!
OH...
WAKE UP
OH...
TOMORROW'S THE BIG DAY, CLARA!
WE'LL BE STACKING CHAIRS ALL NIGHT!
YES, DEAR, I'LL SEE WHAT I CAN SPARE.
GOOD NIGHT.

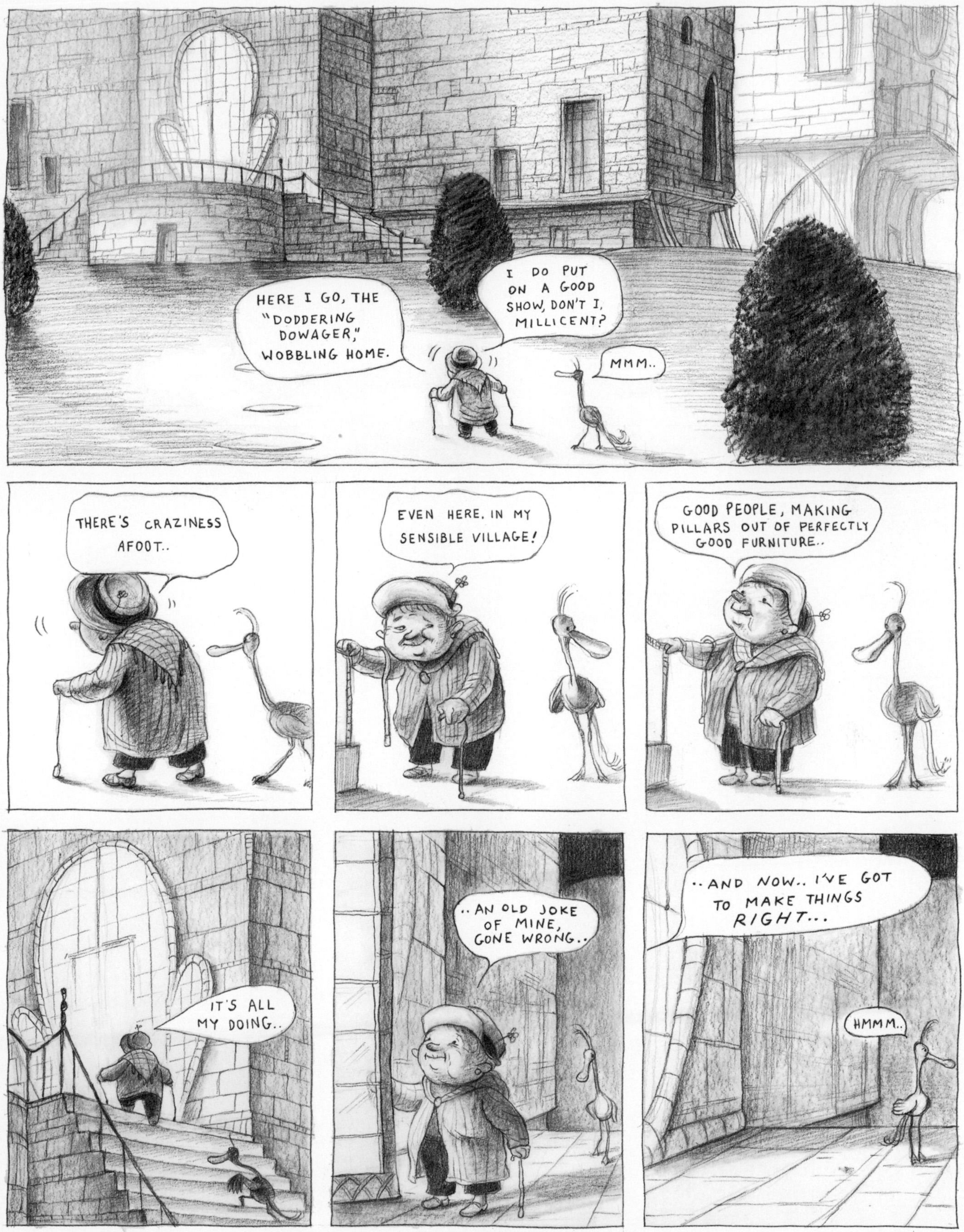
HERE I GO, THE "DODDERING DOWAGER," WOBBLING HOME.
I DO PUT ON A GOOD SHOW, DON'T I, MILLICENT?
MMM..
THERE'S CRAZINESS AFOOT..
EVEN HERE, IN MY SENSIBLE VILLAGE!
GOOD PEOPLE, MAKING PILLARS OUT OF PERFECTLY GOOD FURNITURE..
IT'S ALL MY DOING..
..AN OLD JOKE OF MINE, GONE WRONG..
..AND NOW.. I'VE GOT TO MAKE THINGS *RIGHT*...
HMMM..

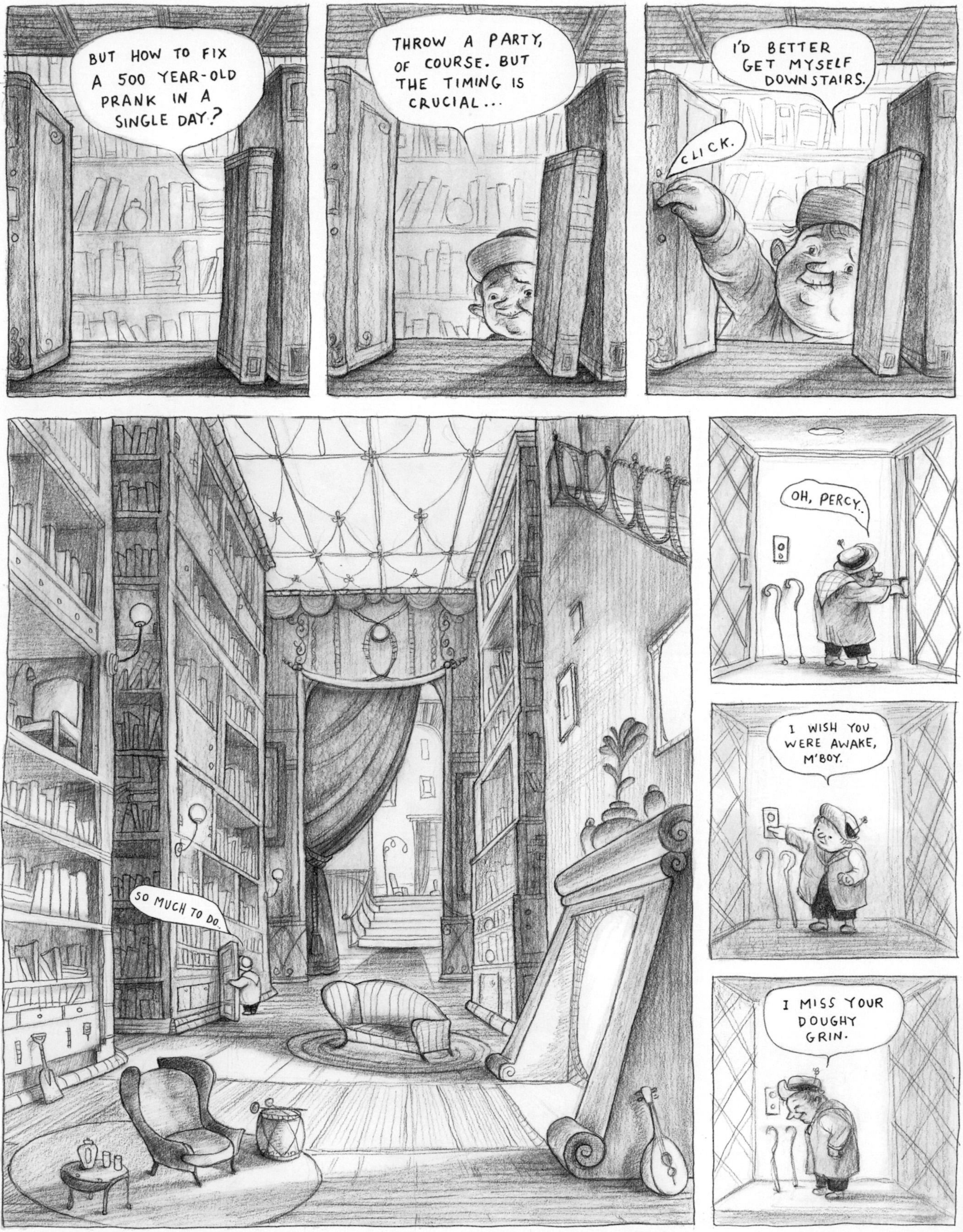
BUT HOW TO FIX A 500 YEAR-OLD PRANK IN A SINGLE DAY?
THROW A PARTY, OF COURSE. BUT THE TIMING IS CRUCIAL...
I'D BETTER GET MYSELF DOWNSTAIRS.
CLICK.
SO MUCH TO DO..
OH, PERCY..
I WISH YOU WERE AWAKE, M'BOY.
I MISS YOUR DOUGHY GRIN.

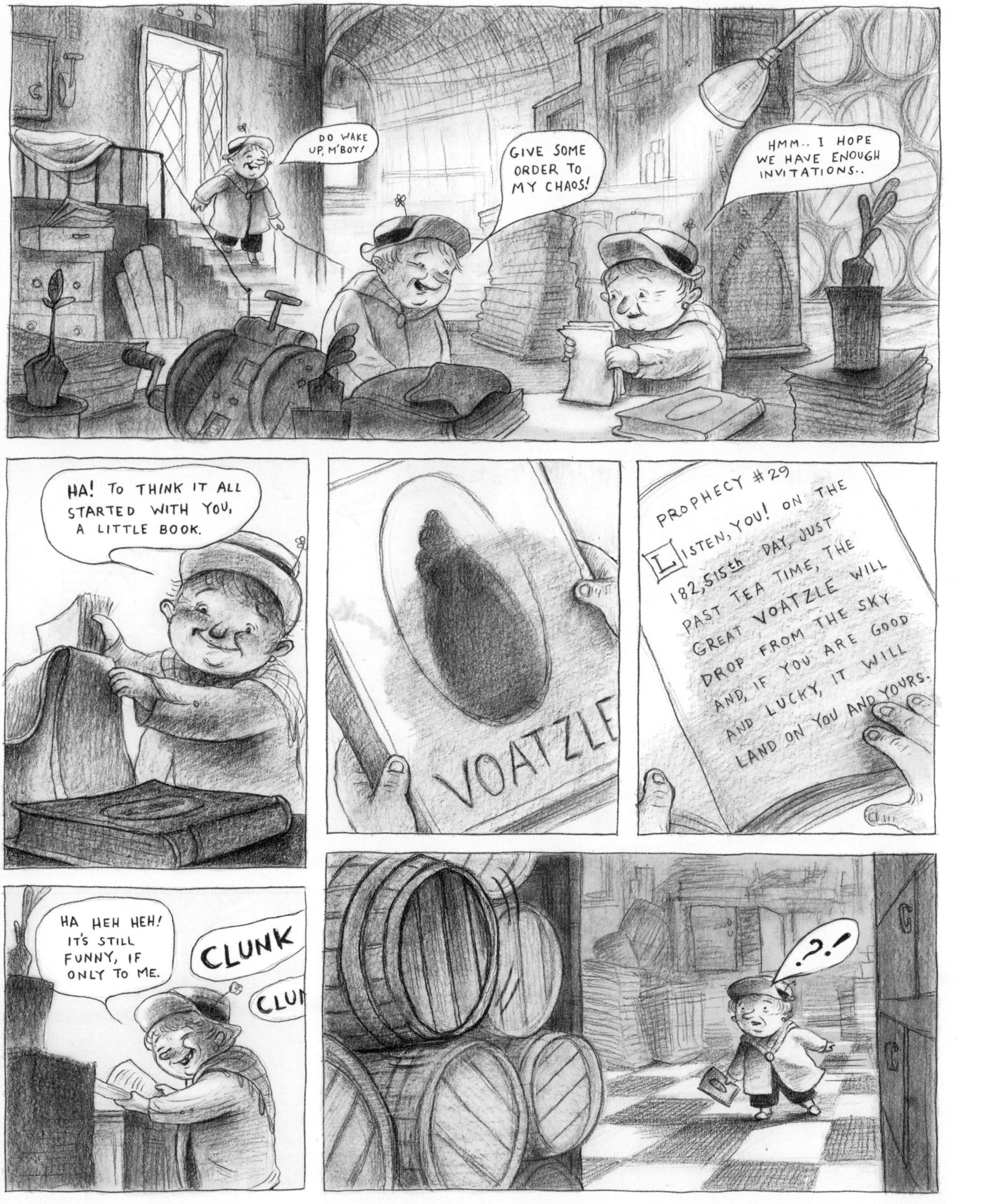
DO WAKE UP, M'BOY!
GIVE SOME ORDER TO MY CHAOS!
HMM.. I HOPE WE HAVE ENOUGH INVITATIONS..
HA! TO THINK IT ALL STARTED WITH YOU, A LITTLE BOOK.
VOATZLE
PROPHECY #29
LISTEN, YOU! ON THE 182,515th DAY, JUST PAST TEA TIME, THE GREAT VOATZLE WILL DROP FROM THE SKY AND, IF YOU ARE GOOD AND LUCKY, IT WILL LAND ON YOU AND YOURS.
HA HEH HEH! IT'S STILL FUNNY, IF ONLY TO ME.
CLUNK
CLUN
?.!

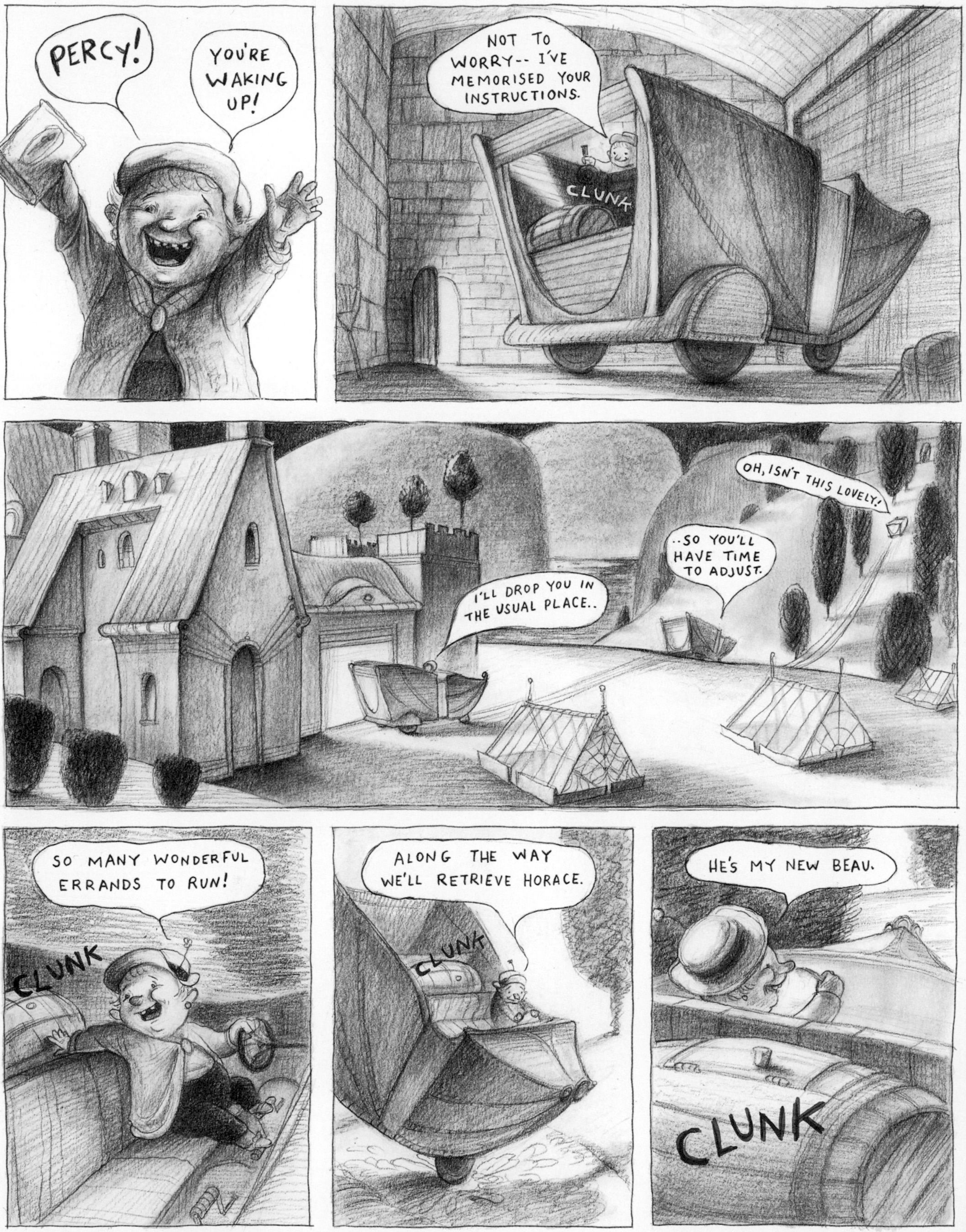
PERCY!
YOU'RE WAKING UP!
NOT TO WORRY-- I'VE MEMORISED YOUR INSTRUCTIONS.
CLUNK
I'LL DROP YOU IN THE USUAL PLACE..
..SO YOU'LL HAVE TIME TO ADJUST.
OH, ISN'T THIS LOVELY!
SO MANY WONDERFUL ERRANDS TO RUN!
CLUNK
ALONG THE WAY WE'LL RETRIEVE HORACE.
CLUNK
HE'S MY NEW BEAU.
CLUNK

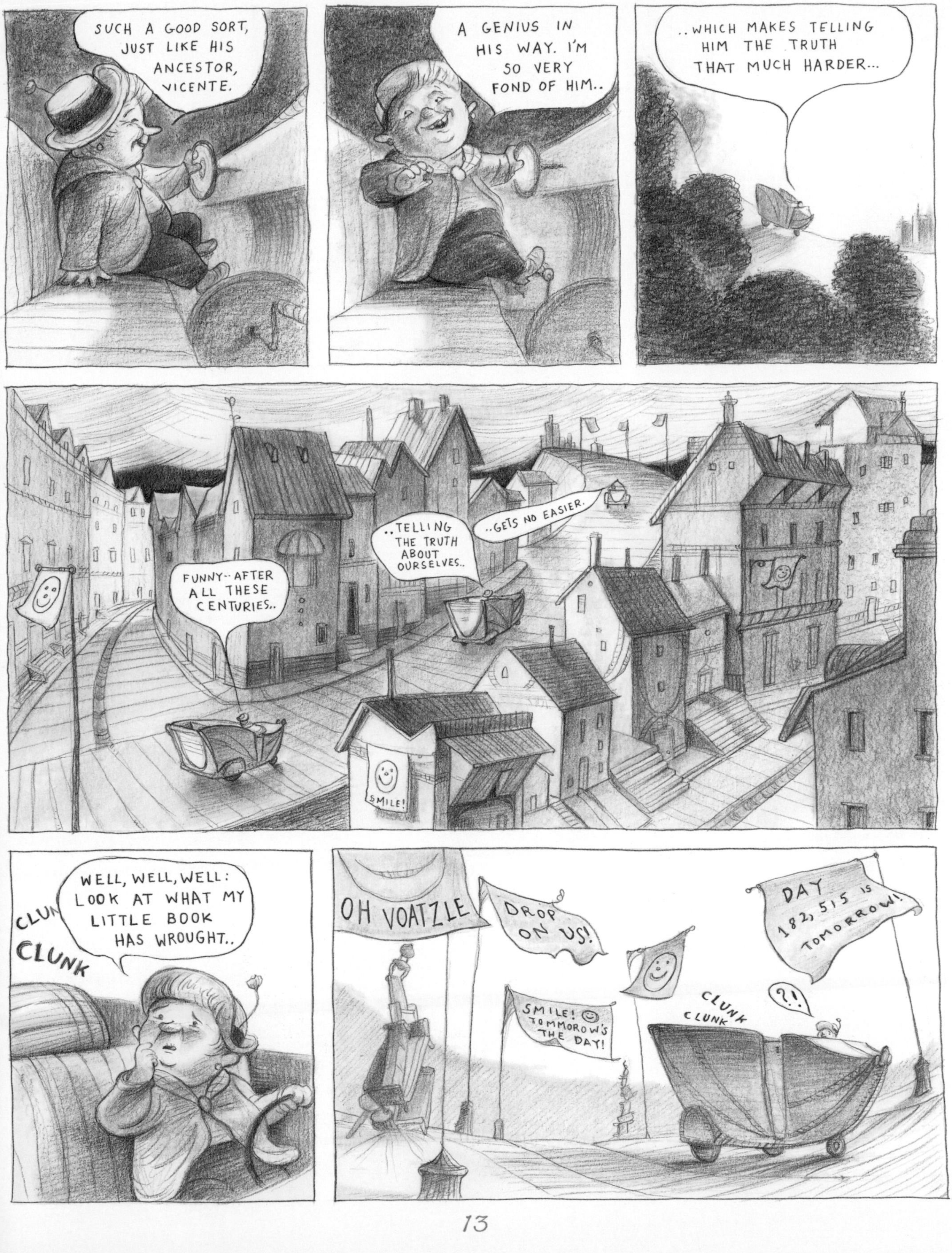
SUCH A GOOD SORT, JUST LIKE HIS ANCESTOR, VICENTE.
A GENIUS IN HIS WAY. I'M SO VERY FOND OF HIM..
..WHICH MAKES TELLING HIM THE TRUTH THAT MUCH HARDER...
FUNNY-- AFTER ALL THESE CENTURIES..
..TELLING THE TRUTH ABOUT OURSELVES..
..GETS NO EASIER.
SMILE!
CLUNK
CLUNK
WELL, WELL, WELL: LOOK AT WHAT MY LITTLE BOOK HAS WROUGHT..
OH VOATZLE
DROP ON US!
DAY 182,515 IS TOMORROW!
SMILE! ☺ TOMMOROW'S THE DAY!
CLUNK
CLUNK
?!

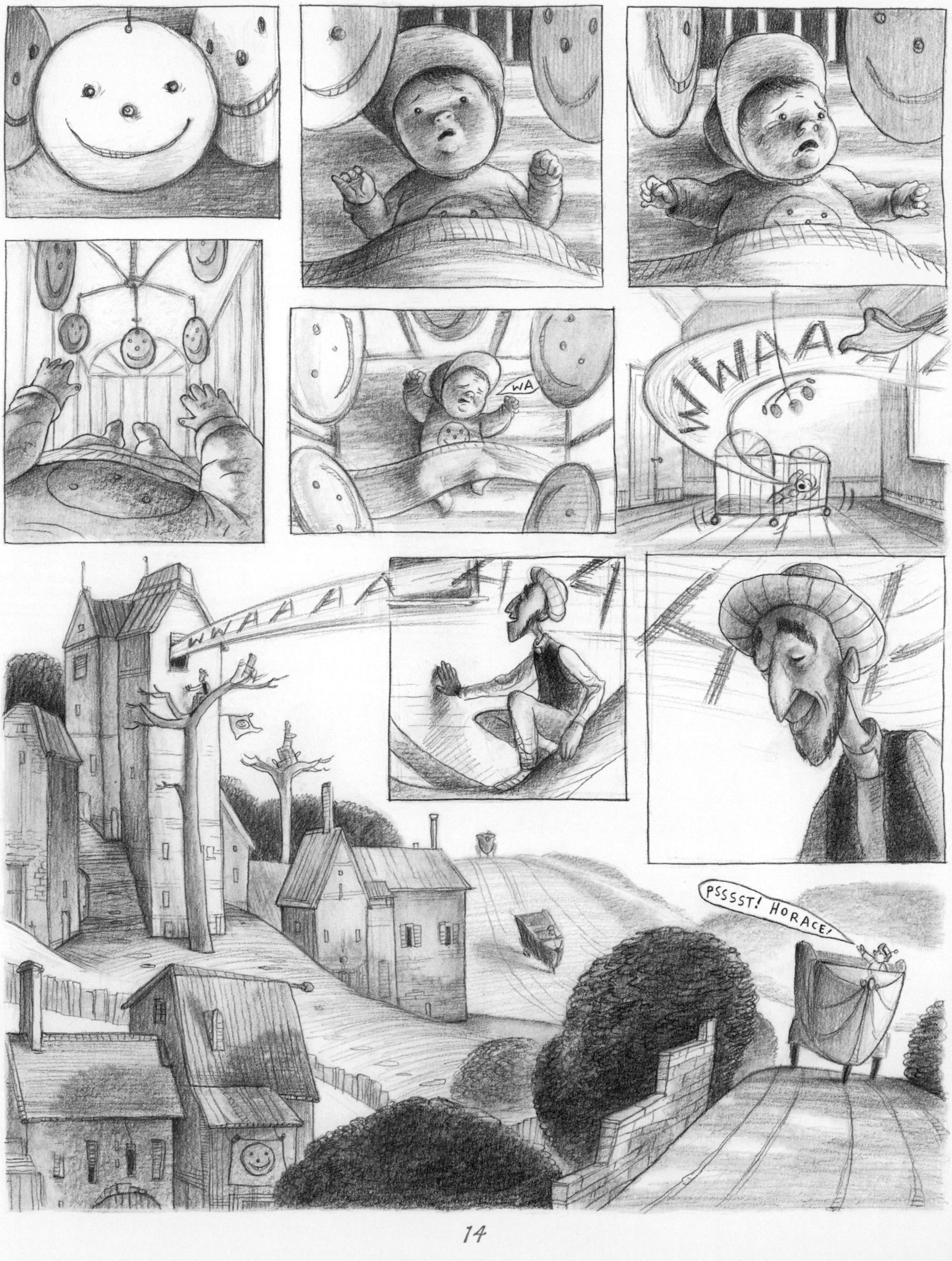
WA
WWAA
WWAAAAA
PSSSST! HORACE!

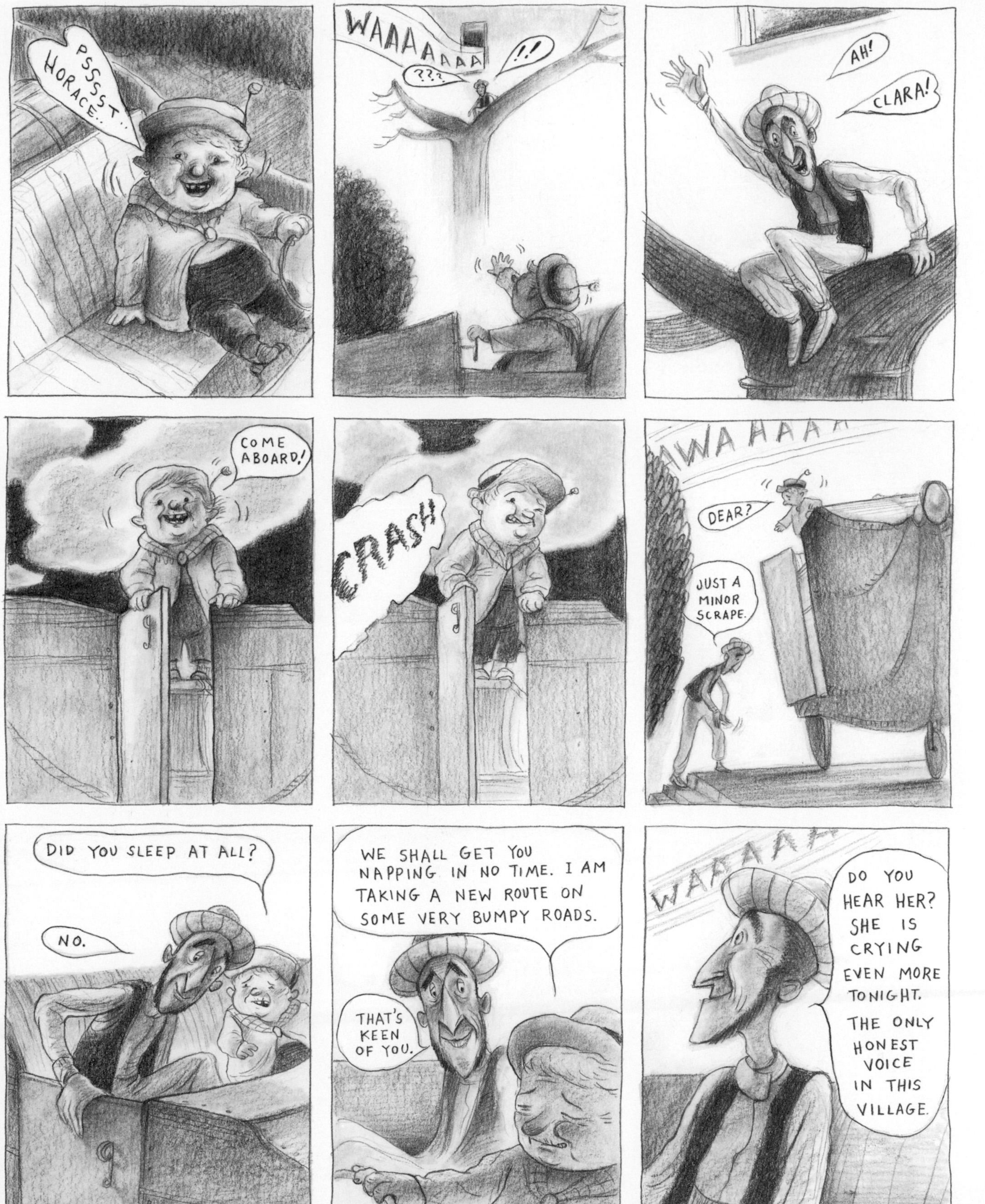
PSSSSST.. HORACE..
WAAAAAAAA
???
!!
AH!
CLARA!
COME ABOARD!
CRASH
WAAAAA
DEAR?
JUST A MINOR SCRAPE.
DID YOU SLEEP AT ALL?
NO.
WE SHALL GET YOU NAPPING IN NO TIME. I AM TAKING A NEW ROUTE ON SOME VERY BUMPY ROADS.
THAT'S KEEN OF YOU.
WAAAAAA
DO YOU HEAR HER? SHE IS CRYING EVEN MORE TONIGHT.
THE ONLY HONEST VOICE IN THIS VILLAGE.

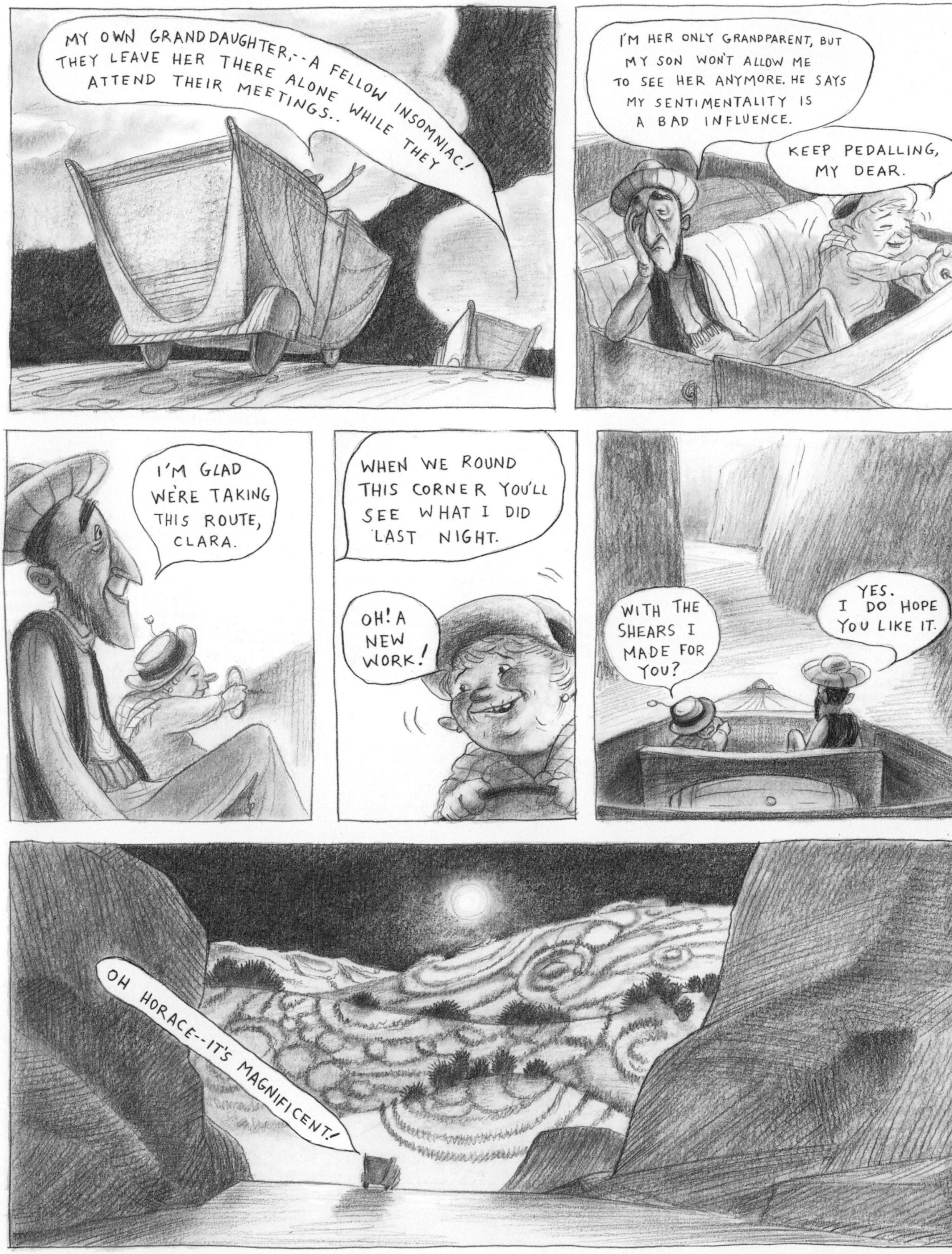

MY OWN GRANDDAUGHTER,--A FELLOW INSOMNIAC! THEY LEAVE HER THERE ALONE WHILE THEY ATTEND THEIR MEETINGS..
I'M HER ONLY GRANDPARENT, BUT MY SON WON'T ALLOW ME TO SEE HER ANYMORE. HE SAYS MY SENTIMENTALITY IS A BAD INFLUENCE.
KEEP PEDALLING, MY DEAR.
I'M GLAD WE'RE TAKING THIS ROUTE, CLARA.
WHEN WE ROUND THIS CORNER YOU'LL SEE WHAT I DID LAST NIGHT.
OH! A NEW WORK!
WITH THE SHEARS I MADE FOR YOU?
YES. I DO HOPE YOU LIKE IT.
OH HORACE--IT'S MAGNIFICENT!

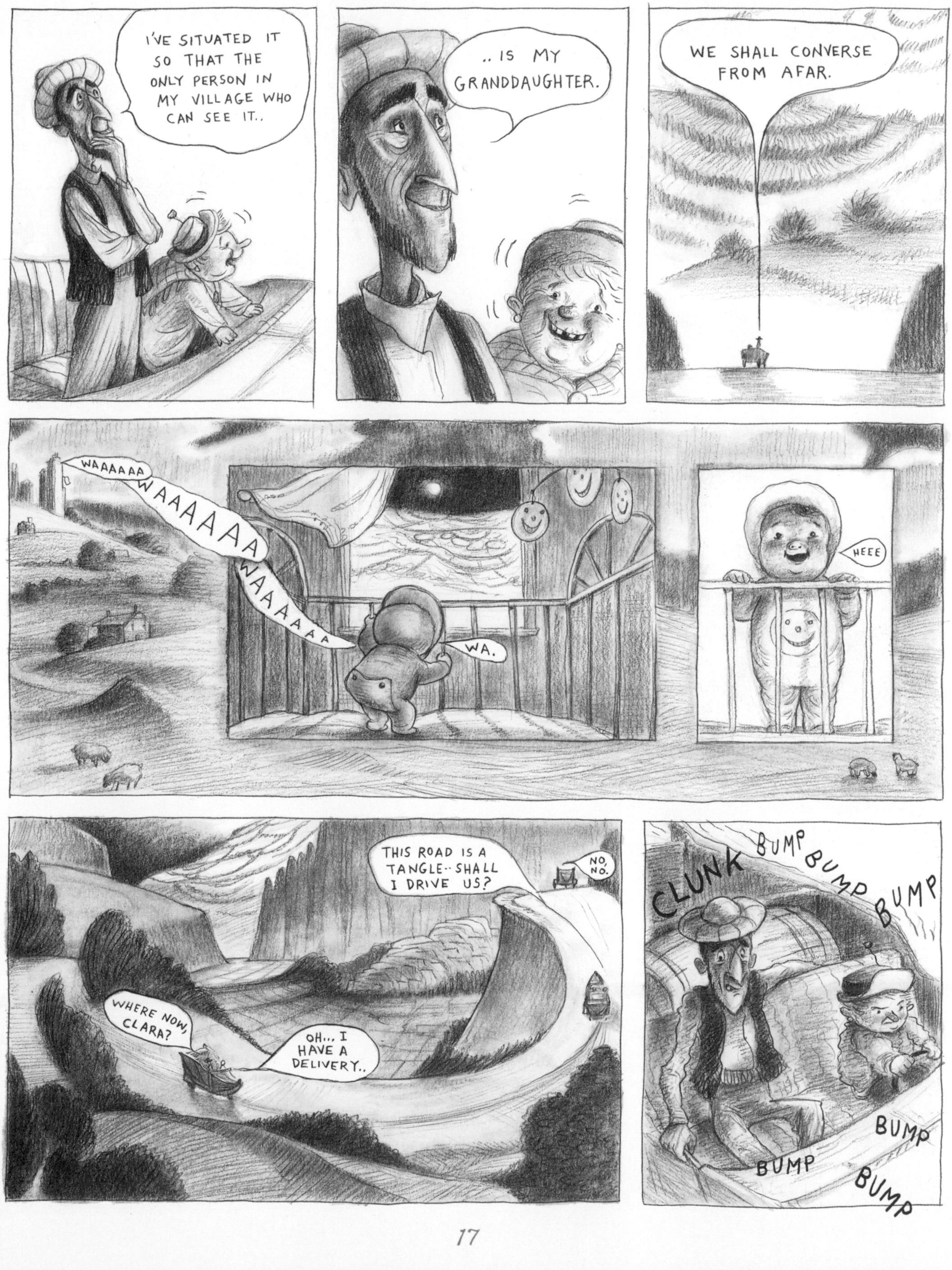
I'VE SITUATED IT SO THAT THE ONLY PERSON IN MY VILLAGE WHO CAN SEE IT..
.. IS MY GRANDDAUGHTER.
WE SHALL CONVERSE FROM AFAR.
WAAAAAA
WAAAAAAA
WAAAAAAA
WA.
HEEE
THIS ROAD IS A TANGLE.. SHALL I DRIVE US?
NO, NO.
WHERE NOW, CLARA?
OH... I HAVE A DELIVERY..
CLUNK
BUMP BUMP BUMP
BUMP
BUMP
BUMP

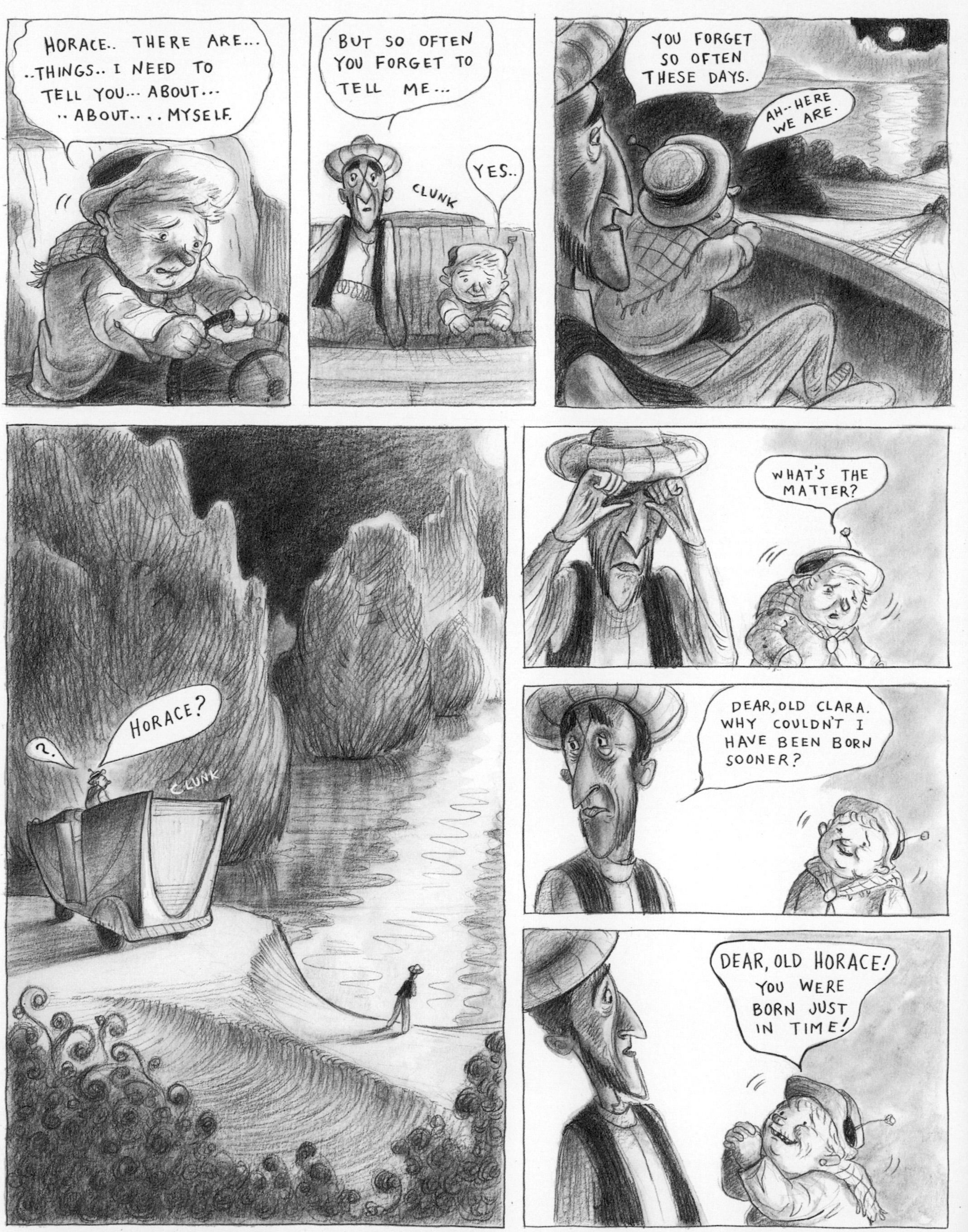

HORACE.. THERE ARE... ..THINGS.. I NEED TO TELL YOU... ABOUT... .. ABOUT.. . . MYSELF.
BUT SO OFTEN YOU FORGET TO TELL ME...
CLUNK
YES..
YOU FORGET SO OFTEN THESE DAYS.
AH-- HERE WE ARE.
HORACE?
?
CLUNK
WHAT'S THE MATTER?
DEAR, OLD CLARA. WHY COULDN'T I HAVE BEEN BORN SOONER?
DEAR, OLD HORACE! YOU WERE BORN JUST IN TIME!

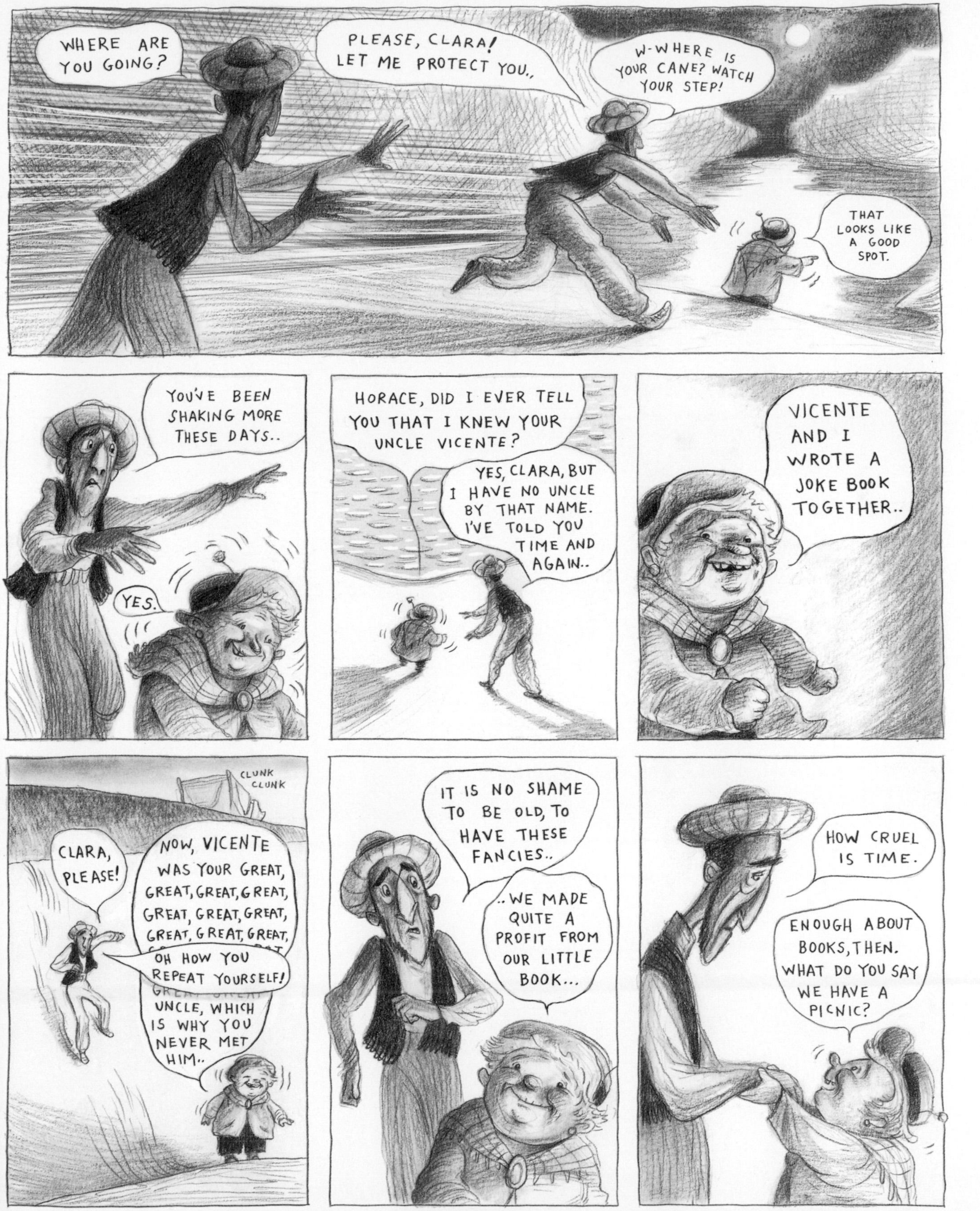

WHERE ARE YOU GOING?
PLEASE, CLARA! LET ME PROTECT YOU..
W-WHERE IS YOUR CANE? WATCH YOUR STEP!
THAT LOOKS LIKE A GOOD SPOT.
YOU'VE BEEN SHAKING MORE THESE DAYS..
YES.
HORACE, DID I EVER TELL YOU THAT I KNEW YOUR UNCLE VICENTE?
YES, CLARA, BUT I HAVE NO UNCLE BY THAT NAME. I'VE TOLD YOU TIME AND AGAIN..
VICENTE AND I WROTE A JOKE BOOK TOGETHER..
CLUNK CLUNK
CLARA, PLEASE!
NOW, VICENTE WAS YOUR GREAT, GREAT, GREAT, GREAT, GREAT, GREAT, GREAT, GREAT, GREAT, GREAT,
OH HOW YOU REPEAT YOURSELF!
UNCLE, WHICH IS WHY YOU NEVER MET HIM..
IT IS NO SHAME TO BE OLD, TO HAVE THESE FANCIES..
..WE MADE QUITE A PROFIT FROM OUR LITTLE BOOK...
HOW CRUEL IS TIME.
ENOUGH ABOUT BOOKS, THEN. WHAT DO YOU SAY WE HAVE A PICNIC?

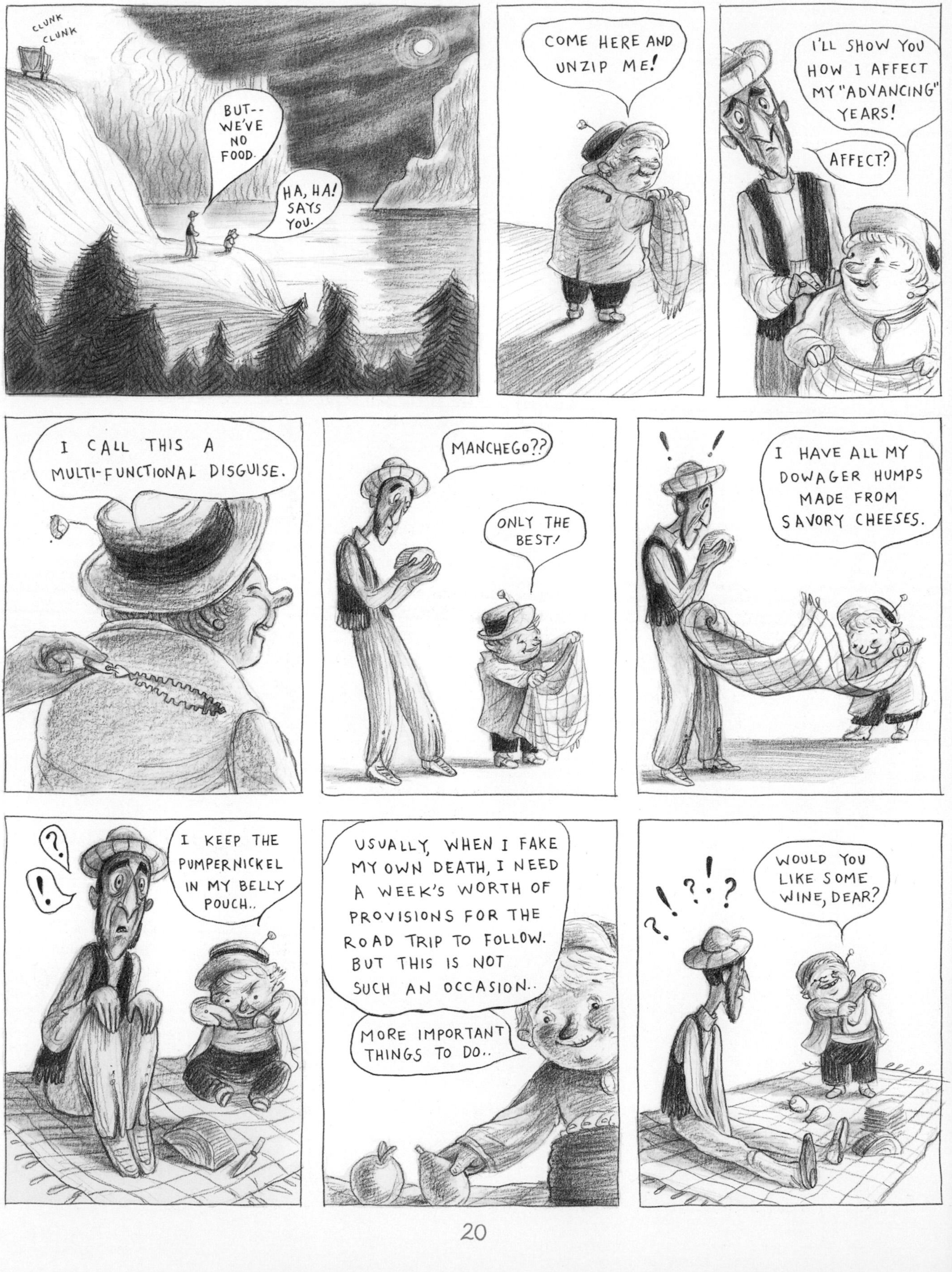
CLUNK CLUNK
BUT-- WE'VE NO FOOD.
HA, HA! SAYS YOU.
COME HERE AND UNZIP ME!
I'LL SHOW YOU HOW I AFFECT MY "ADVANCING" YEARS!
AFFECT?
I CALL THIS A MULTI-FUNCTIONAL DISGUISE.
MANCHEGO??
ONLY THE BEST!
! !
I HAVE ALL MY DOWAGER HUMPS MADE FROM SAVORY CHEESES.
? !
I KEEP THE PUMPERNICKEL IN MY BELLY POUCH..
USUALLY, WHEN I FAKE MY OWN DEATH, I NEED A WEEK'S WORTH OF PROVISIONS FOR THE ROAD TRIP TO FOLLOW. BUT THIS IS NOT SUCH AN OCCASION..
MORE IMPORTANT THINGS TO DO..
?! ?!?
WOULD YOU LIKE SOME WINE, DEAR?

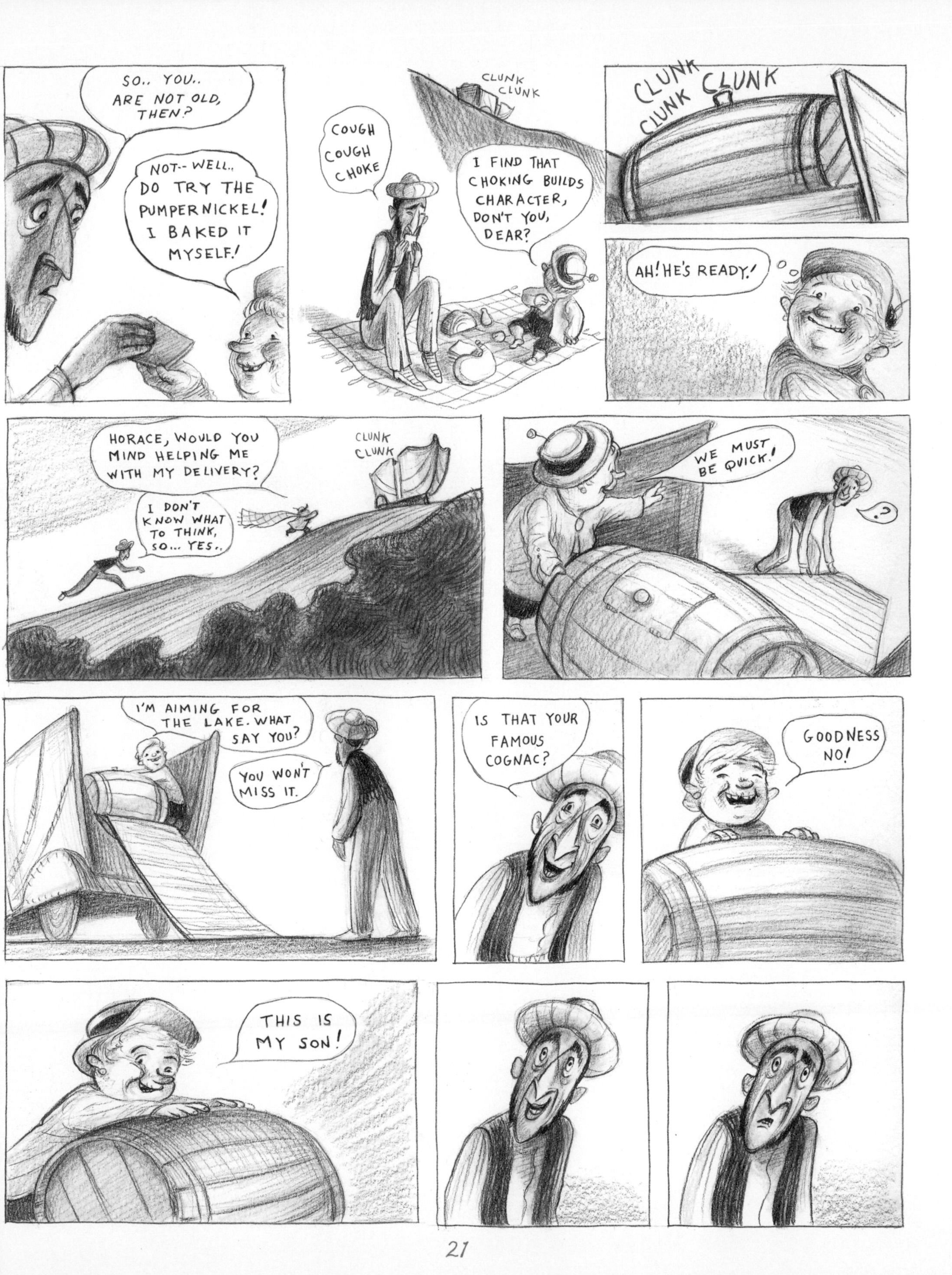
SO.. YOU.. ARE NOT OLD, THEN?
NOT-- WELL.. DO TRY THE PUMPERNICKEL! I BAKED IT MYSELF!
CLUNK CLUNK
COUGH COUGH CHOKE
I FIND THAT CHOKING BUILDS CHARACTER, DON'T YOU, DEAR?
CLUNK CLUNK CLUNK
AH! HE'S READY!
HORACE, WOULD YOU MIND HELPING ME WITH MY DELIVERY?
CLUNK CLUNK
I DON'T KNOW WHAT TO THINK, SO... YES..
WE MUST BE QUICK!
?
I'M AIMING FOR THE LAKE. WHAT SAY YOU?
YOU WON'T MISS IT.
IS THAT YOUR FAMOUS COGNAC?
GOODNESS NO!
THIS IS MY SON!

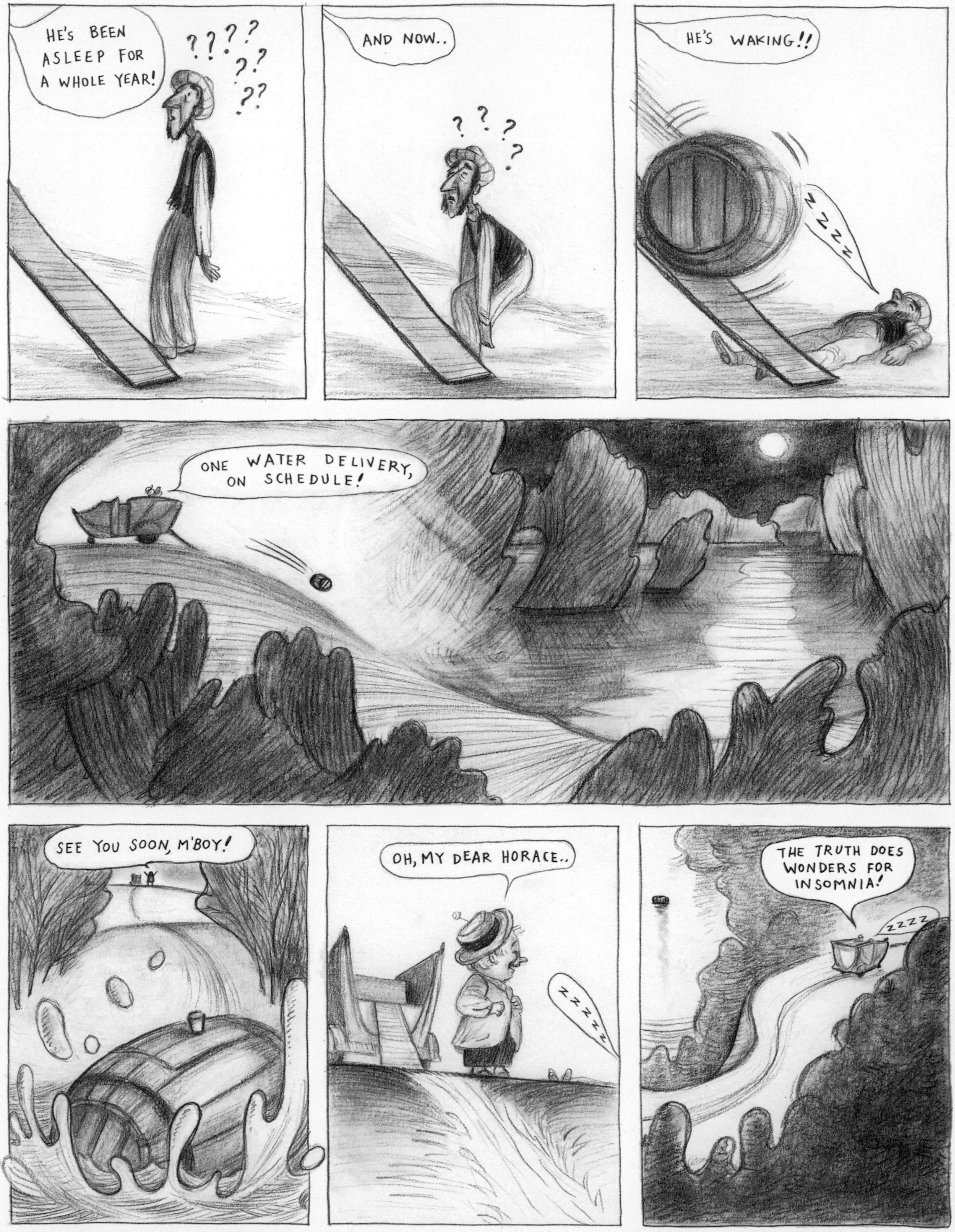
HE'S BEEN ASLEEP FOR A WHOLE YEAR!
????
??
??
AND NOW..
????
HE'S WAKING!!
ZZZZ
ONE WATER DELIVERY, ON SCHEDULE!
SEE YOU SOON, M'BOY!
OH, MY DEAR HORACE..
ZZZZZ
THE TRUTH DOES WONDERS FOR INSOMNIA!
ZZZZ

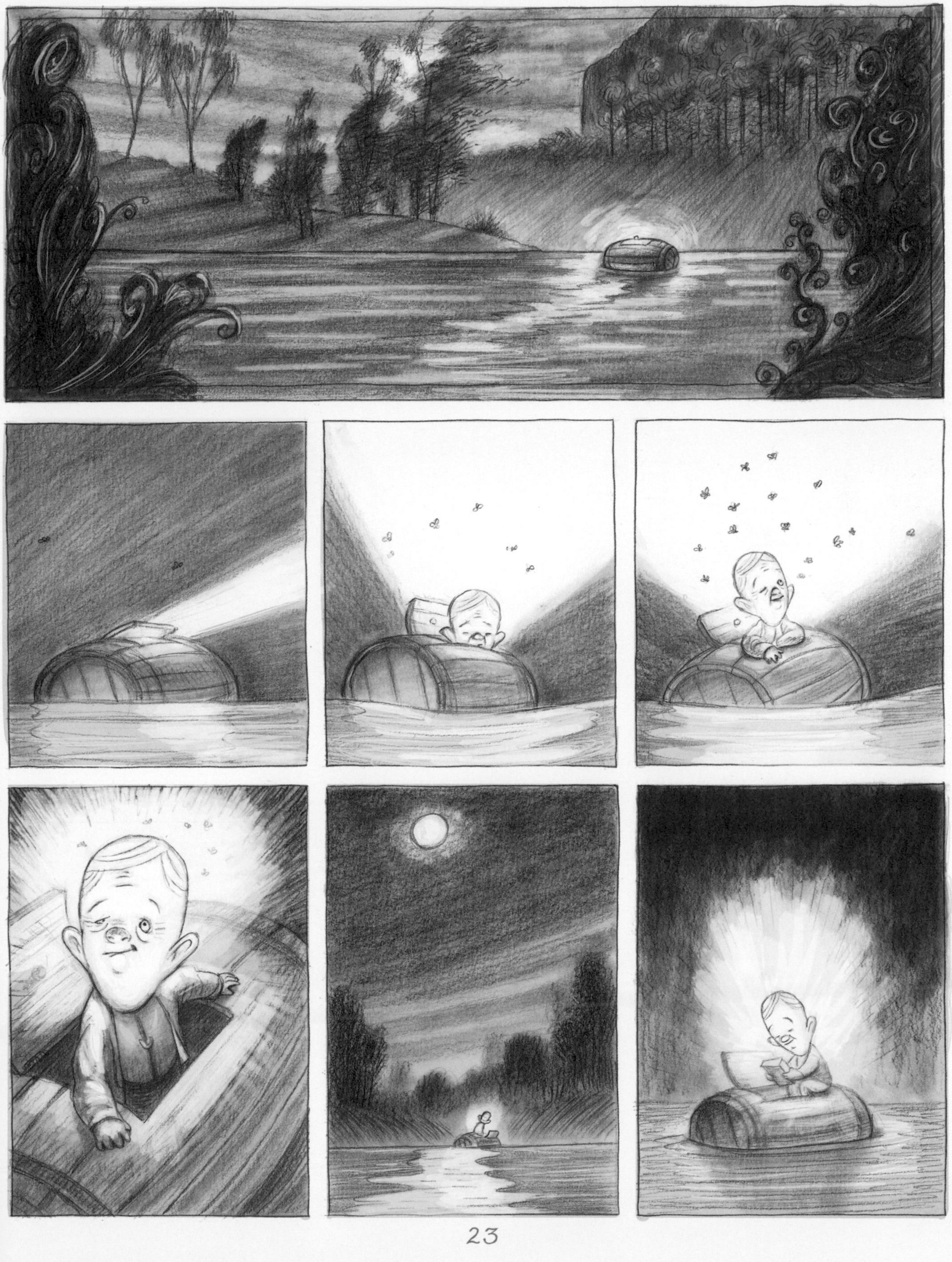

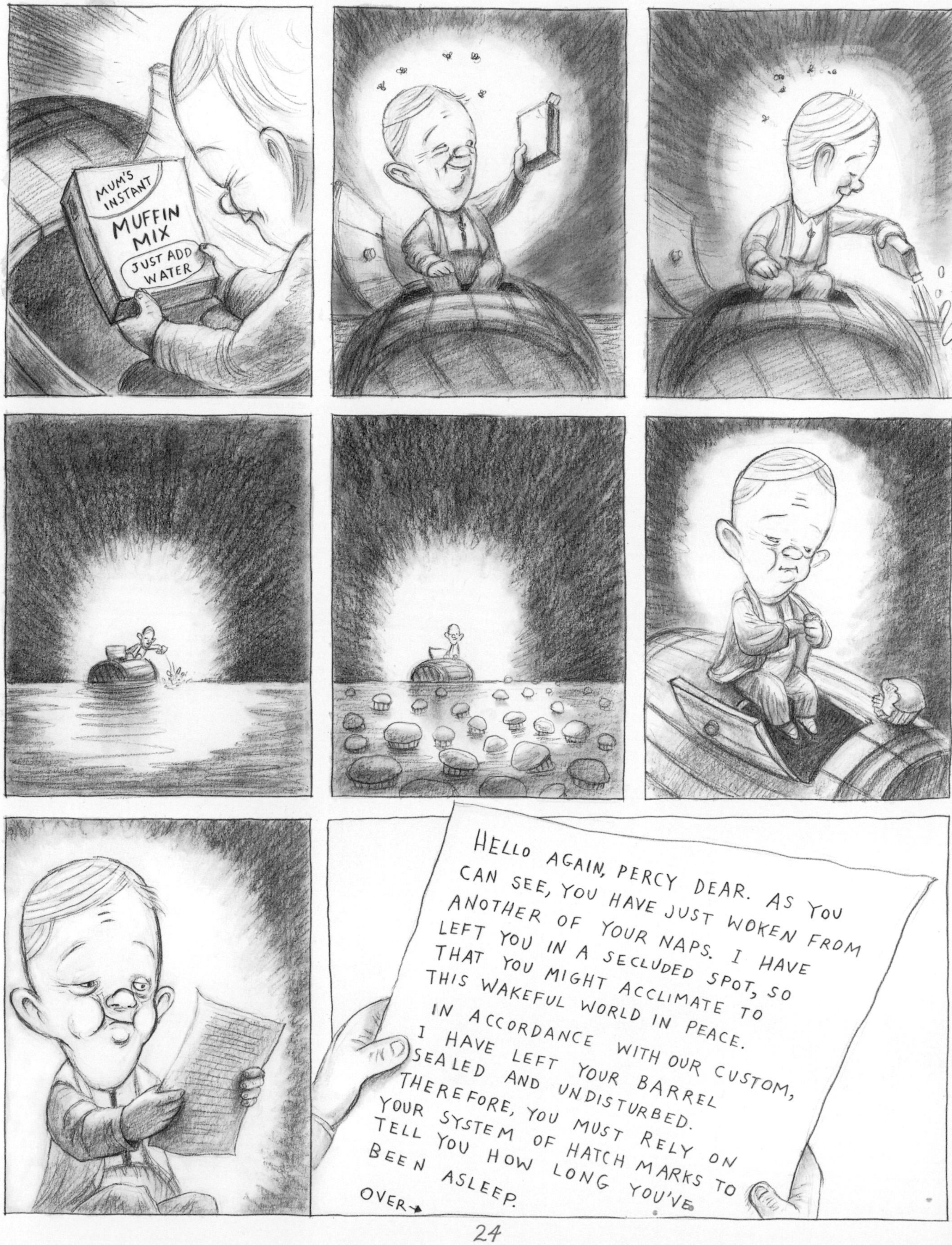
MUM'S INSTANT
MUFFIN MIX
JUST ADD WATER
HELLO AGAIN, PERCY DEAR. AS YOU CAN SEE, YOU HAVE JUST WOKEN FROM ANOTHER OF YOUR NAPS. I HAVE LEFT YOU IN A SECLUDED SPOT, SO THAT YOU MIGHT ACCLIMATE TO THIS WAKEFUL WORLD IN PEACE.
IN ACCORDANCE WITH OUR CUSTOM, I HAVE LEFT YOUR BARREL SEALED AND UNDISTURBED. THEREFORE, YOU MUST RELY ON YOUR SYSTEM OF HATCH MARKS TO TELL YOU HOW LONG YOU'VE BEEN ASLEEP.
OVER→

HERE ARE A FEW REMINDERS:
1. THE WORLD HAS CHANGED.
2. THE WORLD HAS STAYED THE SAME.
3. PROPER HYGIENE IS NEVER OUT OF FASHION.
4. WHEN MEETING THE HUMORLESS, ENDEAVOR TO HUMOR THEM.
5. TRUE SMILES DO NOT BLOOM FROM FALSE HEARTS.
6. YOUR MUM LOVES YOU BOUNDLESSLY.
GOOD LUCK,
MUM
MUM, YOU MAKE A STURDY BARREL.
MUSTN'T FORGET MY HAT.
?
MARGARET'S RIBBON!
DEAR, DEAR MARGARET! I LONG TO SEE YOU.

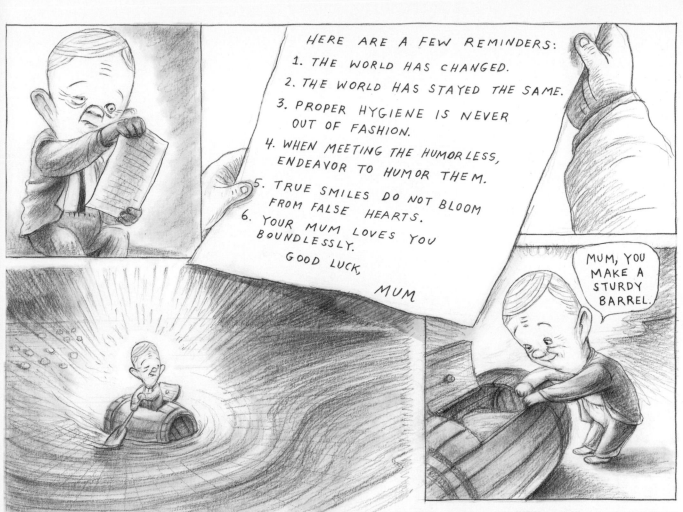

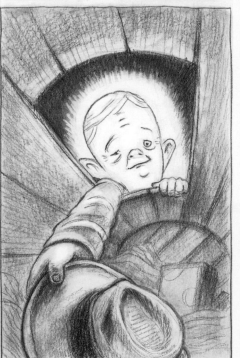

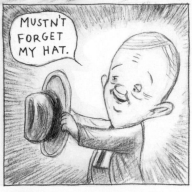

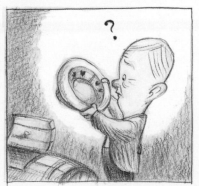

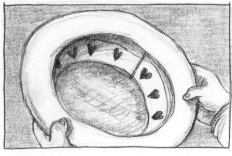

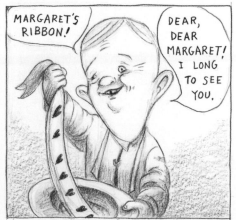

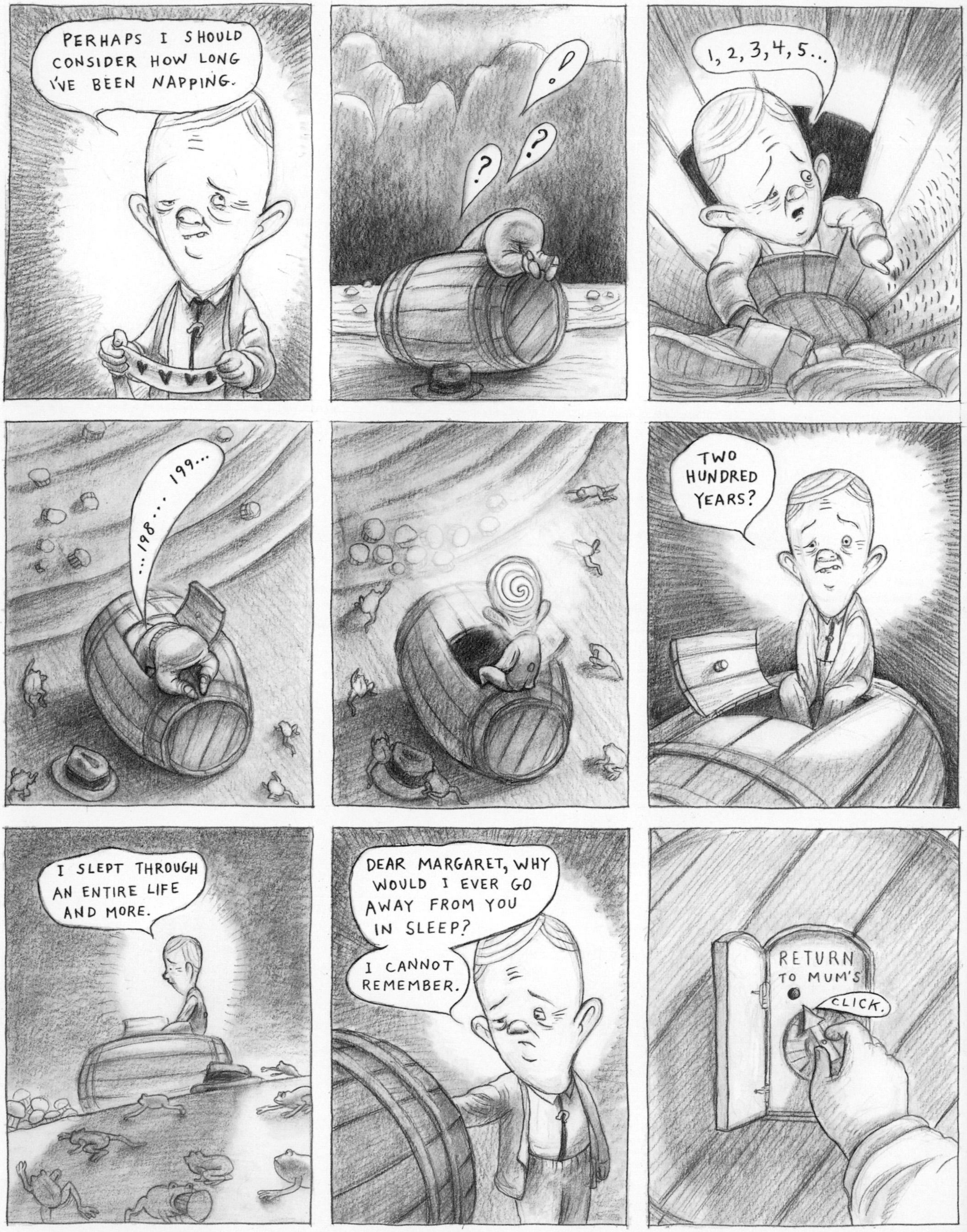
PERHAPS I SHOULD CONSIDER HOW LONG I'VE BEEN NAPPING.
!
?
?
1, 2, 3, 4, 5...
...198.... 199...
TWO HUNDRED YEARS?
I SLEPT THROUGH AN ENTIRE LIFE AND MORE.
DEAR MARGARET, WHY WOULD I EVER GO AWAY FROM YOU IN SLEEP?
I CANNOT REMEMBER.
RETURN TO MUM'S
CLICK.

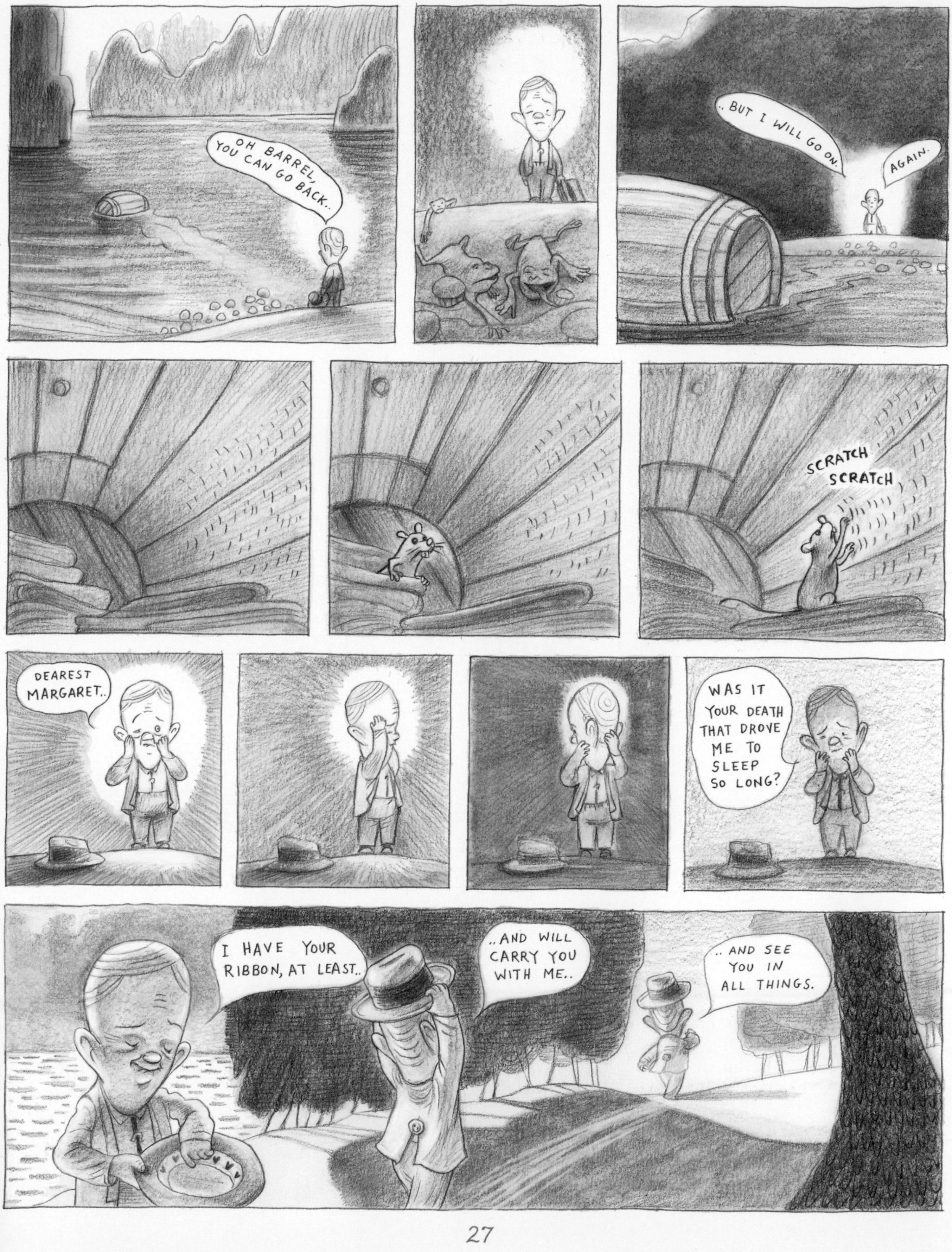
OH BARREL,
YOU CAN GO BACK..
.. BUT I WILL GO ON.
AGAIN.
SCRATCH
SCRATCH
DEAREST
MARGARET..
WAS IT
YOUR DEATH
THAT DROVE
ME TO
SLEEP
SO LONG?
I HAVE YOUR
RIBBON, AT LEAST..
..AND WILL
CARRY YOU
WITH ME..
.. AND SEE
YOU IN
ALL THINGS.

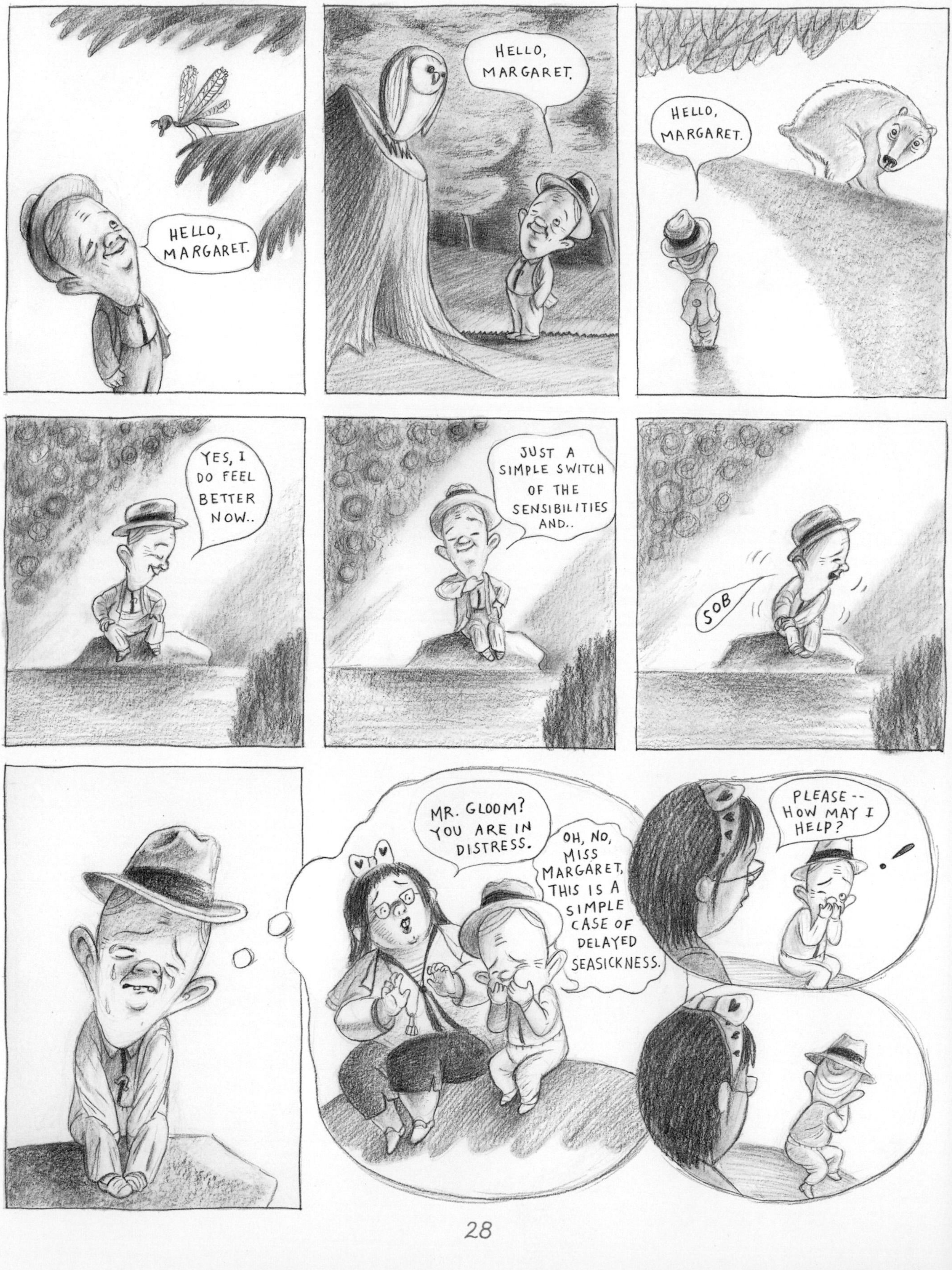
HELLO, MARGARET.
HELLO, MARGARET.
HELLO, MARGARET.
YES, I DO FEEL BETTER NOW..
JUST A SIMPLE SWITCH OF THE SENSIBILITIES AND..
SOB
MR. GLOOM? YOU ARE IN DISTRESS.
OH, NO, MISS MARGARET, THIS IS A SIMPLE CASE OF DELAYED SEASICKNESS.
PLEASE -- HOW MAY I HELP?
!

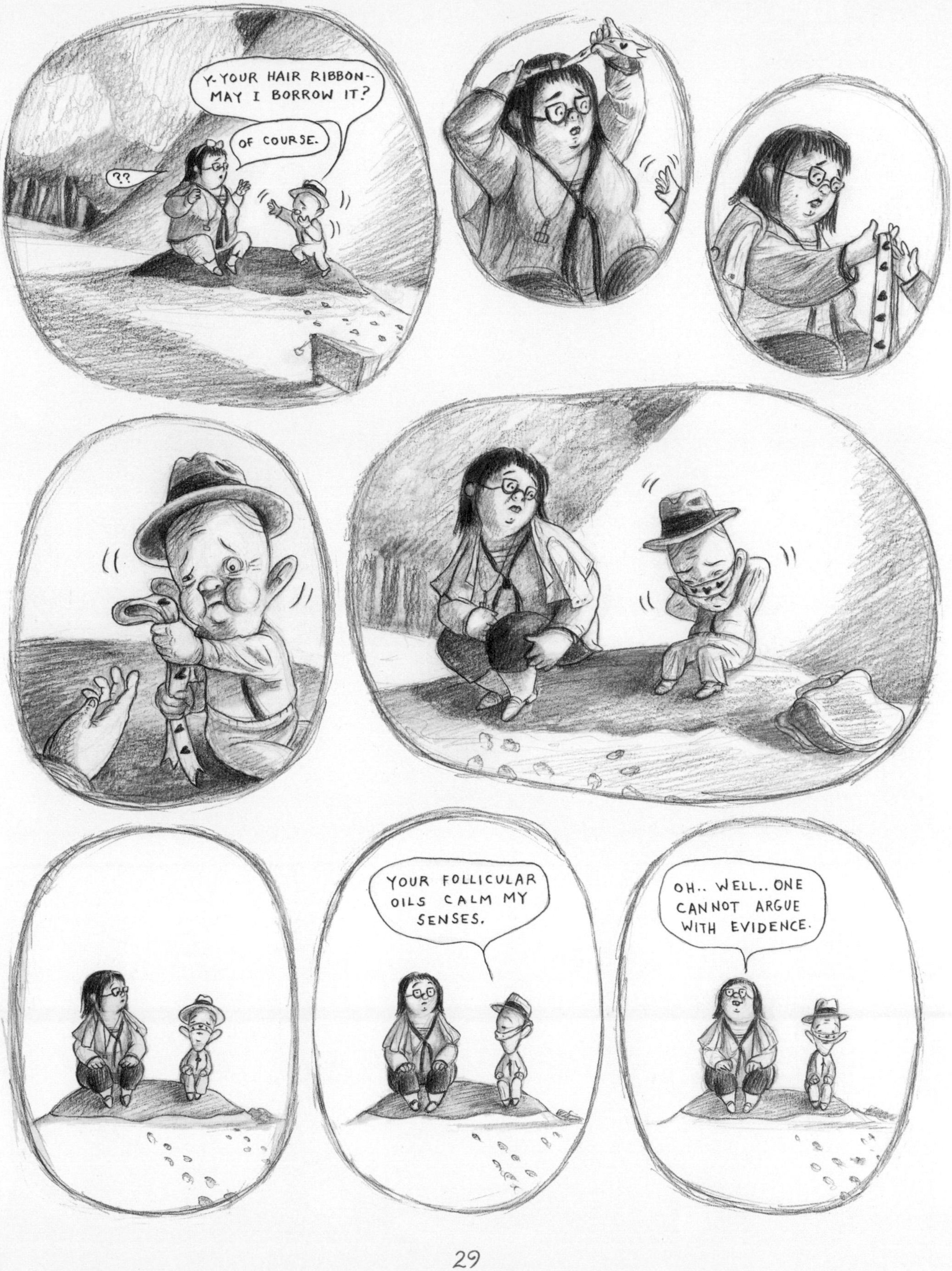
Y-YOUR HAIR RIBBON-- MAY I BORROW IT?
OF COURSE.
??
YOUR FOLLICULAR OILS CALM MY SENSES.
OH.. WELL.. ONE CANNOT ARGUE WITH EVIDENCE.

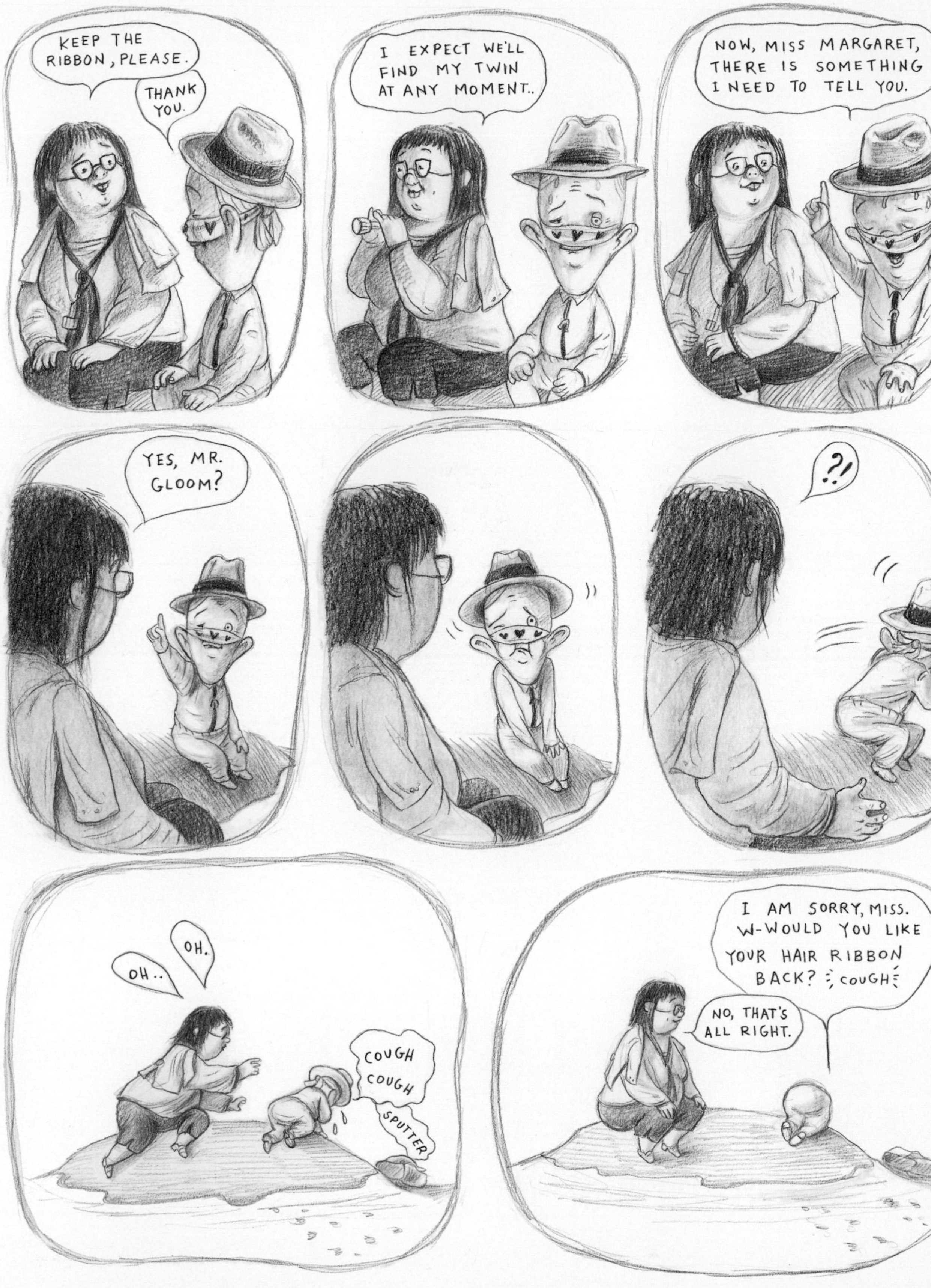
KEEP THE RIBBON, PLEASE.
THANK YOU.
I EXPECT WE'LL FIND MY TWIN AT ANY MOMENT..
NOW, MISS MARGARET, THERE IS SOMETHING I NEED TO TELL YOU.
YES, MR. GLOOM?
?!
OH..
OH.
COUGH COUGH
SPUTTER
I AM SORRY, MISS. W-WOULD YOU LIKE YOUR HAIR RIBBON BACK? COUGH
NO, THAT'S ALL RIGHT.

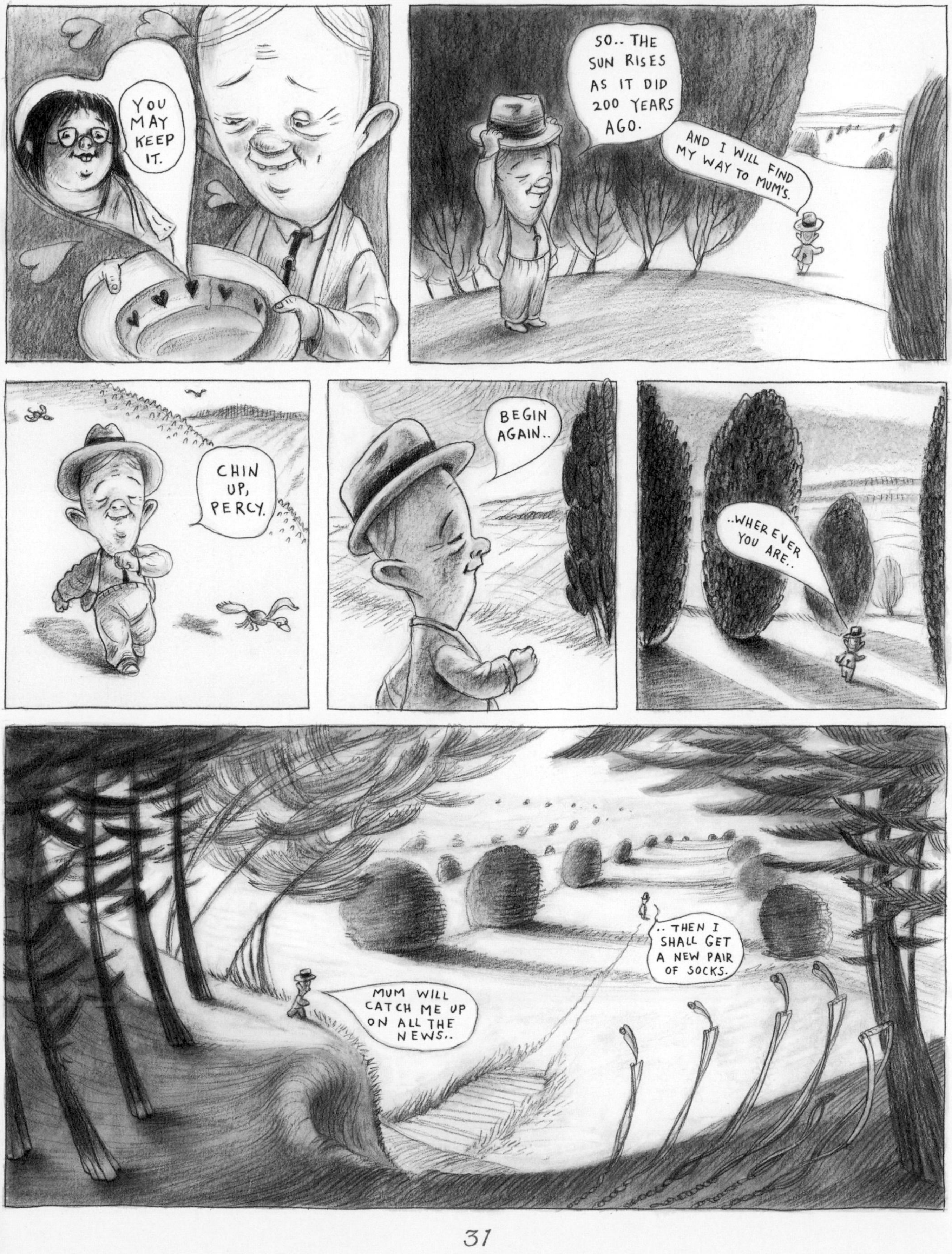
YOU MAY KEEP IT.
SO.. THE SUN RISES AS IT DID 200 YEARS AGO.
AND I WILL FIND MY WAY TO MUM'S.
CHIN UP, PERCY.
BEGIN AGAIN..
..WHEREVER YOU ARE..
MUM WILL CATCH ME UP ON ALL THE NEWS..
.. THEN I SHALL GET A NEW PAIR OF SOCKS.

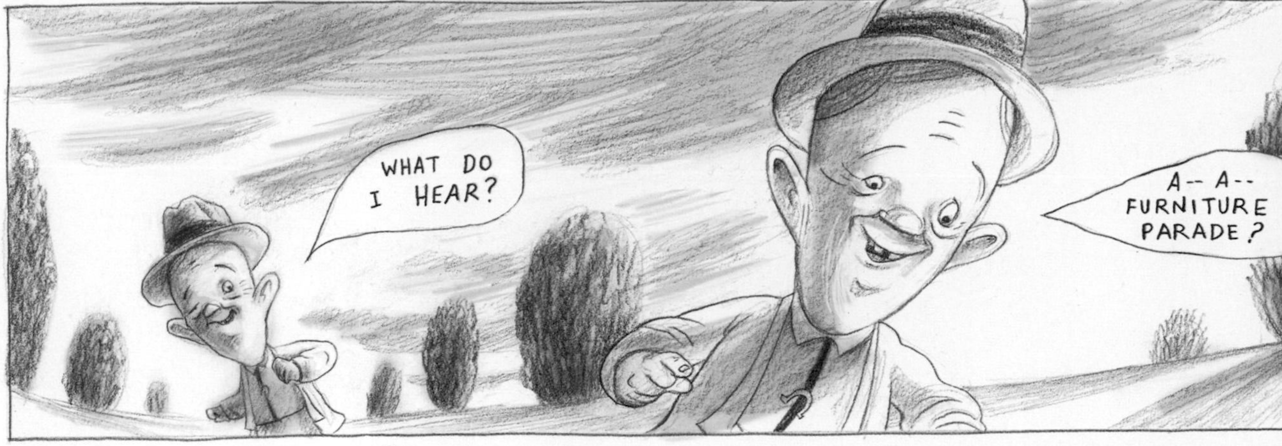
WHAT DO I HEAR?
A-- A-- FURNITURE PARADE?

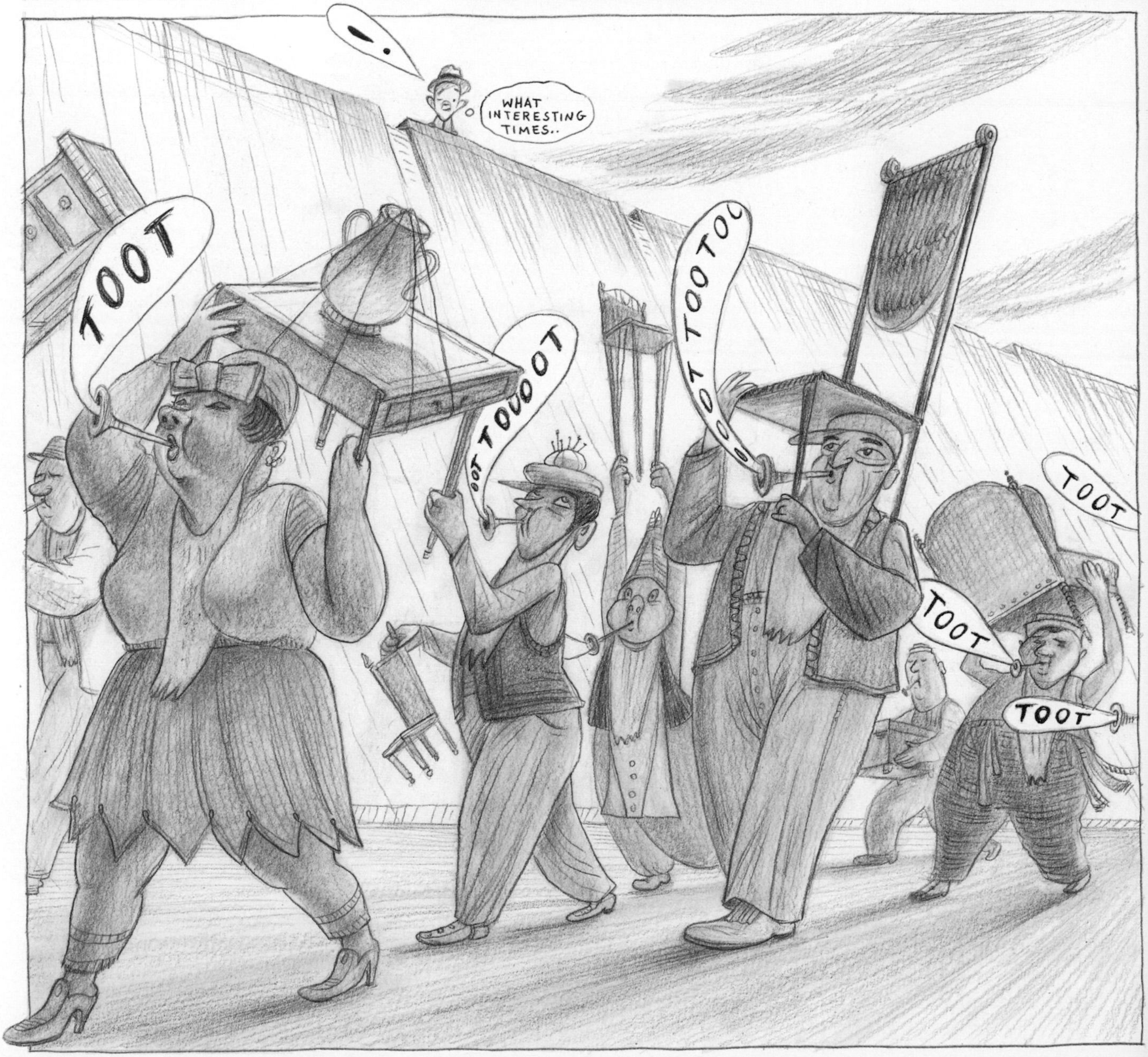
!
WHAT INTERESTING TIMES..
TOOT
TOOT
TOOT
TOOT

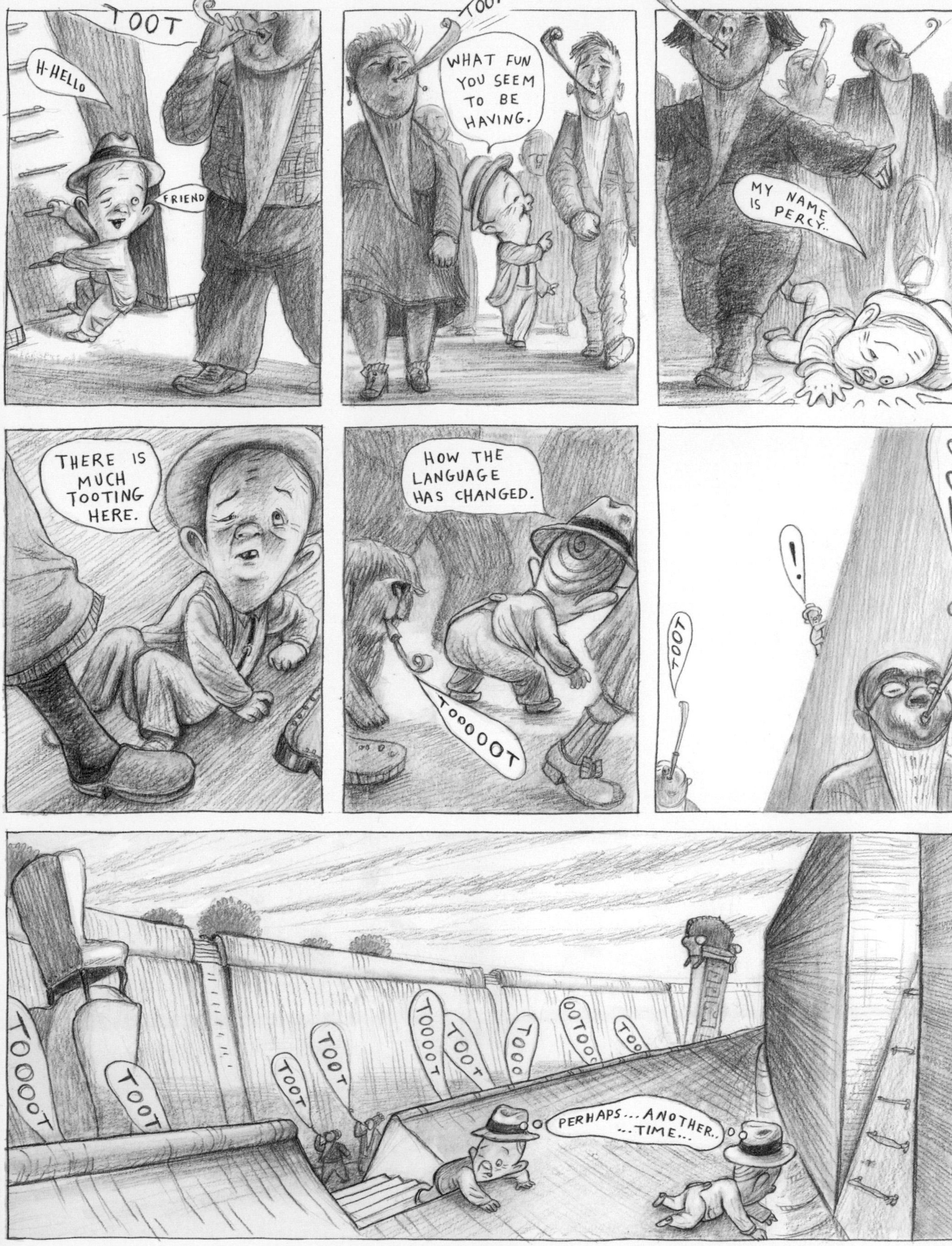
TOOT
H-HELLO
FRIEND
TOOT
WHAT FUN YOU SEEM TO BE HAVING.
MY NAME IS PERCY..
THERE IS MUCH TOOTING HERE.
HOW THE LANGUAGE HAS CHANGED.
TOOOOOT
TOOT
!
TOOT
TOOOOT
TOOT
TOOT
TOOT
TOOOOT
TOOT
TOOO
OOTOOO
TOO
PERHAPS... ANOTHER.. ...TIME...

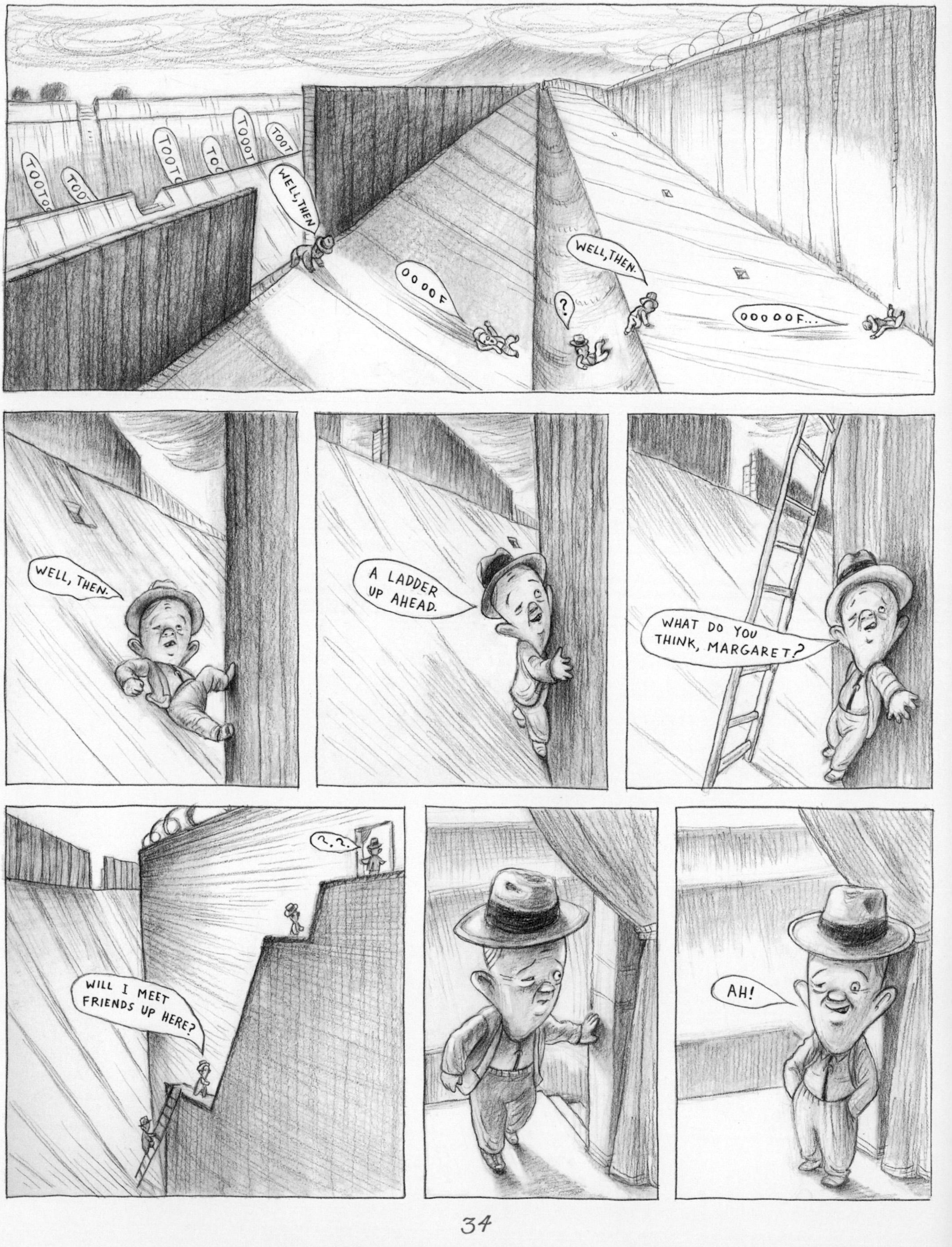
TOOTOO
TOOT
TOOTO
TOO
TOOOT
TOOT
WELL, THEN
OOOOF
?
WELL, THEN.
OOOOOF...
WELL, THEN.
A LADDER UP AHEAD.
WHAT DO YOU THINK, MARGARET?
?.?.
WILL I MEET FRIENDS UP HERE?
AH!

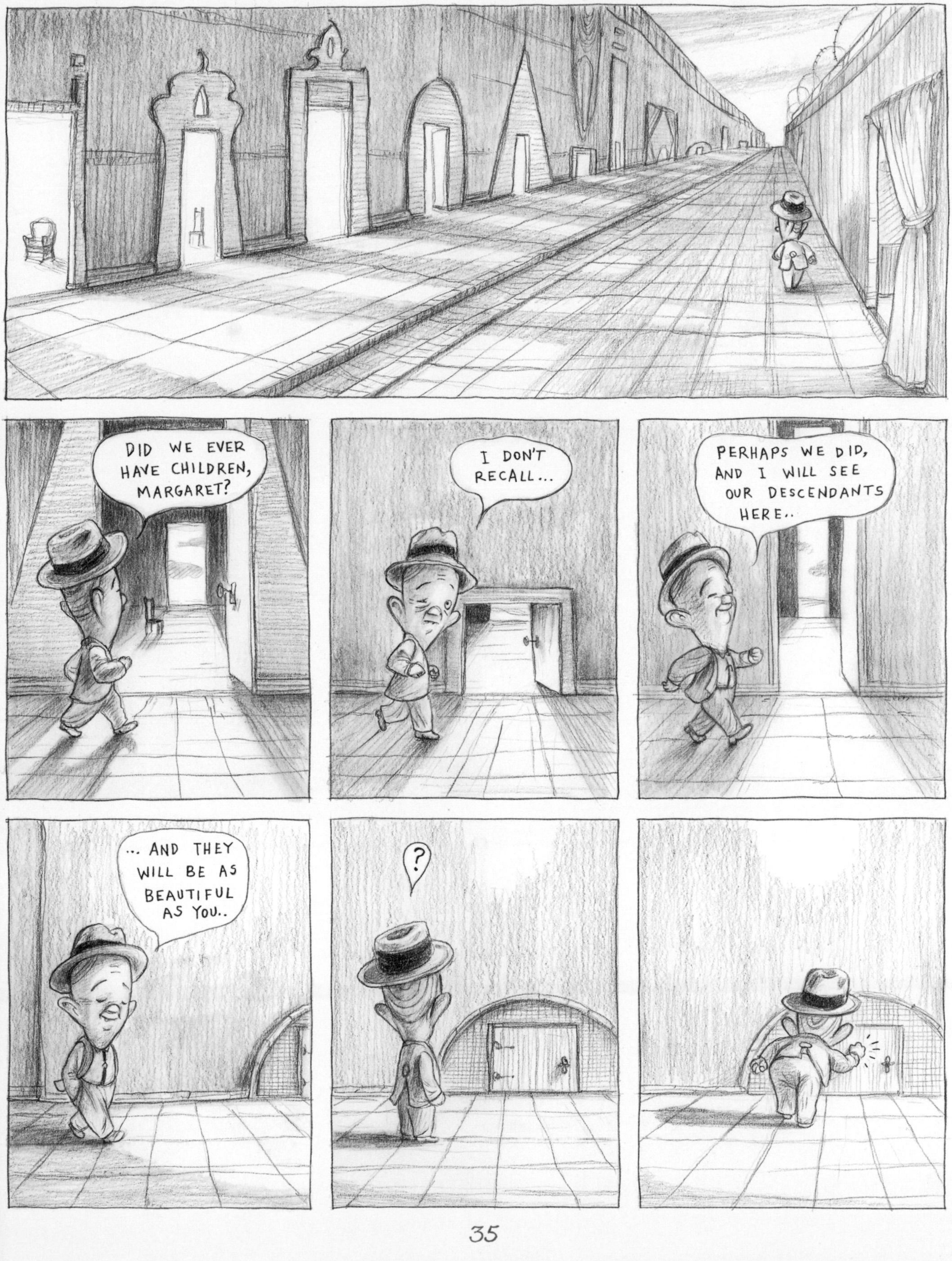
DID WE EVER HAVE CHILDREN, MARGARET?
I DON'T RECALL...
PERHAPS WE DID, AND I WILL SEE OUR DESCENDANTS HERE..
... AND THEY WILL BE AS BEAUTIFUL AS YOU..
?

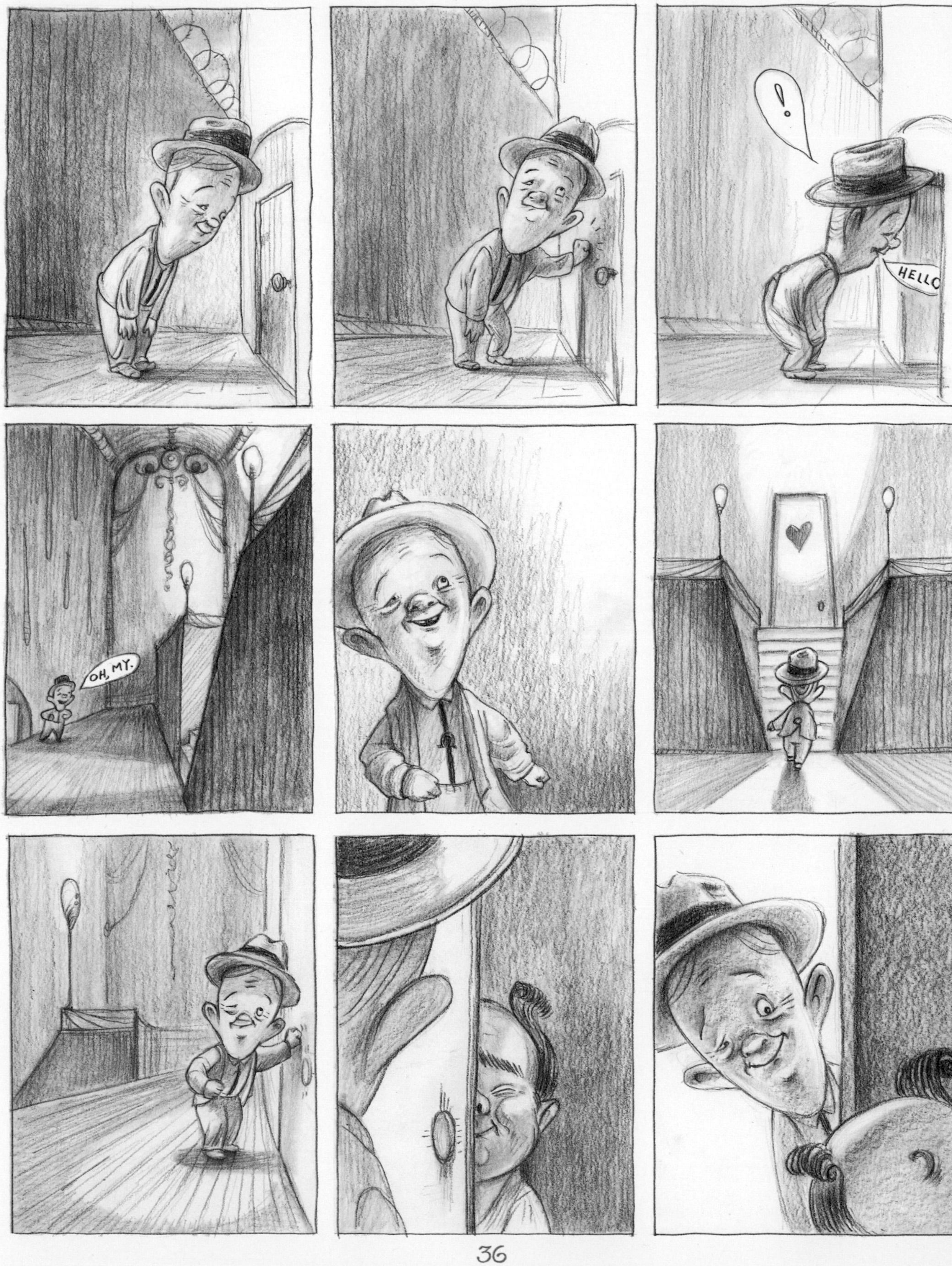
!
HELLO
OH, MY.

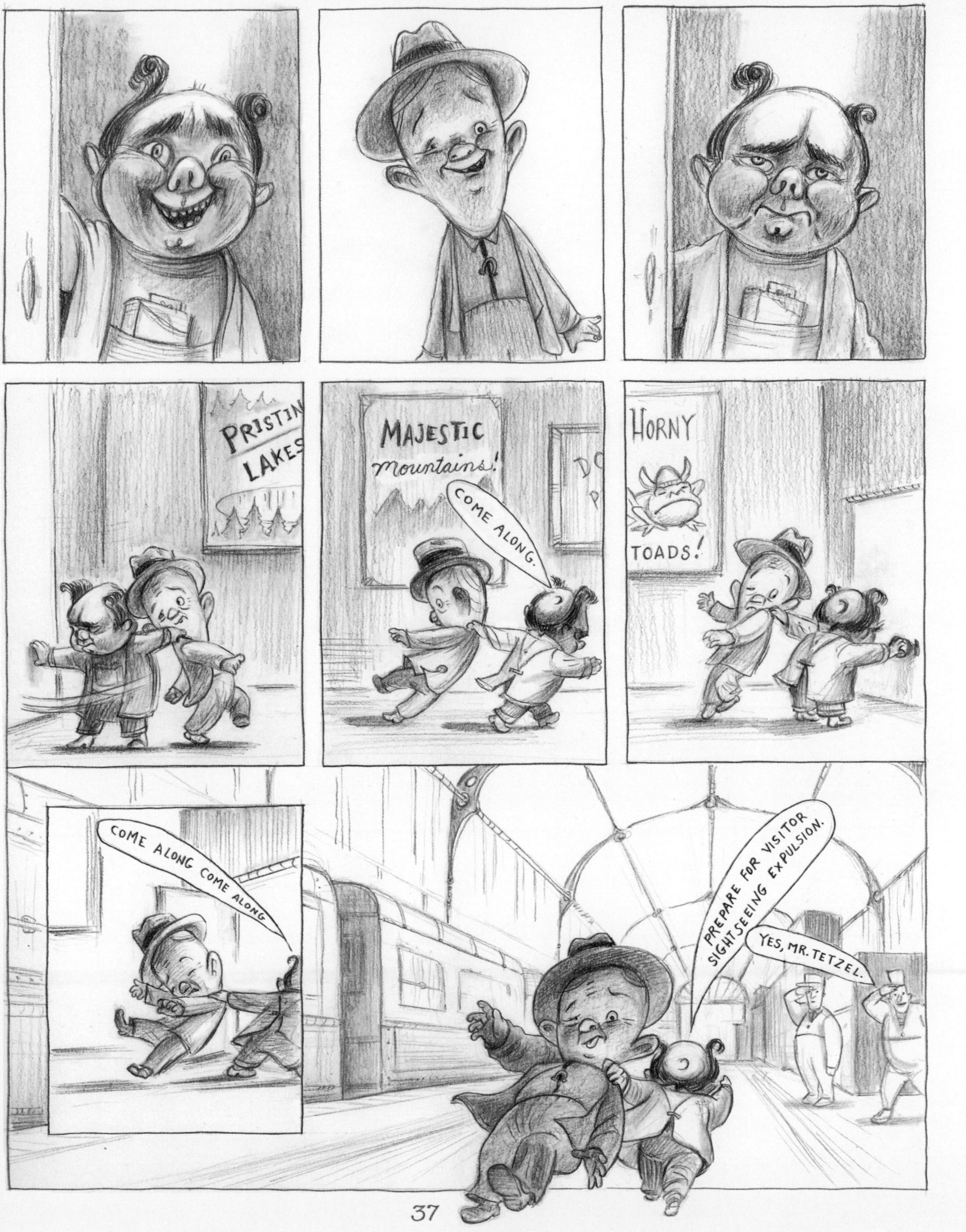
PRISTIN
LAKES
MAJESTIC
mountains!
COME ALONG.
HORNY
TOADS!
COME ALONG COME ALONG
PREPARE FOR VISITOR SIGHTSEEING EXPULSION.
YES, MR. TETZEL.

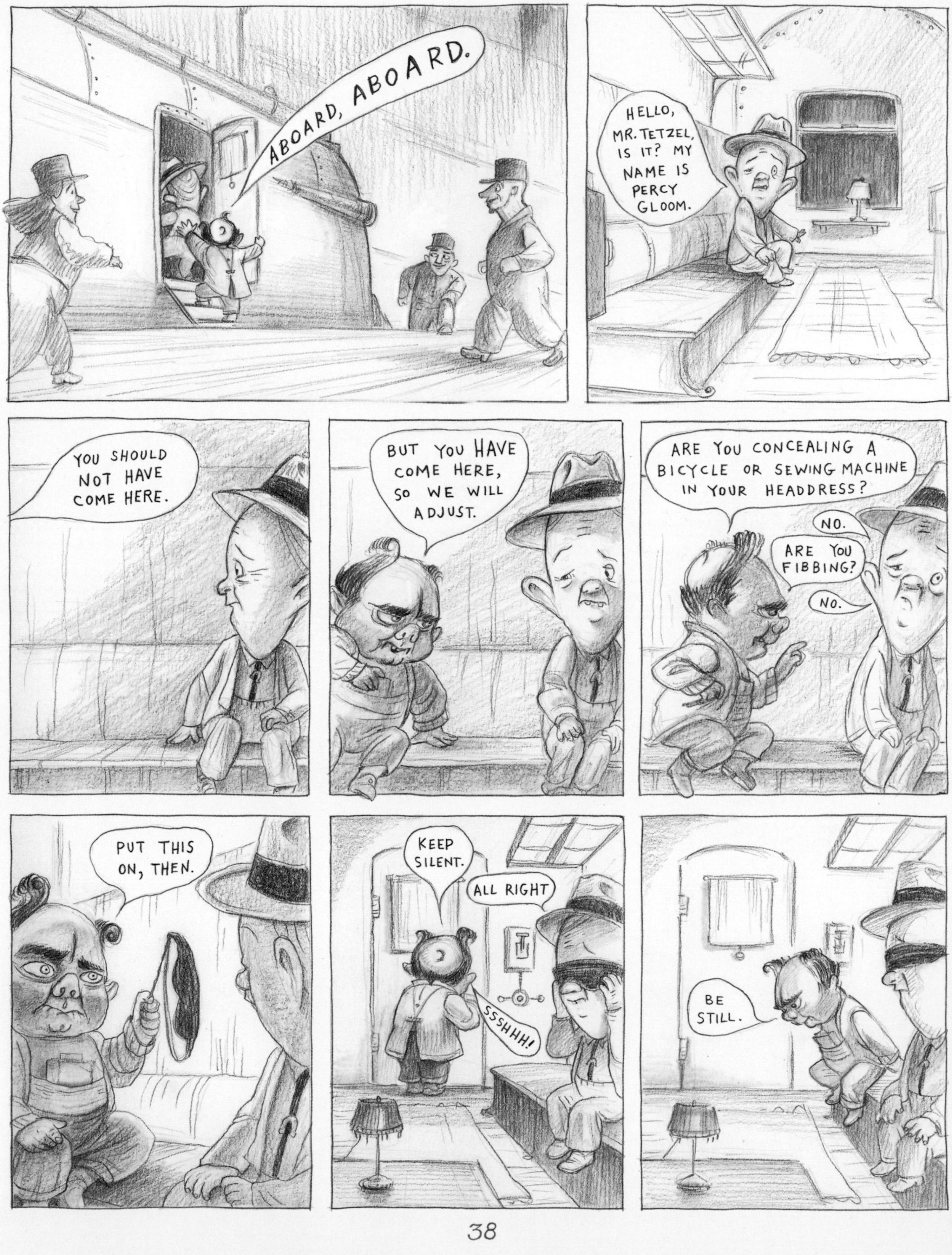
ABOARD, ABOARD.
HELLO, MR. TETZEL, IS IT? MY NAME IS PERCY GLOOM.
YOU SHOULD NOT HAVE COME HERE.
BUT YOU HAVE COME HERE, SO WE WILL ADJUST.
ARE YOU CONCEALING A BICYCLE OR SEWING MACHINE IN YOUR HEADDRESS?
NO.
ARE YOU FIBBING?
NO.
PUT THIS ON, THEN.
KEEP SILENT.
ALL RIGHT
SSSHHH!
BE STILL.

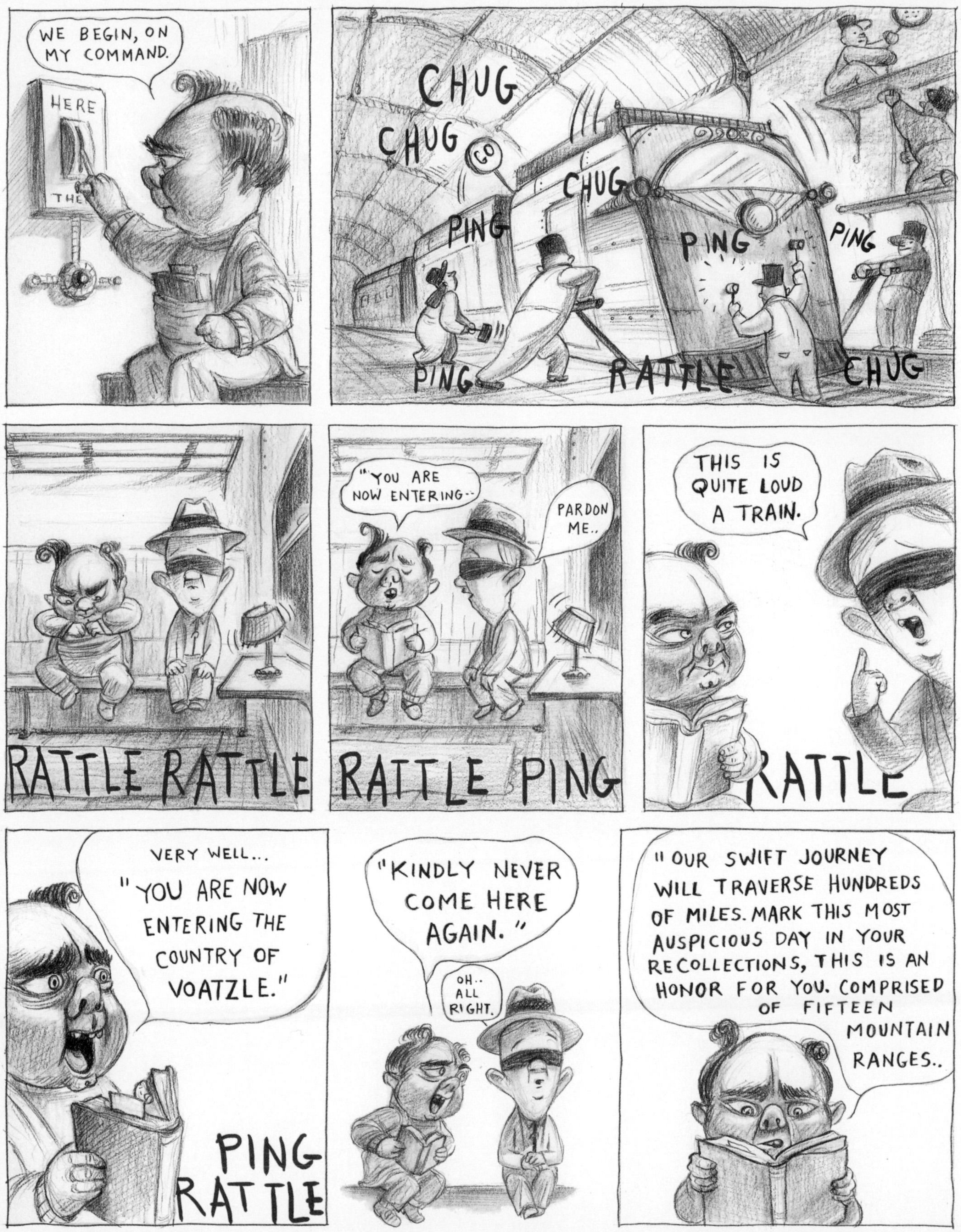
WE BEGIN, ON MY COMMAND.
HERE
THE
CHUG
CHUG
GO
CHUG
PING
PING
PING
PING
RATTLE
CHUG
RATTLE RATTLE
"YOU ARE NOW ENTERING..
PARDON ME..
RATTLE PING
THIS IS QUITE LOUD A TRAIN.
RATTLE
VERY WELL...
"YOU ARE NOW ENTERING THE COUNTRY OF VOATZLE."
PING
RATTLE
"KINDLY NEVER COME HERE AGAIN."
OH.. ALL RIGHT.
"OUR SWIFT JOURNEY WILL TRAVERSE HUNDREDS OF MILES. MARK THIS MOST AUSPICIOUS DAY IN YOUR RECOLLECTIONS, THIS IS AN HONOR FOR YOU. COMPRISED OF FIFTEEN MOUNTAIN RANGES..

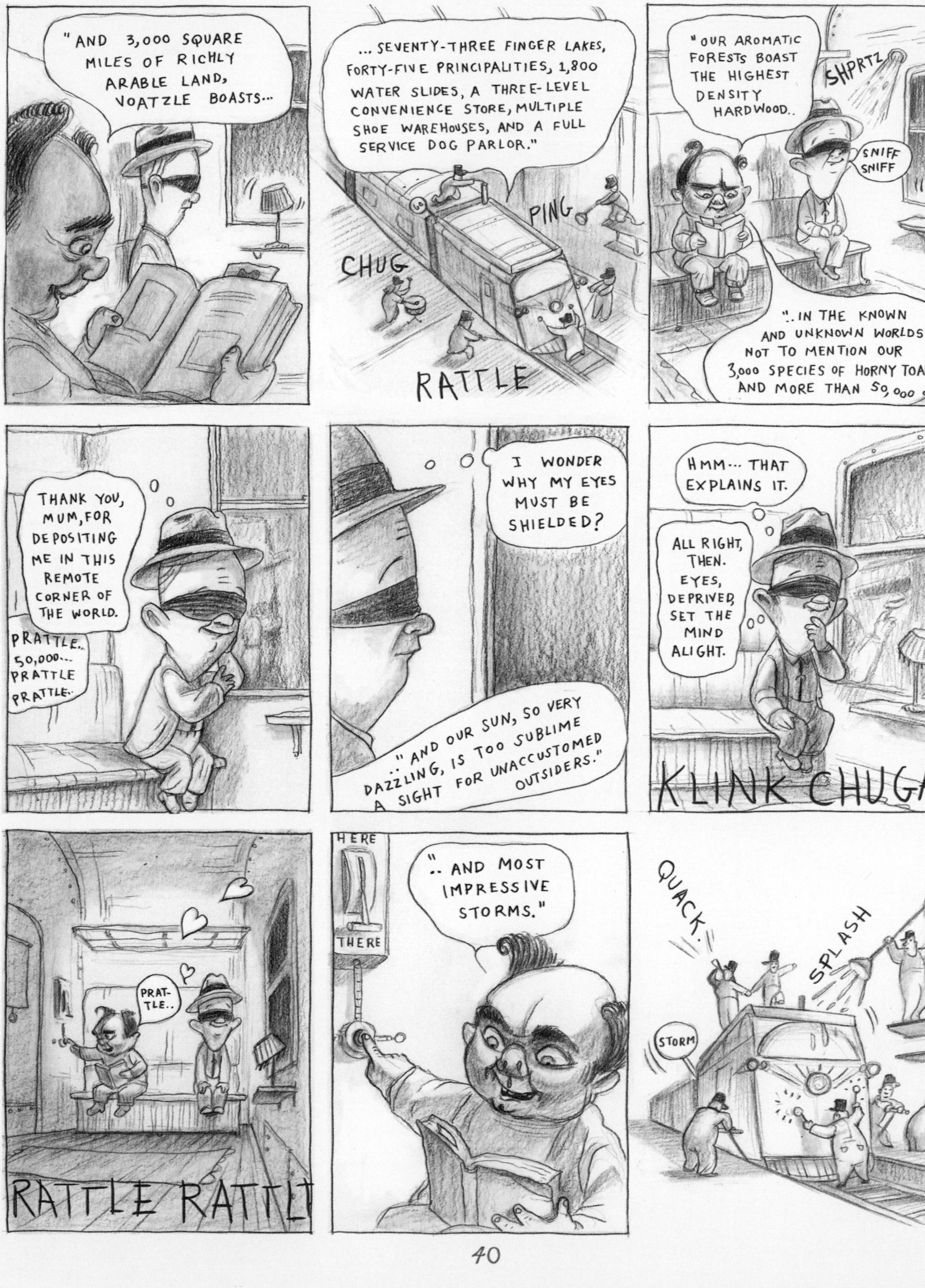
"AND 3,000 SQUARE MILES OF RICHLY ARABLE LAND, VOATZLE BOASTS...
... SEVENTY-THREE FINGER LAKES, FORTY-FIVE PRINCIPALITIES, 1,800 WATER SLIDES, A THREE-LEVEL CONVENIENCE STORE, MULTIPLE SHOE WAREHOUSES, AND A FULL SERVICE DOG PARLOR."
PING
CHUG
RATTLE
"OUR AROMATIC FORESTS BOAST THE HIGHEST DENSITY HARDWOOD..
SHPRTZ
SNIFF SNIFF
"..IN THE KNOWN AND UNKNOWN WORLDS NOT TO MENTION OUR 3,000 SPECIES OF HORNY TOAD AND MORE THAN 50,000
THANK YOU, MUM, FOR DEPOSITING ME IN THIS REMOTE CORNER OF THE WORLD.
PRATTLE.. 50,000... PRATTLE PRATTLE..
I WONDER WHY MY EYES MUST BE SHIELDED?
.." AND OUR SUN, SO VERY DAZZLING, IS TOO SUBLIME A SIGHT FOR UNACCUSTOMED OUTSIDERS."
HMM... THAT EXPLAINS IT.
ALL RIGHT, THEN. EYES, DEPRIVED, SET THE MIND ALIGHT.
KLINK CHUGA
PRAT-TLE..
RATTLE RATTLE
HERE
THERE
".. AND MOST IMPRESSIVE STORMS."
QUACK.
SPLASH
STORM

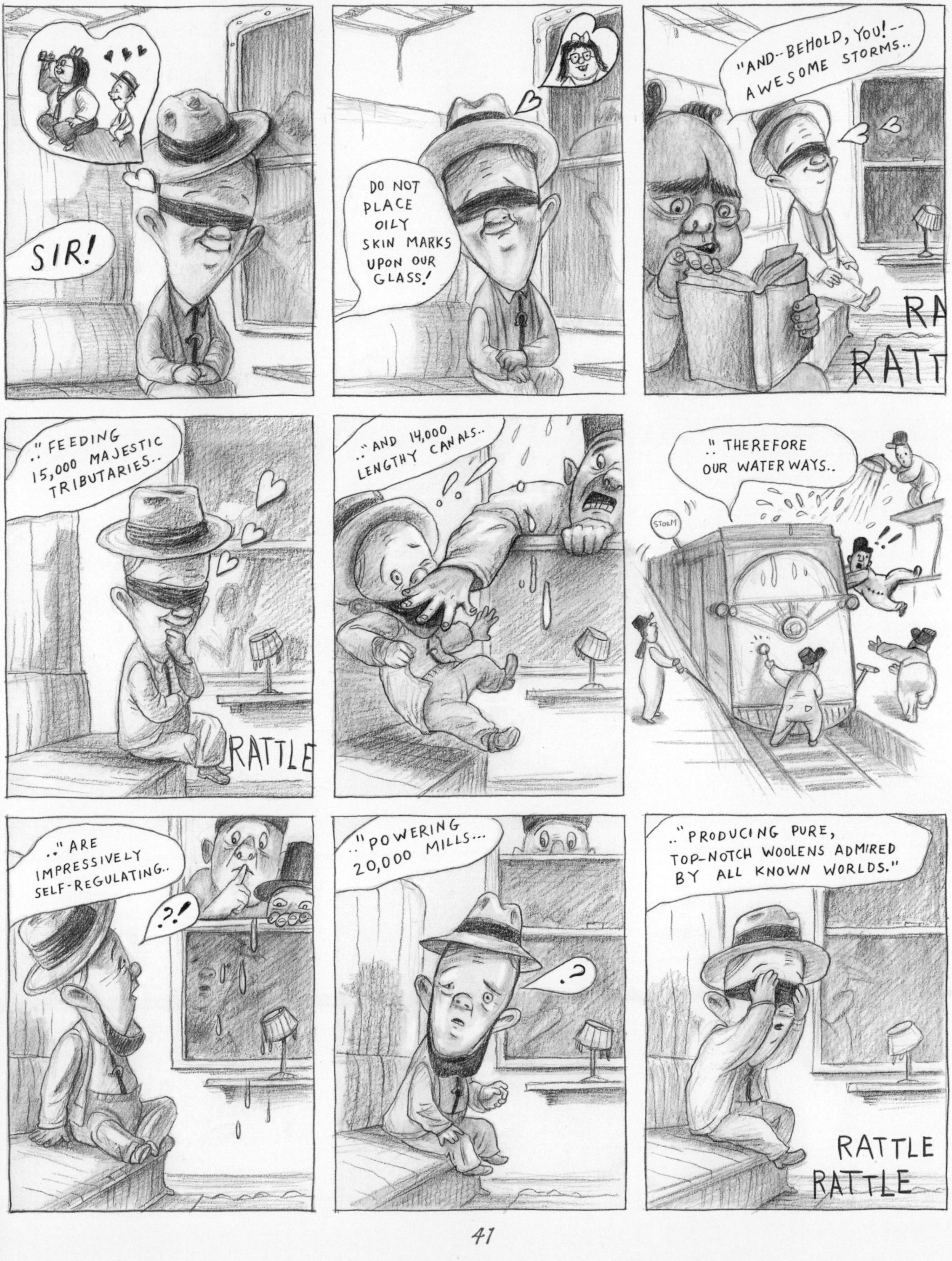
SIR!
DO NOT PLACE OILY SKIN MARKS UPON OUR GLASS!
"AND--BEHOLD, YOU!-- AWESOME STORMS..
RA
RATT
.."FEEDING 15,000 MAJESTIC TRIBUTARIES..
RATTLE
.."AND 14,000 LENGTHY CANALS..
.."THEREFORE OUR WATERWAYS..
STORM
..."ARE IMPRESSIVELY SELF-REGULATING..
?!
.."POWERING 20,000 MILLS...
?
.."PRODUCING PURE, TOP-NOTCH WOOLENS ADMIRED BY ALL KNOWN WORLDS."
RATTLE
RATTLE

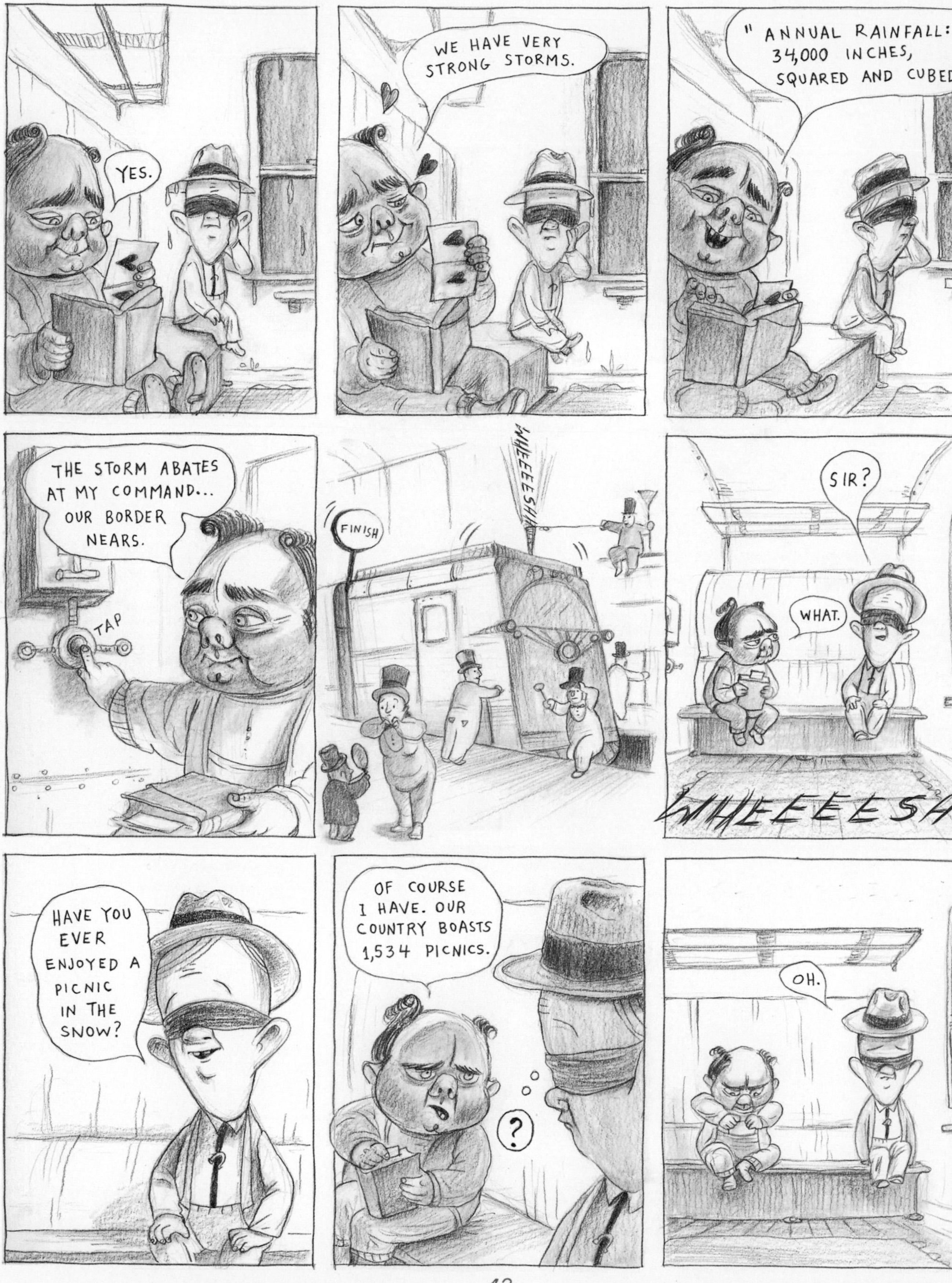
YES.
WE HAVE VERY STRONG STORMS.
" ANNUAL RAINFALL: 34,000 INCHES, SQUARED AND CUBED."
THE STORM ABATES AT MY COMMAND... OUR BORDER NEARS.
TAP
WHEEEESH
FINISH
SIR?
WHAT.
WHEEEESHH
HAVE YOU EVER ENJOYED A PICNIC IN THE SNOW?
OF COURSE I HAVE. OUR COUNTRY BOASTS 1,534 PICNICS.
?
OH.

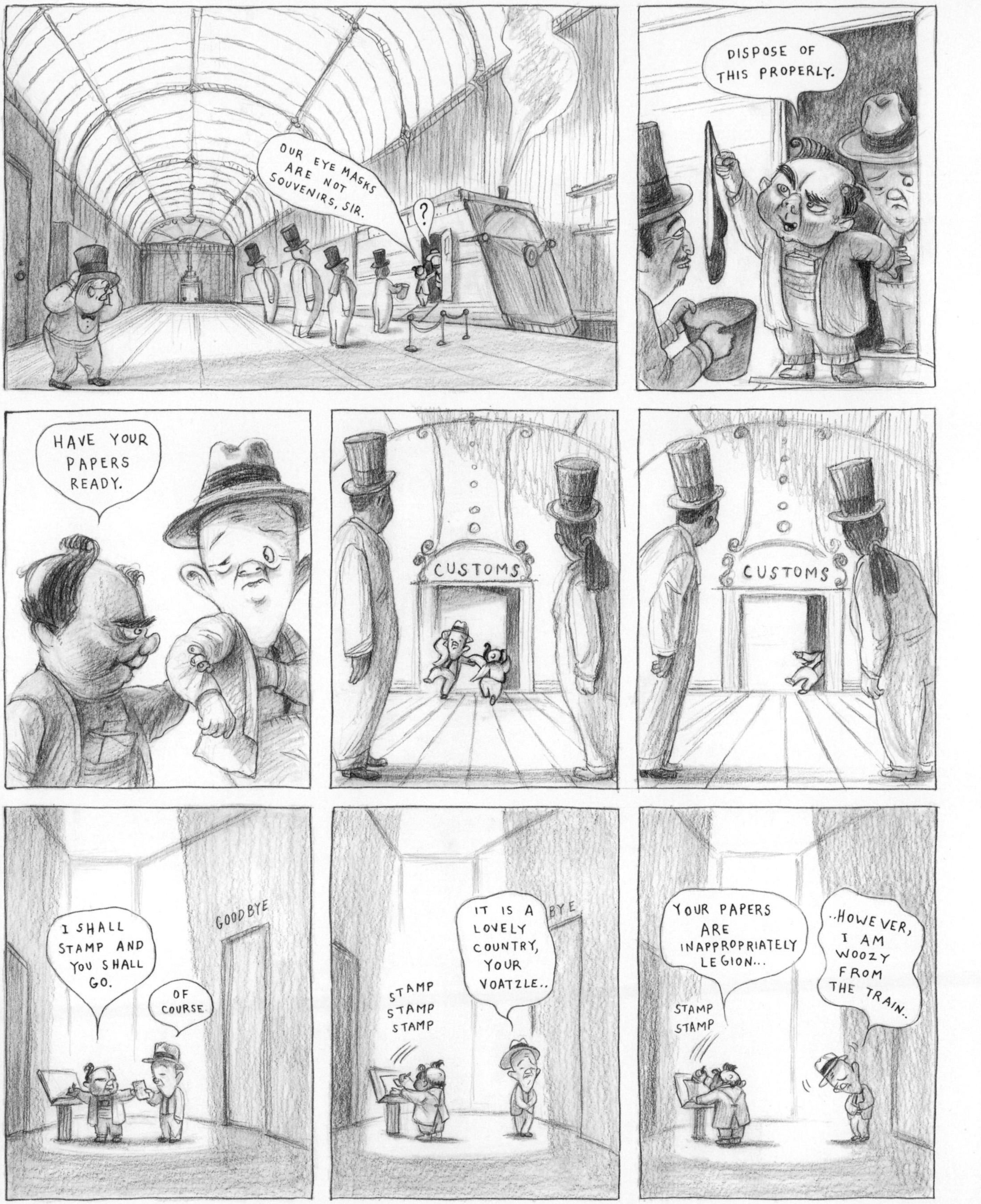
OUR EYE MASKS ARE NOT SOUVENIRS, SIR.
?
DISPOSE OF THIS PROPERLY.
HAVE YOUR PAPERS READY.
CUSTOMS
CUSTOMS
GOODBYE
I SHALL STAMP AND YOU SHALL GO.
OF COURSE.
STAMP STAMP STAMP
IT IS A LOVELY COUNTRY, YOUR VOATZLE..
BYE
YOUR PAPERS ARE INAPPROPRIATELY LEGION...
STAMP STAMP
..HOWEVER, I AM WOOZY FROM THE TRAIN..

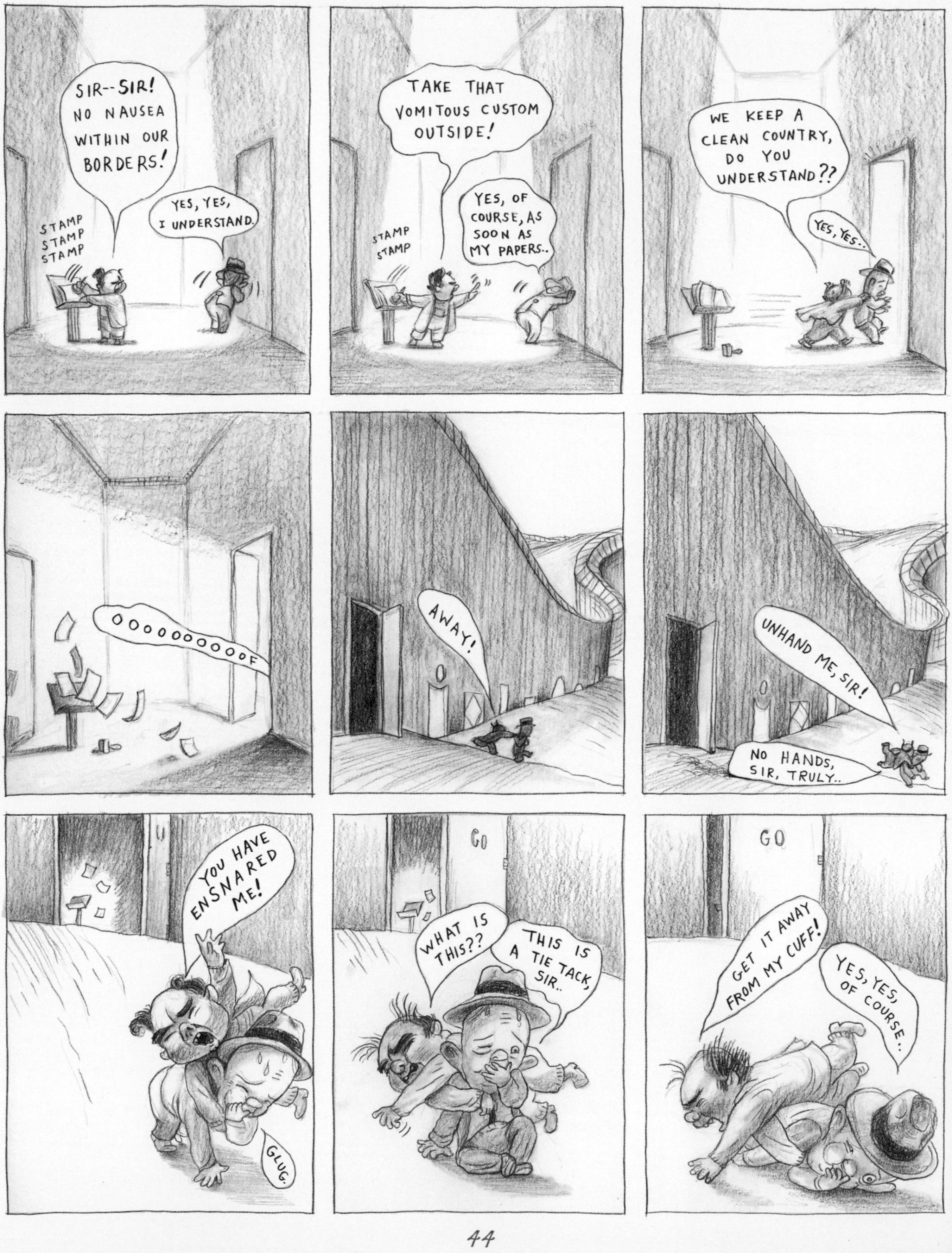
SIR--SIR! NO NAUSEA WITHIN OUR BORDERS!
STAMP STAMP STAMP
YES, YES, I UNDERSTAND.
TAKE THAT VOMITOUS CUSTOM OUTSIDE!
STAMP STAMP
YES, OF COURSE, AS SOON AS MY PAPERS..
WE KEEP A CLEAN COUNTRY, DO YOU UNDERSTAND??
YES, YES..
OOOOOOOOOOF
AWAY!
UNHAND ME, SIR!
NO HANDS, SIR, TRULY..
YOU HAVE ENSNARED ME!
GLUG.
GO
WHAT IS THIS??
THIS IS A TIE TACK, SIR..
GO
GET IT AWAY FROM MY CUFF!
YES, YES, OF COURSE..

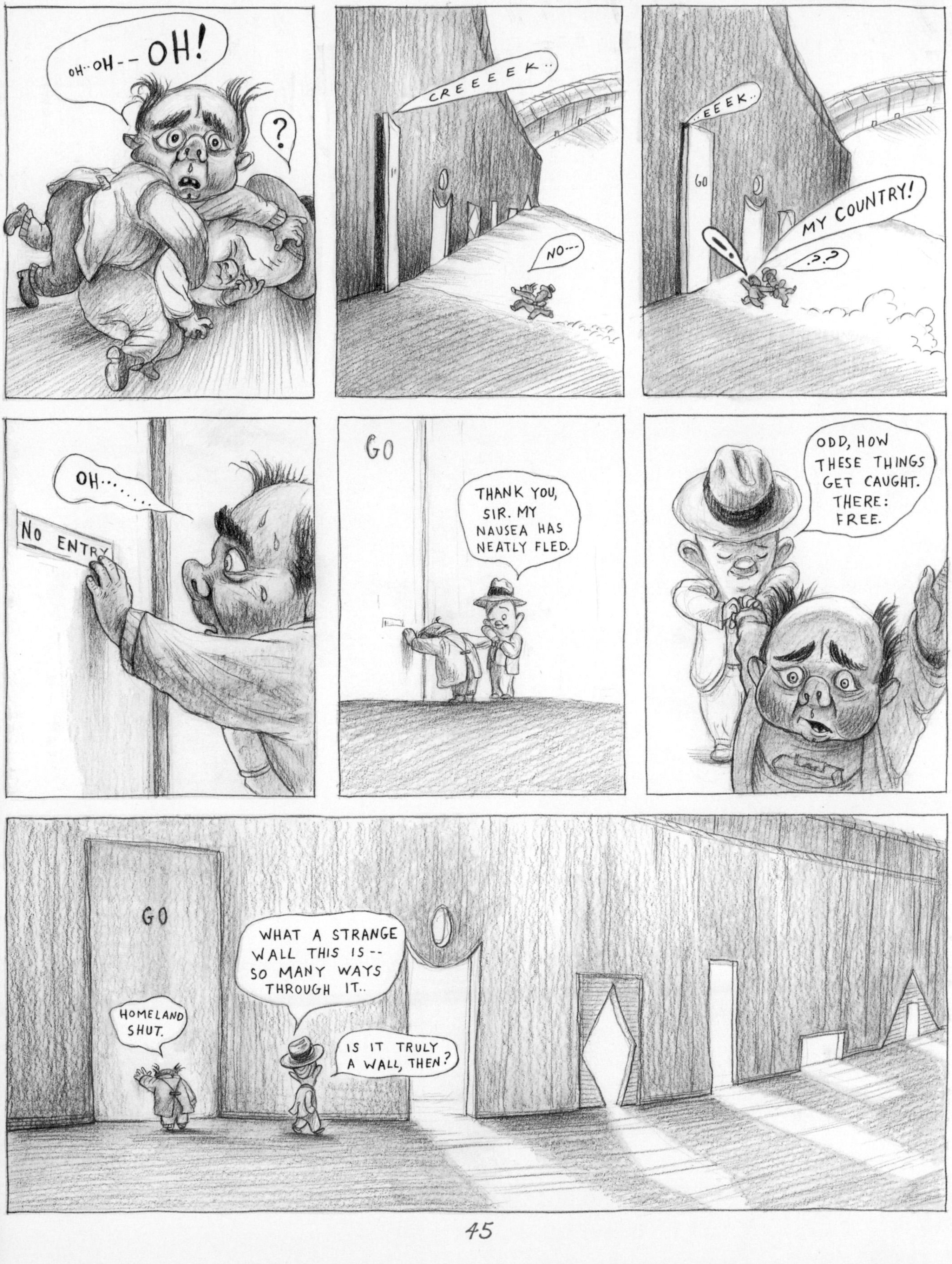
OH··OH-- OH!
?
CREEEEEK..
NO---
..EEEK..
GO
MY COUNTRY!
!
?.?
OH·········
NO ENTRY
GO
THANK YOU, SIR. MY NAUSEA HAS NEATLY FLED.
ODD, HOW THESE THINGS GET CAUGHT. THERE: FREE.
GO
WHAT A STRANGE WALL THIS IS -- SO MANY WAYS THROUGH IT..
HOMELAND SHUT.
IS IT TRULY A WALL, THEN?

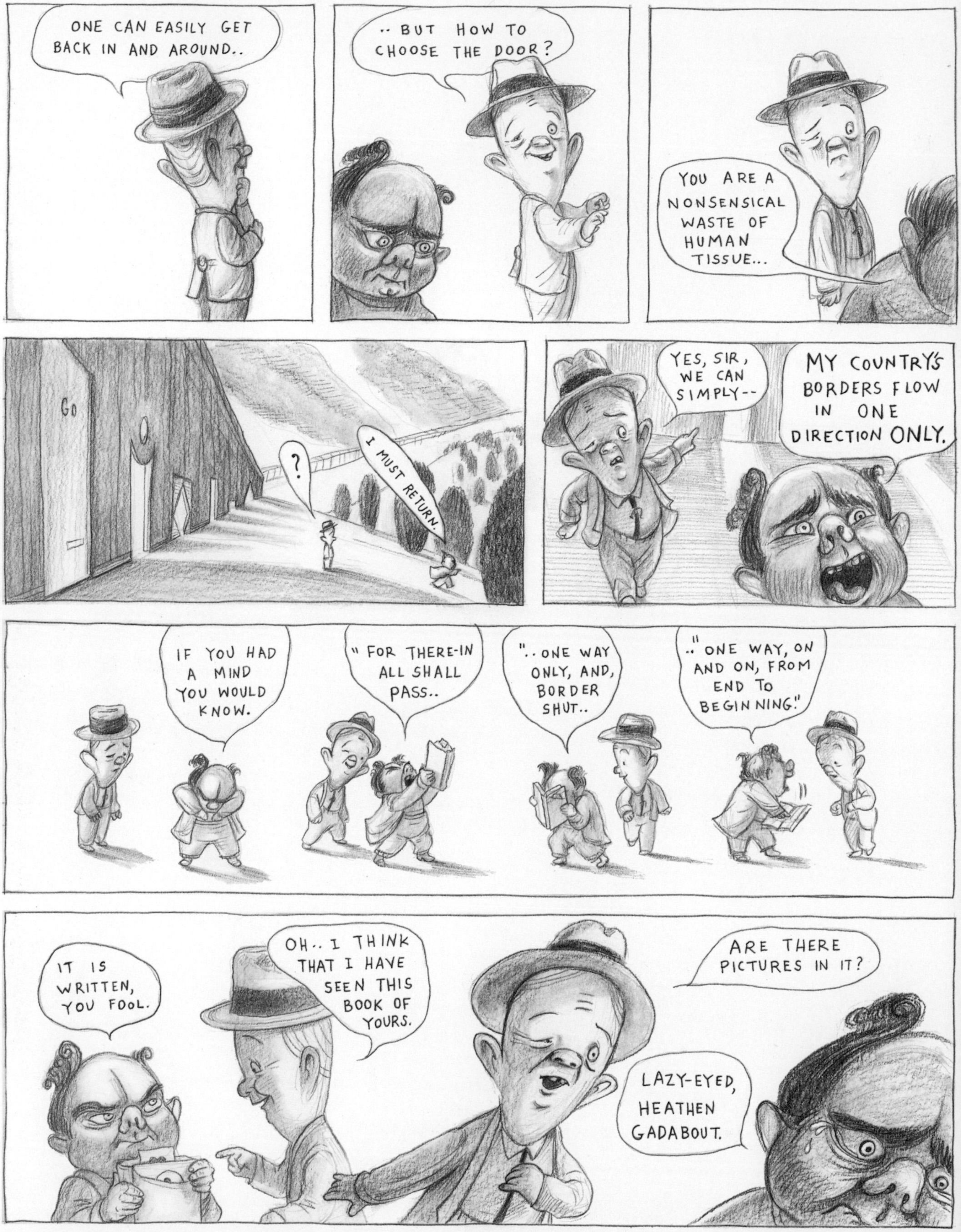
ONE CAN EASILY GET BACK IN AND AROUND..
.. BUT HOW TO CHOOSE THE DOOR?
YOU ARE A NONSENSICAL WASTE OF HUMAN TISSUE...
GO
?
I MUST RETURN.
YES, SIR, WE CAN SIMPLY--
MY COUNTRY'S BORDERS FLOW IN ONE DIRECTION ONLY.
IF YOU HAD A MIND YOU WOULD KNOW.
" FOR THERE-IN ALL SHALL PASS..
".. ONE WAY ONLY, AND, BORDER SHUT..
.." ONE WAY, ON AND ON, FROM END TO BEGINNING."
IT IS WRITTEN, YOU FOOL.
OH.. I THINK THAT I HAVE SEEN THIS BOOK OF YOURS.
ARE THERE PICTURES IN IT?
LAZY-EYED, HEATHEN GADABOUT.

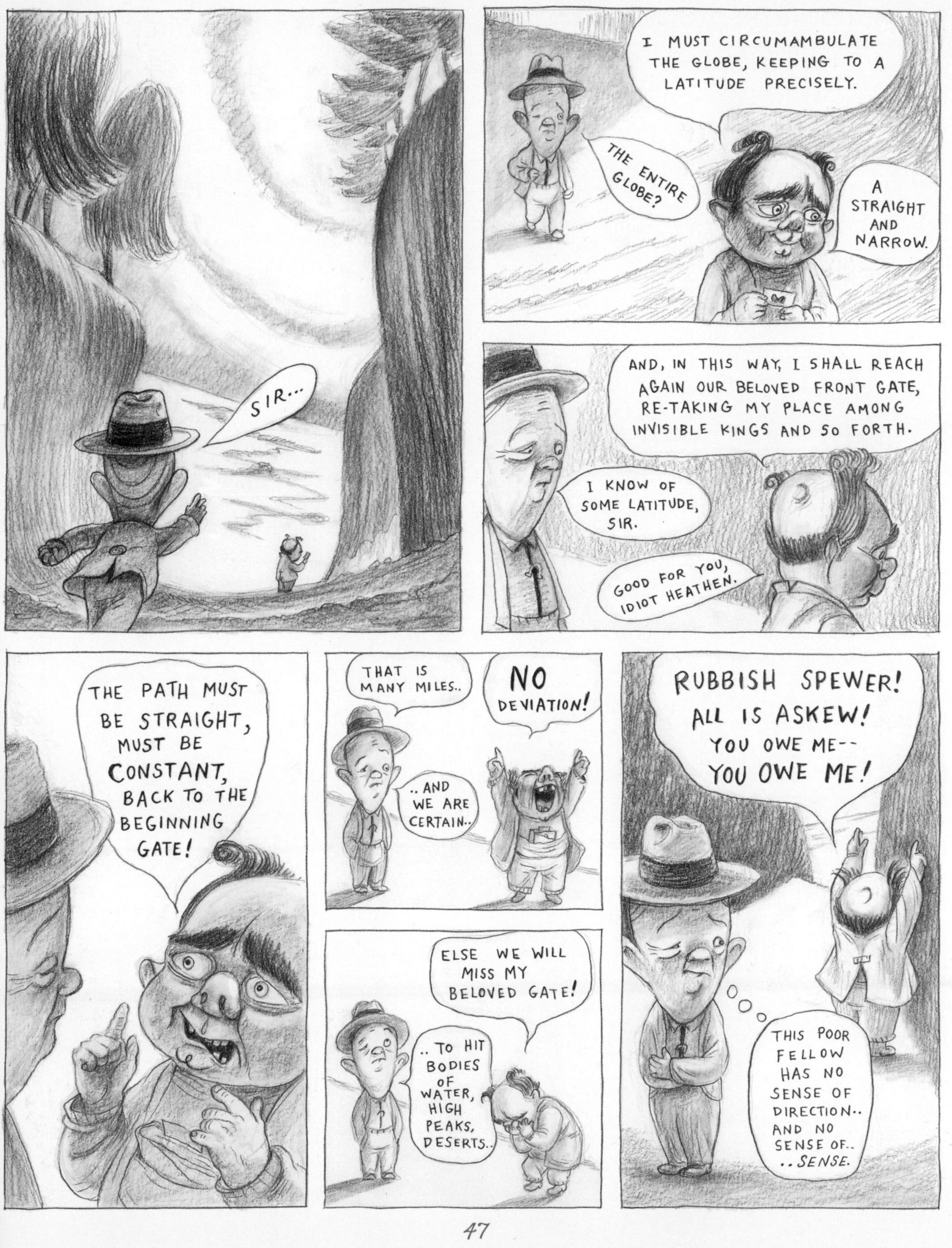
SIR...
I MUST CIRCUMAMBULATE THE GLOBE, KEEPING TO A LATITUDE PRECISELY.
THE ENTIRE GLOBE?
A STRAIGHT AND NARROW.
AND, IN THIS WAY, I SHALL REACH AGAIN OUR BELOVED FRONT GATE, RE-TAKING MY PLACE AMONG INVISIBLE KINGS AND SO FORTH.
I KNOW OF SOME LATITUDE, SIR.
GOOD FOR YOU, IDIOT HEATHEN.
THE PATH MUST BE STRAIGHT, MUST BE CONSTANT, BACK TO THE BEGINNING GATE!
THAT IS MANY MILES..
NO DEVIATION!
.. AND WE ARE CERTAIN..
ELSE WE WILL MISS MY BELOVED GATE!
.. TO HIT BODIES OF WATER, HIGH PEAKS, DESERTS..
RUBBISH SPEWER! ALL IS ASKEW! YOU OWE ME-- YOU OWE ME!
THIS POOR FELLOW HAS NO SENSE OF DIRECTION.. AND NO SENSE OF.. ..SENSE.

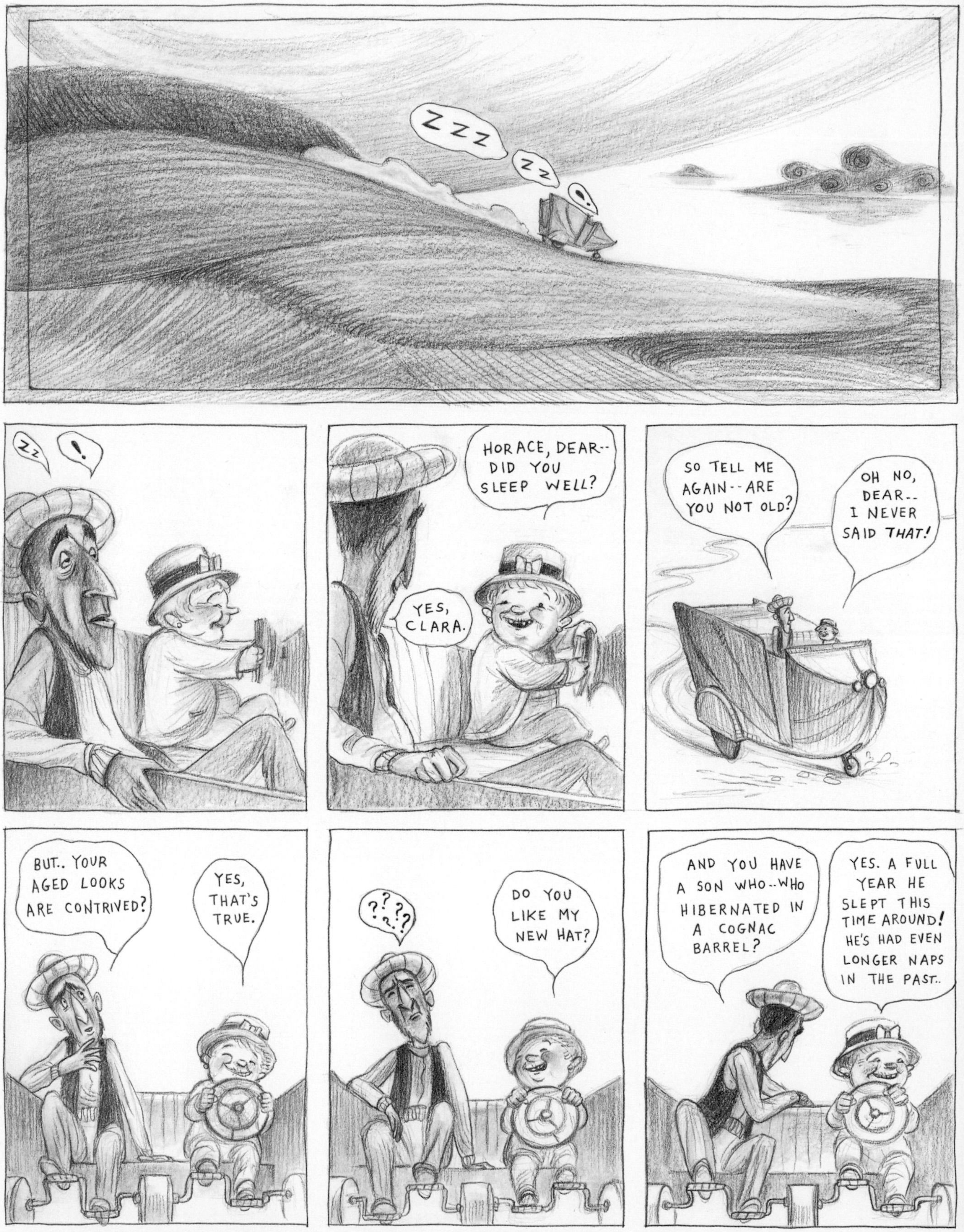
Z Z Z
Z Z
!
Z Z
!
HORACE, DEAR--
DID YOU
SLEEP WELL?
YES,
CLARA.
SO TELL ME
AGAIN--ARE
YOU NOT OLD?
OH NO,
DEAR--
I NEVER
SAID THAT!
BUT.. YOUR
AGED LOOKS
ARE CONTRIVED?
YES,
THAT'S
TRUE.
??
???
DO YOU
LIKE MY
NEW HAT?
AND YOU HAVE
A SON WHO..WHO
HIBERNATED IN
A COGNAC
BARREL?
YES. A FULL
YEAR HE
SLEPT THIS
TIME AROUND!
HE'S HAD EVEN
LONGER NAPS
IN THE PAST..

ONCE, AFTER A PARTICULARLY RIGOROUS CHECKERS MATCH..

..HE NAPPED FOR FIFTEEN YEARS!

FIFTEEN?!

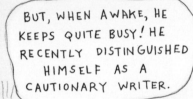
BUT, WHEN AWAKE, HE KEEPS QUITE BUSY! HE RECENTLY DISTINGUISHED HIMSELF AS A CAUTIONARY WRITER.

AND HE WAS STELLAR IN HIS FIRST PROFESSION AS WELL. THAT WAS SOME TIME AGO..

OH-- HERE WE GO...

CLARA THIS IS STEEP!

KEEP PEDALLING, DEAR.

FOR YEARS MY BOY WORKED AS A PROFESSIONAL SCAPEGOAT, SERVING AS A LAST-MINUTE PROXY FOR PEOPLE ON THEIR WAY TO THE GALLOWS. THEY THEN ESCAPED IN ANY NUMBER OF DISGUISES MADE BY YOUR UNCLE VICENTE.

MY PERCY NEVER DIED, OF COURSE. HE MODESTLY SAVED MANY A GREAT AND HELPFUL MIND FROM THE CLUTCHES OF SUPERSTITION.

49

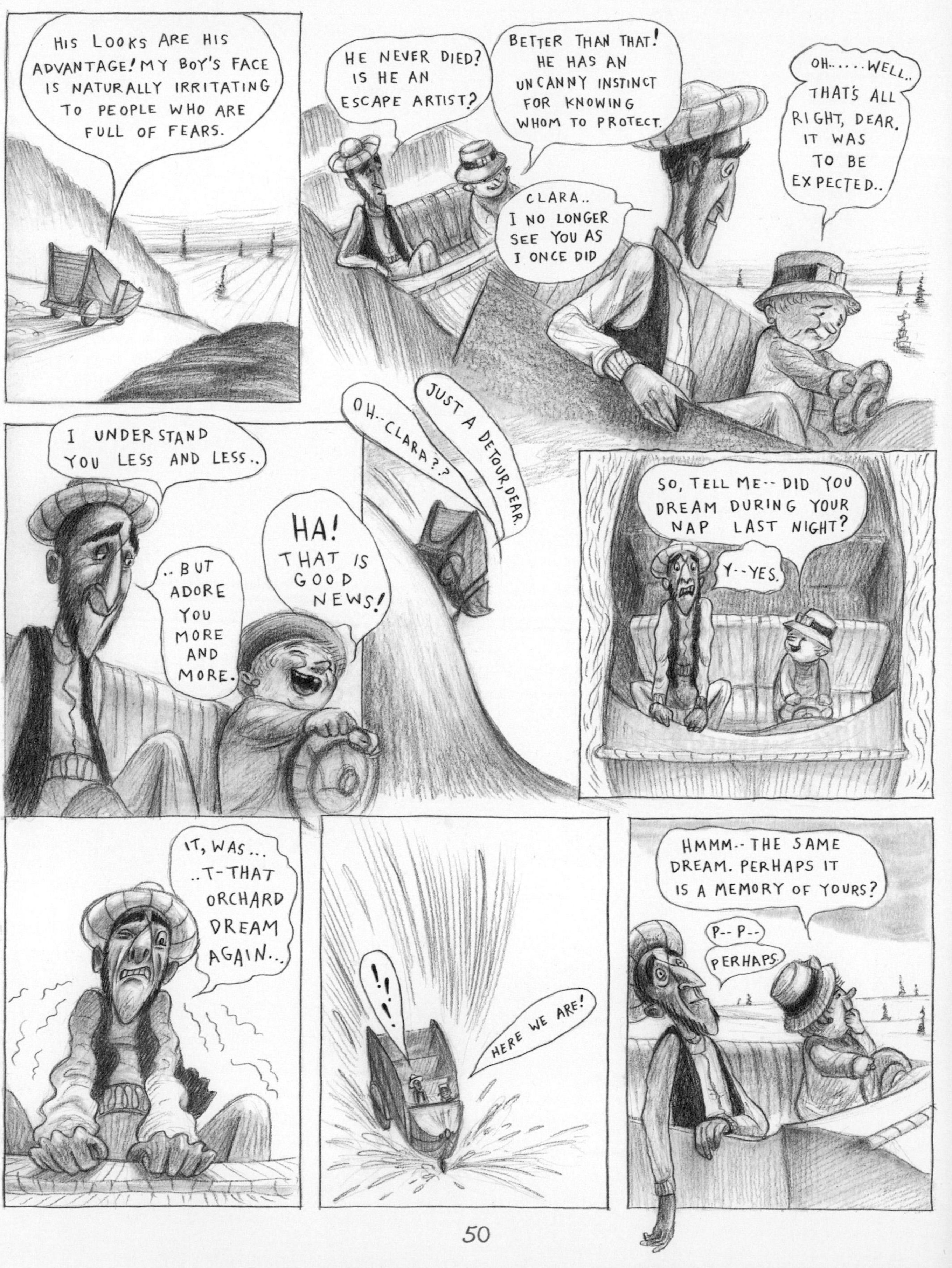
HIS LOOKS ARE HIS ADVANTAGE! MY BOY'S FACE IS NATURALLY IRRITATING TO PEOPLE WHO ARE FULL OF FEARS.
HE NEVER DIED? IS HE AN ESCAPE ARTIST?
BETTER THAN THAT! HE HAS AN UNCANNY INSTINCT FOR KNOWING WHOM TO PROTECT.
CLARA.. I NO LONGER SEE YOU AS I ONCE DID
OH.....WELL.. THAT'S ALL RIGHT, DEAR. IT WAS TO BE EXPECTED..
I UNDERSTAND YOU LESS AND LESS..
..BUT ADORE YOU MORE AND MORE.
HA! THAT IS GOOD NEWS!
OH--CLARA??
JUST A DETOUR, DEAR.
SO, TELL ME-- DID YOU DREAM DURING YOUR NAP LAST NIGHT?
Y--YES.
IT, WAS... ..T-THAT ORCHARD DREAM AGAIN...
!!!
HERE WE ARE!
HMMM-- THE SAME DREAM. PERHAPS IT IS A MEMORY OF YOURS?
P-- P-- PERHAPS.

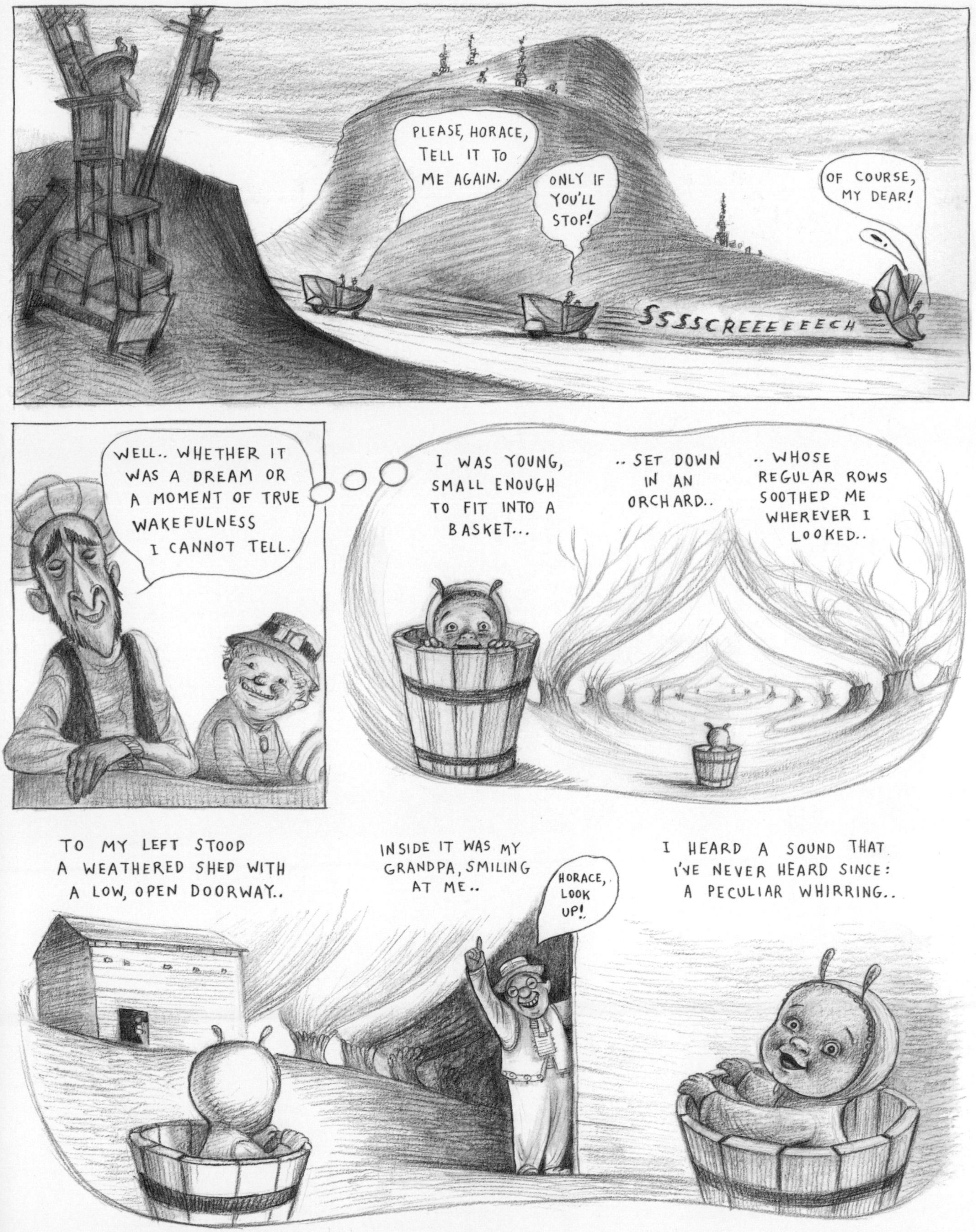
PLEASE, HORACE, TELL IT TO ME AGAIN.
ONLY IF YOU'LL STOP!
SSSSCREEEEEEECH
OF COURSE, MY DEAR!
WELL.. WHETHER IT WAS A DREAM OR A MOMENT OF TRUE WAKEFULNESS I CANNOT TELL.
I WAS YOUNG, SMALL ENOUGH TO FIT INTO A BASKET...
.. SET DOWN IN AN ORCHARD..
.. WHOSE REGULAR ROWS SOOTHED ME WHEREVER I LOOKED..
TO MY LEFT STOOD A WEATHERED SHED WITH A LOW, OPEN DOORWAY..
INSIDE IT WAS MY GRANDPA, SMILING AT ME..
HORACE, LOOK UP!
I HEARD A SOUND THAT I'VE NEVER HEARD SINCE: A PECULIAR WHIRRING..

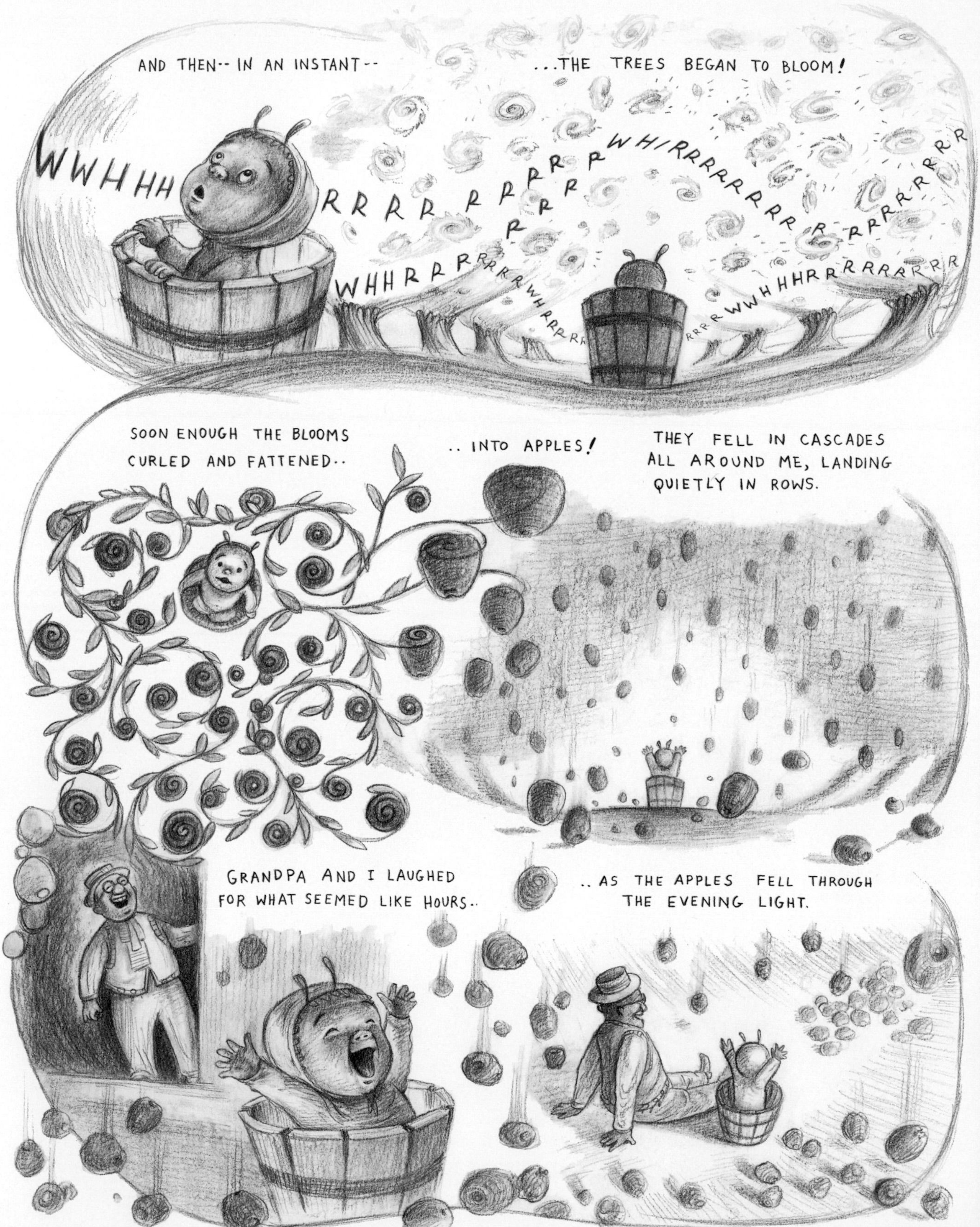

AND THEN-- IN AN INSTANT--
...THE TREES BEGAN TO BLOOM!
WWHHHRRRR RRR
WHIRRRRRRRR
WHHRRRRRRRWHRRRR
WWHHHRRRRRRR
SOON ENOUGH THE BLOOMS CURLED AND FATTENED..
.. INTO APPLES!
THEY FELL IN CASCADES ALL AROUND ME, LANDING QUIETLY IN ROWS.
GRANDPA AND I LAUGHED FOR WHAT SEEMED LIKE HOURS..
.. AS THE APPLES FELL THROUGH THE EVENING LIGHT.

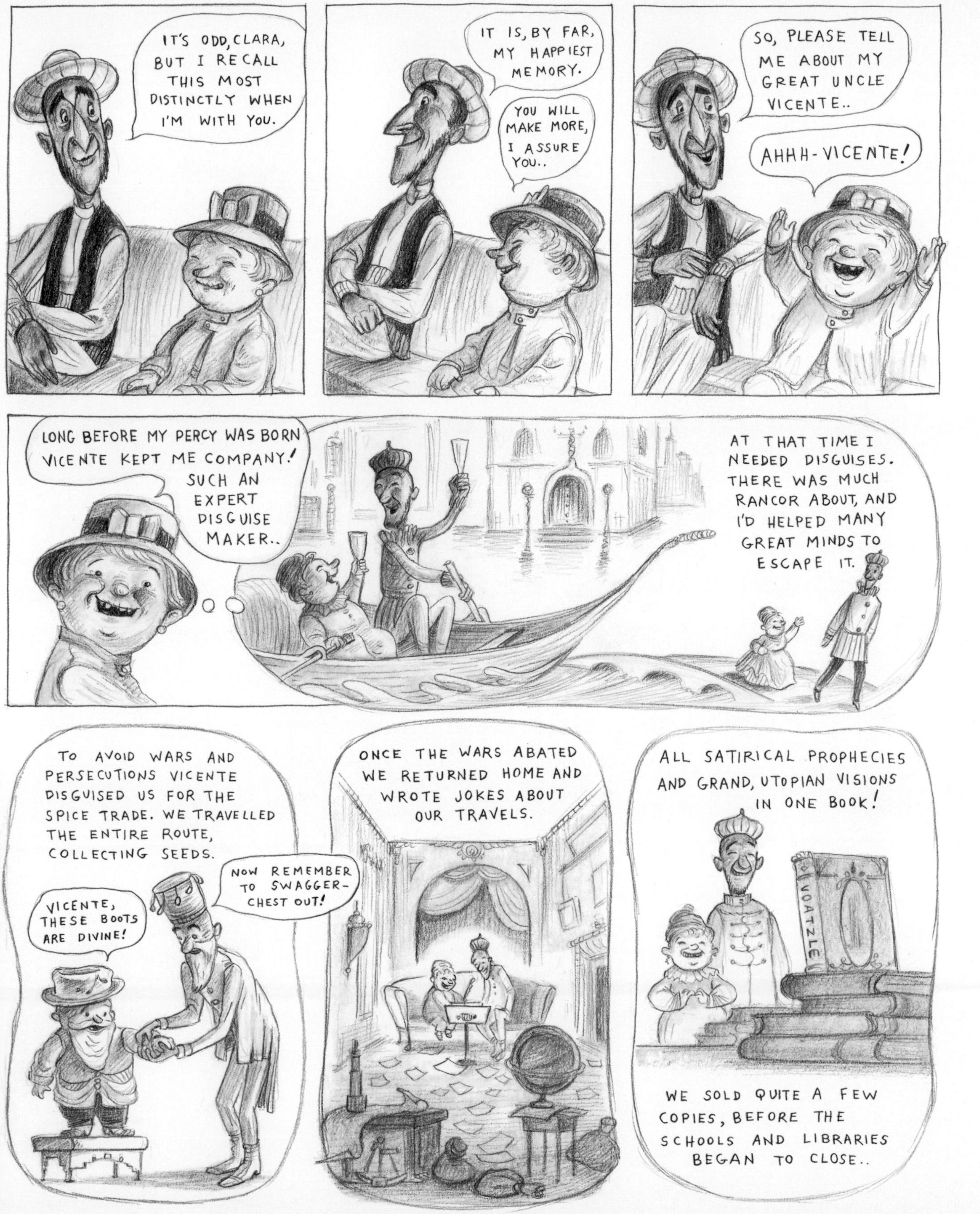
IT'S ODD, CLARA, BUT I RECALL THIS MOST DISTINCTLY WHEN I'M WITH YOU.
IT IS, BY FAR, MY HAPPIEST MEMORY.
YOU WILL MAKE MORE, I ASSURE YOU..
SO, PLEASE TELL ME ABOUT MY GREAT UNCLE VICENTE..
AHHH-VICENTE!
LONG BEFORE MY PERCY WAS BORN VICENTE KEPT ME COMPANY! SUCH AN EXPERT DISGUISE MAKER..
AT THAT TIME I NEEDED DISGUISES. THERE WAS MUCH RANCOR ABOUT, AND I'D HELPED MANY GREAT MINDS TO ESCAPE IT.
TO AVOID WARS AND PERSECUTIONS VICENTE DISGUISED US FOR THE SPICE TRADE. WE TRAVELLED THE ENTIRE ROUTE, COLLECTING SEEDS.
VICENTE, THESE BOOTS ARE DIVINE!
NOW REMEMBER TO SWAGGER-CHEST OUT!
ONCE THE WARS ABATED WE RETURNED HOME AND WROTE JOKES ABOUT OUR TRAVELS.
ALL SATIRICAL PROPHECIES AND GRAND, UTOPIAN VISIONS IN ONE BOOK!
VOATZLE
WE SOLD QUITE A FEW COPIES, BEFORE THE SCHOOLS AND LIBRARIES BEGAN TO CLOSE..

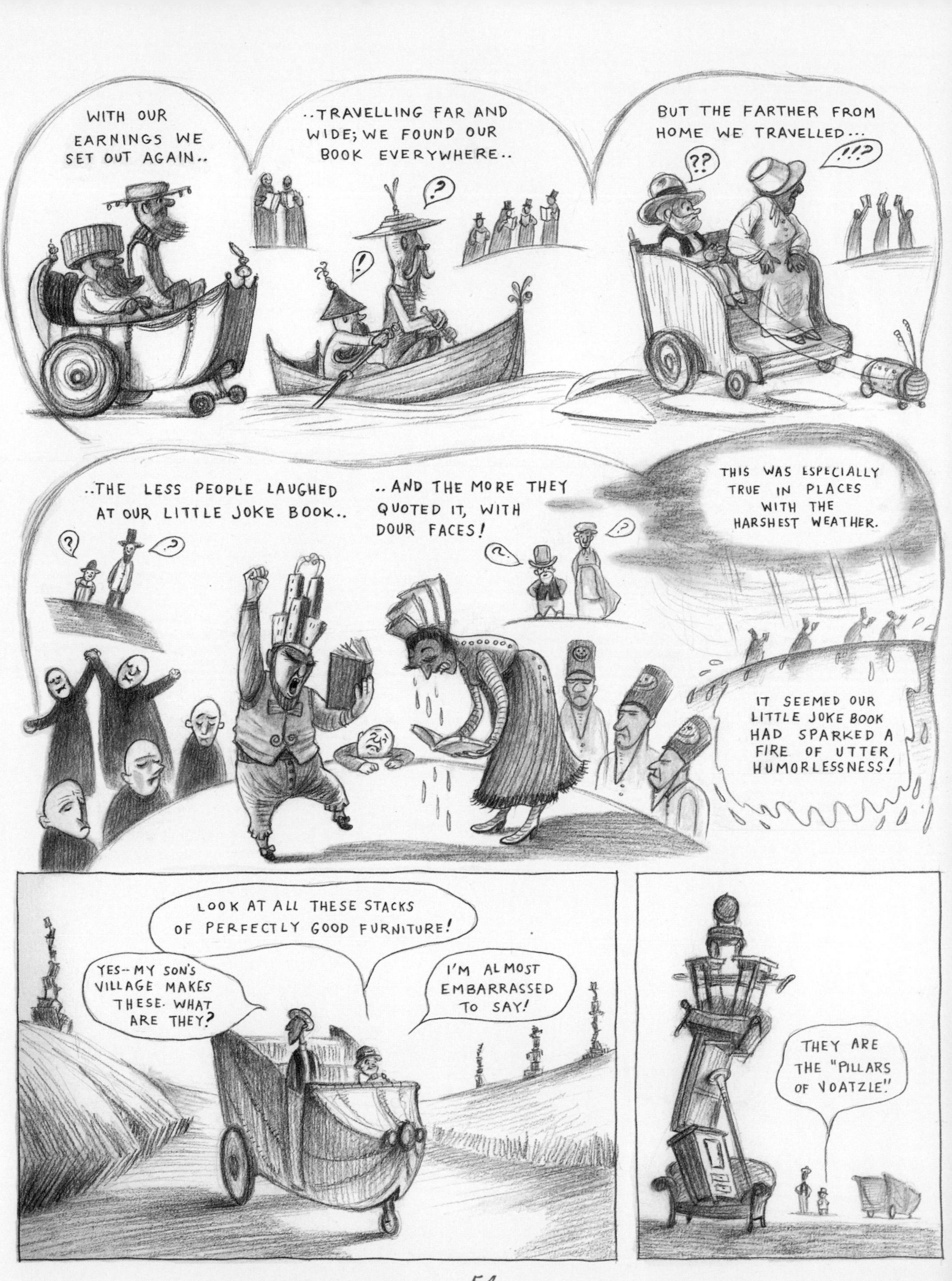
WITH OUR EARNINGS WE SET OUT AGAIN..
..TRAVELLING FAR AND WIDE; WE FOUND OUR BOOK EVERYWHERE..
?
!
BUT THE FARTHER FROM HOME WE TRAVELLED...
??
!!?
..THE LESS PEOPLE LAUGHED AT OUR LITTLE JOKE BOOK..
..AND THE MORE THEY QUOTED IT, WITH DOUR FACES!
THIS WAS ESPECIALLY TRUE IN PLACES WITH THE HARSHEST WEATHER.
?
?
?
?
IT SEEMED OUR LITTLE JOKE BOOK HAD SPARKED A FIRE OF UTTER HUMORLESSNESS!
LOOK AT ALL THESE STACKS OF PERFECTLY GOOD FURNITURE!
YES-- MY SON'S VILLAGE MAKES THESE. WHAT ARE THEY?
I'M ALMOST EMBARRASSED TO SAY!
THEY ARE THE "PILLARS OF VOATZLE."

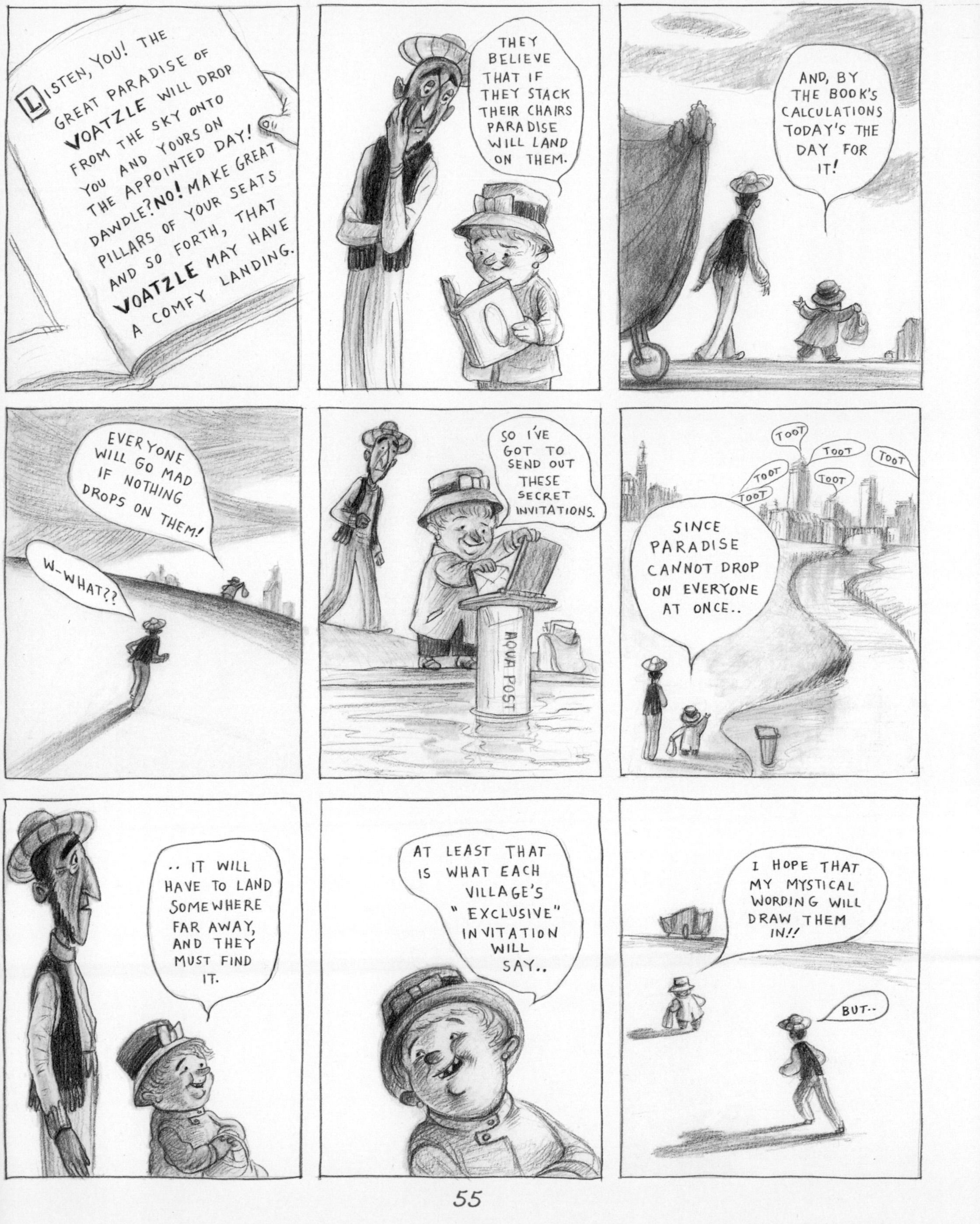
LISTEN, YOU! THE GREAT PARADISE OF VOATZLE WILL DROP FROM THE SKY ONTO YOU AND YOURS ON THE APPOINTED DAY! DAWDLE? NO! MAKE GREAT PILLARS OF YOUR SEATS AND SO FORTH, THAT VOATZLE MAY HAVE A COMFY LANDING.
THEY BELIEVE THAT IF THEY STACK THEIR CHAIRS PARADISE WILL LAND ON THEM.
AND, BY THE BOOK'S CALCULATIONS TODAY'S THE DAY FOR IT!
EVERYONE WILL GO MAD IF NOTHING DROPS ON THEM!
W-WHAT??
SO I'VE GOT TO SEND OUT THESE SECRET INVITATIONS.
AQUA POST
TOOT
TOOT
TOOT
TOOT
TOOT
TOOT
SINCE PARADISE CANNOT DROP ON EVERYONE AT ONCE..
.. IT WILL HAVE TO LAND SOMEWHERE FAR AWAY, AND THEY MUST FIND IT.
AT LEAST THAT IS WHAT EACH VILLAGE'S "EXCLUSIVE" INVITATION WILL SAY..
I HOPE THAT MY MYSTICAL WORDING WILL DRAW THEM IN!!
BUT..

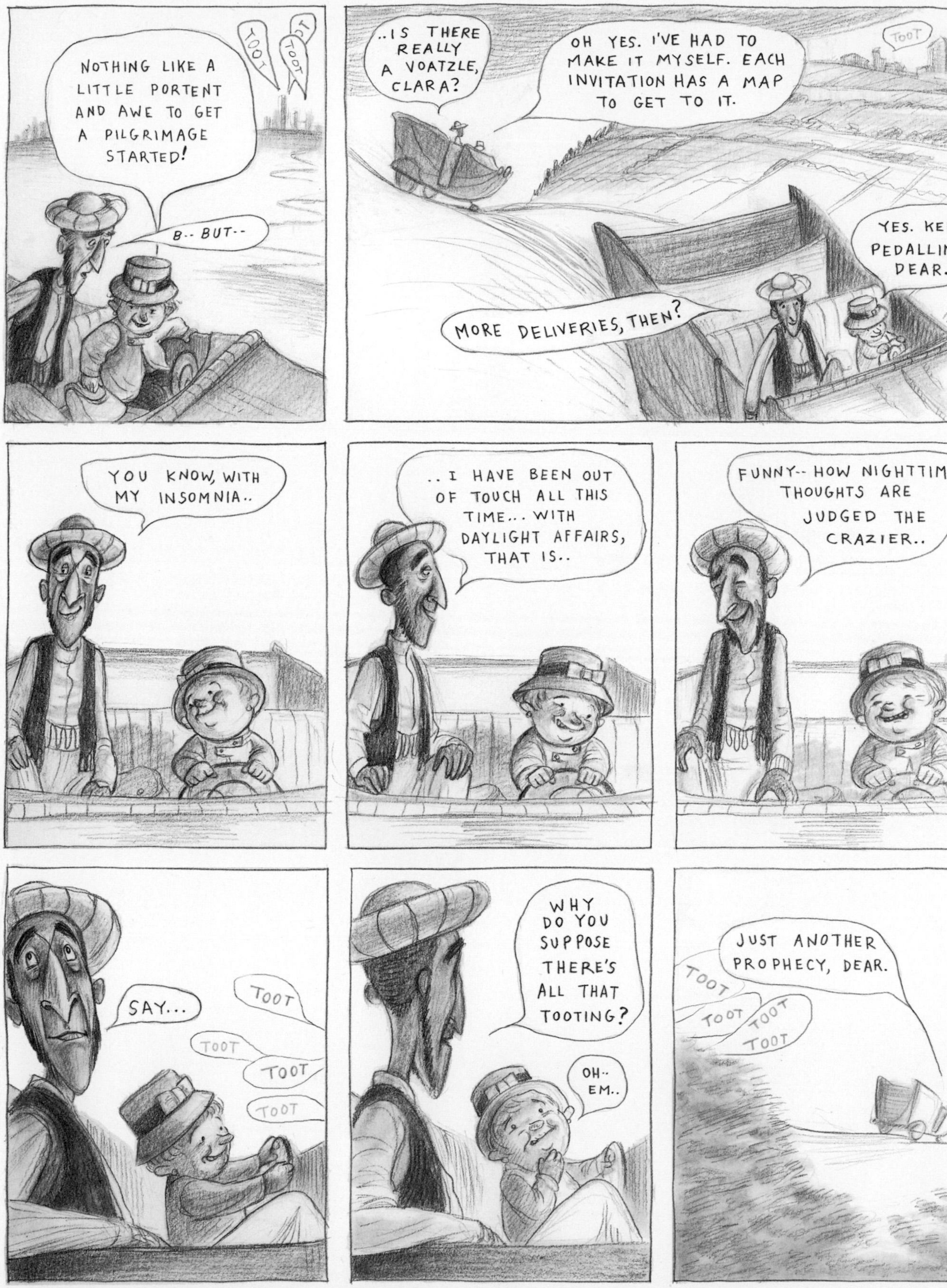
NOTHING LIKE A LITTLE PORTENT AND AWE TO GET A PILGRIMAGE STARTED!
TOOT
TOOT
TOOT
B-- BUT--
..IS THERE REALLY A VOATZLE, CLARA?
OH YES. I'VE HAD TO MAKE IT MYSELF. EACH INVITATION HAS A MAP TO GET TO IT.
TOOT
MORE DELIVERIES, THEN?
YES. KEEP PEDALLING, DEAR.
YOU KNOW, WITH MY INSOMNIA..
.. I HAVE BEEN OUT OF TOUCH ALL THIS TIME... WITH DAYLIGHT AFFAIRS, THAT IS..
FUNNY-- HOW NIGHTTIME THOUGHTS ARE JUDGED THE CRAZIER..
SAY...
TOOT
TOOT
TOOT
TOOT
WHY DO YOU SUPPOSE THERE'S ALL THAT TOOTING?
OH.. EM..
JUST ANOTHER PROPHECY, DEAR.
TOOT
TOOT
TOOT
TOOT

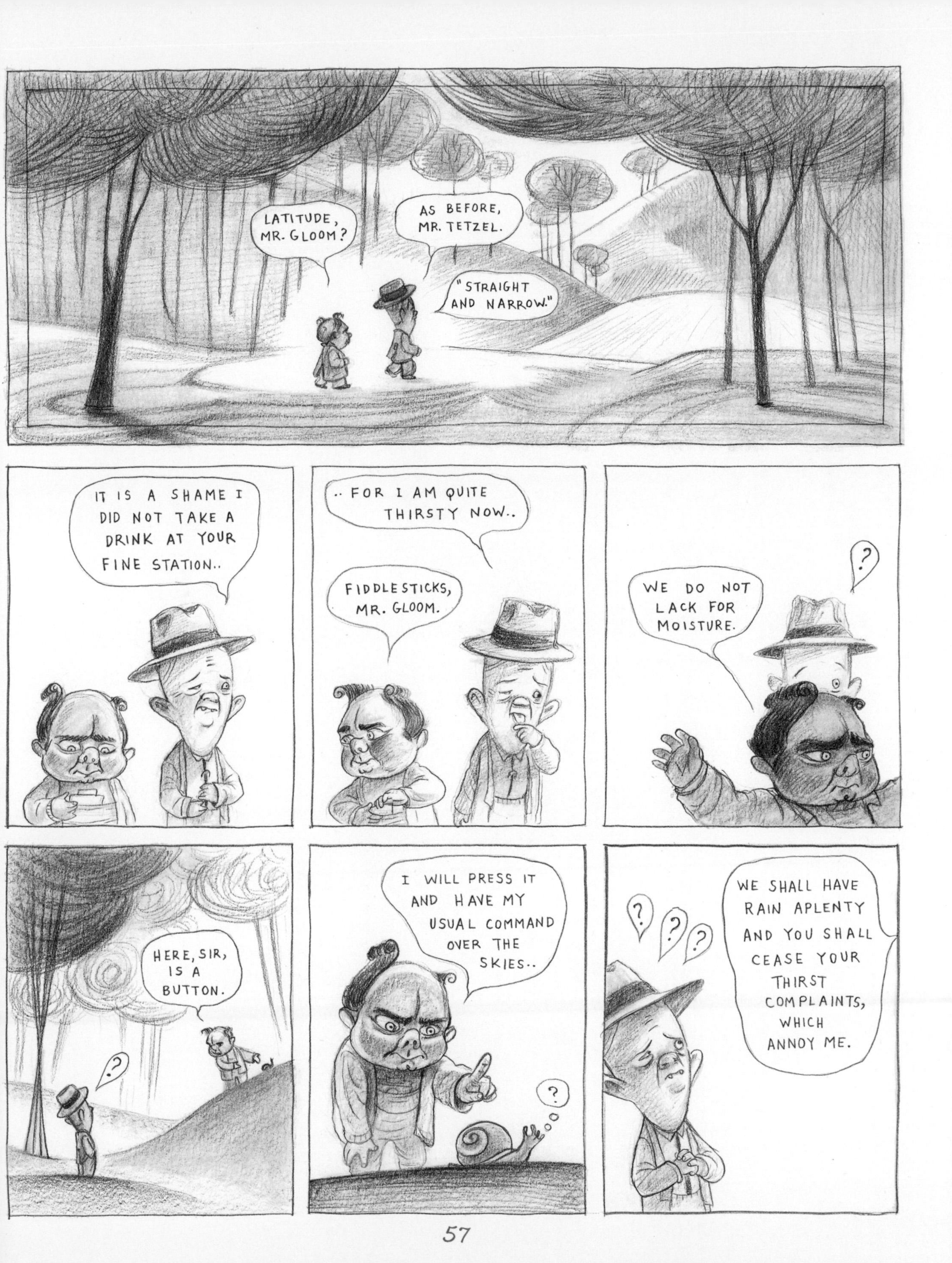
LATITUDE, MR. GLOOM?
AS BEFORE, MR. TETZEL.
"STRAIGHT AND NARROW."
IT IS A SHAME I DID NOT TAKE A DRINK AT YOUR FINE STATION..
.. FOR I AM QUITE THIRSTY NOW..
FIDDLESTICKS, MR. GLOOM.
WE DO NOT LACK FOR MOISTURE.
?
HERE, SIR, IS A BUTTON.
?
I WILL PRESS IT AND HAVE MY USUAL COMMAND OVER THE SKIES..
?
? ? ?
WE SHALL HAVE RAIN APLENTY AND YOU SHALL CEASE YOUR THIRST COMPLAINTS, WHICH ANNOY ME.

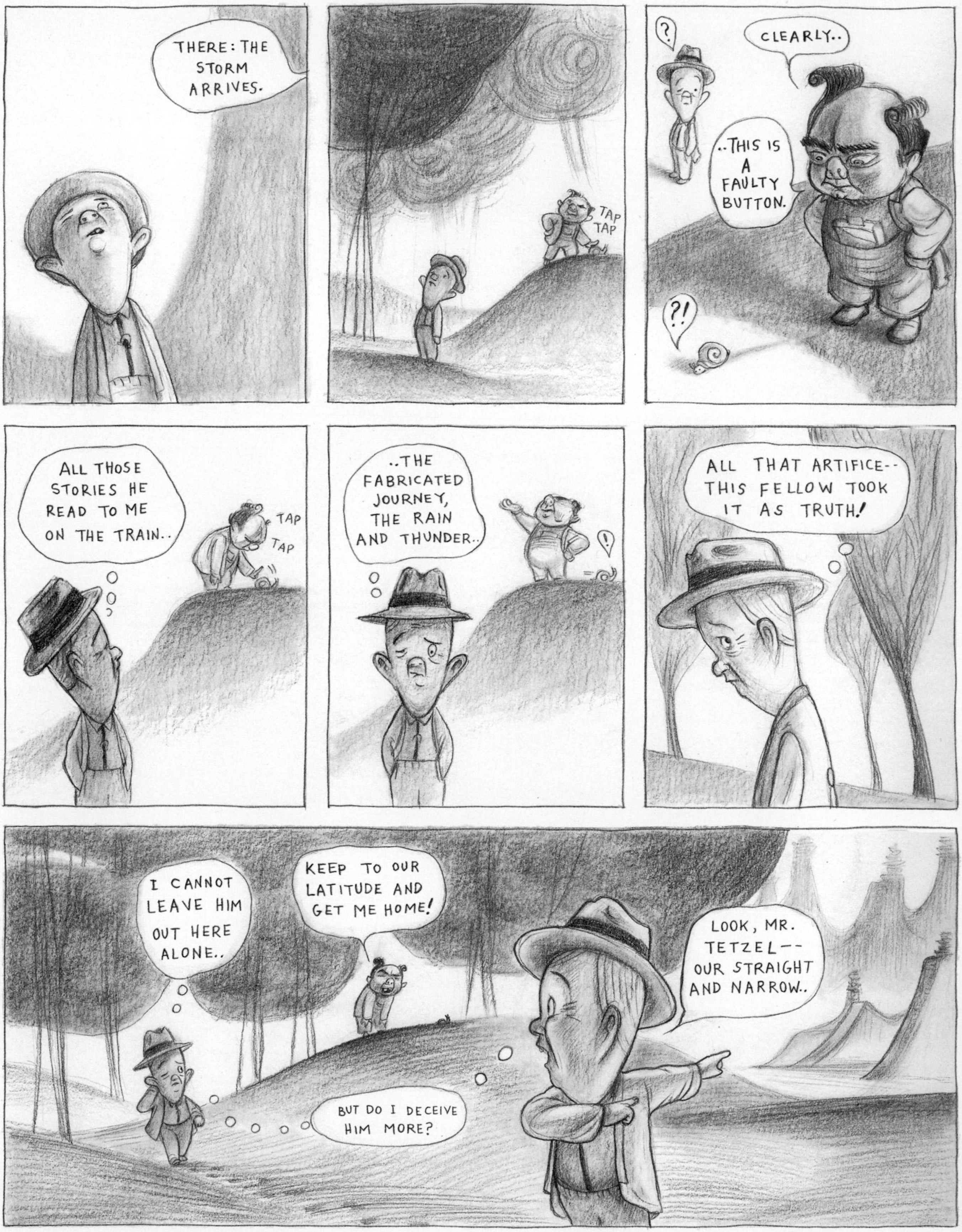
THERE: THE STORM ARRIVES.
TAP TAP
?
CLEARLY..
..THIS IS A FAULTY BUTTON.
?!
ALL THOSE STORIES HE READ TO ME ON THE TRAIN..
TAP TAP
..THE FABRICATED JOURNEY, THE RAIN AND THUNDER..
!
ALL THAT ARTIFICE-- THIS FELLOW TOOK IT AS TRUTH!
I CANNOT LEAVE HIM OUT HERE ALONE..
KEEP TO OUR LATITUDE AND GET ME HOME!
LOOK, MR. TETZEL-- OUR STRAIGHT AND NARROW..
BUT DO I DECEIVE HIM MORE?

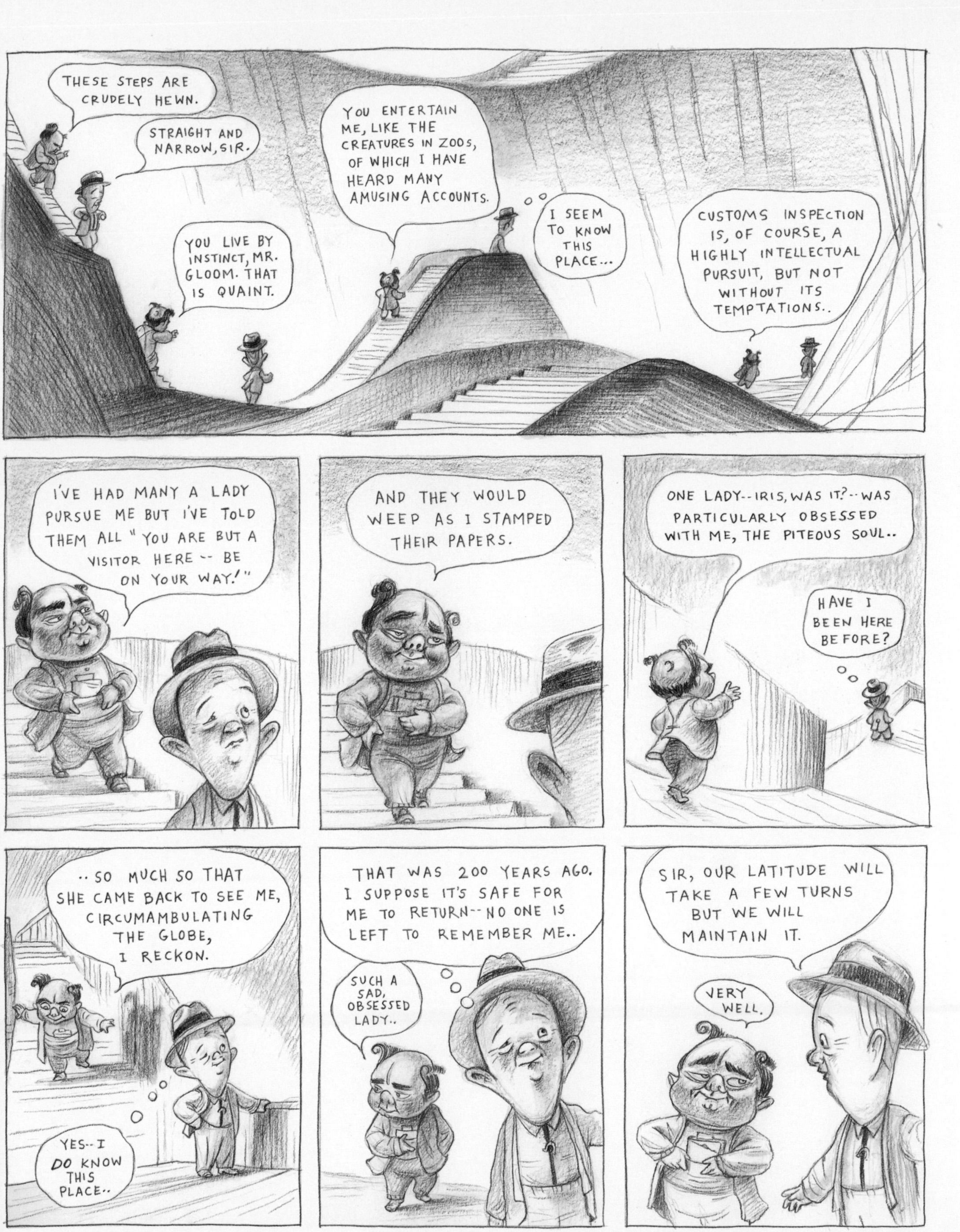
THESE STEPS ARE CRUDELY HEWN.
STRAIGHT AND NARROW, SIR.
YOU LIVE BY INSTINCT, MR. GLOOM. THAT IS QUAINT.
YOU ENTERTAIN ME, LIKE THE CREATURES IN ZOOS, OF WHICH I HAVE HEARD MANY AMUSING ACCOUNTS.
I SEEM TO KNOW THIS PLACE...
CUSTOMS INSPECTION IS, OF COURSE, A HIGHLY INTELLECTUAL PURSUIT, BUT NOT WITHOUT ITS TEMPTATIONS..
I'VE HAD MANY A LADY PURSUE ME BUT I'VE TOLD THEM ALL "YOU ARE BUT A VISITOR HERE -- BE ON YOUR WAY!"
AND THEY WOULD WEEP AS I STAMPED THEIR PAPERS.
ONE LADY--IRIS, WAS IT?--WAS PARTICULARLY OBSESSED WITH ME, THE PITEOUS SOUL..
HAVE I BEEN HERE BEFORE?
..SO MUCH SO THAT SHE CAME BACK TO SEE ME, CIRCUMAMBULATING THE GLOBE, I RECKON.
YES--I *DO* KNOW THIS PLACE..
THAT WAS 200 YEARS AGO. I SUPPOSE IT'S SAFE FOR ME TO RETURN--NO ONE IS LEFT TO REMEMBER ME..
SUCH A SAD, OBSESSED LADY..
SIR, OUR LATITUDE WILL TAKE A FEW TURNS BUT WE WILL MAINTAIN IT.
VERY WELL.

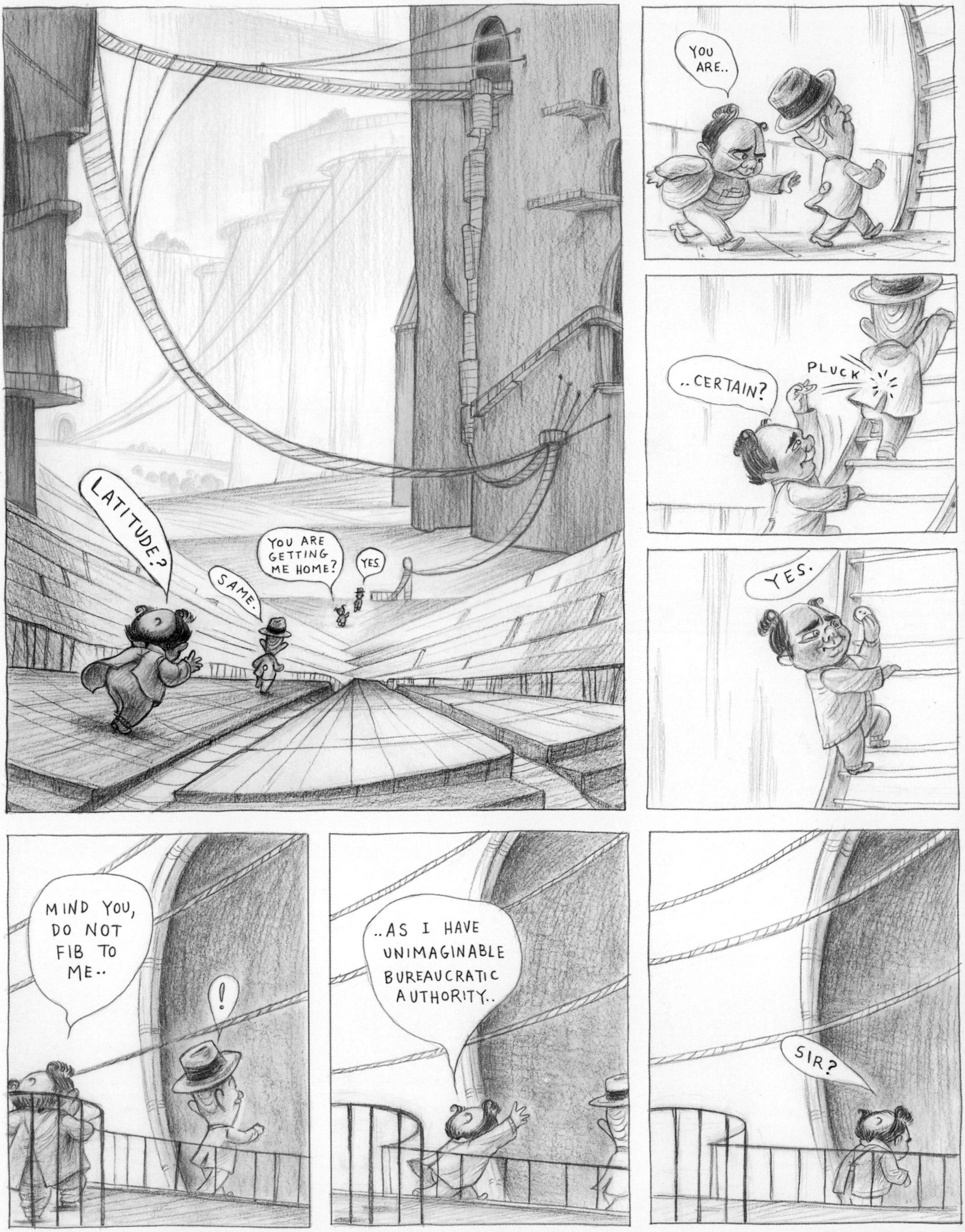
LATITUDE?
SAME.
YOU ARE GETTING ME HOME?
YES.
YOU ARE..
..CERTAIN?
PLUCK
YES.
MIND YOU, DO NOT FIB TO ME..
!
..AS I HAVE UNIMAGINABLE BUREAUCRATIC AUTHORITY..
SIR?

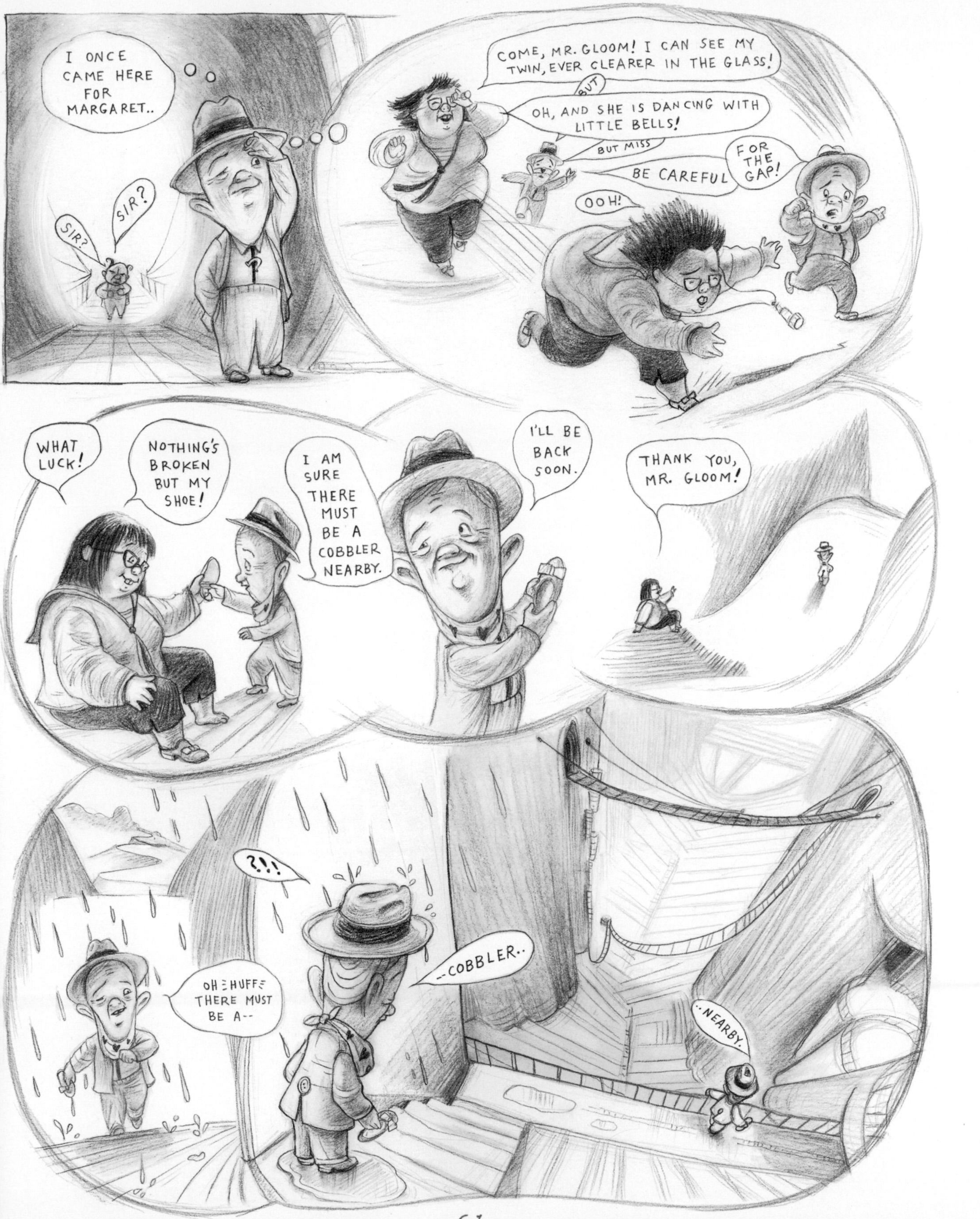
I ONCE CAME HERE FOR MARGARET..
SIR?
SIR?
COME, MR. GLOOM! I CAN SEE MY TWIN, EVER CLEARER IN THE GLASS!
BUT
OH, AND SHE IS DANCING WITH LITTLE BELLS!
BUT MISS
BE CAREFUL
FOR THE GAP!
OOH!
WHAT LUCK!
NOTHING'S BROKEN BUT MY SHOE!
I AM SURE THERE MUST BE A COBBLER NEARBY.
I'LL BE BACK SOON.
THANK YOU, MR. GLOOM!
?!!
OH HUFF THERE MUST BE A--
--COBBLER..
..NEARBY.

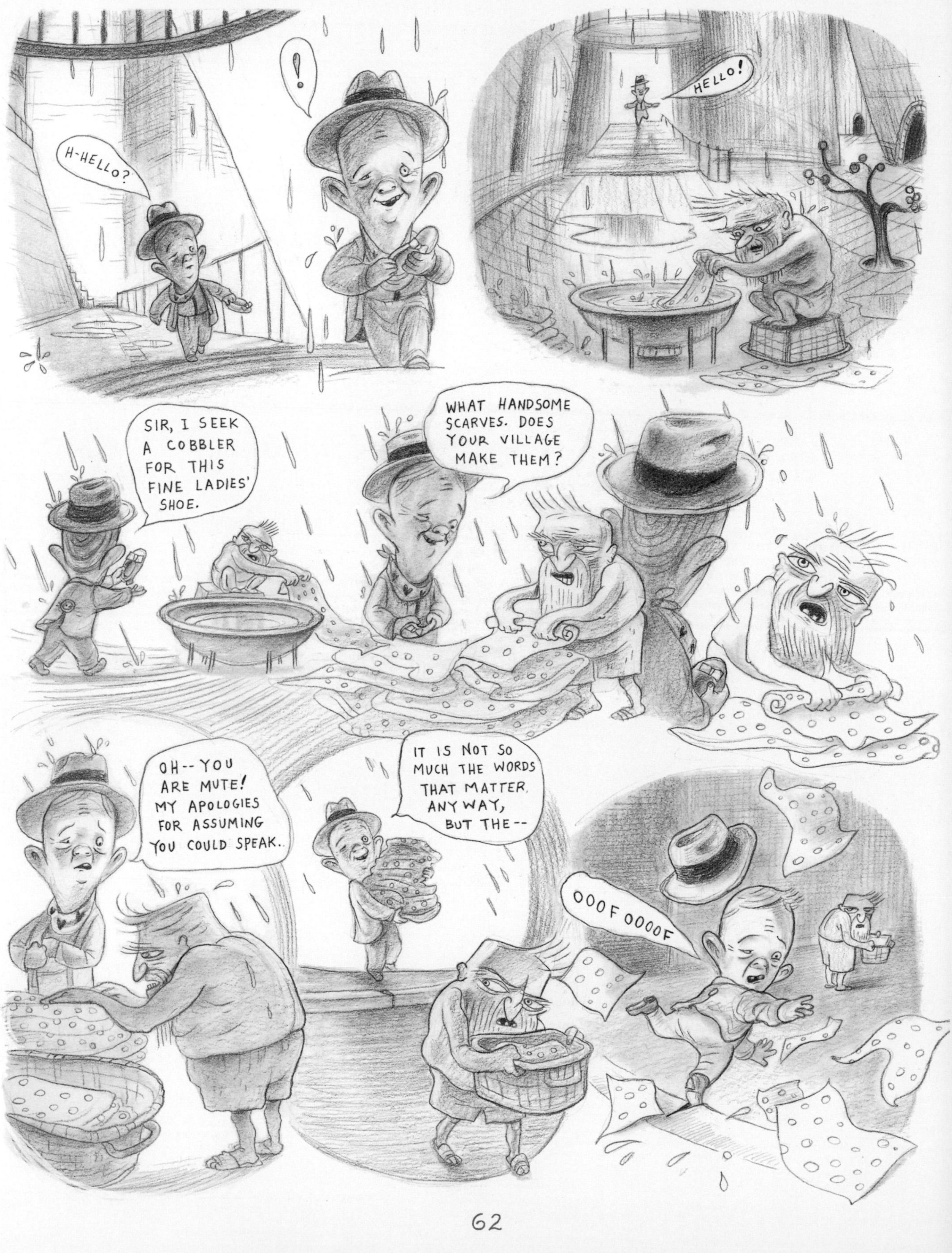
H-HELLO?
!
HELLO!
SIR, I SEEK A COBBLER FOR THIS FINE LADIES' SHOE.
WHAT HANDSOME SCARVES. DOES YOUR VILLAGE MAKE THEM?
OH-- YOU ARE MUTE! MY APOLOGIES FOR ASSUMING YOU COULD SPEAK..
IT IS NOT SO MUCH THE WORDS THAT MATTER, ANYWAY, BUT THE--
OOOF OOOOF

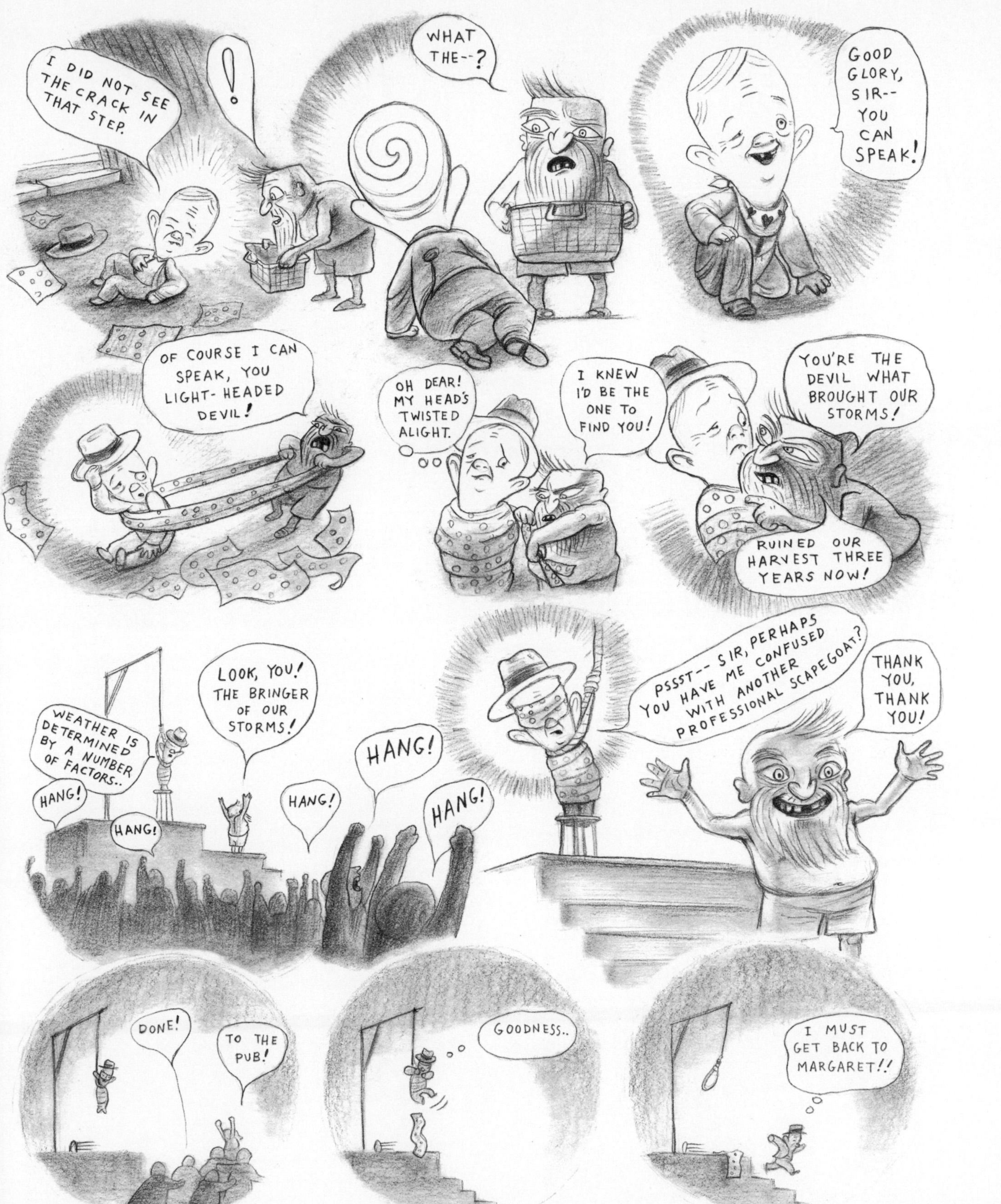
I DID NOT SEE THE CRACK IN THAT STEP.
!
WHAT THE--?
GOOD GLORY, SIR-- YOU CAN SPEAK!
OF COURSE I CAN SPEAK, YOU LIGHT-HEADED DEVIL!
OH DEAR! MY HEAD'S TWISTED ALIGHT.
I KNEW I'D BE THE ONE TO FIND YOU!
YOU'RE THE DEVIL WHAT BROUGHT OUR STORMS!
RUINED OUR HARVEST THREE YEARS NOW!
WEATHER IS DETERMINED BY A NUMBER OF FACTORS..
LOOK, YOU! THE BRINGER OF OUR STORMS!
HANG!
HANG!
HANG!
HANG!
HANG!
PSSST-- SIR, PERHAPS YOU HAVE ME CONFUSED WITH ANOTHER PROFESSIONAL SCAPEGOAT?
THANK YOU, THANK YOU!
DONE!
TO THE PUB!
GOODNESS..
I MUST GET BACK TO MARGARET!!

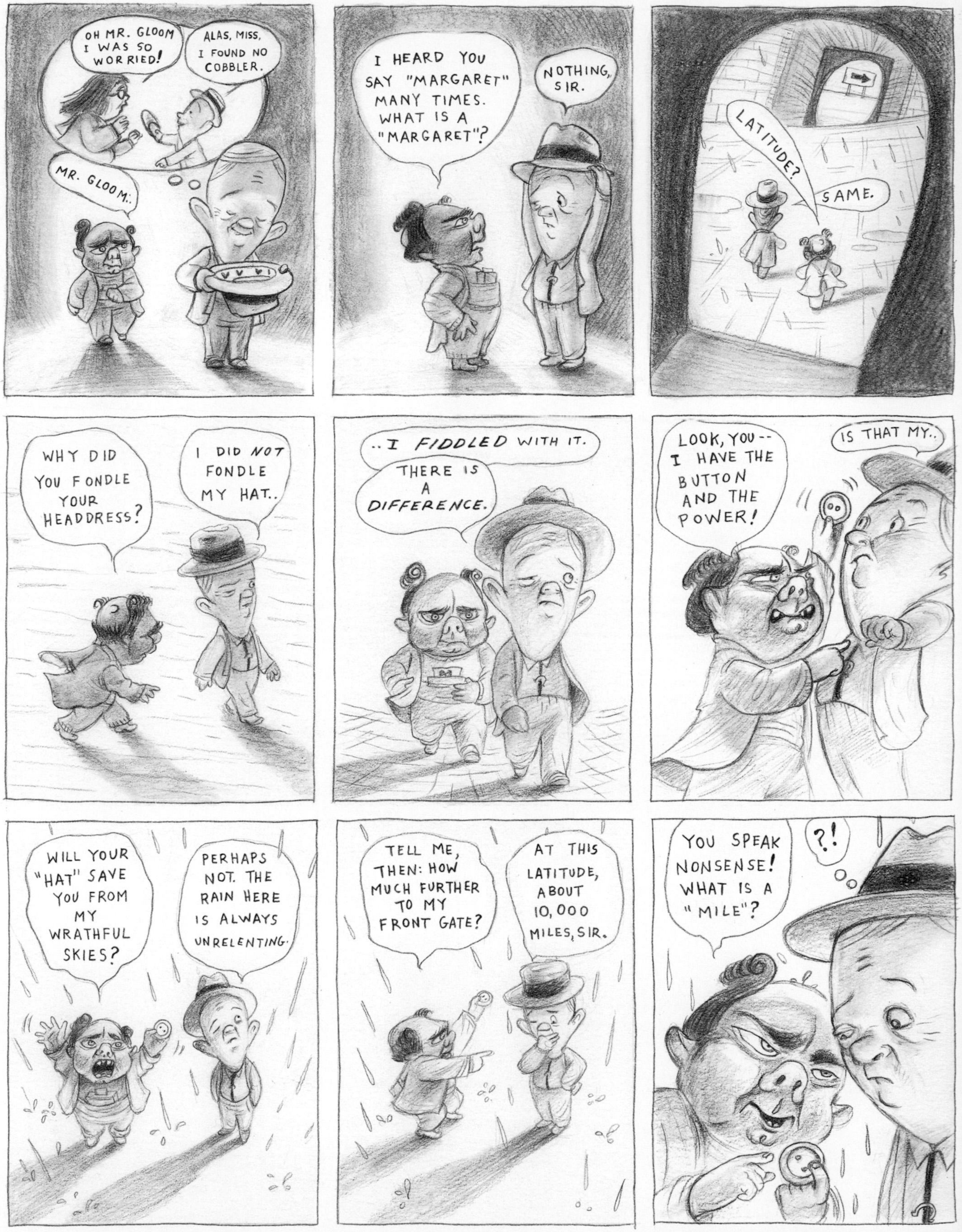
OH MR. GLOOM I WAS SO WORRIED!
ALAS, MISS, I FOUND NO COBBLER.
MR. GLOOM..
I HEARD YOU SAY "MARGARET" MANY TIMES. WHAT IS A "MARGARET"?
NOTHING, SIR.
LATITUDE?
SAME.
WHY DID YOU FONDLE YOUR HEADDRESS?
I DID NOT FONDLE MY HAT..
..I FIDDLED WITH IT.
THERE IS A DIFFERENCE.
LOOK, YOU-- I HAVE THE BUTTON AND THE POWER!
IS THAT MY..
WILL YOUR "HAT" SAVE YOU FROM MY WRATHFUL SKIES?
PERHAPS NOT. THE RAIN HERE IS ALWAYS UNRELENTING.
TELL ME, THEN: HOW MUCH FURTHER TO MY FRONT GATE?
AT THIS LATITUDE, ABOUT 10,000 MILES, SIR.
YOU SPEAK NONSENSE! WHAT IS A "MILE"?
?!

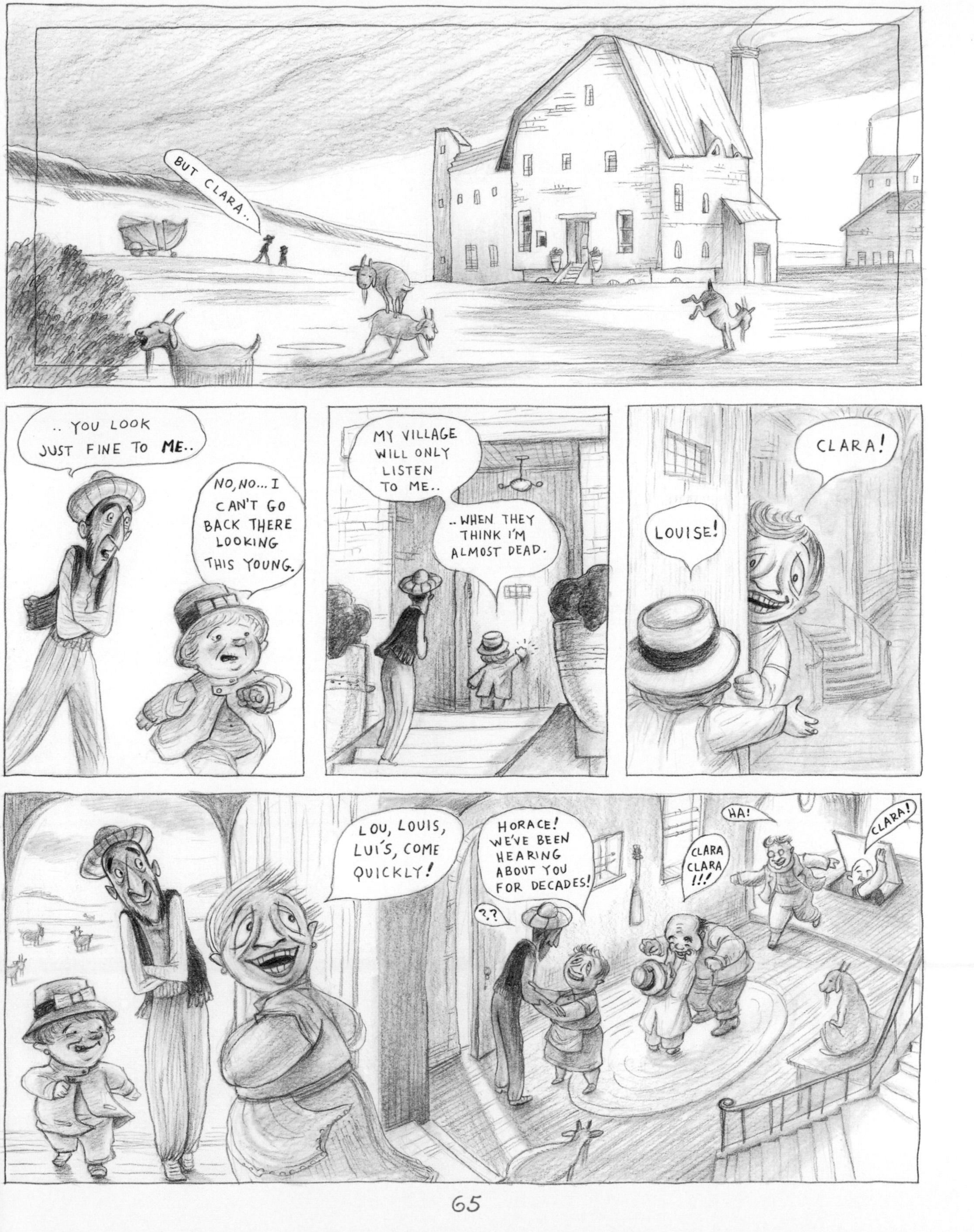
BUT CLARA..
.. YOU LOOK JUST FINE TO ME..
NO, NO... I CAN'T GO BACK THERE LOOKING THIS YOUNG.
MY VILLAGE WILL ONLY LISTEN TO ME..
.. WHEN THEY THINK I'M ALMOST DEAD.
CLARA!
LOUISE!
LOU, LOUIS, LUI'S, COME QUICKLY!
HORACE! WE'VE BEEN HEARING ABOUT YOU FOR DECADES!
??
CLARA CLARA !!!
HA!
CLARA!

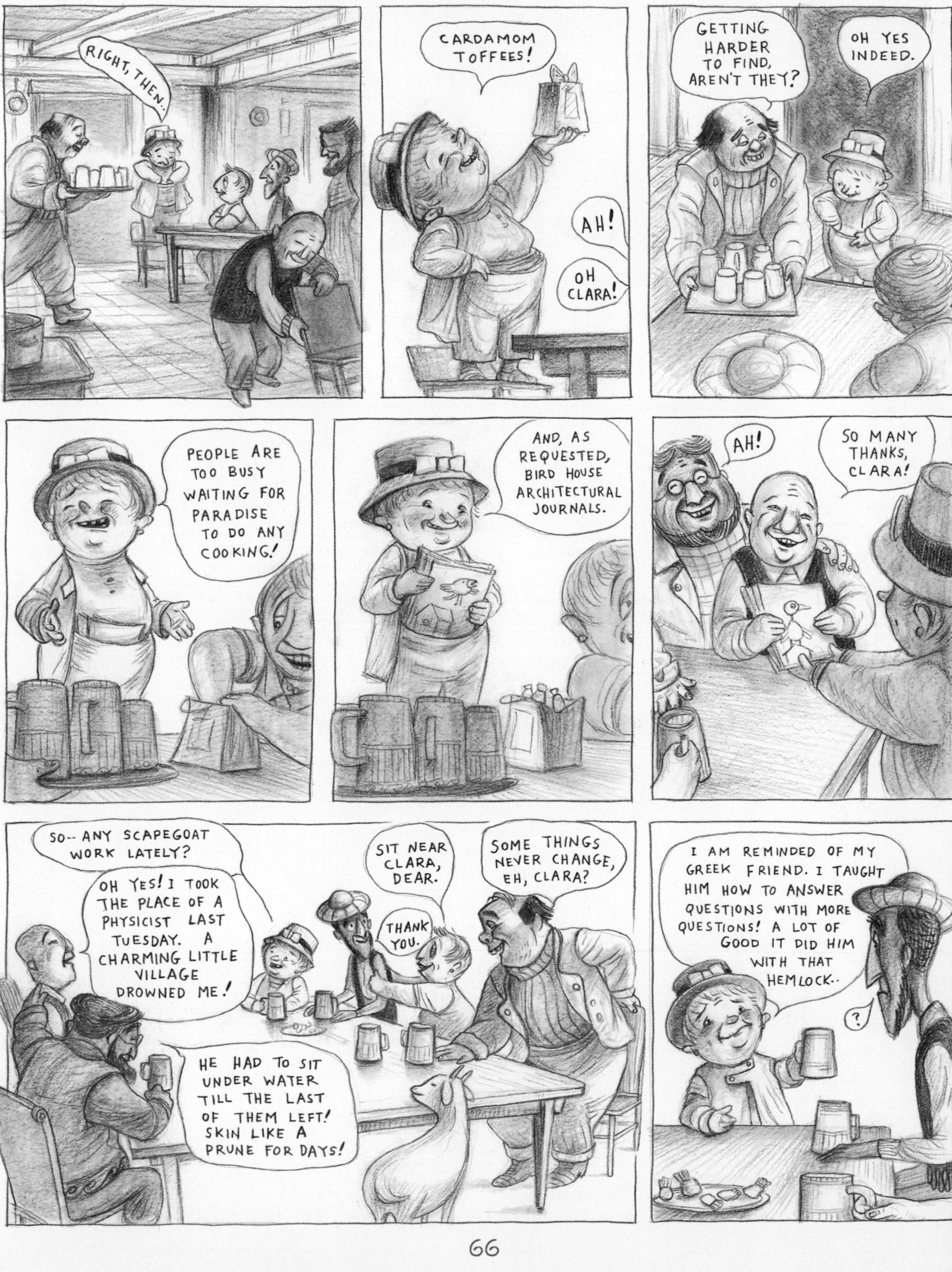
RIGHT, THEN..
CARDAMOM TOFFEES!
AH!
OH CLARA!
GETTING HARDER TO FIND, AREN'T THEY?
OH YES INDEED.
PEOPLE ARE TOO BUSY WAITING FOR PARADISE TO DO ANY COOKING!
AND, AS REQUESTED, BIRD HOUSE ARCHITECTURAL JOURNALS.
AH!
SO MANY THANKS, CLARA!
SO-- ANY SCAPEGOAT WORK LATELY?
OH YES! I TOOK THE PLACE OF A PHYSICIST LAST TUESDAY. A CHARMING LITTLE VILLAGE DROWNED ME!
HE HAD TO SIT UNDER WATER TILL THE LAST OF THEM LEFT! SKIN LIKE A PRUNE FOR DAYS!
SIT NEAR CLARA, DEAR.
THANK YOU.
SOME THINGS NEVER CHANGE, EH, CLARA?
I AM REMINDED OF MY GREEK FRIEND. I TAUGHT HIM HOW TO ANSWER QUESTIONS WITH MORE QUESTIONS! A LOT OF GOOD IT DID HIM WITH THAT HEMLOCK..
?

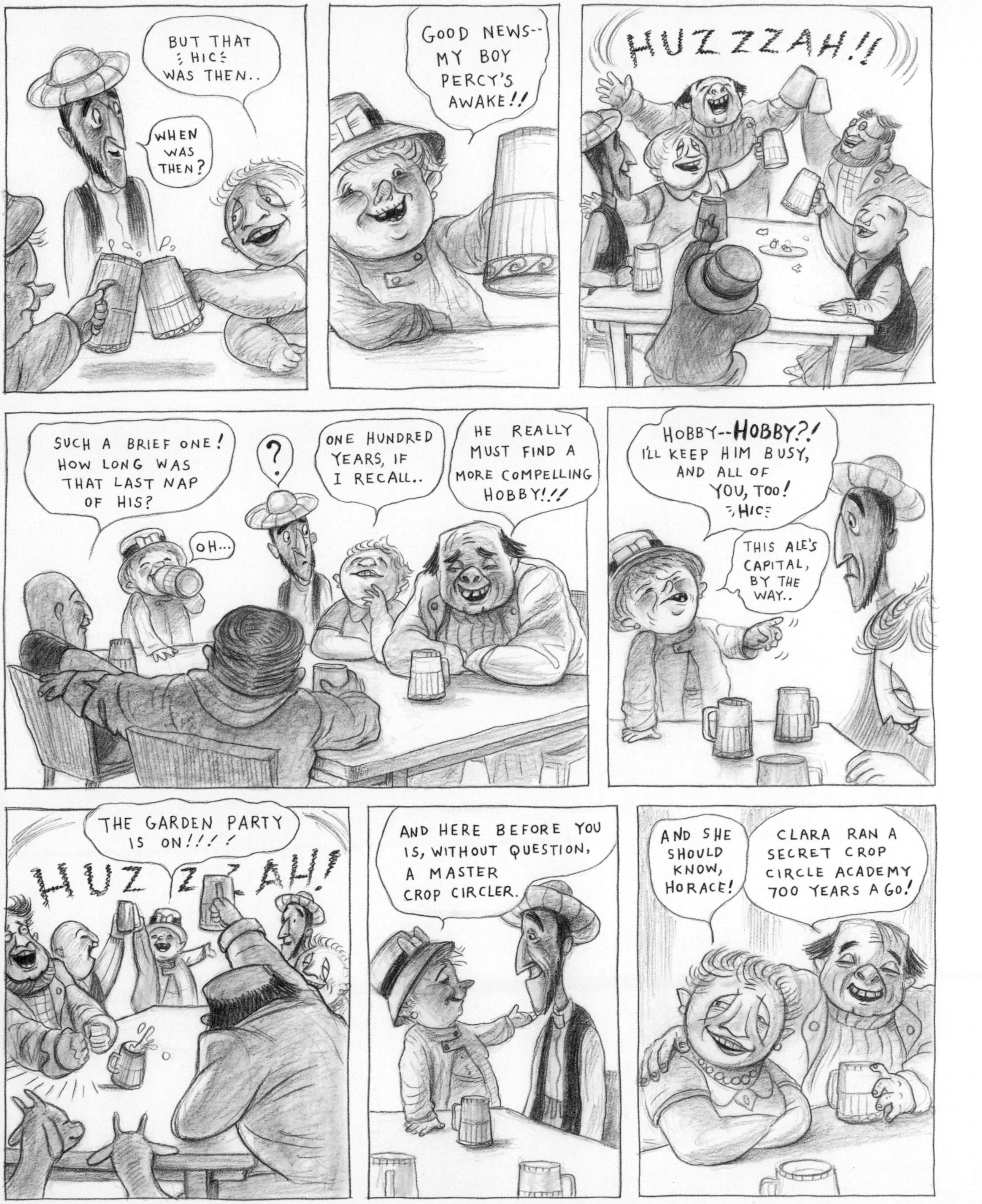
BUT THAT HIC WAS THEN..
WHEN WAS THEN?
GOOD NEWS-- MY BOY PERCY'S AWAKE!!
HUZZZAH!!
SUCH A BRIEF ONE! HOW LONG WAS THAT LAST NAP OF HIS?
?
OH...
ONE HUNDRED YEARS, IF I RECALL..
HE REALLY MUST FIND A MORE COMPELLING HOBBY!!!
HOBBY--HOBBY?! I'LL KEEP HIM BUSY, AND ALL OF YOU, TOO! HIC
THIS ALE'S CAPITAL, BY THE WAY..
THE GARDEN PARTY IS ON!!!!
HUZZAH!
AND HERE BEFORE YOU IS, WITHOUT QUESTION, A MASTER CROP CIRCLER.
AND SHE SHOULD KNOW, HORACE!
CLARA RAN A SECRET CROP CIRCLE ACADEMY 700 YEARS AGO!

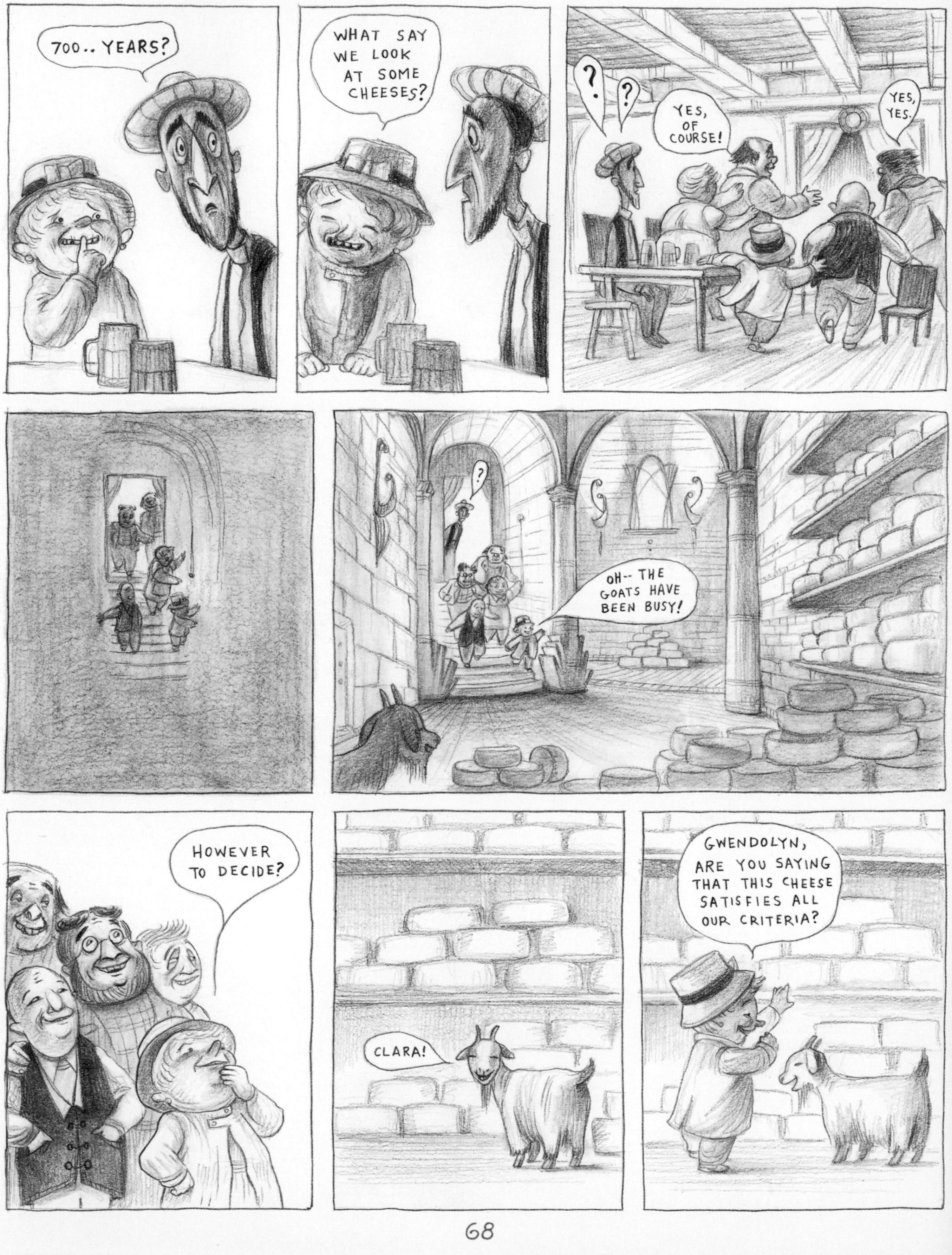
700.. YEARS?
WHAT SAY WE LOOK AT SOME CHEESES?
?
?
YES, OF COURSE!
YES, YES.
?
OH-- THE GOATS HAVE BEEN BUSY!
HOWEVER TO DECIDE?
CLARA!
GWENDOLYN, ARE YOU SAYING THAT THIS CHEESE SATISFIES ALL OUR CRITERIA?

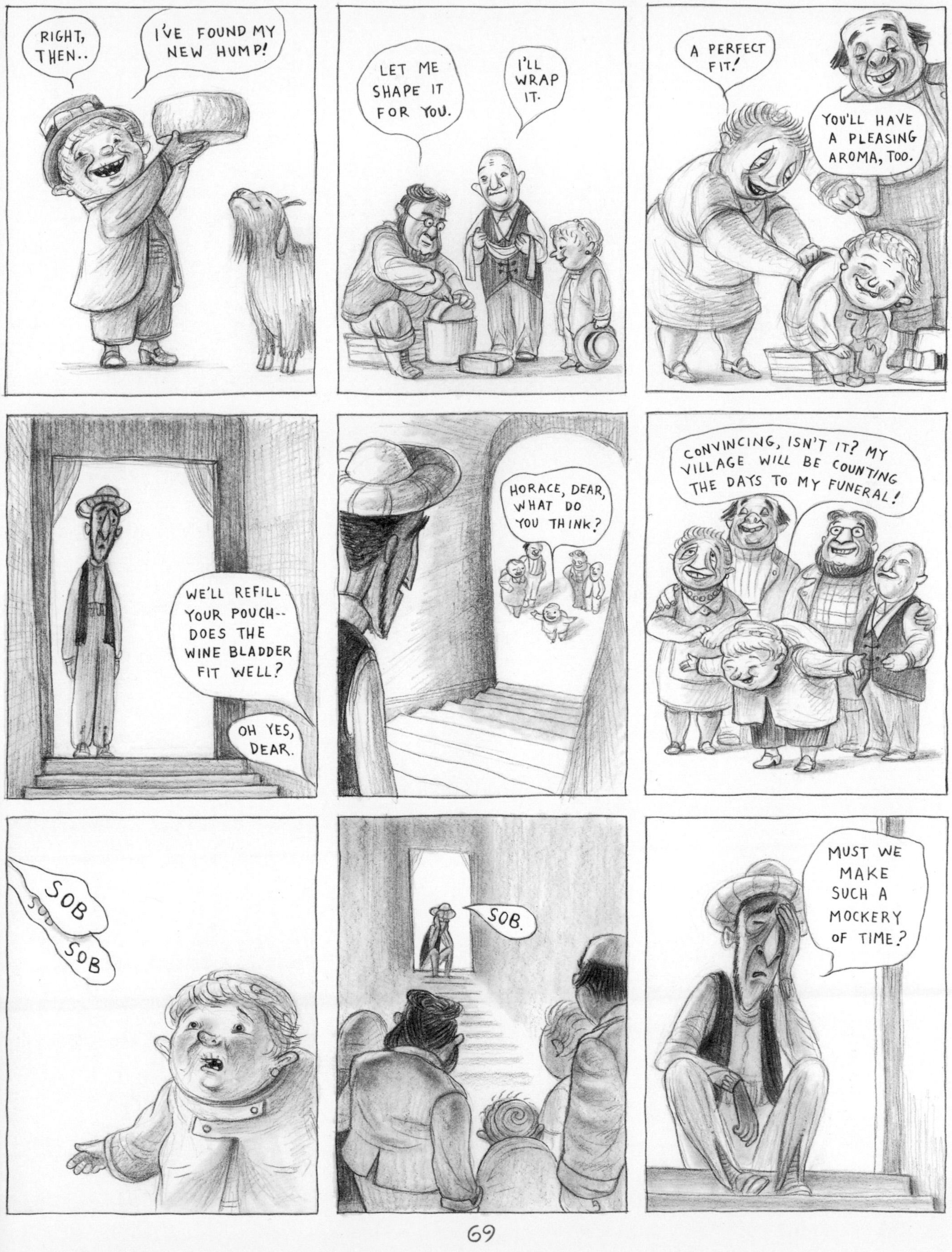
RIGHT, THEN..
I'VE FOUND MY NEW HUMP!
LET ME SHAPE IT FOR YOU.
I'LL WRAP IT.
A PERFECT FIT!
YOU'LL HAVE A PLEASING AROMA, TOO.
WE'LL REFILL YOUR POUCH-- DOES THE WINE BLADDER FIT WELL?
OH YES, DEAR.
HORACE, DEAR, WHAT DO YOU THINK?
CONVINCING, ISN'T IT? MY VILLAGE WILL BE COUNTING THE DAYS TO MY FUNERAL!
SOB
SOB
SOB
SOB.
MUST WE MAKE SUCH A MOCKERY OF TIME?

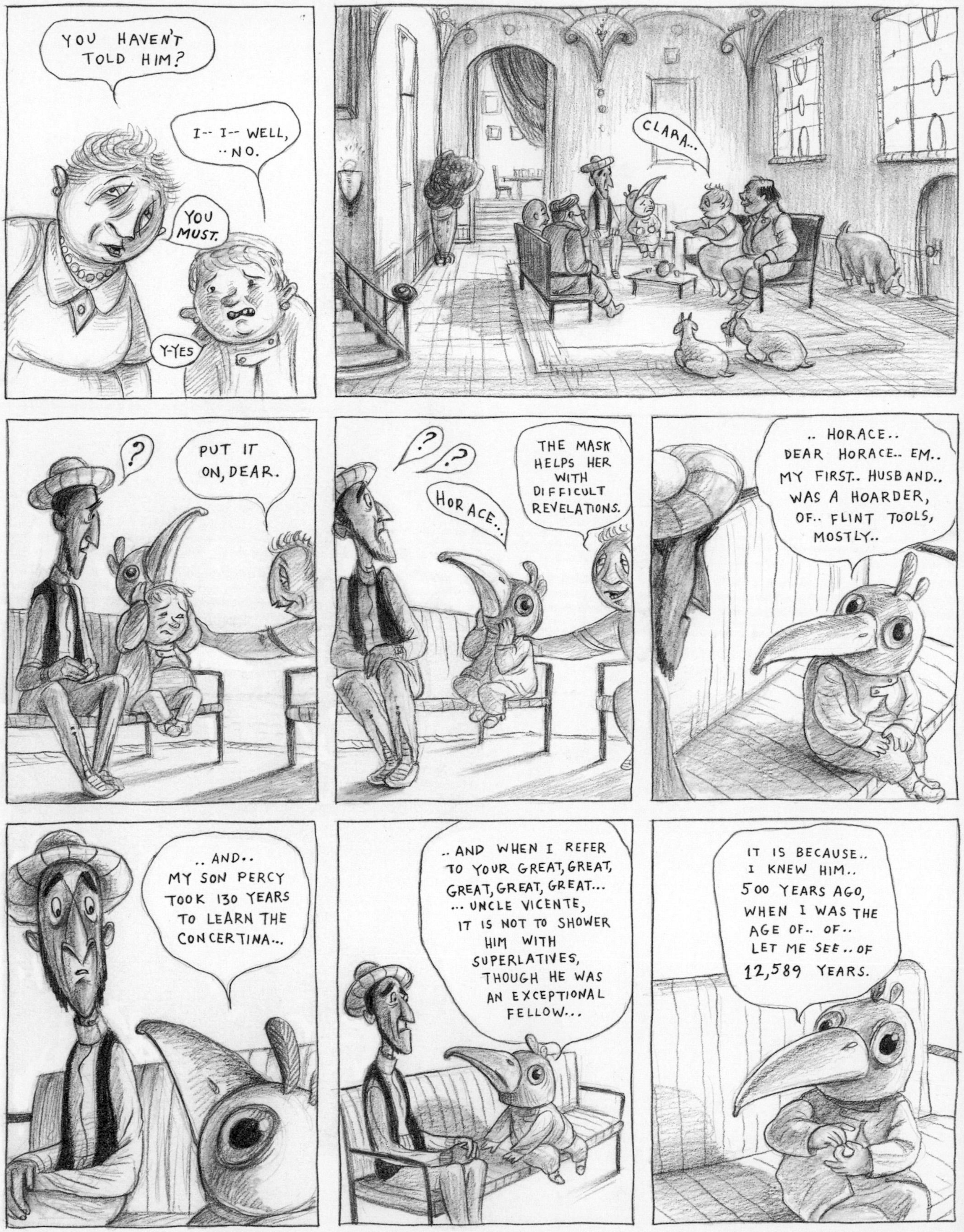
YOU HAVEN'T TOLD HIM?
I-- I-- WELL, ..NO.
YOU MUST.
Y-YES
CLARA...
?
PUT IT ON, DEAR.
?
?
HORACE...
THE MASK HELPS HER WITH DIFFICULT REVELATIONS.
.. HORACE.. DEAR HORACE.. EM.. MY FIRST.. HUSBAND.. WAS A HOARDER, OF.. FLINT TOOLS, MOSTLY..
.. AND.. MY SON PERCY TOOK 130 YEARS TO LEARN THE CONCERTINA...
.. AND WHEN I REFER TO YOUR GREAT, GREAT, GREAT, GREAT, GREAT... ... UNCLE VICENTE, IT IS NOT TO SHOWER HIM WITH SUPERLATIVES, THOUGH HE WAS AN EXCEPTIONAL FELLOW...
IT IS BECAUSE.. I KNEW HIM.. 500 YEARS AGO, WHEN I WAS THE AGE OF.. OF.. LET ME SEE.. OF 12,589 YEARS.

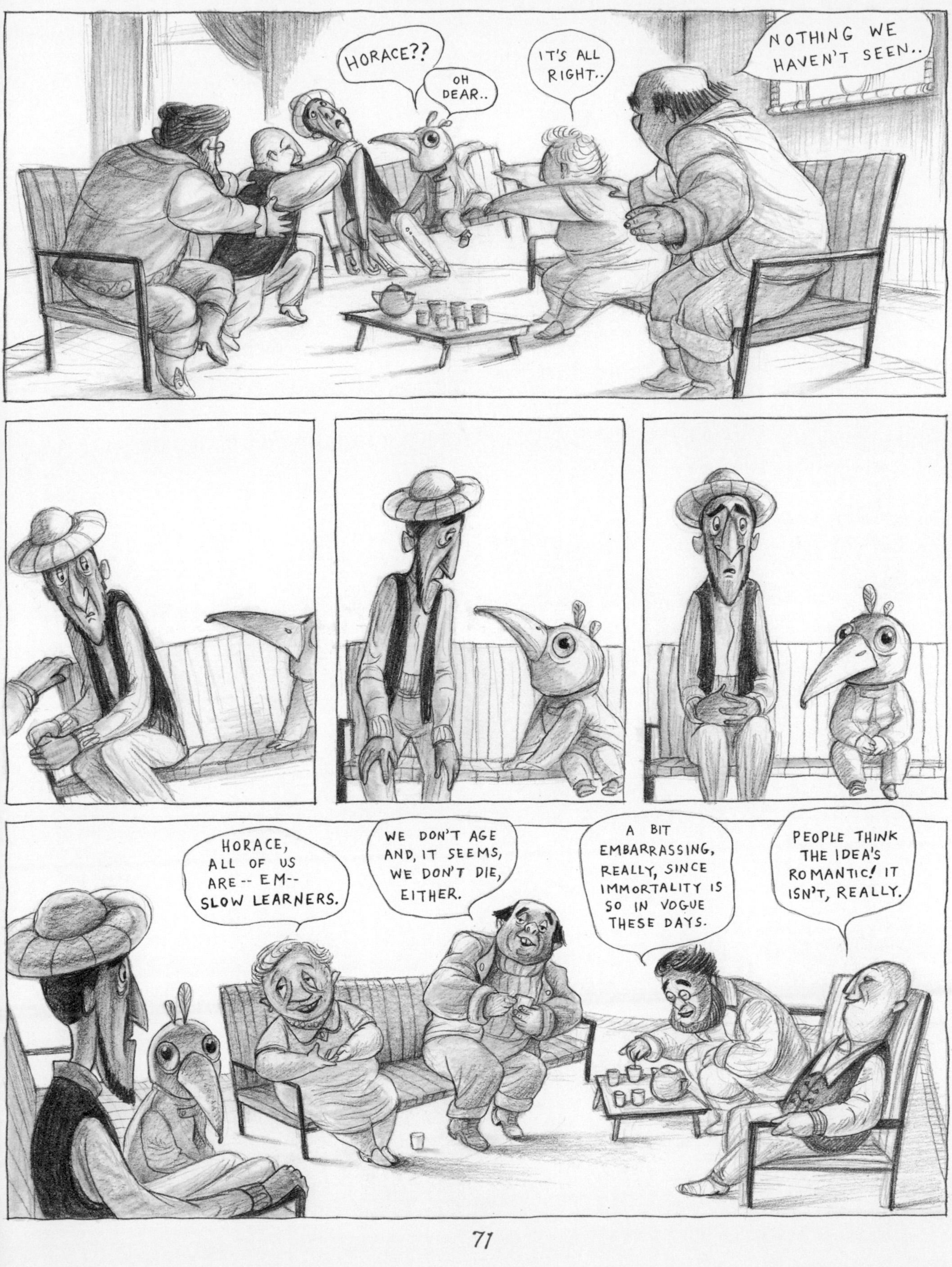
HORACE??
OH DEAR..
IT'S ALL RIGHT..
NOTHING WE HAVEN'T SEEN..
HORACE, ALL OF US ARE -- EM-- SLOW LEARNERS.
WE DON'T AGE AND, IT SEEMS, WE DON'T DIE, EITHER.
A BIT EMBARRASSING, REALLY, SINCE IMMORTALITY IS SO IN VOGUE THESE DAYS.
PEOPLE THINK THE IDEA'S ROMANTIC! IT ISN'T, REALLY.

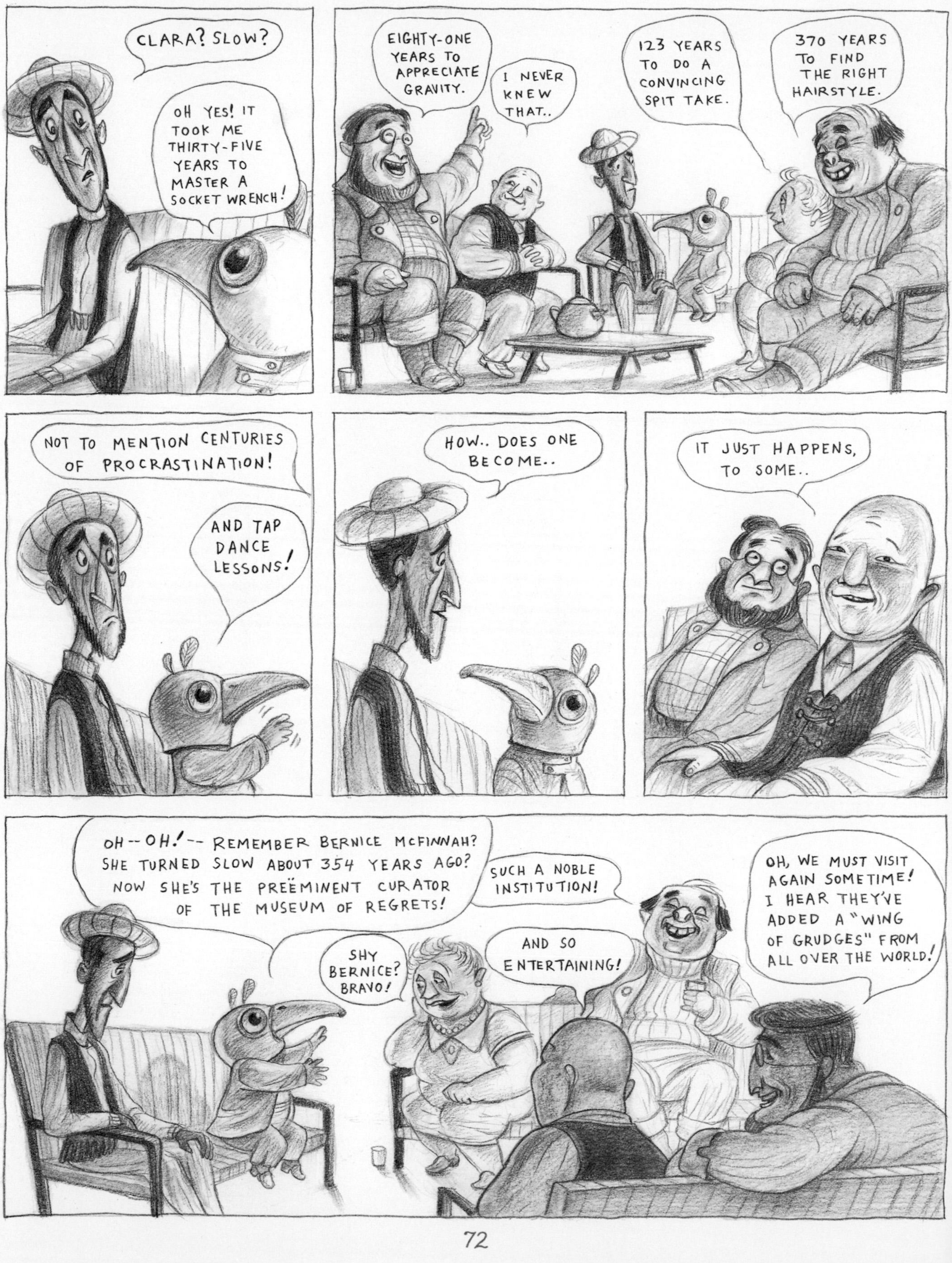
CLARA? SLOW?
OH YES! IT TOOK ME THIRTY-FIVE YEARS TO MASTER A SOCKET WRENCH!
EIGHTY-ONE YEARS TO APPRECIATE GRAVITY.
I NEVER KNEW THAT..
123 YEARS TO DO A CONVINCING SPIT TAKE.
370 YEARS TO FIND THE RIGHT HAIRSTYLE.
NOT TO MENTION CENTURIES OF PROCRASTINATION!
AND TAP DANCE LESSONS!
HOW.. DOES ONE BECOME..
IT JUST HAPPENS, TO SOME..
OH -- OH! -- REMEMBER BERNICE MCFINNAH? SHE TURNED SLOW ABOUT 354 YEARS AGO? NOW SHE'S THE PREËMINENT CURATOR OF THE MUSEUM OF REGRETS!
SHY BERNICE? BRAVO!
SUCH A NOBLE INSTITUTION!
AND SO ENTERTAINING!
OH, WE MUST VISIT AGAIN SOMETIME! I HEAR THEY'VE ADDED A "WING OF GRUDGES" FROM ALL OVER THE WORLD!

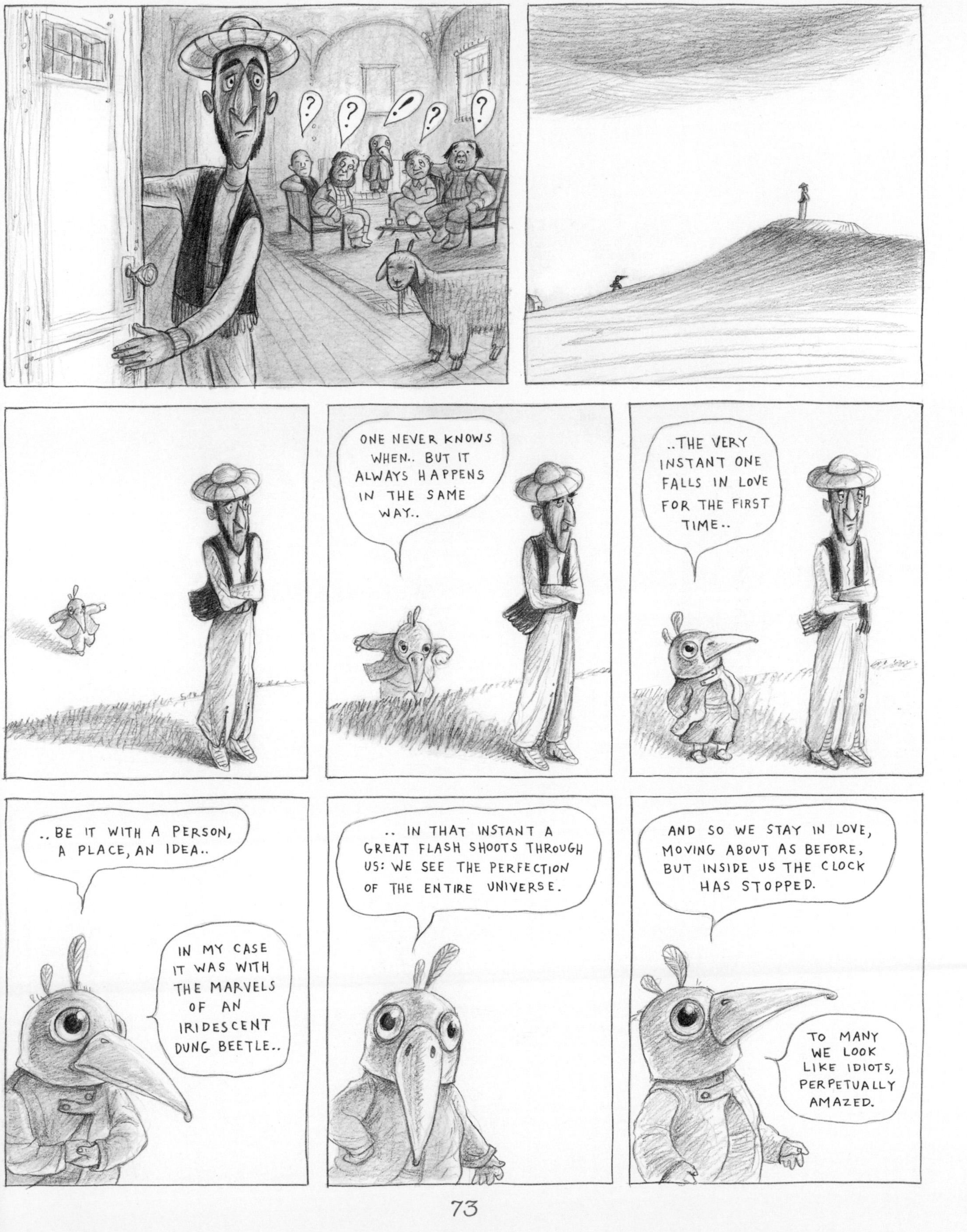
?
?
!
?
?
ONE NEVER KNOWS WHEN.. BUT IT ALWAYS HAPPENS IN THE SAME WAY..
..THE VERY INSTANT ONE FALLS IN LOVE FOR THE FIRST TIME..
..BE IT WITH A PERSON, A PLACE, AN IDEA..
IN MY CASE IT WAS WITH THE MARVELS OF AN IRIDESCENT DUNG BEETLE..
.. IN THAT INSTANT A GREAT FLASH SHOOTS THROUGH US: WE SEE THE PERFECTION OF THE ENTIRE UNIVERSE.
AND SO WE STAY IN LOVE, MOVING ABOUT AS BEFORE, BUT INSIDE US THE CLOCK HAS STOPPED.
TO MANY WE LOOK LIKE IDIOTS, PERPETUALLY AMAZED.

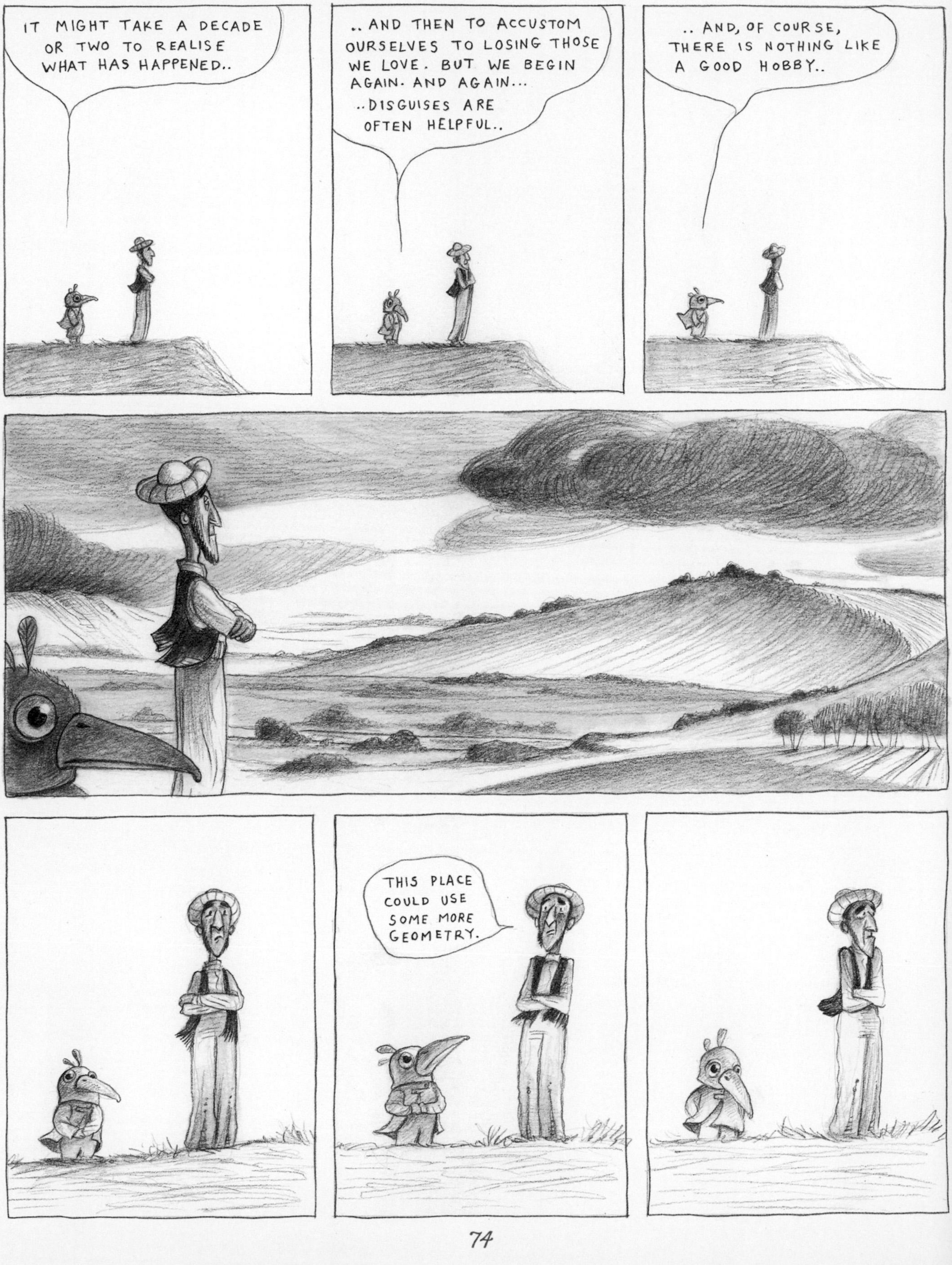
IT MIGHT TAKE A DECADE OR TWO TO REALISE WHAT HAS HAPPENED..
.. AND THEN TO ACCUSTOM OURSELVES TO LOSING THOSE WE LOVE. BUT WE BEGIN AGAIN. AND AGAIN...
..DISGUISES ARE OFTEN HELPFUL..
.. AND, OF COURSE, THERE IS NOTHING LIKE A GOOD HOBBY..
THIS PLACE COULD USE SOME MORE GEOMETRY.

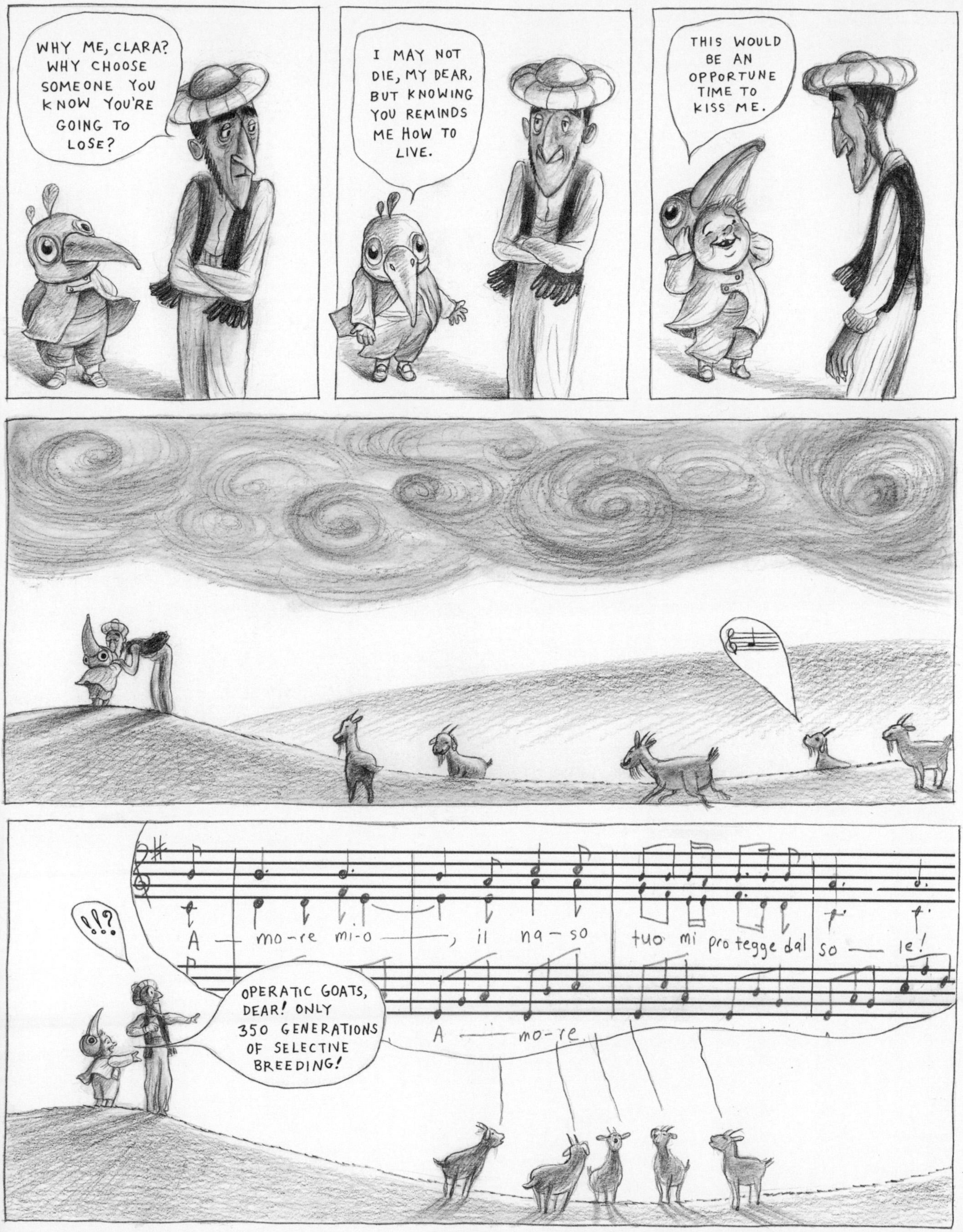

WHY ME, CLARA? WHY CHOOSE SOMEONE YOU KNOW YOU'RE GOING TO LOSE?
I MAY NOT DIE, MY DEAR, BUT KNOWING YOU REMINDS ME HOW TO LIVE.
THIS WOULD BE AN OPPORTUNE TIME TO KISS ME.
!!?
A — mo-re mi-o ——, il na-so tuo mi pro tegge dal so — le!
A —— mo-re
OPERATIC GOATS, DEAR! ONLY 350 GENERATIONS OF SELECTIVE BREEDING!

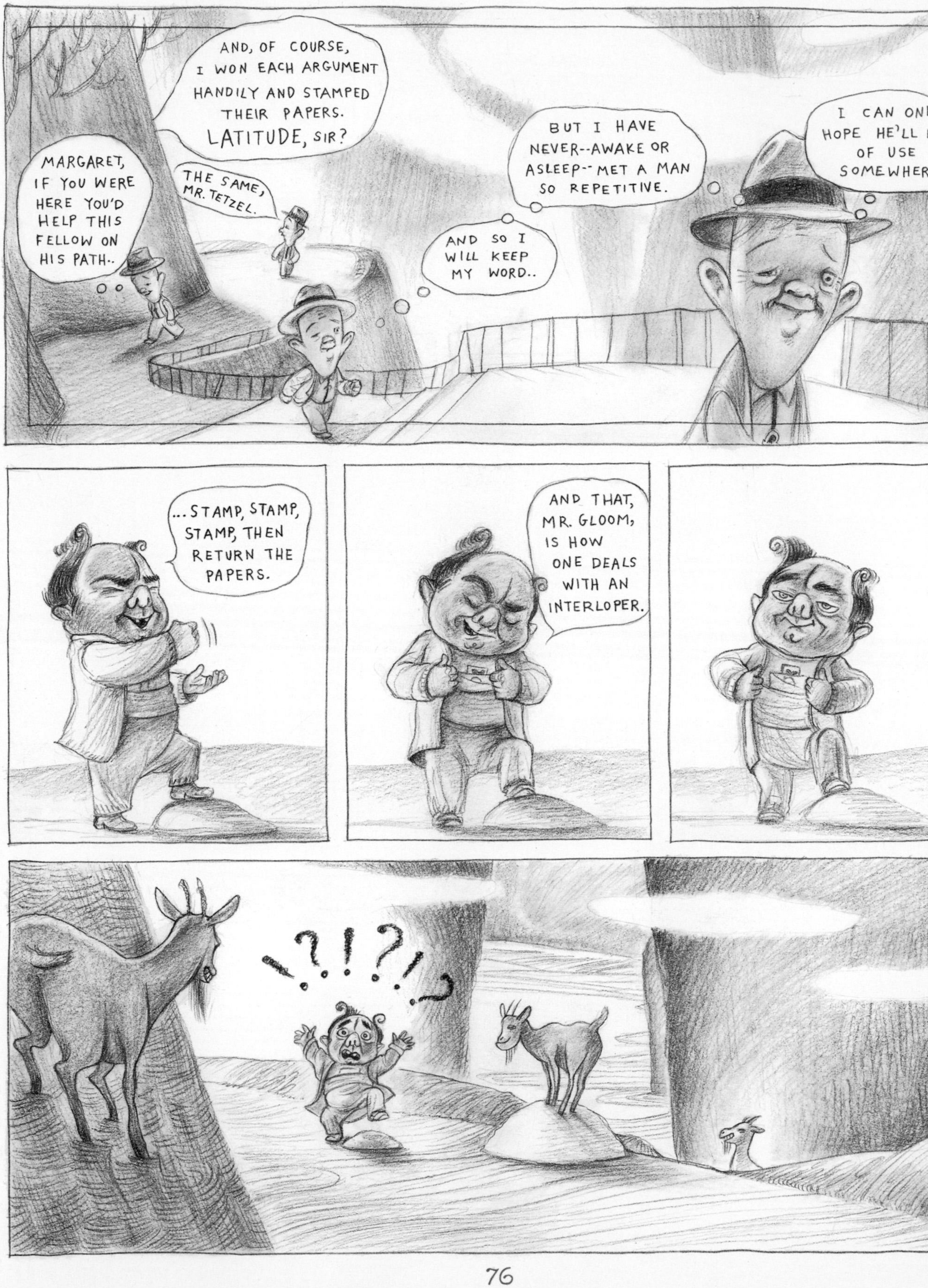
MARGARET, IF YOU WERE HERE YOU'D HELP THIS FELLOW ON HIS PATH..
AND, OF COURSE, I WON EACH ARGUMENT HANDILY AND STAMPED THEIR PAPERS. LATITUDE, SIR?
THE SAME, MR. TETZEL.
AND SO I WILL KEEP MY WORD..
BUT I HAVE NEVER--AWAKE OR ASLEEP--MET A MAN SO REPETITIVE.
I CAN ONLY HOPE HE'LL BE OF USE SOMEWHERE..
...STAMP, STAMP, STAMP, THEN RETURN THE PAPERS.
AND THAT, MR. GLOOM, IS HOW ONE DEALS WITH AN INTERLOPER.
!?!?!?

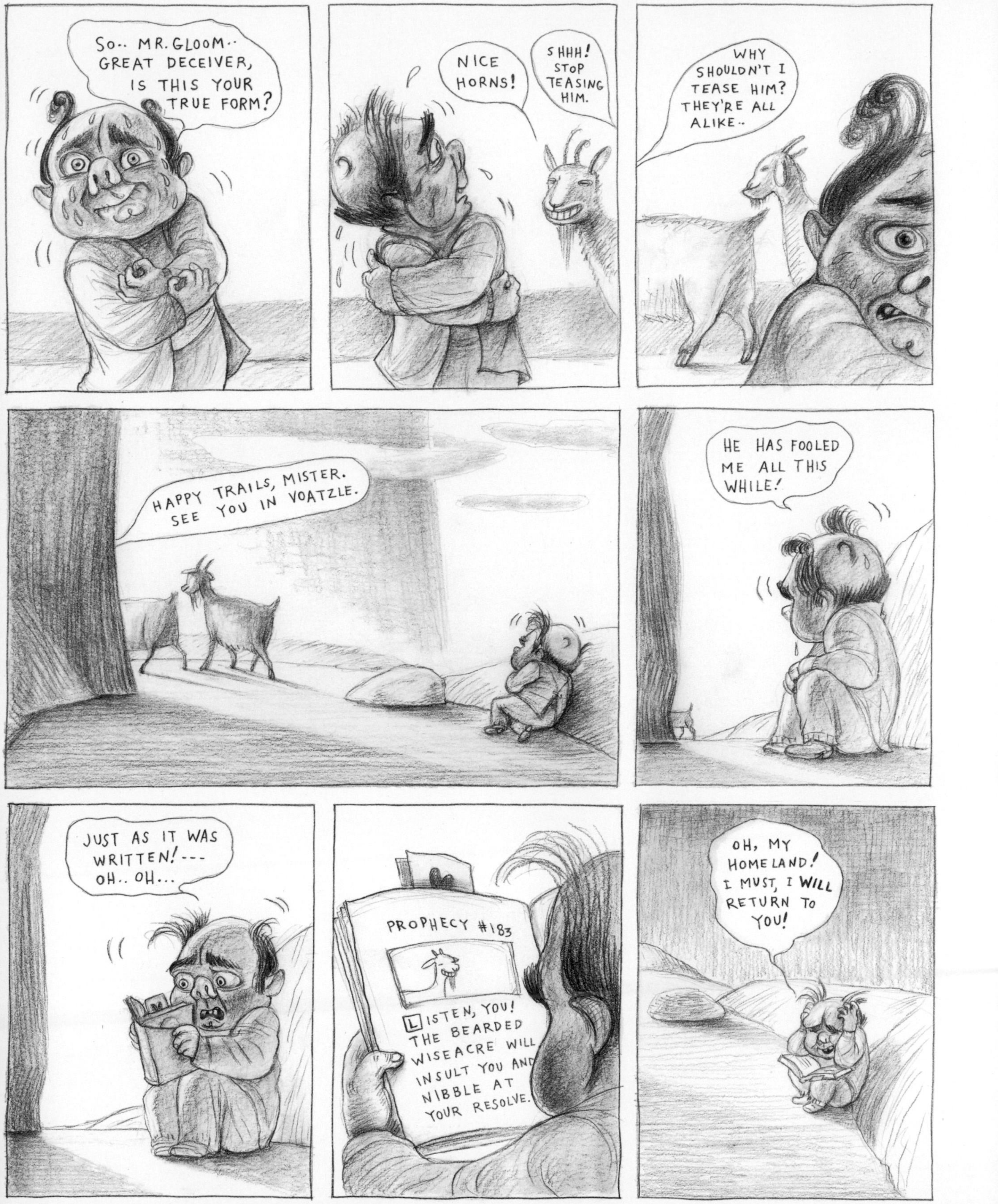
SO.. MR. GLOOM.. GREAT DECEIVER, IS THIS YOUR TRUE FORM?
NICE HORNS!
SHHH! STOP TEASING HIM.
WHY SHOULDN'T I TEASE HIM? THEY'RE ALL ALIKE..
HAPPY TRAILS, MISTER. SEE YOU IN VOATZLE.
HE HAS FOOLED ME ALL THIS WHILE!
JUST AS IT WAS WRITTEN! --- OH.. OH...
PROPHECY #183
LISTEN, YOU! THE BEARDED WISEACRE WILL INSULT YOU AND NIBBLE AT YOUR RESOLVE.
OH, MY HOMELAND! I MUST, I WILL RETURN TO YOU!

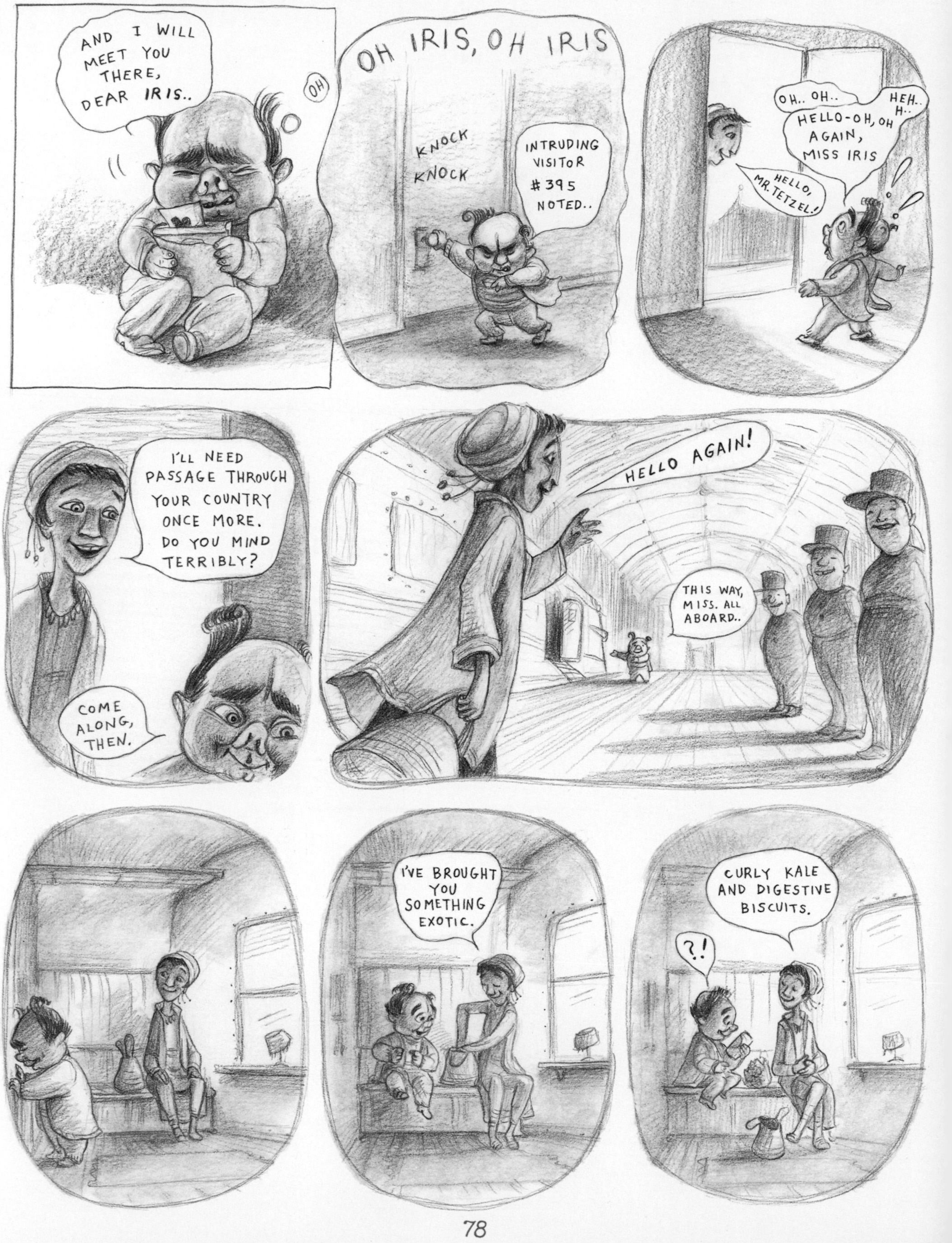
AND I WILL MEET YOU THERE, DEAR IRIS..
OH
OH IRIS, OH IRIS
KNOCK KNOCK
INTRUDING VISITOR #395 NOTED..
OH.. OH..
HEH.. H..
HELLO-OH, OH AGAIN, MISS IRIS
HELLO, MR. TETZEL!
I'LL NEED PASSAGE THROUGH YOUR COUNTRY ONCE MORE. DO YOU MIND TERRIBLY?
COME ALONG, THEN.
HELLO AGAIN!
THIS WAY, MISS. ALL ABOARD..
I'VE BROUGHT YOU SOMETHING EXOTIC.
CURLY KALE AND DIGESTIVE BISCUITS.
?!

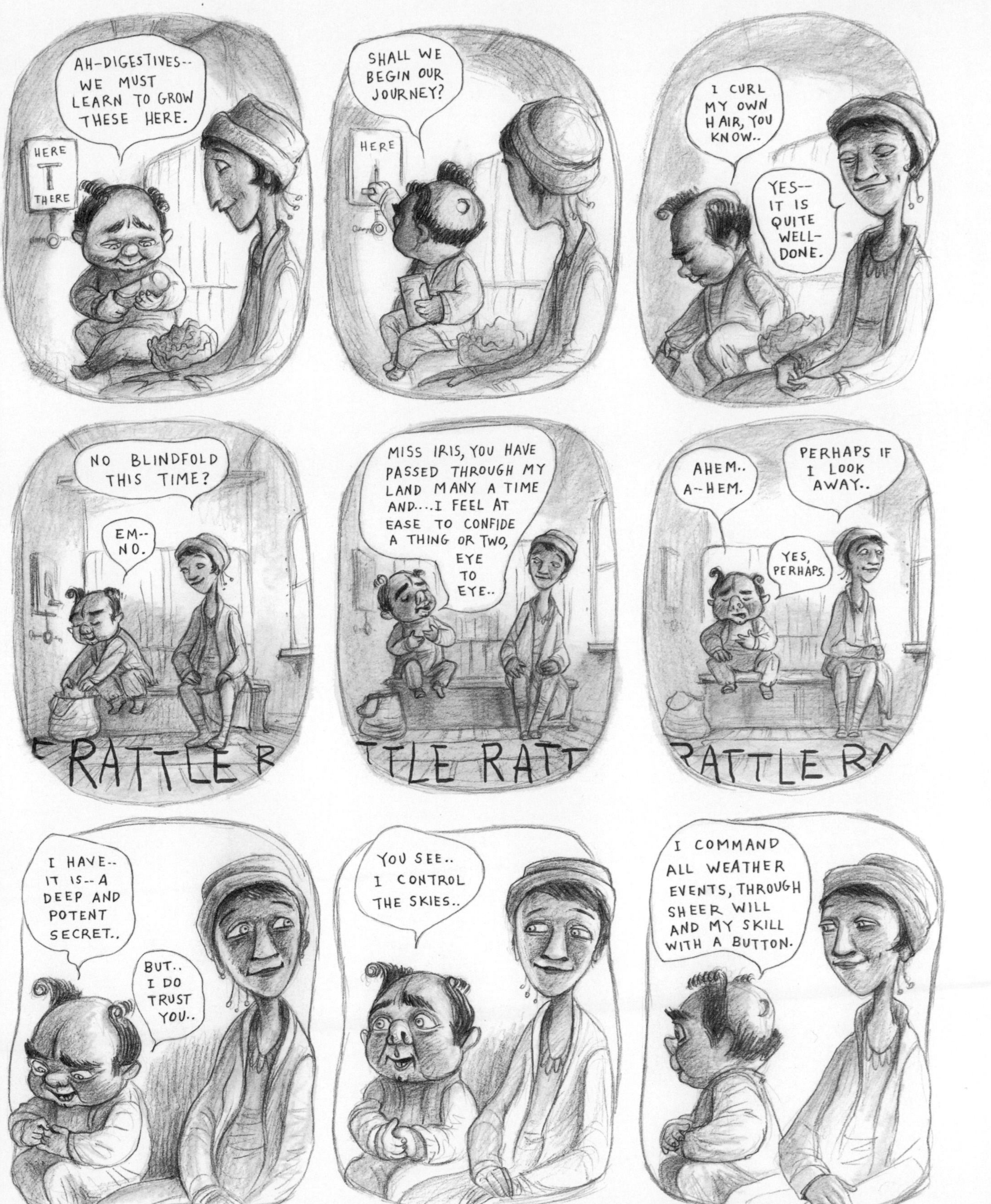
AH-DIGESTIVES-- WE MUST LEARN TO GROW THESE HERE.
HERE
THERE
SHALL WE BEGIN OUR JOURNEY?
HERE
I CURL MY OWN HAIR, YOU KNOW..
YES-- IT IS QUITE WELL-DONE.
NO BLINDFOLD THIS TIME?
EM-- NO.
MISS IRIS, YOU HAVE PASSED THROUGH MY LAND MANY A TIME AND....I FEEL AT EASE TO CONFIDE A THING OR TWO, EYE TO EYE..
AHEM.. A--HEM.
PERHAPS IF I LOOK AWAY..
YES, PERHAPS.
RATTLE RATTLE RATTLE
I HAVE-- IT IS-- A DEEP AND POTENT SECRET..
BUT.. I DO TRUST YOU..
YOU SEE.. I CONTROL THE SKIES..
I COMMAND ALL WEATHER EVENTS, THROUGH SHEER WILL AND MY SKILL WITH A BUTTON.

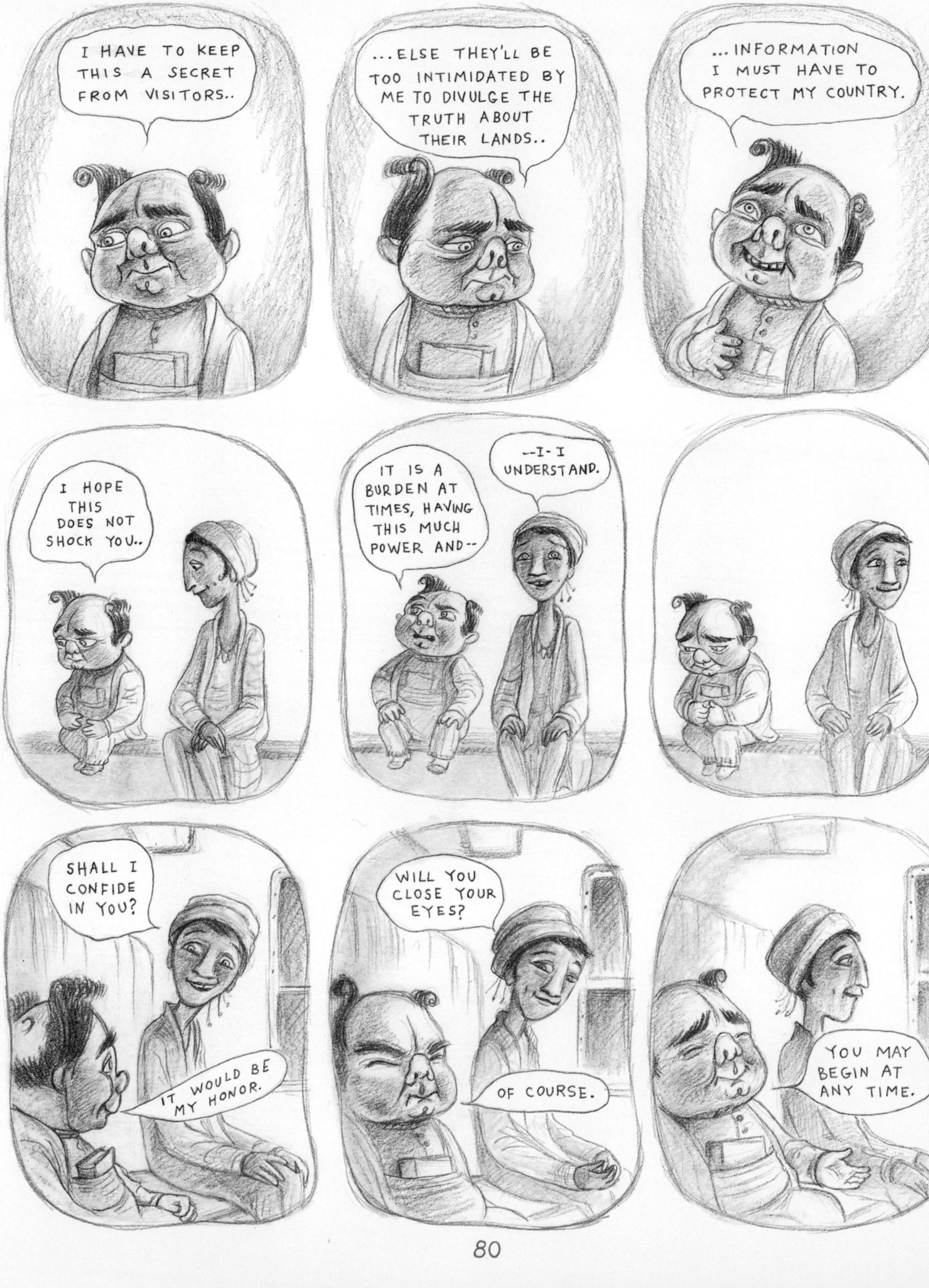
I HAVE TO KEEP THIS A SECRET FROM VISITORS..
...ELSE THEY'LL BE TOO INTIMIDATED BY ME TO DIVULGE THE TRUTH ABOUT THEIR LANDS..
...INFORMATION I MUST HAVE TO PROTECT MY COUNTRY.
I HOPE THIS DOES NOT SHOCK YOU..
IT IS A BURDEN AT TIMES, HAVING THIS MUCH POWER AND--
--I-I UNDERSTAND.
SHALL I CONFIDE IN YOU?
IT WOULD BE MY HONOR.
WILL YOU CLOSE YOUR EYES?
OF COURSE.
YOU MAY BEGIN AT ANY TIME.

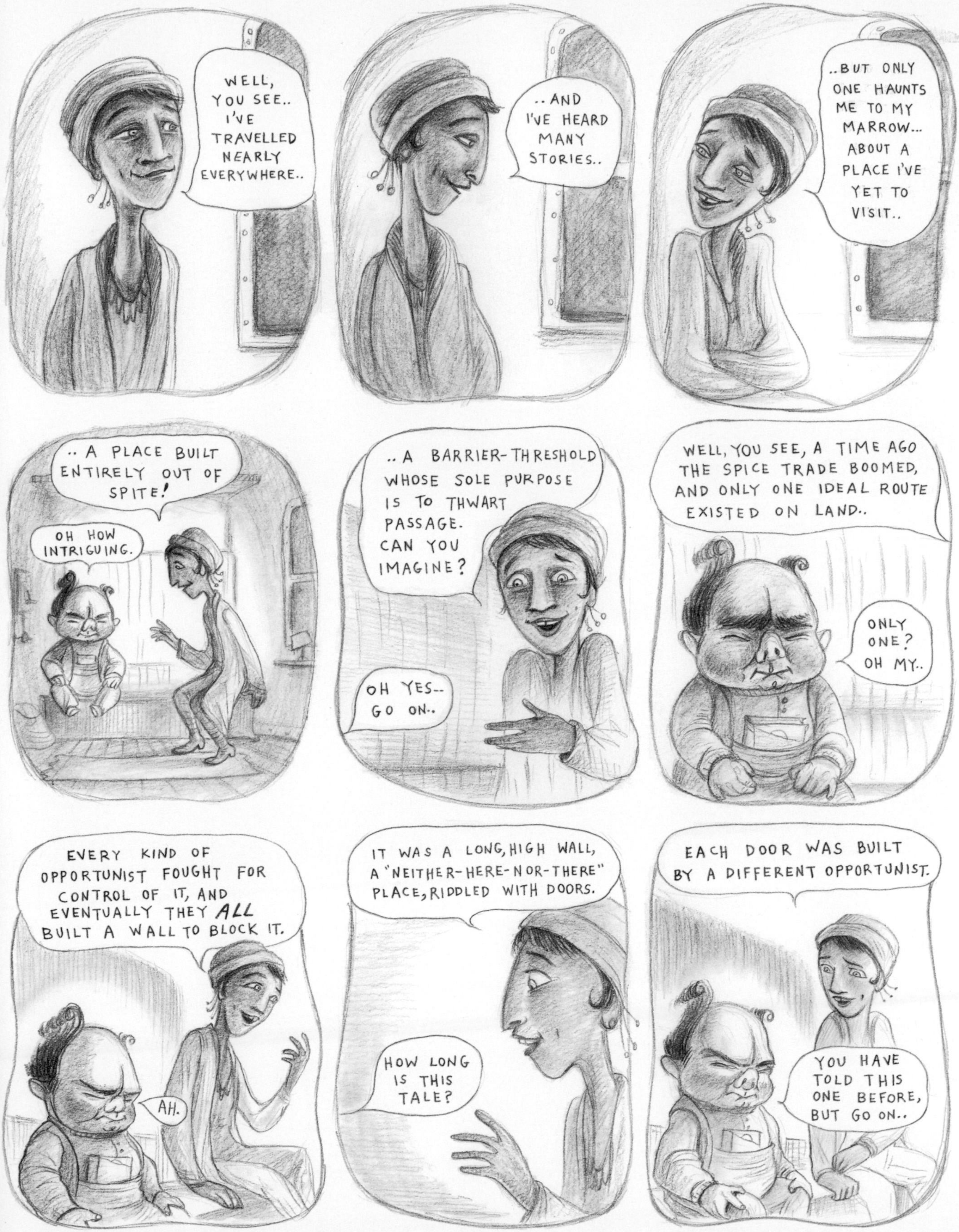
WELL, YOU SEE.. I'VE TRAVELLED NEARLY EVERYWHERE..
..AND I'VE HEARD MANY STORIES..
..BUT ONLY ONE HAUNTS ME TO MY MARROW... ABOUT A PLACE I'VE YET TO VISIT..
.. A PLACE BUILT ENTIRELY OUT OF SPITE!
OH HOW INTRIGUING.
..A BARRIER-THRESHOLD WHOSE SOLE PURPOSE IS TO THWART PASSAGE. CAN YOU IMAGINE?
OH YES-- GO ON..
WELL, YOU SEE, A TIME AGO THE SPICE TRADE BOOMED, AND ONLY ONE IDEAL ROUTE EXISTED ON LAND..
ONLY ONE? OH MY..
EVERY KIND OF OPPORTUNIST FOUGHT FOR CONTROL OF IT, AND EVENTUALLY THEY ALL BUILT A WALL TO BLOCK IT.
AH.
IT WAS A LONG, HIGH WALL, A "NEITHER-HERE-NOR-THERE" PLACE, RIDDLED WITH DOORS.
HOW LONG IS THIS TALE?
EACH DOOR WAS BUILT BY A DIFFERENT OPPORTUNIST.
YOU HAVE TOLD THIS ONE BEFORE, BUT GO ON..

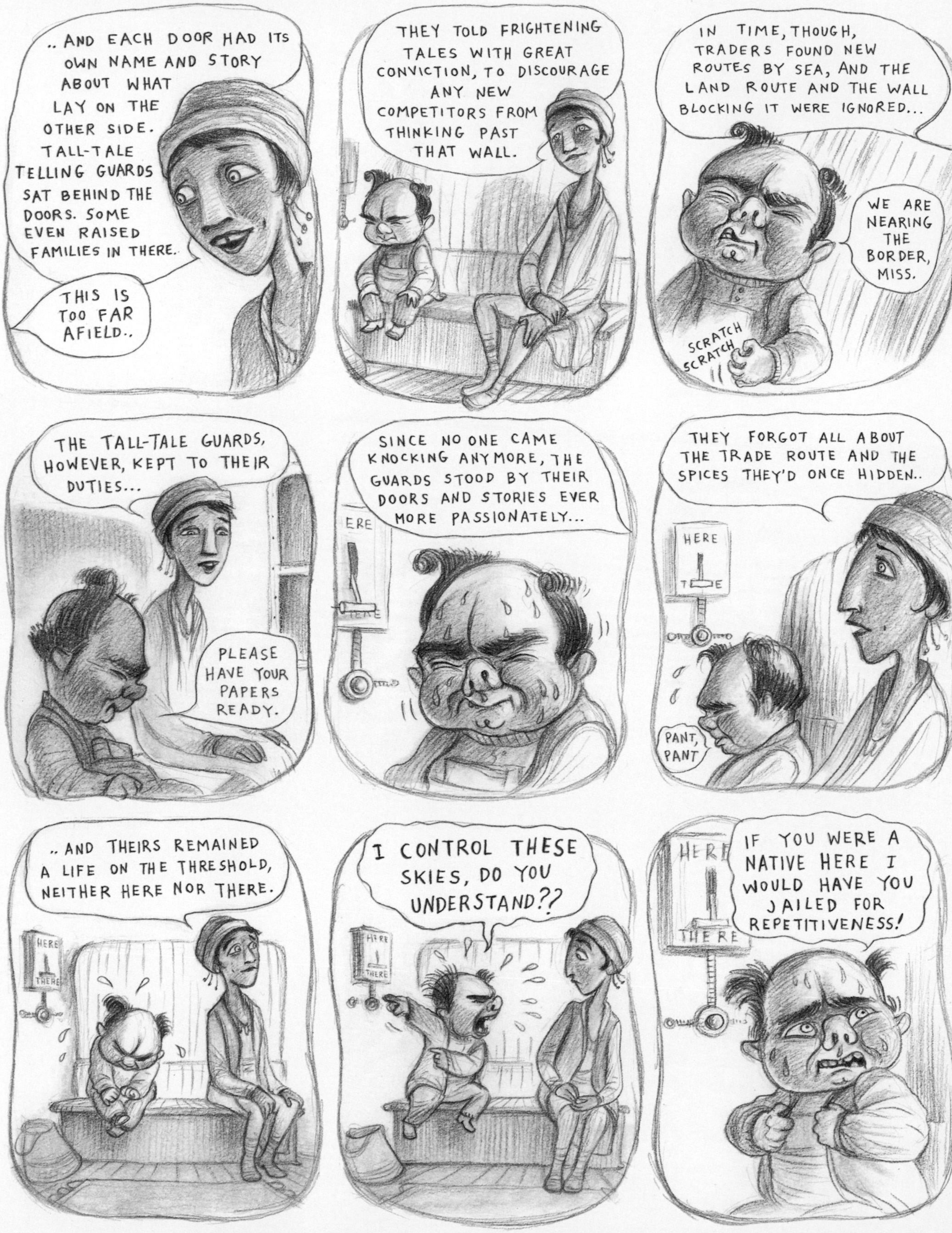
.. AND EACH DOOR HAD ITS OWN NAME AND STORY ABOUT WHAT LAY ON THE OTHER SIDE. TALL-TALE TELLING GUARDS SAT BEHIND THE DOORS. SOME EVEN RAISED FAMILIES IN THERE.
THIS IS TOO FAR AFIELD..
THEY TOLD FRIGHTENING TALES WITH GREAT CONVICTION, TO DISCOURAGE ANY NEW COMPETITORS FROM THINKING PAST THAT WALL.
IN TIME, THOUGH, TRADERS FOUND NEW ROUTES BY SEA, AND THE LAND ROUTE AND THE WALL BLOCKING IT WERE IGNORED...
WE ARE NEARING THE BORDER, MISS.
SCRATCH SCRATCH
THE TALL-TALE GUARDS, HOWEVER, KEPT TO THEIR DUTIES...
PLEASE HAVE YOUR PAPERS READY.
SINCE NO ONE CAME KNOCKING ANYMORE, THE GUARDS STOOD BY THEIR DOORS AND STORIES EVER MORE PASSIONATELY...
THEY FORGOT ALL ABOUT THE TRADE ROUTE AND THE SPICES THEY'D ONCE HIDDEN..
HERE
PANT, PANT
.. AND THEIRS REMAINED A LIFE ON THE THRESHOLD, NEITHER HERE NOR THERE.
I CONTROL THESE SKIES, DO YOU UNDERSTAND??
IF YOU WERE A NATIVE HERE I WOULD HAVE YOU JAILED FOR REPETITIVENESS!

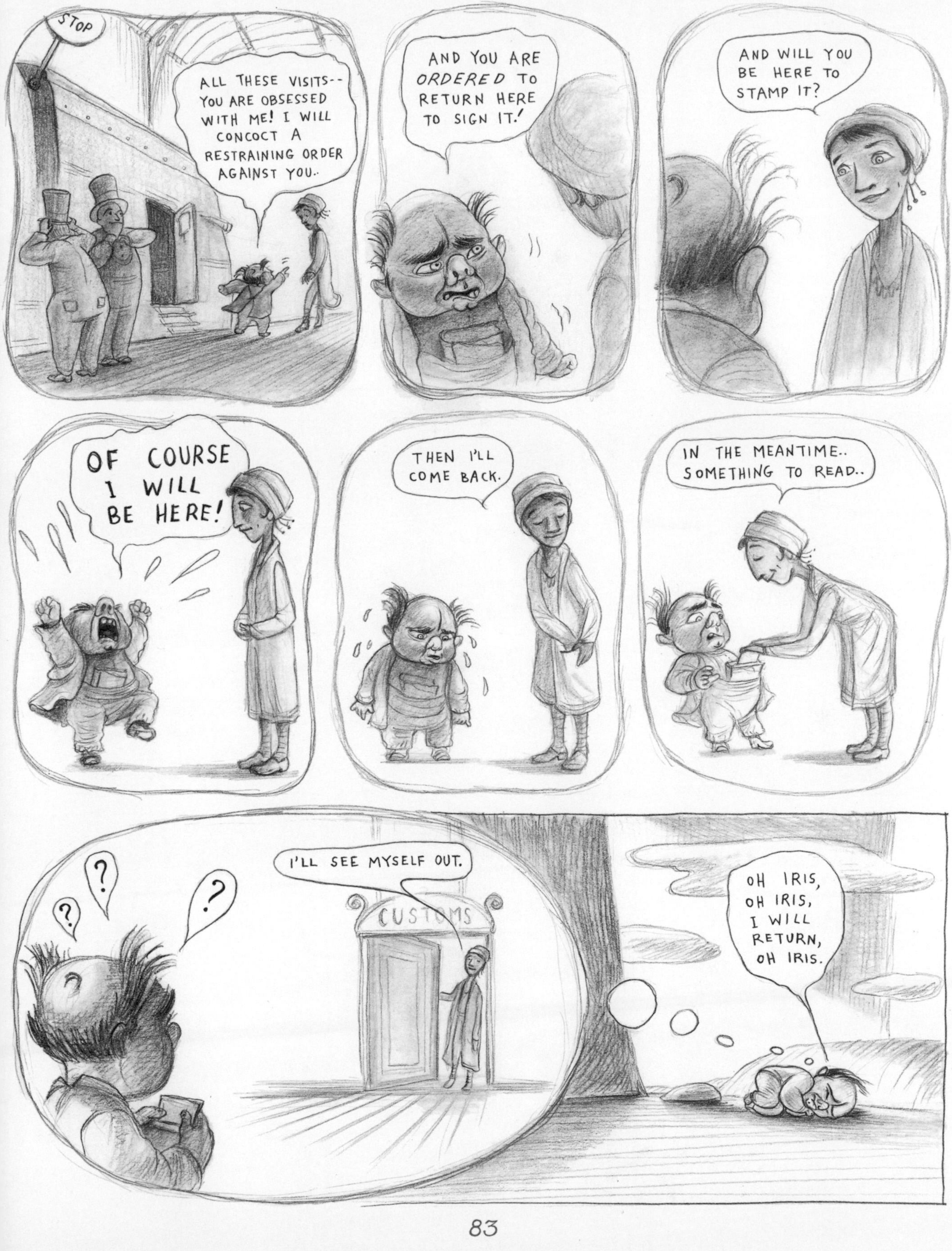
STOP
ALL THESE VISITS-- YOU ARE OBSESSED WITH ME! I WILL CONCOCT A RESTRAINING ORDER AGAINST YOU..
AND YOU ARE *ORDERED* TO RETURN HERE TO SIGN IT.!
AND WILL YOU BE HERE TO STAMP IT?
OF COURSE I WILL BE HERE!
THEN I'LL COME BACK.
IN THE MEANTIME.. SOMETHING TO READ..
?
?
?
I'LL SEE MYSELF OUT.
CUSTOMS
OH IRIS, OH IRIS, I WILL RETURN, OH IRIS.

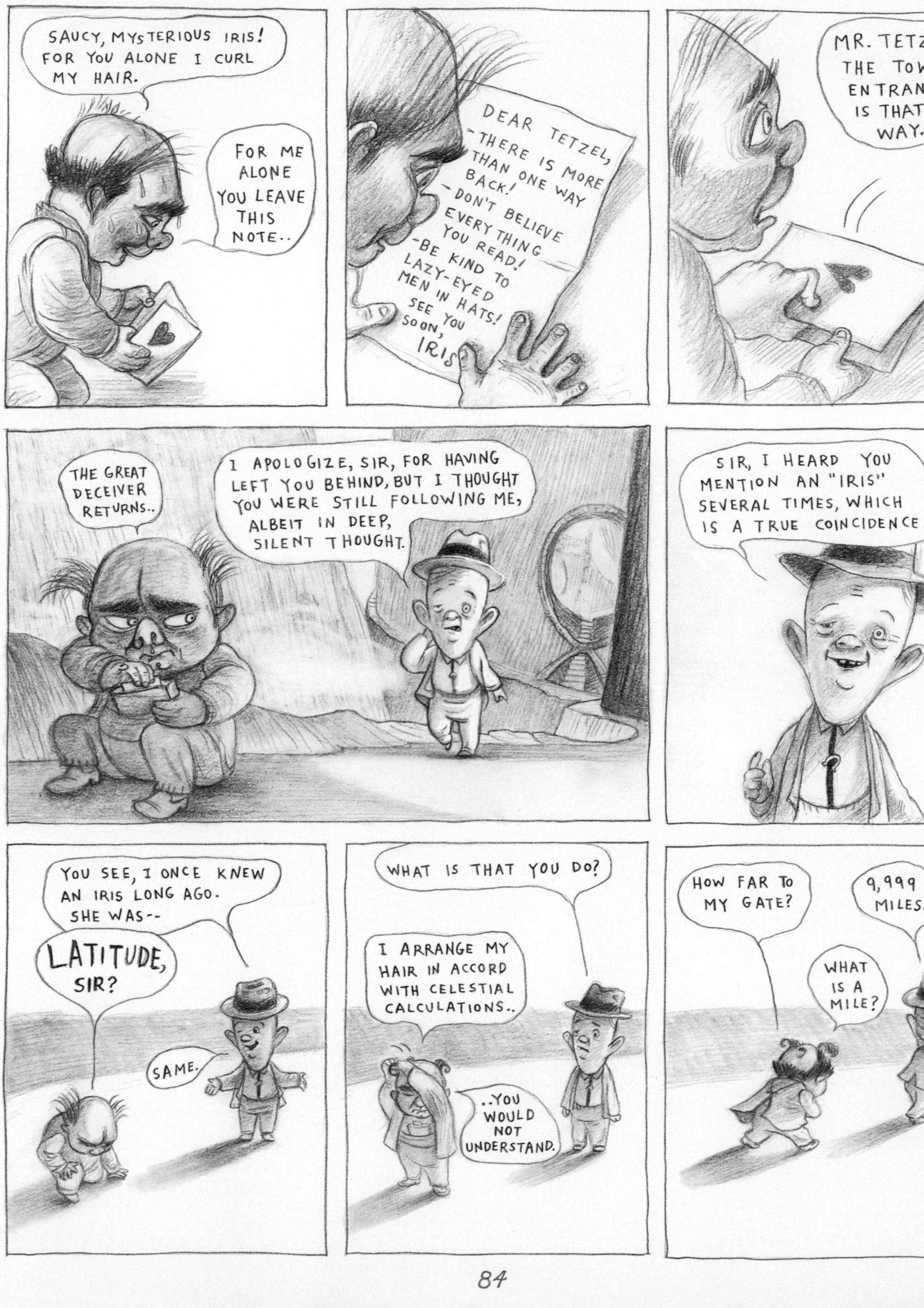
SAUCY, MYSTERIOUS IRIS! FOR YOU ALONE I CURL MY HAIR.
FOR ME ALONE YOU LEAVE THIS NOTE..
DEAR TETZEL, -THERE IS MORE THAN ONE WAY BACK! -DON'T BELIEVE EVERYTHING YOU READ! -BE KIND TO LAZY-EYED MEN IN HATS! SEE YOU SOON, IRIS
MR. TETZEL, THE TOWN'S ENTRANCE IS THAT WAY..
THE GREAT DECEIVER RETURNS..
I APOLOGIZE, SIR, FOR HAVING LEFT YOU BEHIND, BUT I THOUGHT YOU WERE STILL FOLLOWING ME, ALBEIT IN DEEP, SILENT THOUGHT.
SIR, I HEARD YOU MENTION AN "IRIS" SEVERAL TIMES, WHICH IS A TRUE COINCIDENCE.
YOU SEE, I ONCE KNEW AN IRIS LONG AGO. SHE WAS--
LATITUDE, SIR?
SAME.
WHAT IS THAT YOU DO?
I ARRANGE MY HAIR IN ACCORD WITH CELESTIAL CALCULATIONS..
..YOU WOULD NOT UNDERSTAND.
HOW FAR TO MY GATE?
9,999 MILES.
WHAT IS A MILE?

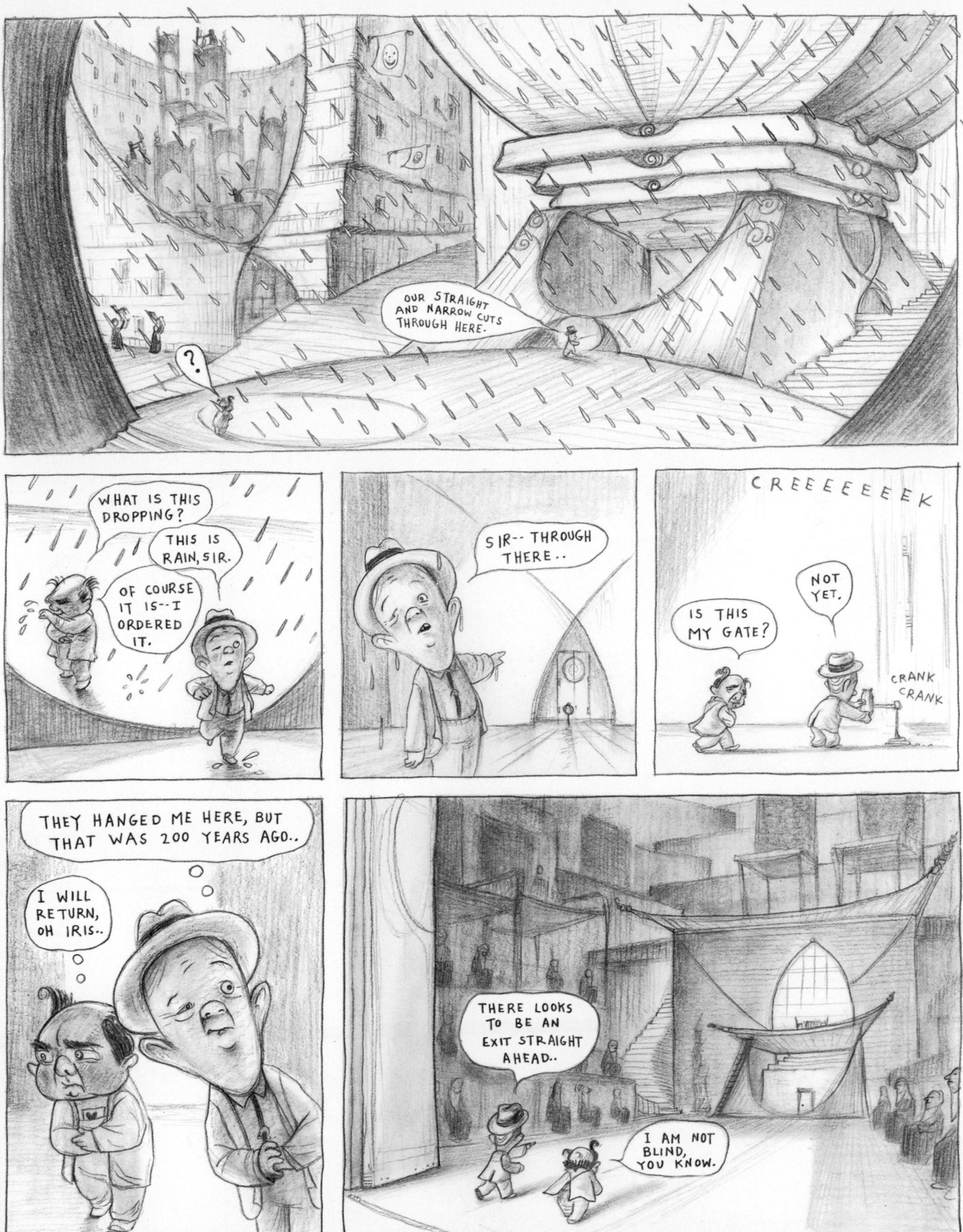
OUR STRAIGHT AND NARROW CUTS THROUGH HERE.
?
WHAT IS THIS DROPPING?
THIS IS RAIN, SIR.
OF COURSE IT IS--I ORDERED IT.
SIR-- THROUGH THERE..
CREEEEEEEEK
IS THIS MY GATE?
NOT YET.
CRANK CRANK
THEY HANGED ME HERE, BUT THAT WAS 200 YEARS AGO..
I WILL RETURN, OH IRIS..
THERE LOOKS TO BE AN EXIT STRAIGHT AHEAD..
I AM NOT BLIND, YOU KNOW.

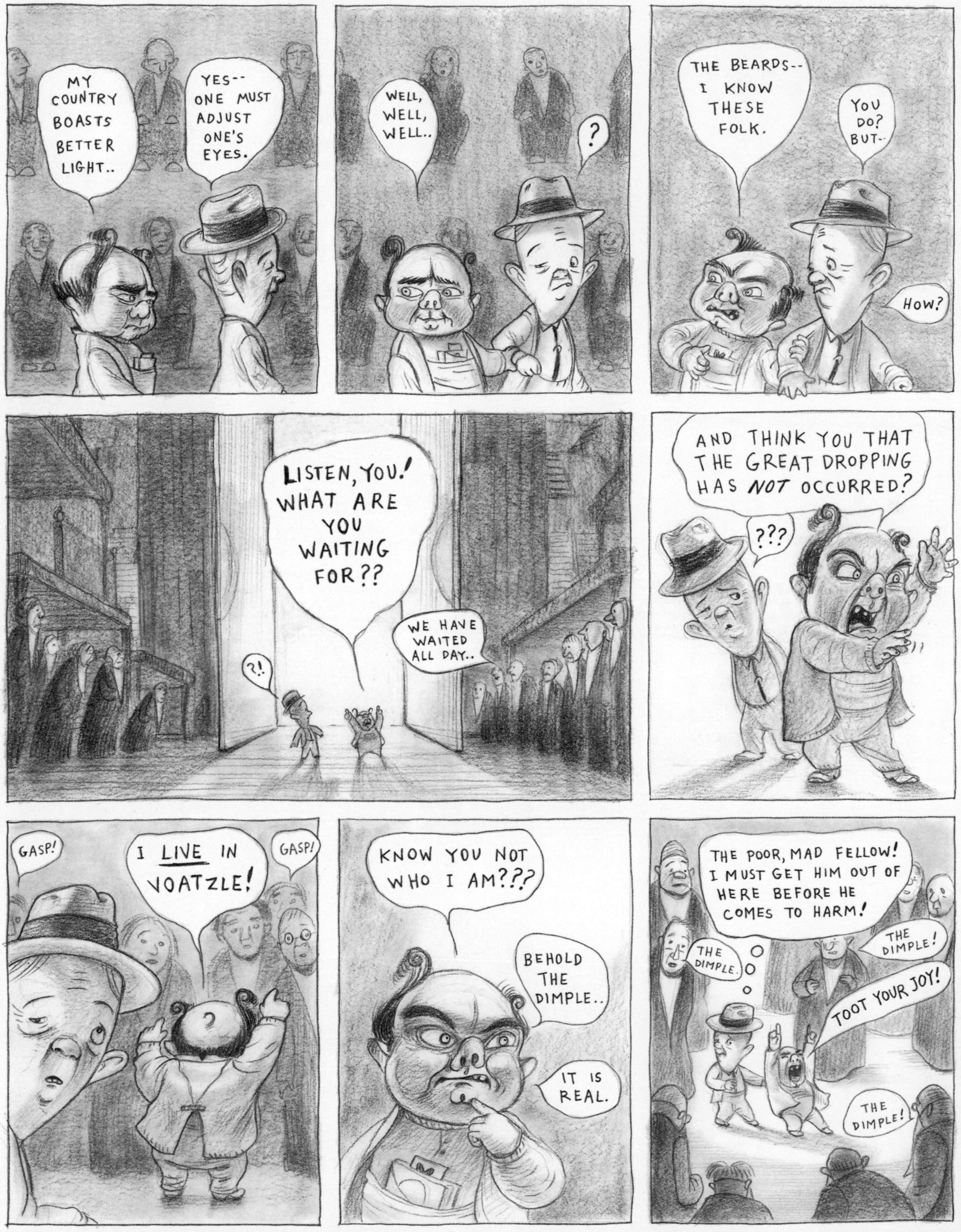
MY COUNTRY BOASTS BETTER LIGHT..
YES-- ONE MUST ADJUST ONE'S EYES.
WELL, WELL, WELL..
?
THE BEARDS-- I KNOW THESE FOLK.
YOU DO? BUT--
HOW?
LISTEN, YOU! WHAT ARE YOU WAITING FOR??
?!
WE HAVE WAITED ALL DAY..
AND THINK YOU THAT THE GREAT DROPPING HAS NOT OCCURRED?
???
GASP!
I LIVE IN VOATZLE!
GASP!
?
KNOW YOU NOT WHO I AM???
BEHOLD THE DIMPLE..
IT IS REAL.
THE POOR, MAD FELLOW! I MUST GET HIM OUT OF HERE BEFORE HE COMES TO HARM!
THE DIMPLE.
THE DIMPLE!
TOOT YOUR JOY!
THE DIMPLE!

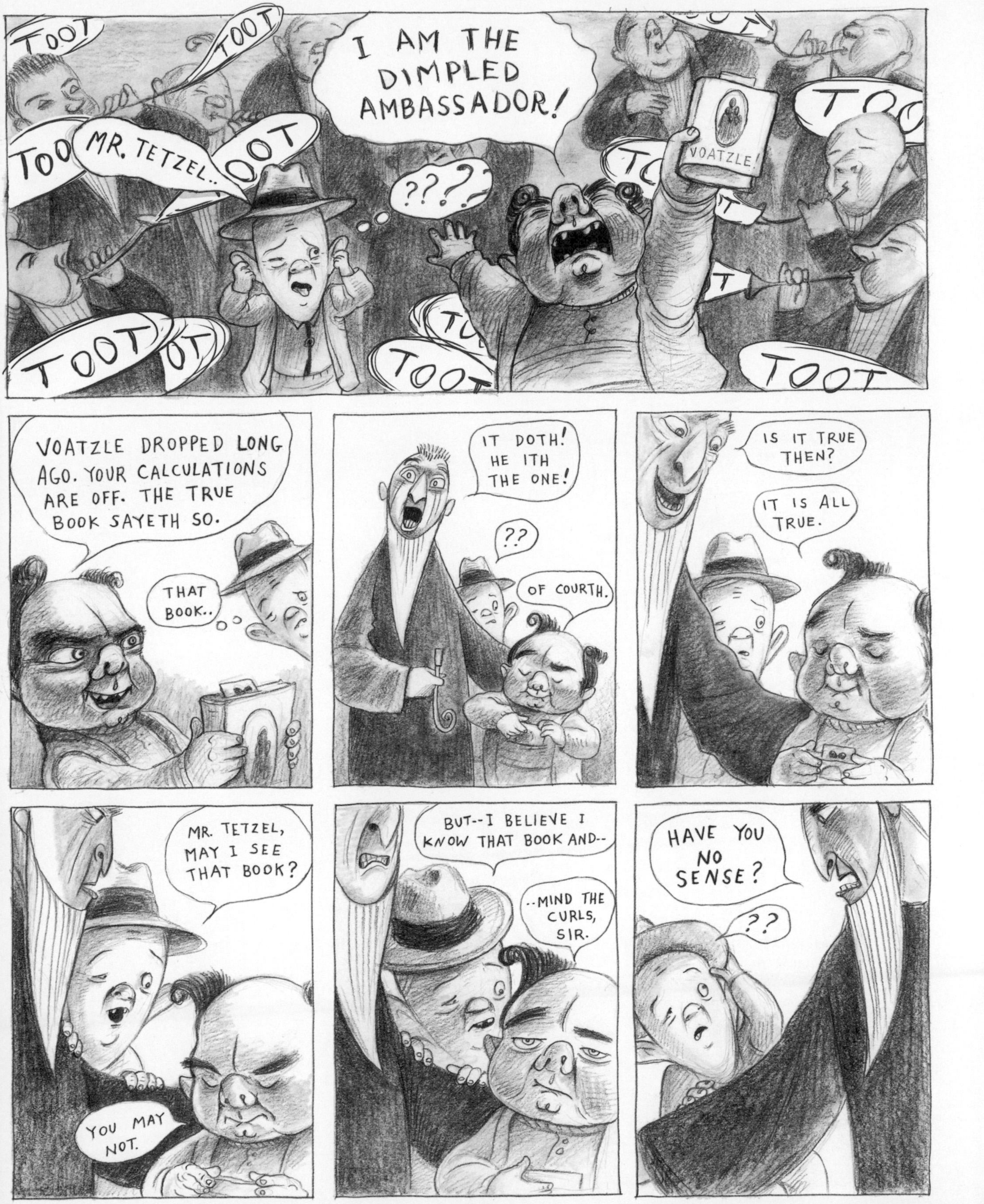
TOOT
TOOT
I AM THE DIMPLED AMBASSADOR!
TOO
MR. TETZEL..
TOOT
???
VOATZLE!
TOOT
TOOT
TOOT
VOATZLE DROPPED LONG AGO. YOUR CALCULATIONS ARE OFF. THE TRUE BOOK SAYETH SO.
THAT BOOK..
IT DOTH! HE ITH THE ONE!
??
OF COURTH.
IS IT TRUE THEN?
IT IS ALL TRUE.
MR. TETZEL, MAY I SEE THAT BOOK?
YOU MAY NOT.
BUT--I BELIEVE I KNOW THAT BOOK AND--
..MIND THE CURLS, SIR.
HAVE YOU NO SENSE?
??

HONOR THE DIMPLED AMBASSADOR!
MAKE YOUR NOISE
S-SIR, WOULD YOU MIND EXPLAINING..
TOOT
TOOT
TOOT
TOOT
TOOT
TOOT
TOOT
TOOT
TOOT
SOME STRANGE EUPHORIA FILLS THIS PLACE.
WHAT BOOK IS THIS? THEY ALL FOLLOW IT.
EVEN MR. TETZEL.
200 YEARS AGO THIS TOWN CALLED FOR MY HANGING...
HAS THIS BOOK CIVILIZED THEM?
TOOT JOY!
NOISE!!
TOOT
PERHAPS I HAVE AWAKENED TO A MORE PERFECT WORLD.
I WISH I COULD GET A BETTER LOOK AT THAT BOOK.
IT HAS ELEVATED MR. TETZEL, A SHUT-IN..
IT HAS ELEVATED EVERYONE, IT SEEMS..
WOMEN, MEN-- THEY ALL WEAR BEARDS NOW..
THIS IS A GOOD SIGN, I SUPPOSE.
TOOT
TOOT
TOOT
TOOT

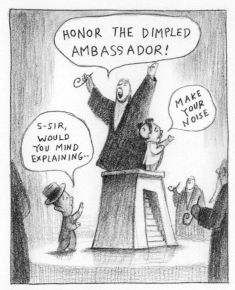

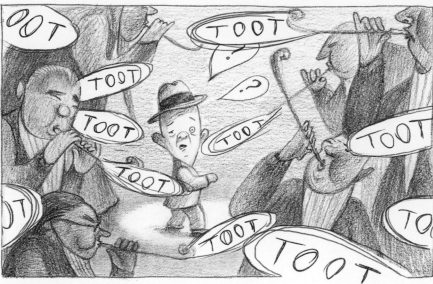

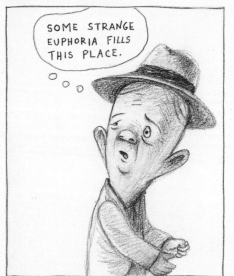

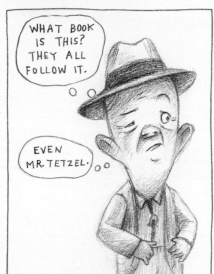

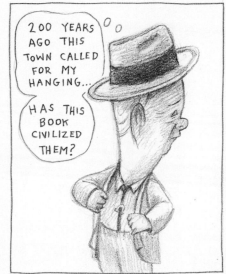

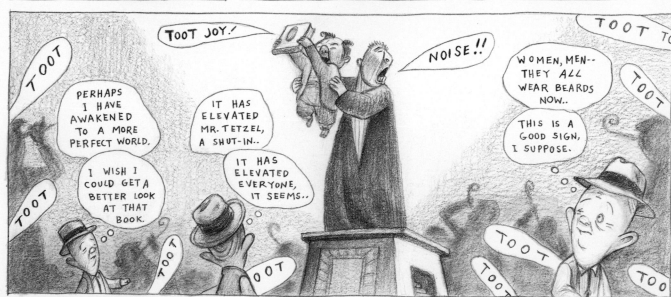

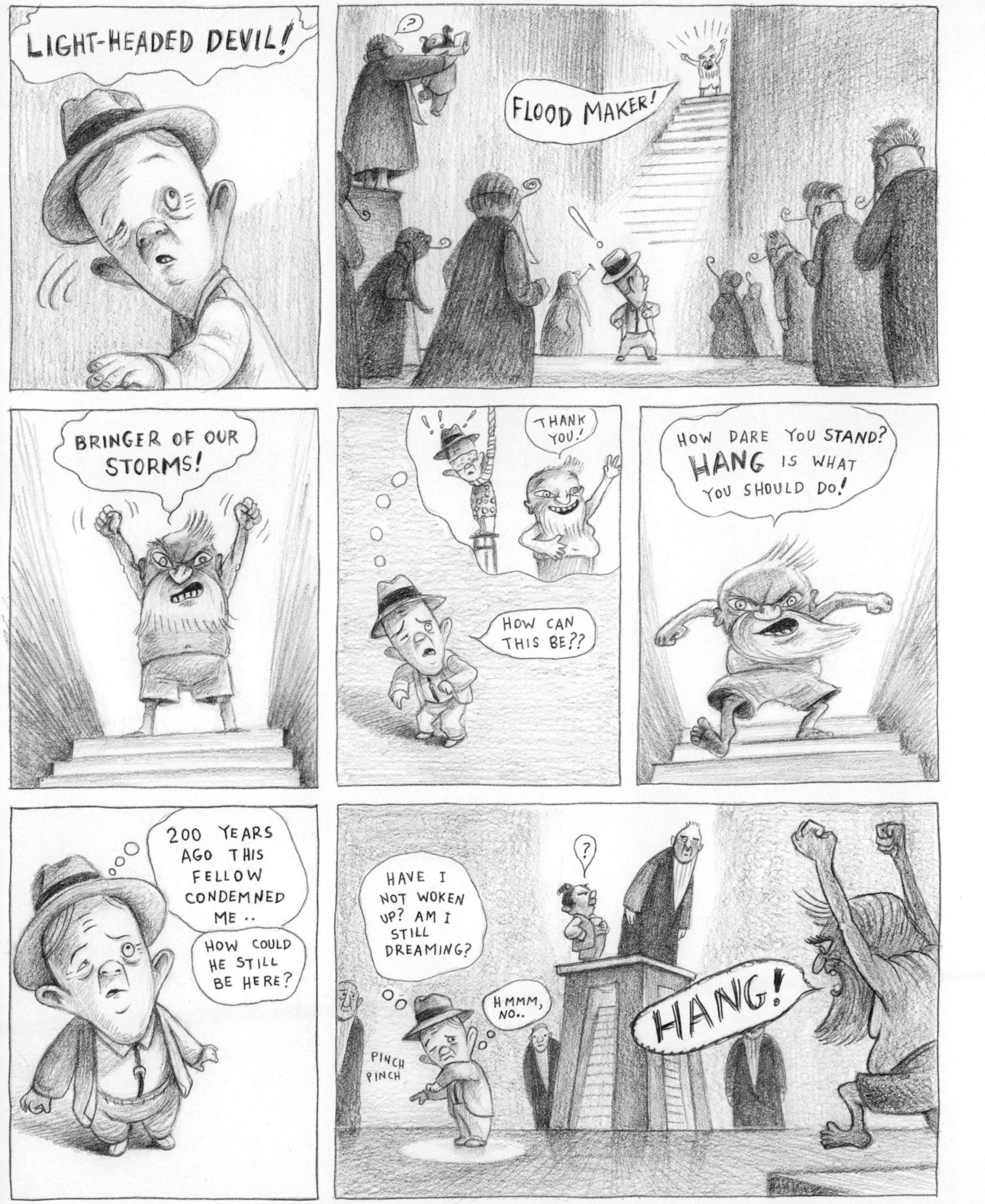
LIGHT-HEADED DEVIL!
?
FLOOD MAKER!
!
BRINGER OF OUR STORMS!
! ! !
THANK YOU!
HOW CAN THIS BE??
HOW DARE YOU STAND? HANG IS WHAT YOU SHOULD DO!
200 YEARS AGO THIS FELLOW CONDEMNED ME..
HOW COULD HE STILL BE HERE?
?
HAVE I NOT WOKEN UP? AM I STILL DREAMING?
HMMM, NO..
PINCH PINCH
HANG!

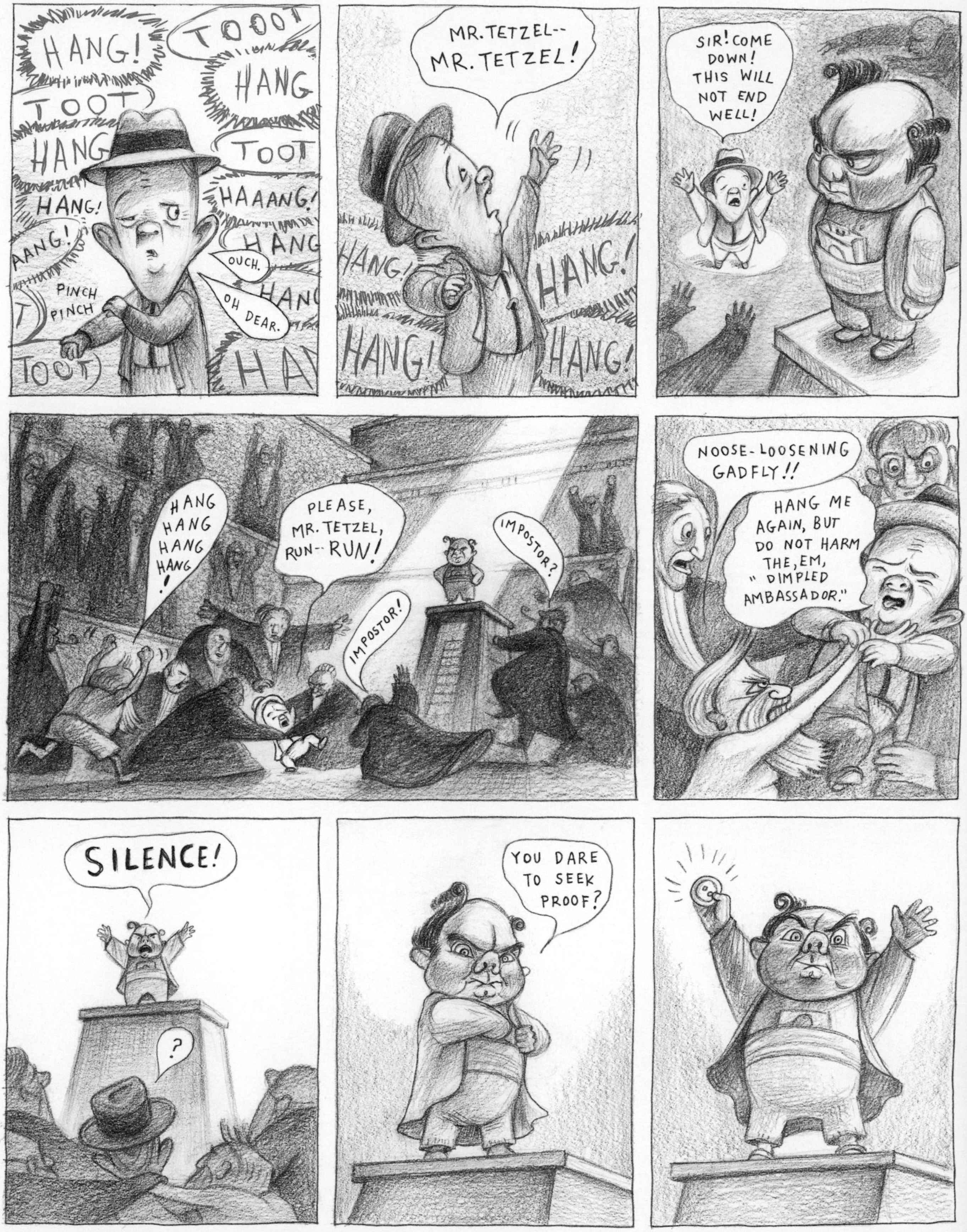
HANG!
TOOOT
HANG
TOOT
HANG
TOOT
HANG!
HAAANG!
AANG!
HANG
OUCH.
PINCH
PINCH
OH DEAR.
TOOT
MR. TETZEL--
MR. TETZEL!
HANG!
HANG!
HANG!
HANG!
SIR! COME DOWN! THIS WILL NOT END WELL!
HANG HANG HANG HANG!
PLEASE, MR. TETZEL, RUN--RUN!
IMPOSTOR?
IMPOSTOR!
NOOSE-LOOSENING GADFLY!!
HANG ME AGAIN, BUT DO NOT HARM THE, EM, "DIMPLED AMBASSADOR."
SILENCE!
?
YOU DARE TO SEEK PROOF?

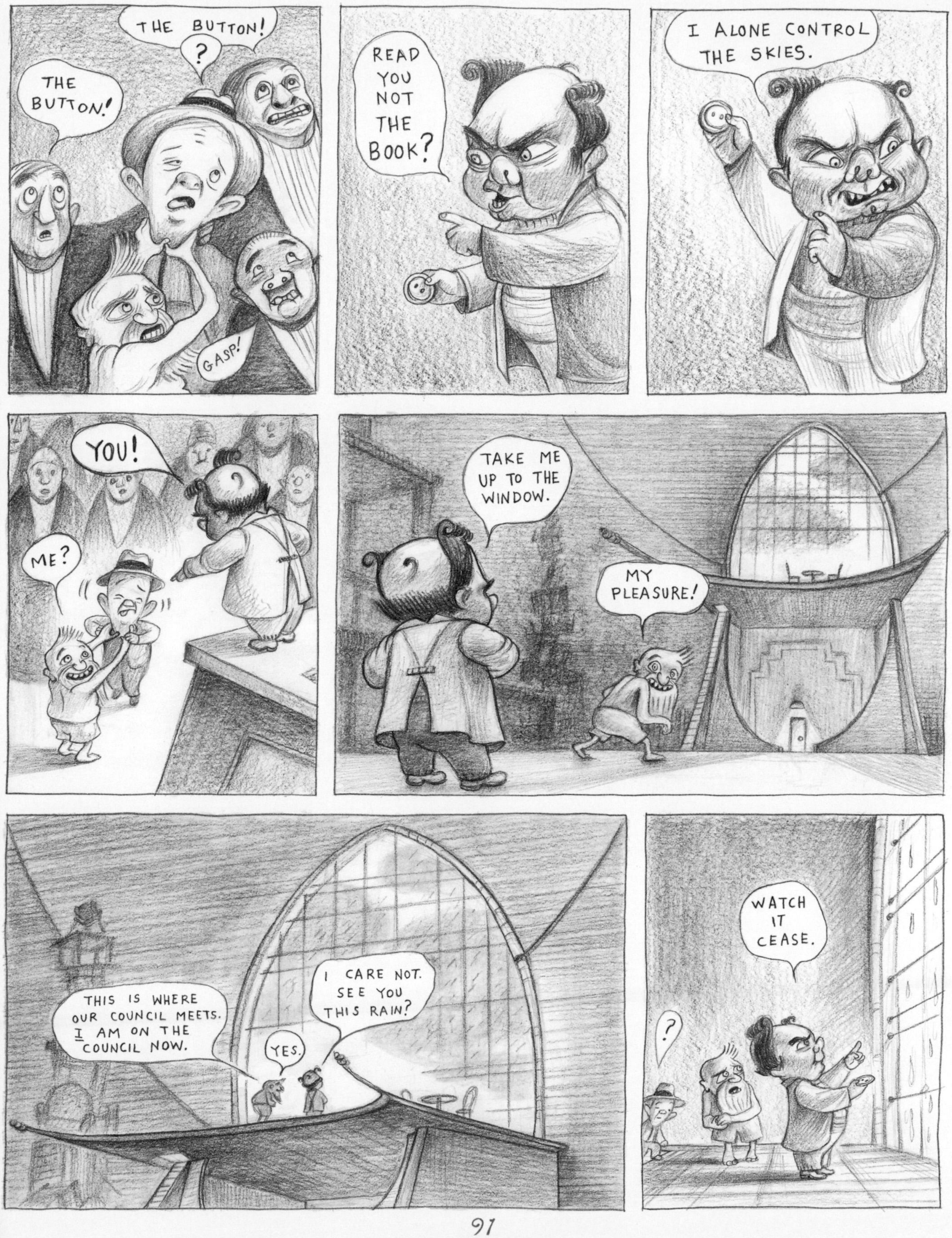
THE BUTTON!
?
THE BUTTON!
GASP!
READ YOU NOT THE BOOK?
I ALONE CONTROL THE SKIES.
YOU!
ME?
TAKE ME UP TO THE WINDOW.
MY PLEASURE!
THIS IS WHERE OUR COUNCIL MEETS. I AM ON THE COUNCIL NOW.
YES.
I CARE NOT. SEE YOU THIS RAIN?
WATCH IT CEASE.
?

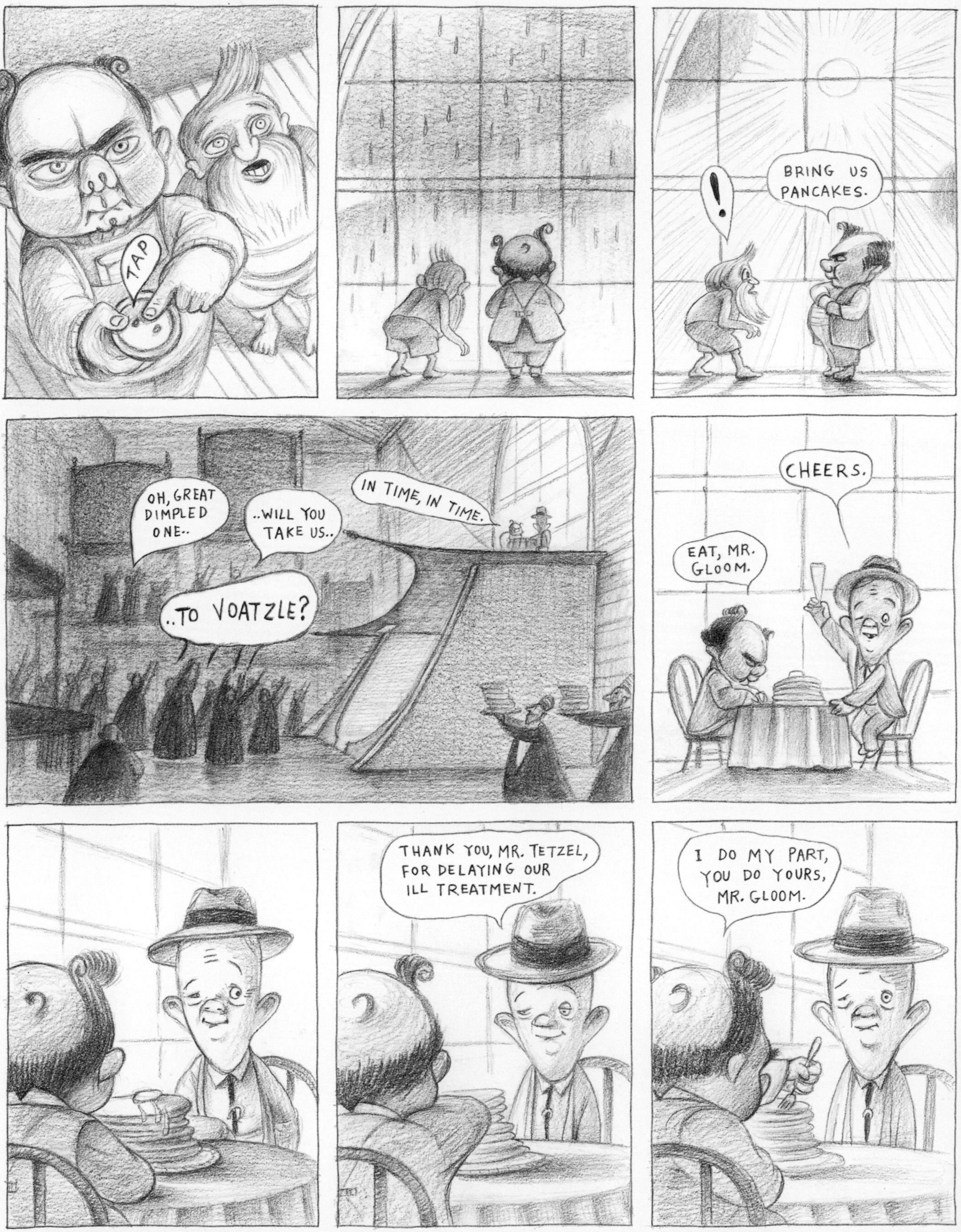
TAP
!
BRING US PANCAKES.
OH, GREAT DIMPLED ONE..
..WILL YOU TAKE US..
..TO VOATZLE?
IN TIME, IN TIME.
CHEERS.
EAT, MR. GLOOM.
THANK YOU, MR. TETZEL, FOR DELAYING OUR ILL TREATMENT.
I DO MY PART, YOU DO YOURS, MR. GLOOM.

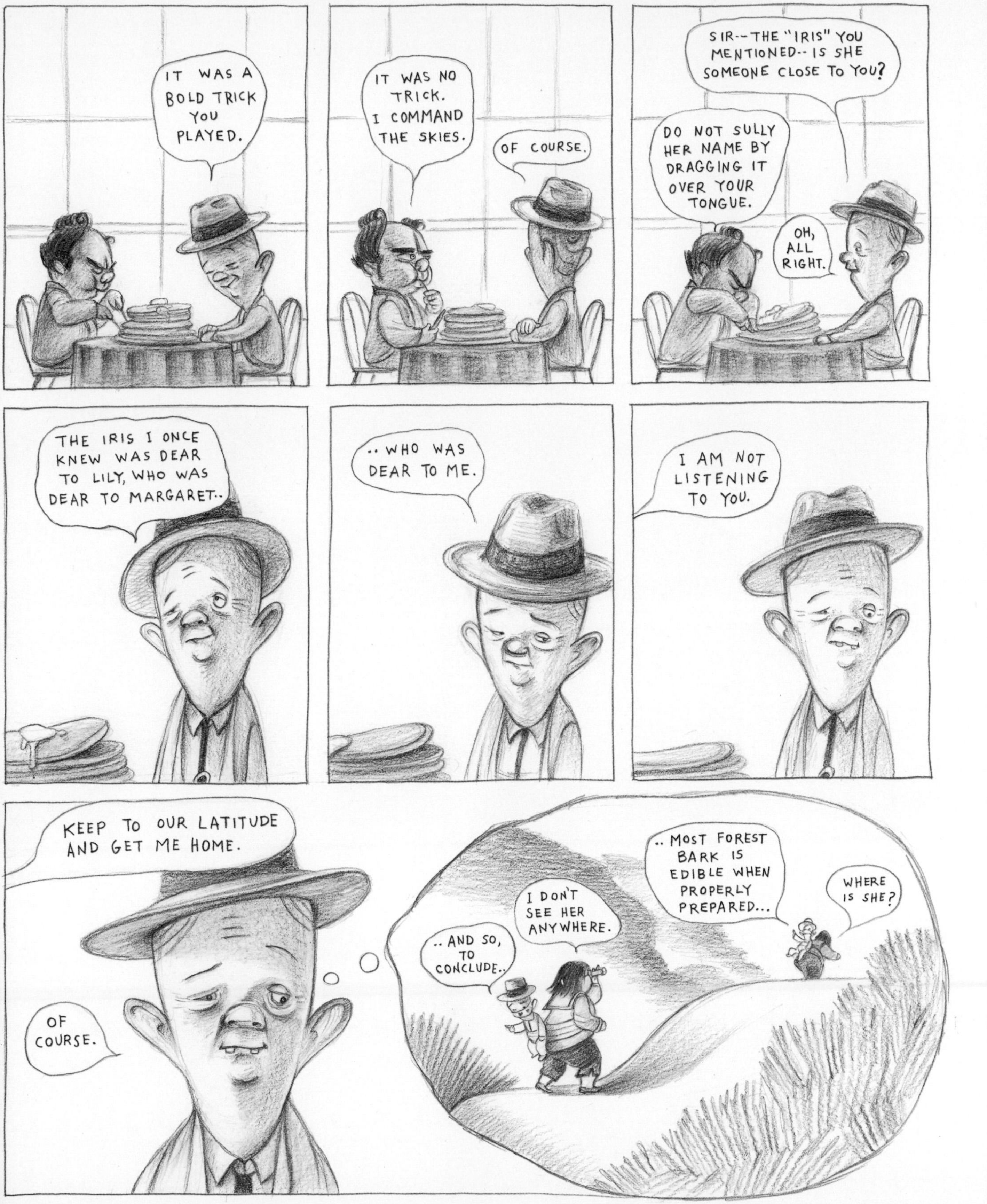
IT WAS A BOLD TRICK YOU PLAYED.
IT WAS NO TRICK. I COMMAND THE SKIES.
OF COURSE.
SIR--THE "IRIS" YOU MENTIONED--IS SHE SOMEONE CLOSE TO YOU?
DO NOT SULLY HER NAME BY DRAGGING IT OVER YOUR TONGUE.
OH, ALL RIGHT.
THE IRIS I ONCE KNEW WAS DEAR TO LILY, WHO WAS DEAR TO MARGARET..
..WHO WAS DEAR TO ME.
I AM NOT LISTENING TO YOU.
KEEP TO OUR LATITUDE AND GET ME HOME.
OF COURSE.
..AND SO, TO CONCLUDE..
I DON'T SEE HER ANYWHERE.
..MOST FOREST BARK IS EDIBLE WHEN PROPERLY PREPARED...
WHERE IS SHE?

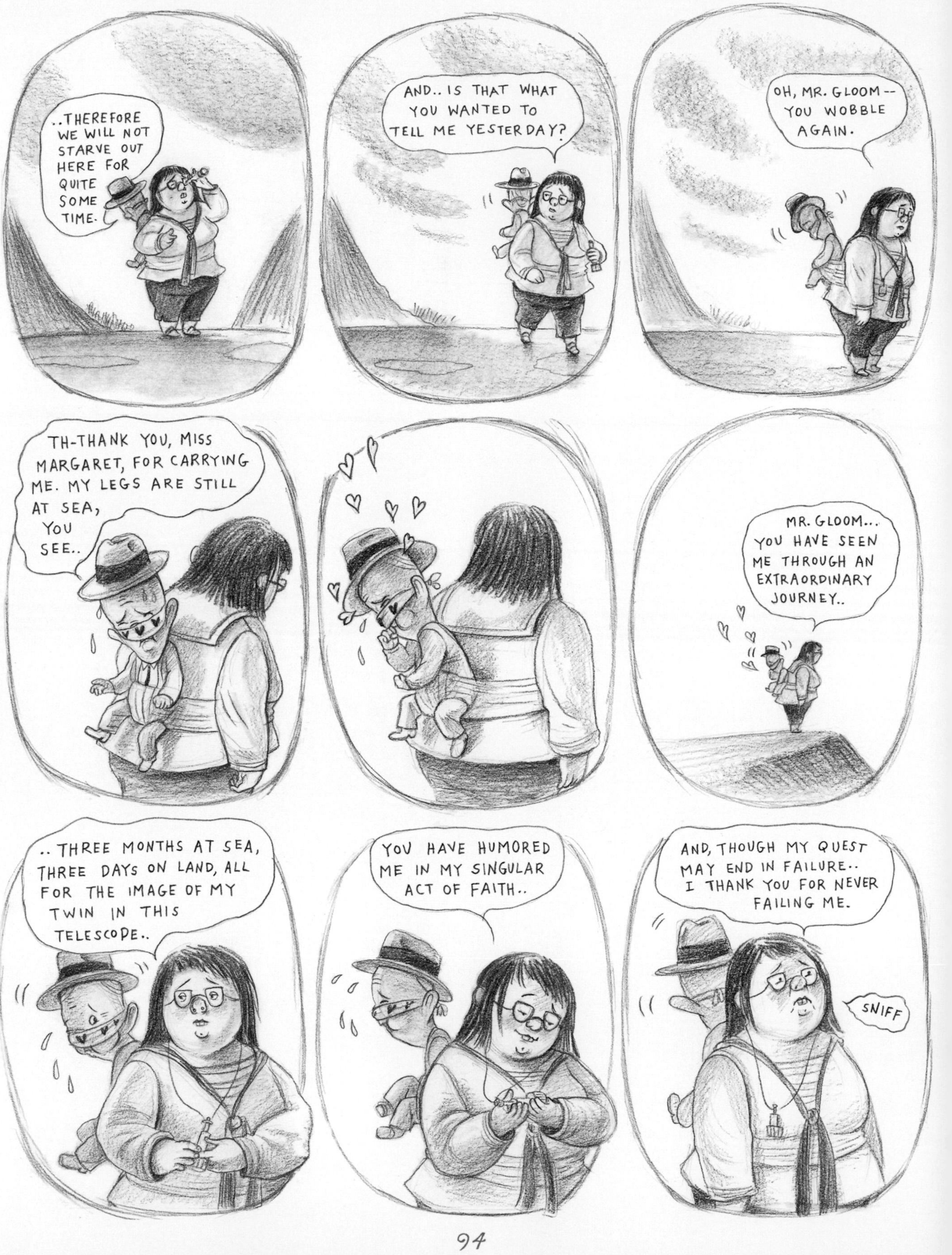
..THEREFORE WE WILL NOT STARVE OUT HERE FOR QUITE SOME TIME.
AND.. IS THAT WHAT YOU WANTED TO TELL ME YESTERDAY?
OH, MR. GLOOM -- YOU WOBBLE AGAIN.
TH-THANK YOU, MISS MARGARET, FOR CARRYING ME. MY LEGS ARE STILL AT SEA, YOU SEE..
MR. GLOOM... YOU HAVE SEEN ME THROUGH AN EXTRAORDINARY JOURNEY..
.. THREE MONTHS AT SEA, THREE DAYS ON LAND, ALL FOR THE IMAGE OF MY TWIN IN THIS TELESCOPE..
YOU HAVE HUMORED ME IN MY SINGULAR ACT OF FAITH..
AND, THOUGH MY QUEST MAY END IN FAILURE.. I THANK YOU FOR NEVER FAILING ME.
SNIFF

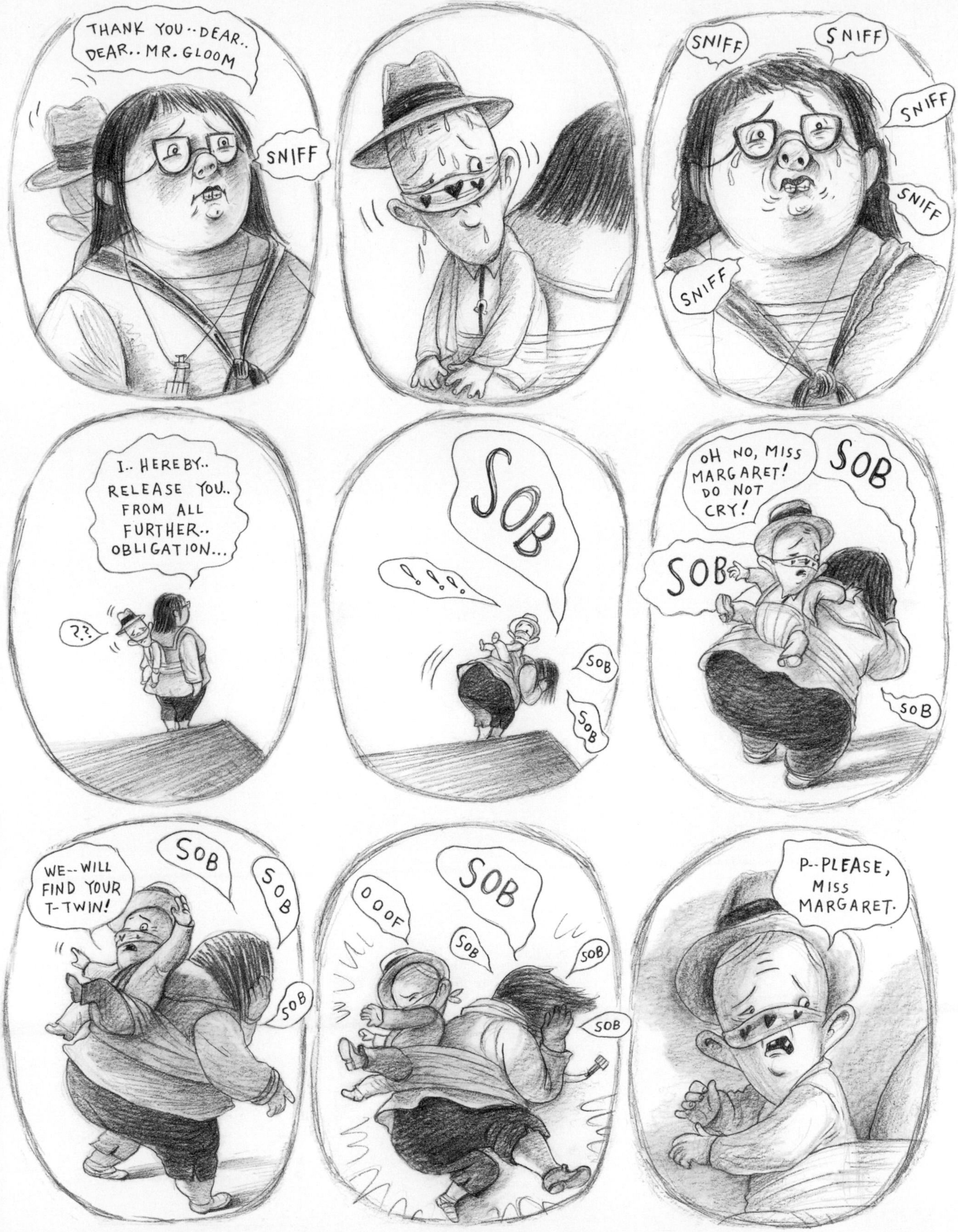
THANK YOU.. DEAR.. DEAR.. MR. GLOOM
SNIFF
SNIFF
SNIFF
SNIFF
SNIFF
SNIFF
I.. HEREBY.. RELEASE YOU.. FROM ALL FURTHER.. OBLIGATION...
??
SOB
!!!
SOB
SOB
OH NO, MISS MARGARET! DO NOT CRY!
SOB
SOB
SOB
WE-- WILL FIND YOUR T-TWIN!
SOB
SOB
SOB
OOOF
SOB
SOB
SOB
SOB
P--PLEASE, MISS MARGARET.

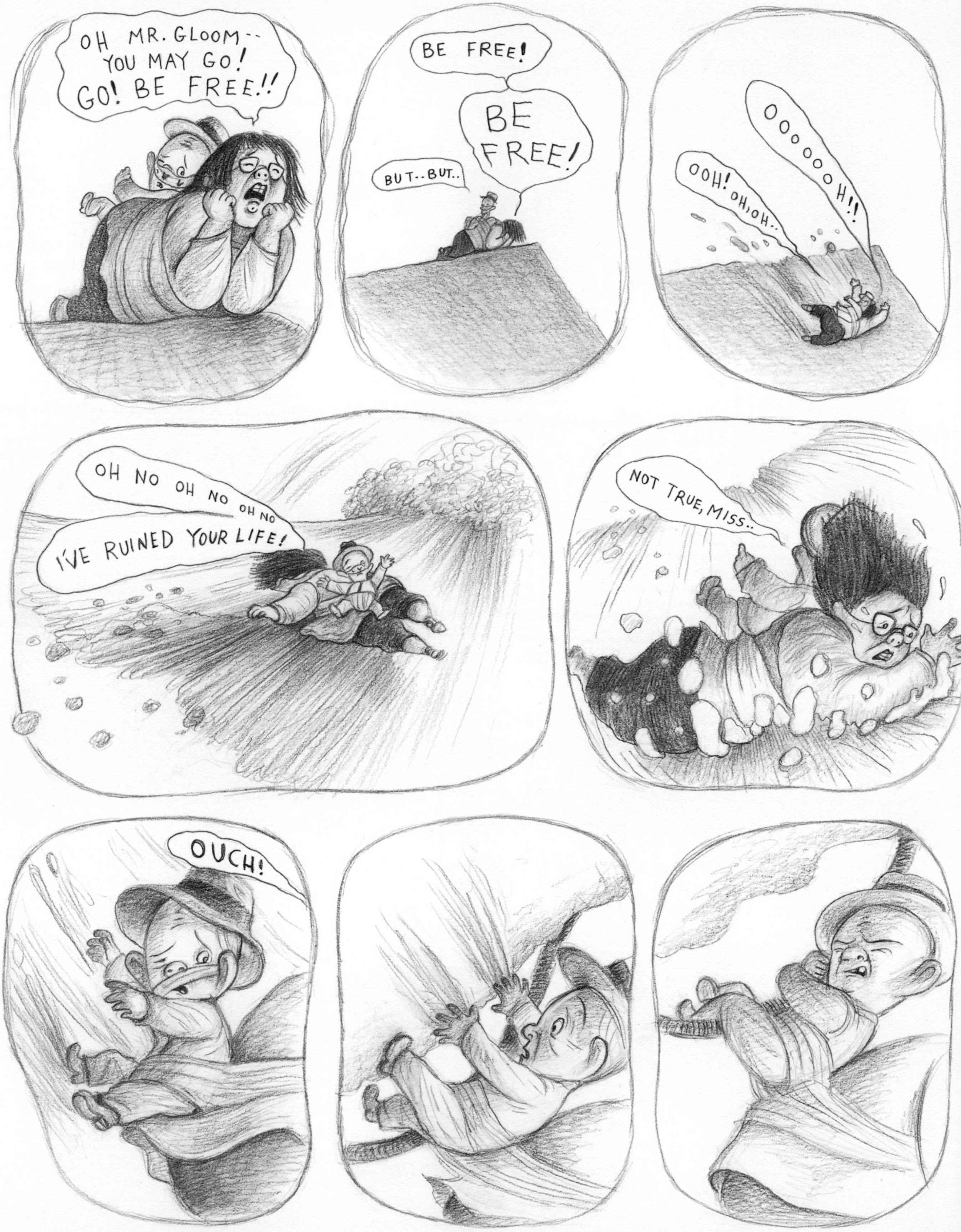
OH MR. GLOOM-- YOU MAY GO! GO! BE FREE!!
BE FREE!
BE FREE!
BUT--BUT..
OOOOOOH!!
OOH! OH, OH..
OH NO OH NO OH NO
I'VE RUINED YOUR LIFE!
NOT TRUE, MISS..
OUCH!

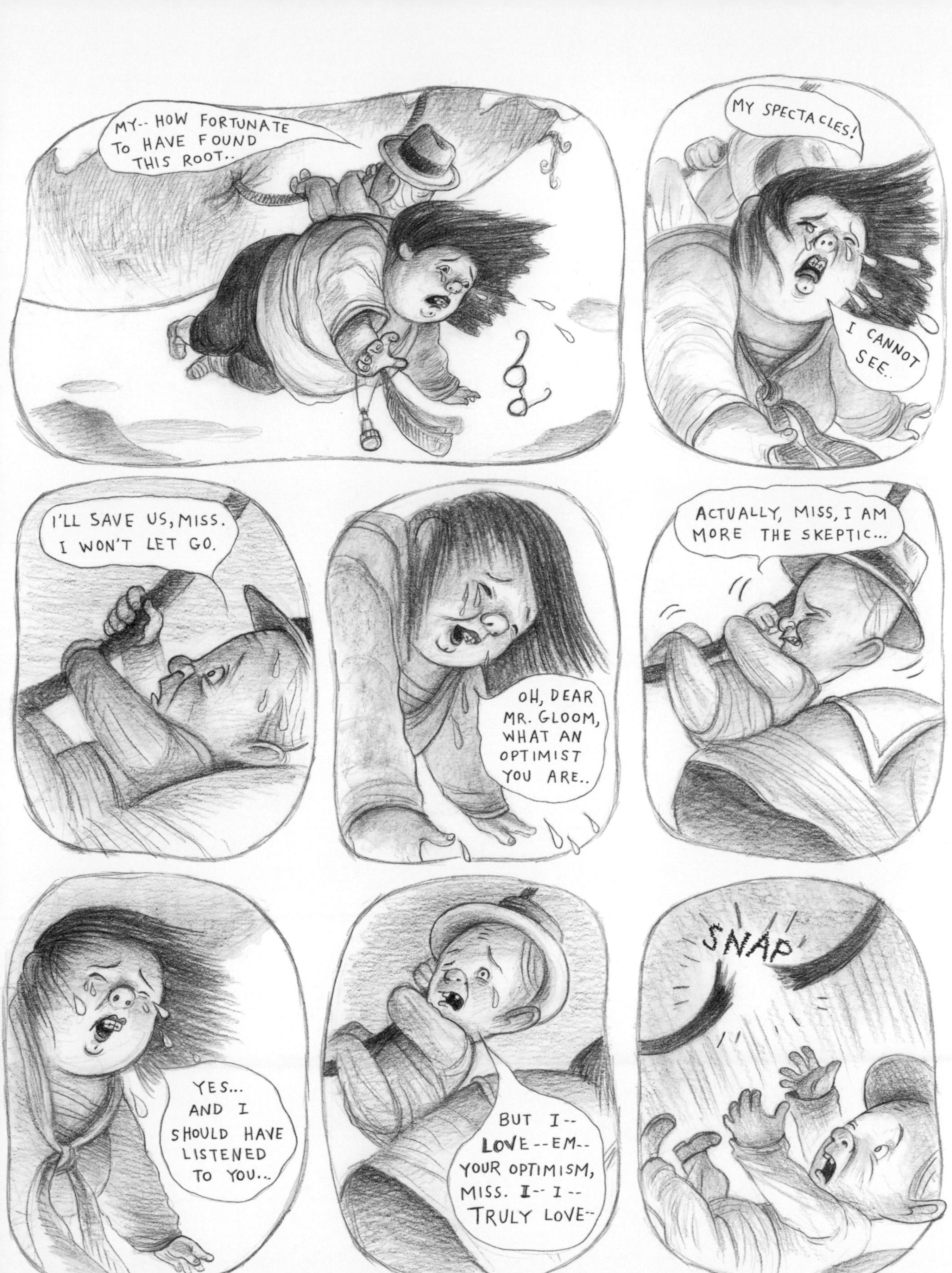
MY-- HOW FORTUNATE TO HAVE FOUND THIS ROOT..
MY SPECTACLES!
I CANNOT SEE..
I'LL SAVE US, MISS. I WON'T LET GO.
OH, DEAR MR. GLOOM, WHAT AN OPTIMIST YOU ARE..
ACTUALLY, MISS, I AM MORE THE SKEPTIC...
YES... AND I SHOULD HAVE LISTENED TO YOU...
BUT I-- LOVE--EM-- YOUR OPTIMISM, MISS. I-- I-- TRULY LOVE--
SNAP

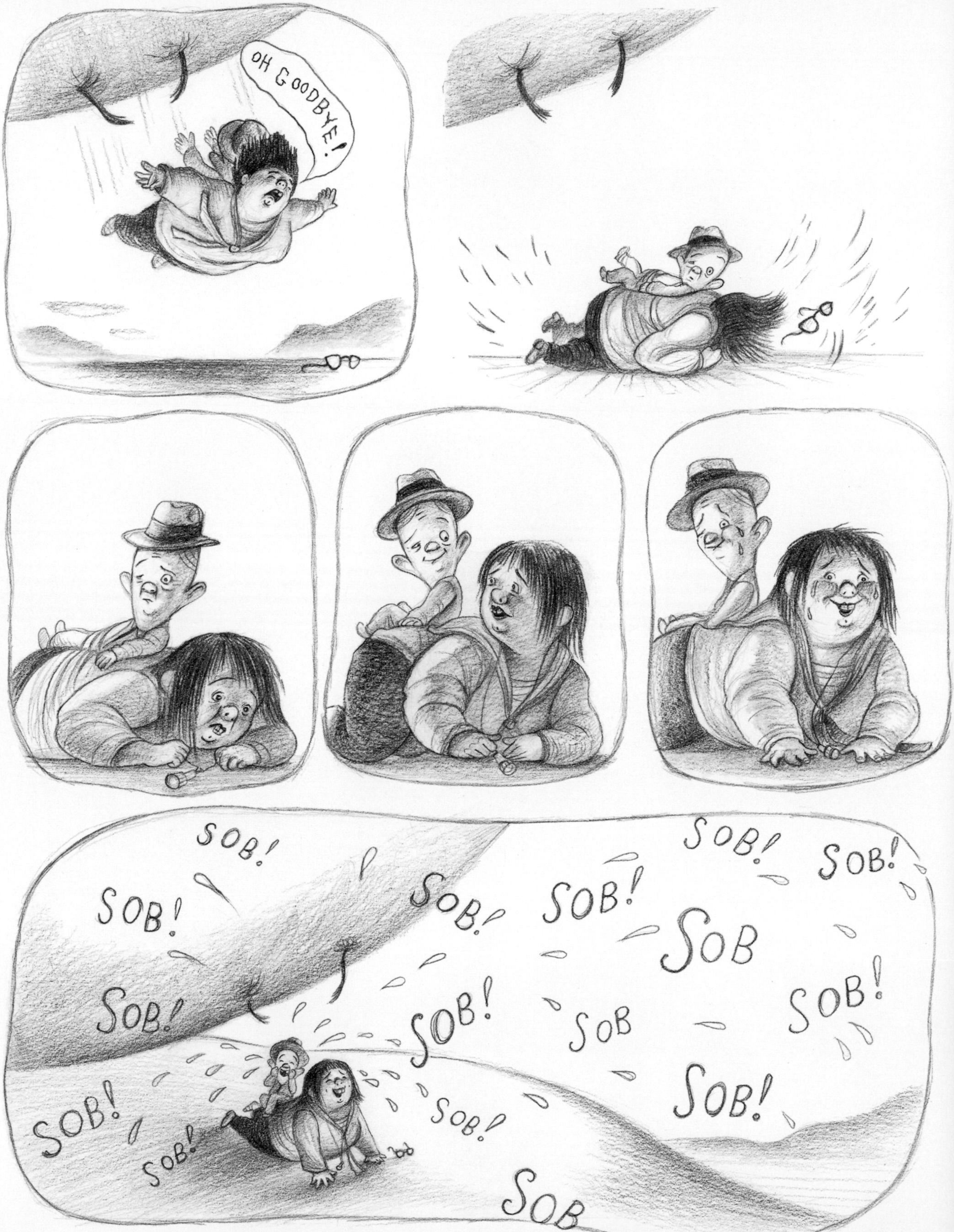
OH GOODBYE!
SOB!
SOB!
SOB!
SOB!
SOB!
SOB!
SOB
SOB!
SOB!
SOB
SOB!
SOB!
SOB!
SOB!
SOB

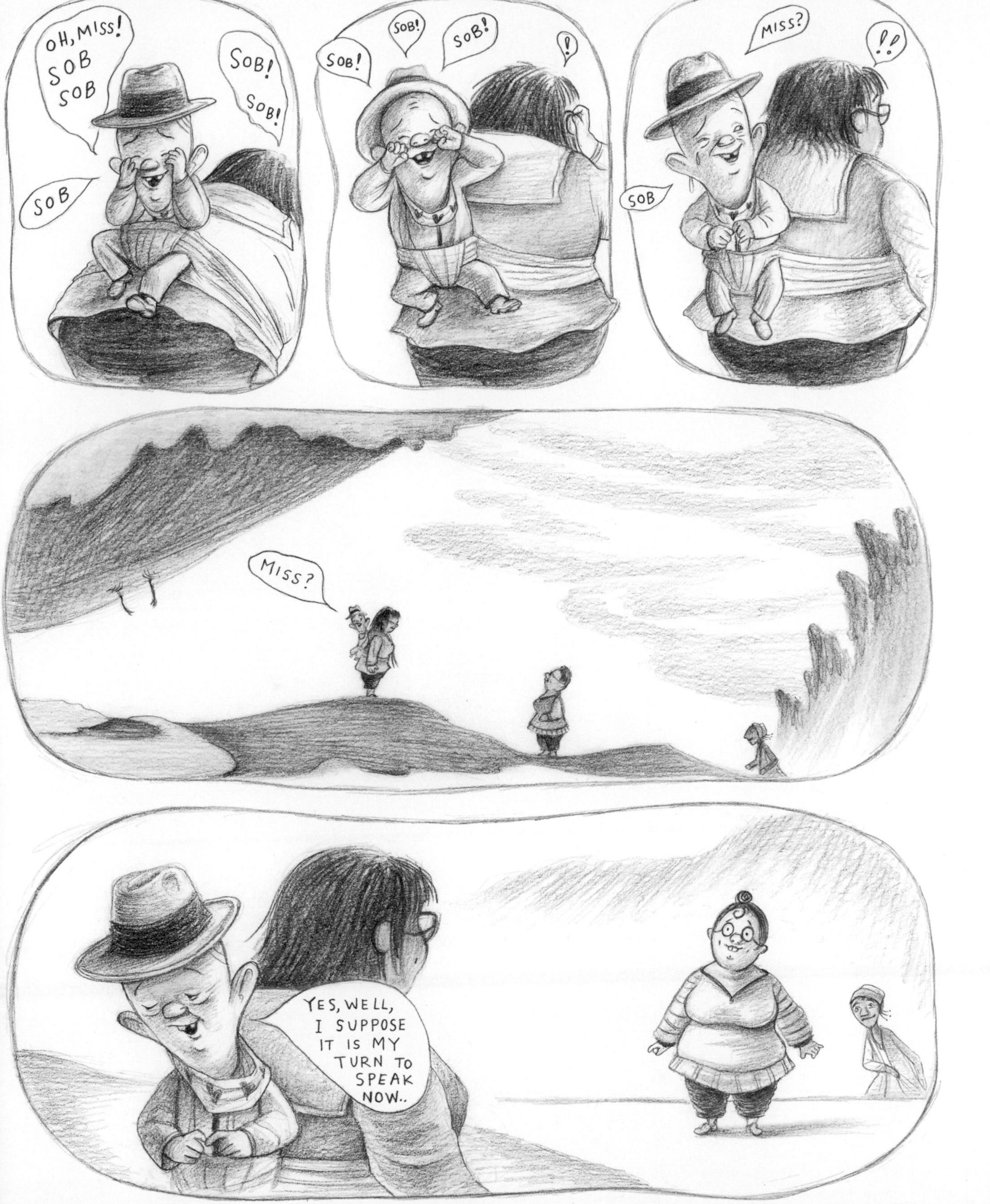
OH, MISS!
SOB
SOB
SOB! SOB!
SOB
SOB!
SOB!
SOB!
!
MISS?
!!
SOB
MISS?
YES, WELL, I SUPPOSE IT IS MY TURN TO SPEAK NOW..

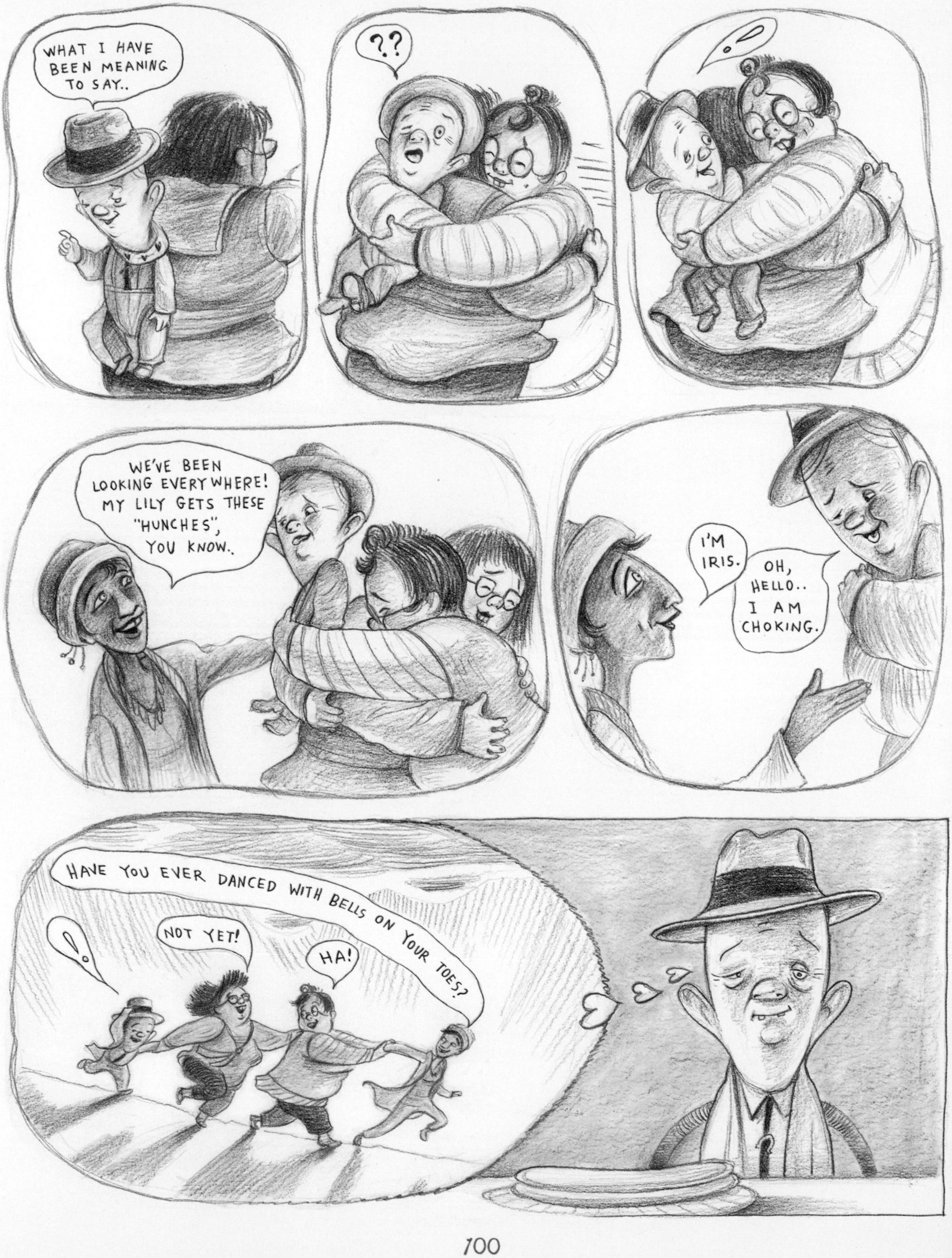
WHAT I HAVE BEEN MEANING TO SAY..
??
!
WE'VE BEEN LOOKING EVERY WHERE! MY LILY GETS THESE "HUNCHES", YOU KNOW..
I'M IRIS.
OH, HELLO.. I AM CHOKING.
HAVE YOU EVER DANCED WITH BELLS ON YOUR TOES?
!
NOT YET!
HA!

MMM.. IN MY COUNTRY THE PORTIONS ARE BIGGER..
WOULD YOU LIKE A GUAVA?
SET IT DOWN.
!
THANK YOU FOR CLEARING OUR SKIES!
DO NOT THANK ME, THANK MY POWER.
DRIP
DROP
!
DRIP
DRIP
!
?
DROP
DROP
!
DROP
DRIP
DRIP
HANG!
WHA.. WHA..?
IMPOSTER!
HANG!
HANG!
HANG!
THIS BUTTON IS FAULTY!
WHY DO THEY CHASE US??

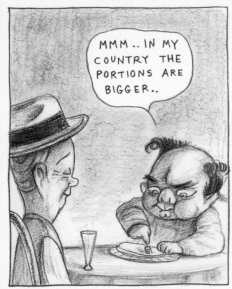

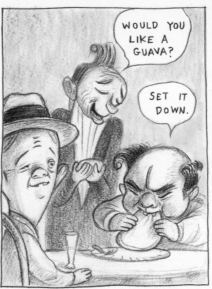

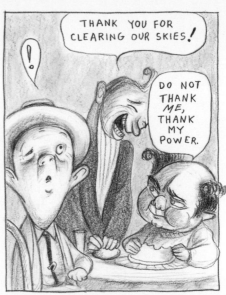

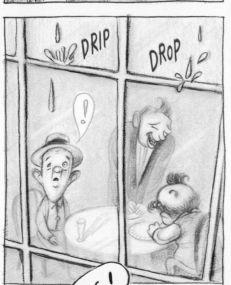

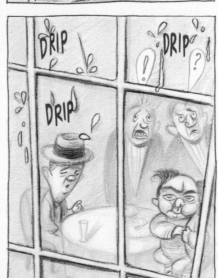

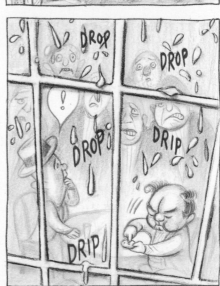

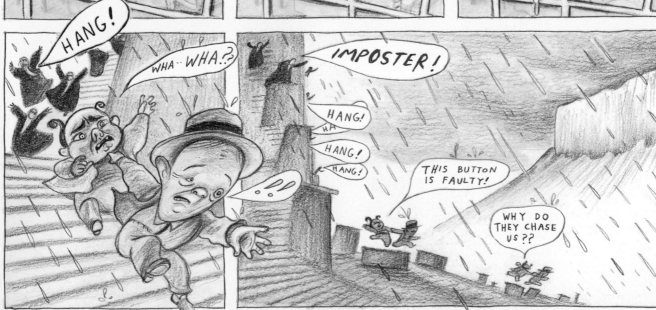

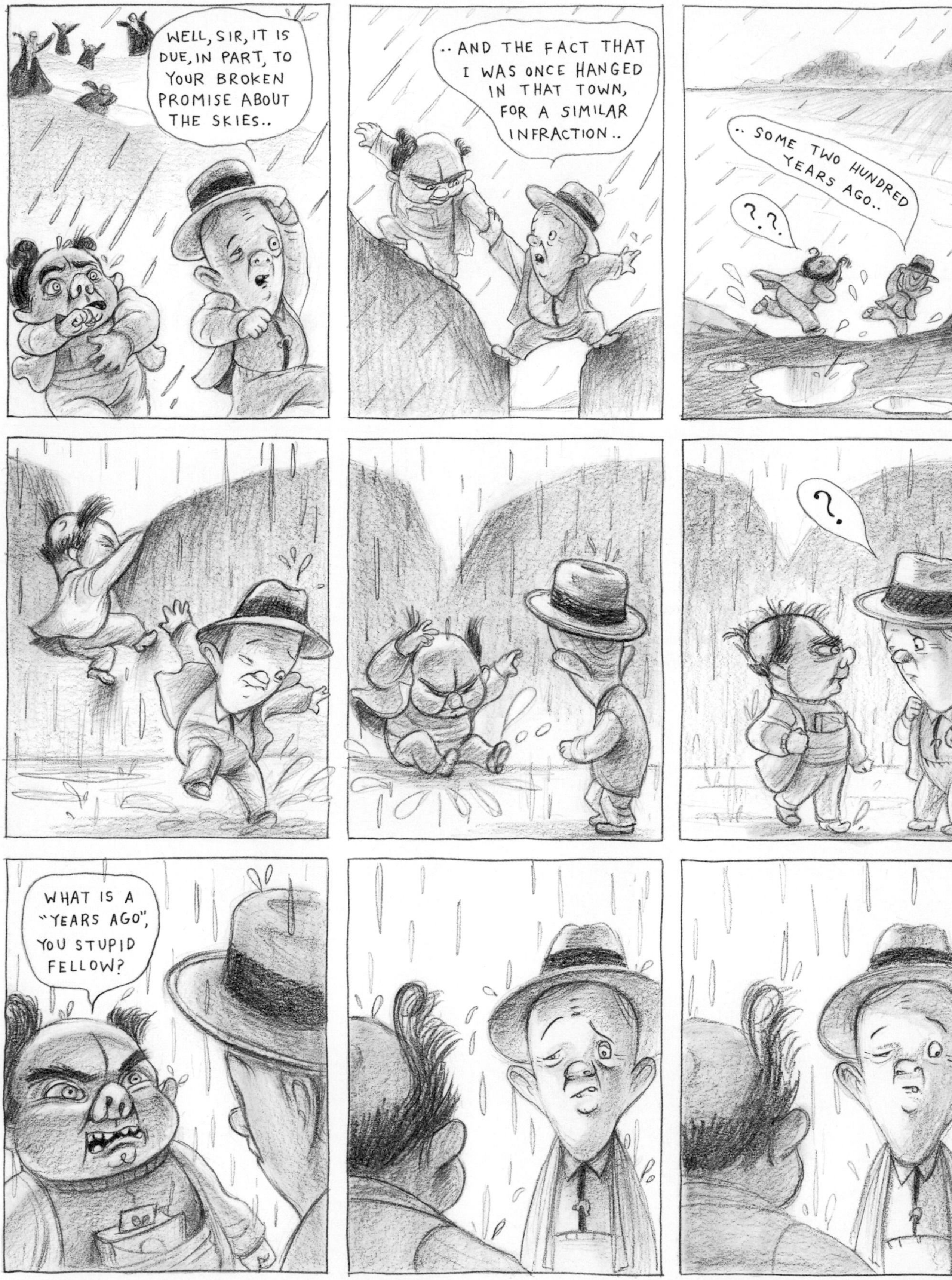
WELL, SIR, IT IS DUE, IN PART, TO YOUR BROKEN PROMISE ABOUT THE SKIES..
..AND THE FACT THAT I WAS ONCE HANGED IN THAT TOWN, FOR A SIMILAR INFRACTION..
.. SOME TWO HUNDRED YEARS AGO..
?.?.
?.
WHAT IS A "YEARS AGO", YOU STUPID FELLOW?

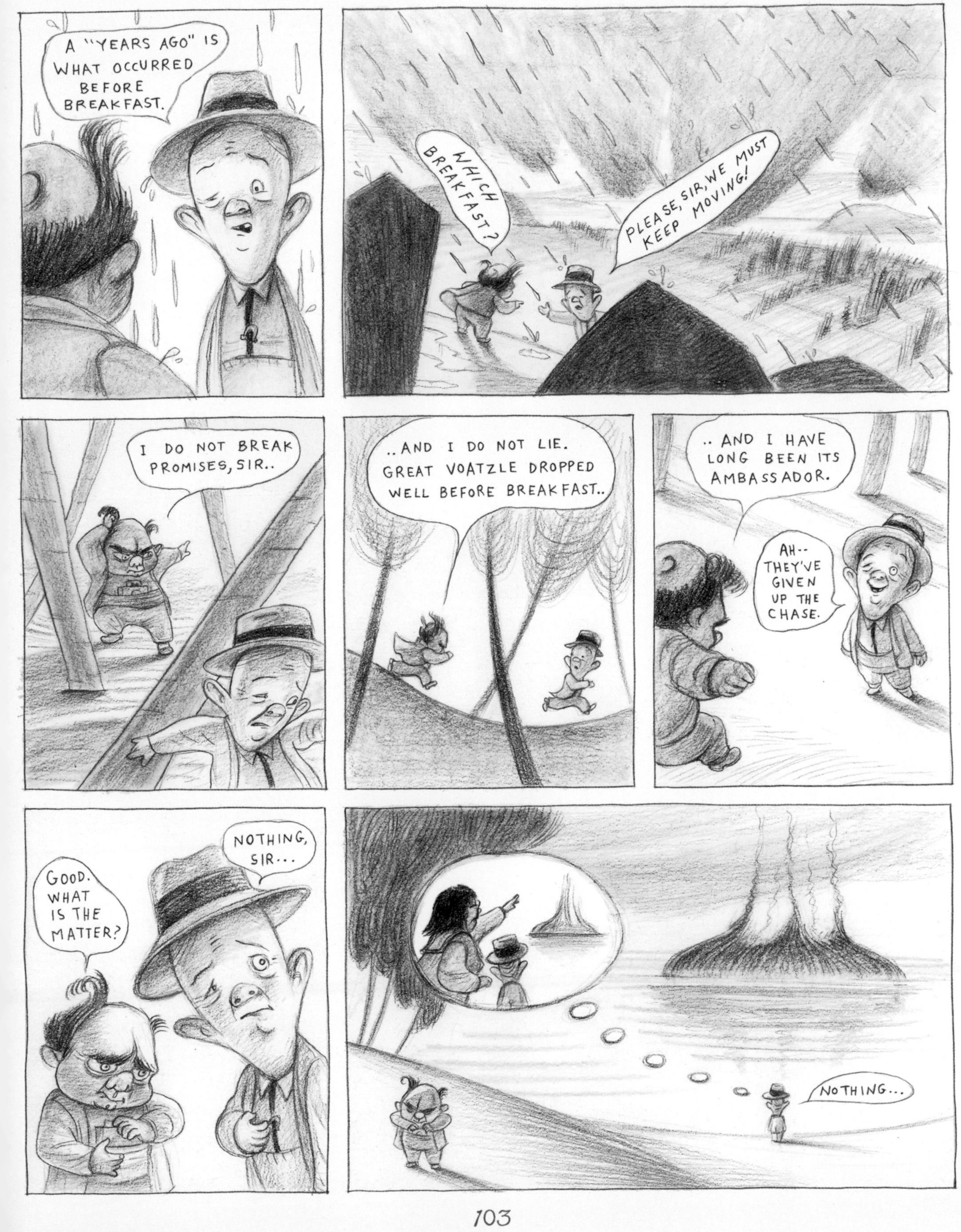

A "YEARS AGO" IS WHAT OCCURRED BEFORE BREAKFAST.
WHICH BREAKFAST?
PLEASE, SIR, WE MUST KEEP MOVING!
I DO NOT BREAK PROMISES, SIR..
..AND I DO NOT LIE. GREAT VOATZLE DROPPED WELL BEFORE BREAKFAST..
..AND I HAVE LONG BEEN ITS AMBASSADOR.
AH-- THEY'VE GIVEN UP THE CHASE.
GOOD. WHAT IS THE MATTER?
NOTHING, SIR...
NOTHING...

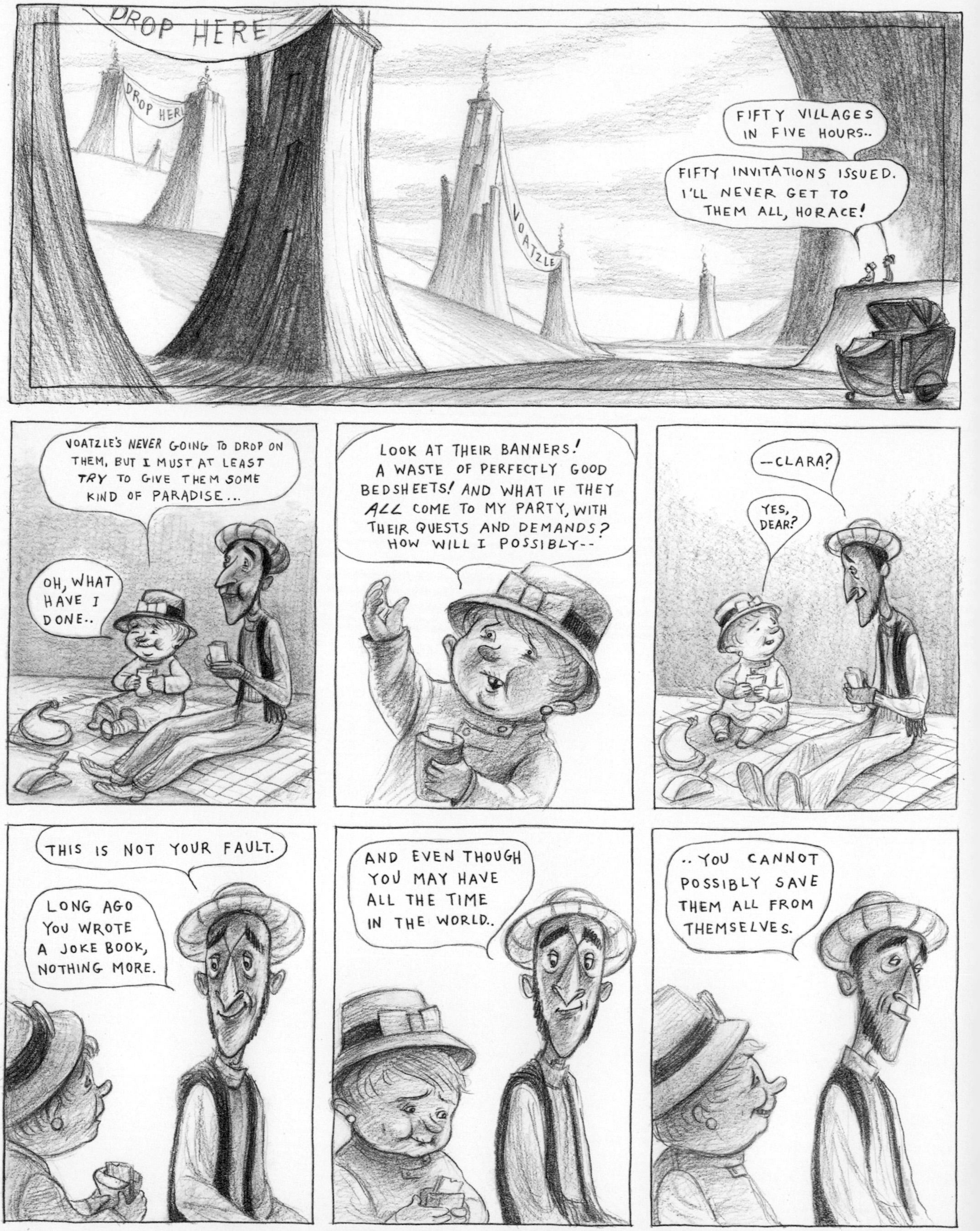
DROP HERE
DROP HERE
VOATZLE
FIFTY VILLAGES IN FIVE HOURS..
FIFTY INVITATIONS ISSUED. I'LL NEVER GET TO THEM ALL, HORACE!
VOATZLE'S NEVER GOING TO DROP ON THEM, BUT I MUST AT LEAST TRY TO GIVE THEM SOME KIND OF PARADISE...
OH, WHAT HAVE I DONE..
LOOK AT THEIR BANNERS! A WASTE OF PERFECTLY GOOD BEDSHEETS! AND WHAT IF THEY ALL COME TO MY PARTY, WITH THEIR QUESTS AND DEMANDS? HOW WILL I POSSIBLY--
--CLARA?
YES, DEAR?
THIS IS NOT YOUR FAULT.
LONG AGO YOU WROTE A JOKE BOOK, NOTHING MORE.
AND EVEN THOUGH YOU MAY HAVE ALL THE TIME IN THE WORLD..
.. YOU CANNOT POSSIBLY SAVE THEM ALL FROM THEMSELVES.

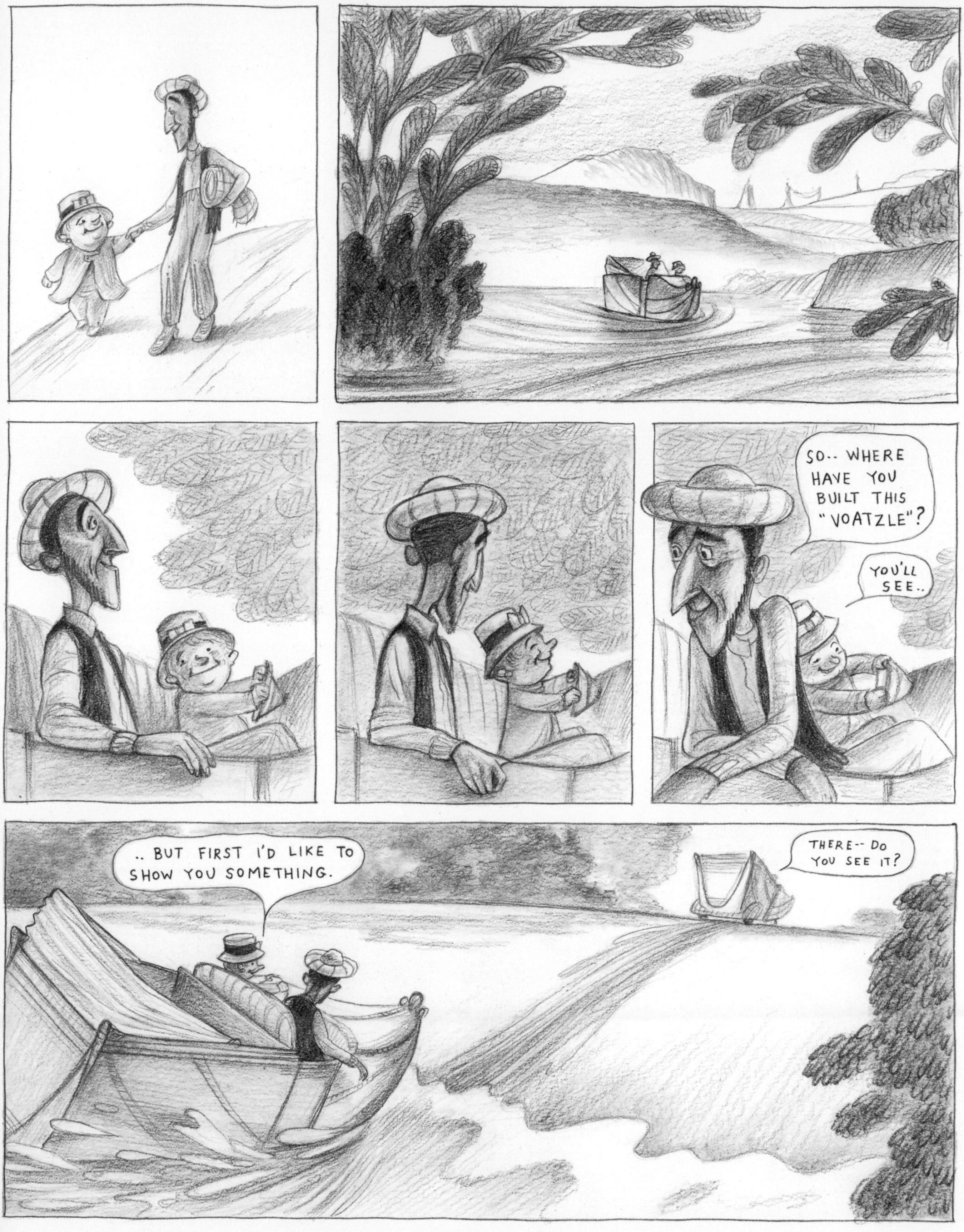
SO.. WHERE HAVE YOU BUILT THIS "VOATZLE"?
YOU'LL SEE..
.. BUT FIRST I'D LIKE TO SHOW YOU SOMETHING.
THERE-- DO YOU SEE IT?

I SEE A LOT OF BRAMBLES TO CLEAR.
YES! THE PERFECT SITE FOR OUR NEXT PICNIC!
SHOULDN'T WE BE IN A HURRY TO YOUR PARADISE?
ALL IN GOOD TIME.
HORACE--BE A DEAR AND HELP ME WITH THIS HEAP..
WHAT AN OVERGROWTH!
THE FINERY OF NEGLECT.
PULL--PULL!
O OOO O O O O OOF!
THERE!

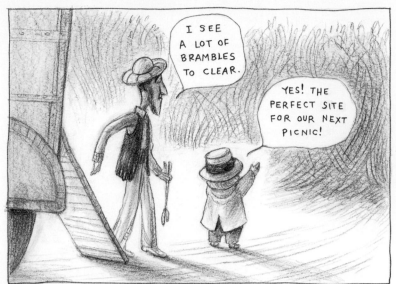

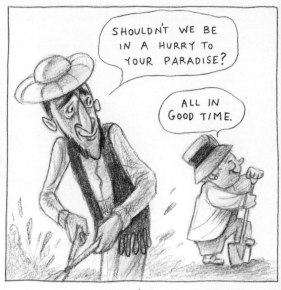

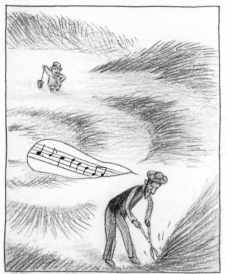

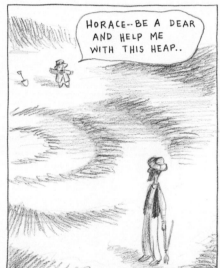

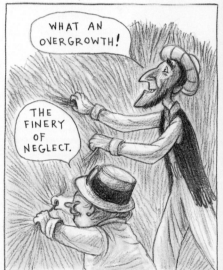

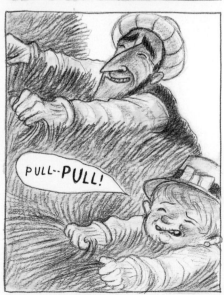

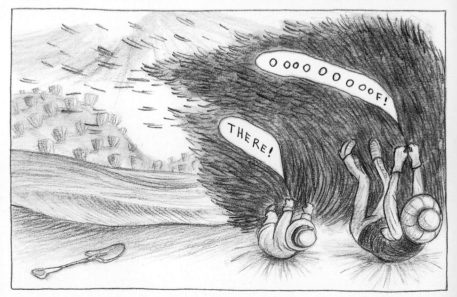

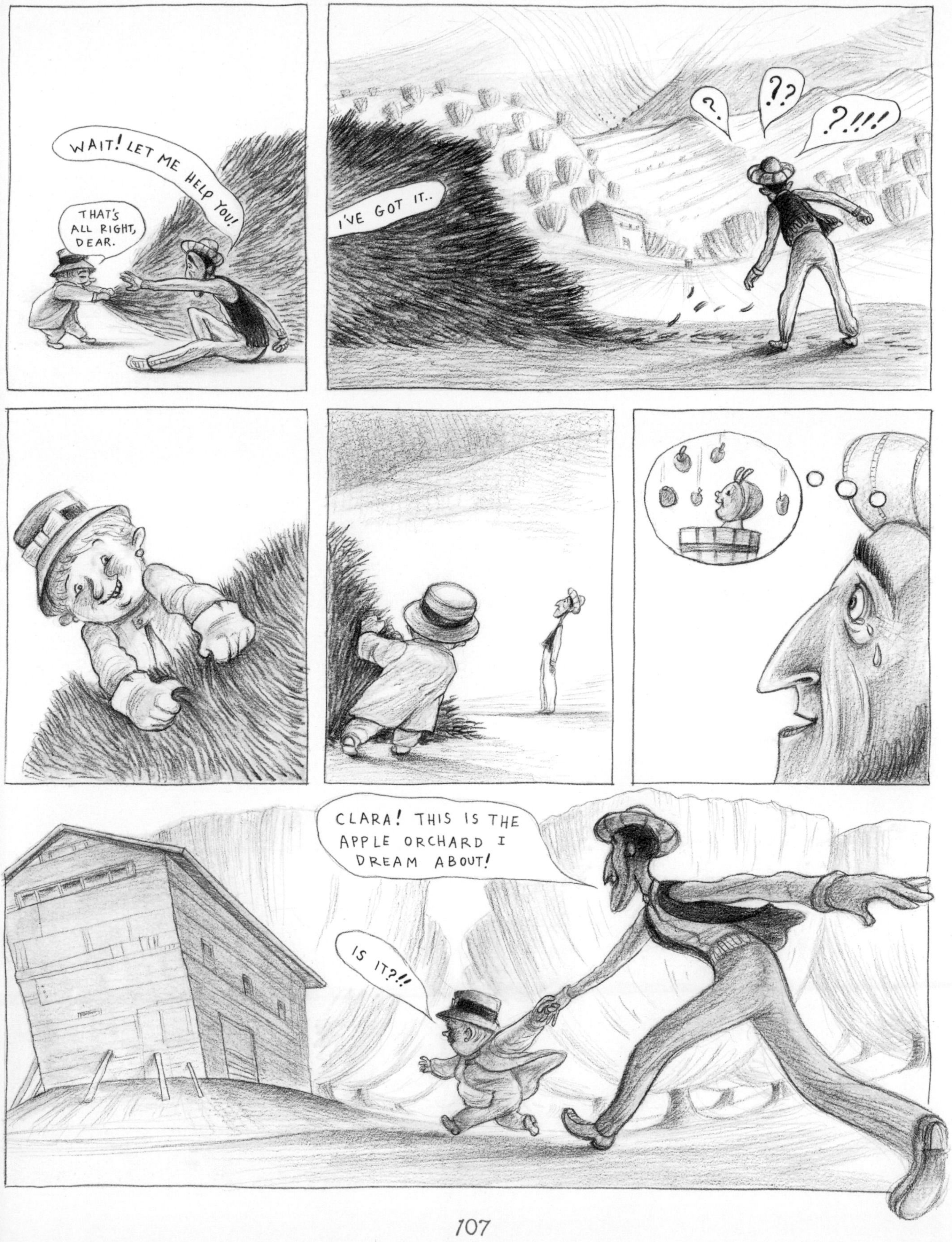
WAIT! LET ME HELP YOU!
THAT'S ALL RIGHT, DEAR.
I'VE GOT IT..
?
??
?!!!
CLARA! THIS IS THE APPLE ORCHARD I DREAM ABOUT!
IS IT?!!

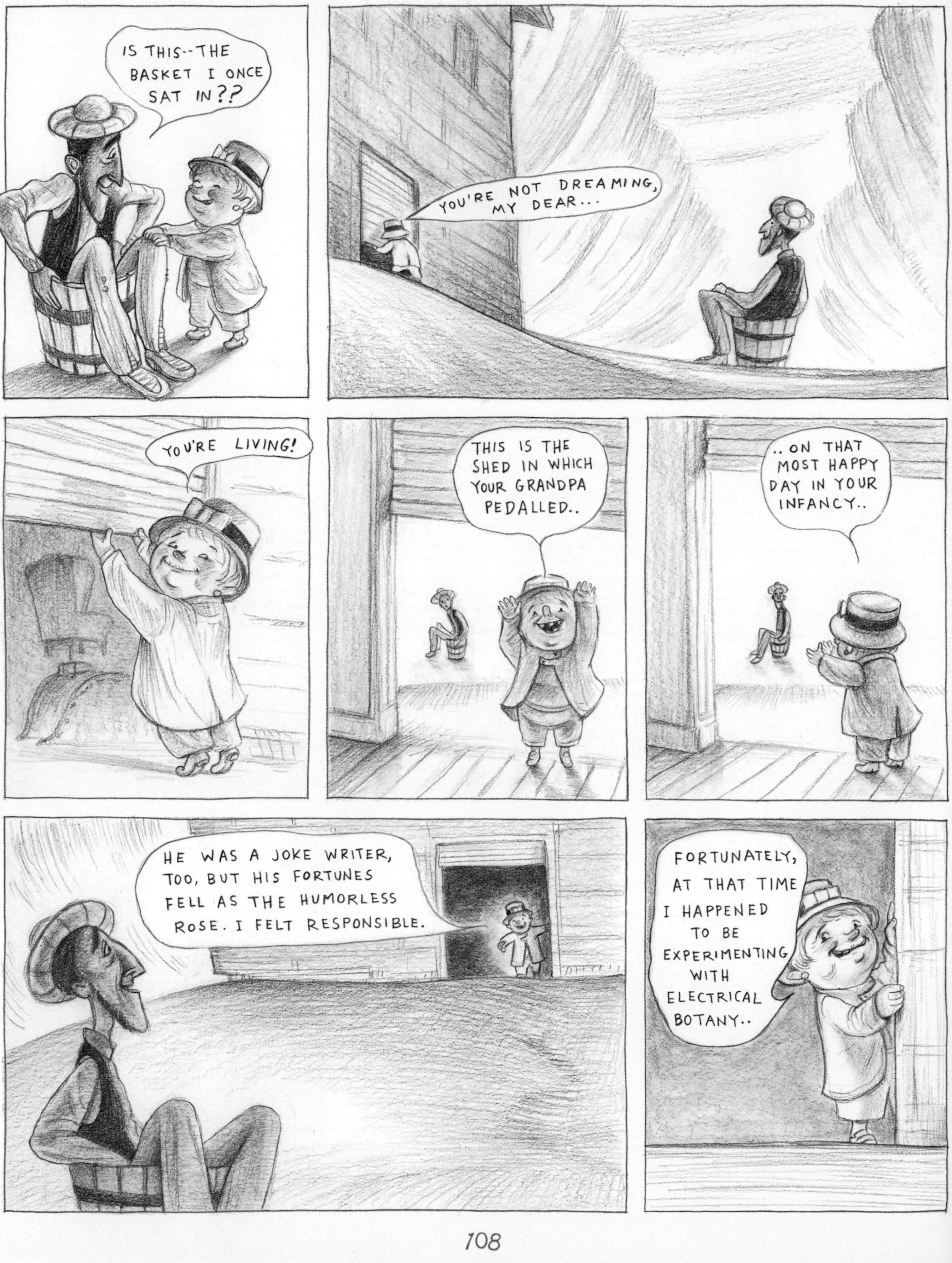
IS THIS--THE BASKET I ONCE SAT IN??
YOU'RE NOT DREAMING, MY DEAR...
YOU'RE LIVING!
THIS IS THE SHED IN WHICH YOUR GRANDPA PEDALLED..
..ON THAT MOST HAPPY DAY IN YOUR INFANCY..
HE WAS A JOKE WRITER, TOO, BUT HIS FORTUNES FELL AS THE HUMORLESS ROSE. I FELT RESPONSIBLE.
FORTUNATELY, AT THAT TIME I HAPPENED TO BE EXPERIMENTING WITH ELECTRICAL BOTANY..

I HELPED HIM TO PRODUCE A PAYING CROP AT WILL.
HA! IT STILL WORKS!
RWHHHHRR
DO YOU HEAR IT, HORACE?
WHHRRRR
!
CLARA! THAT'S THE SOUND!

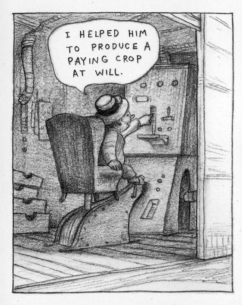

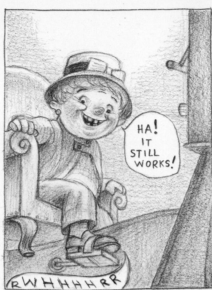

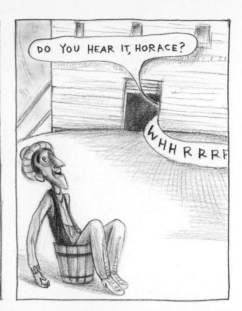

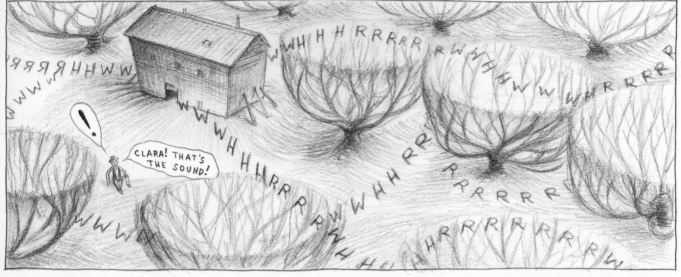

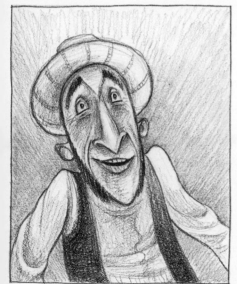

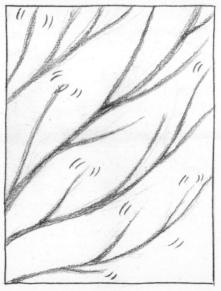

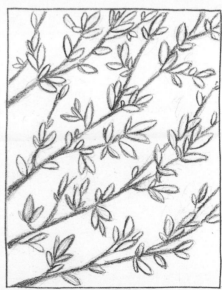

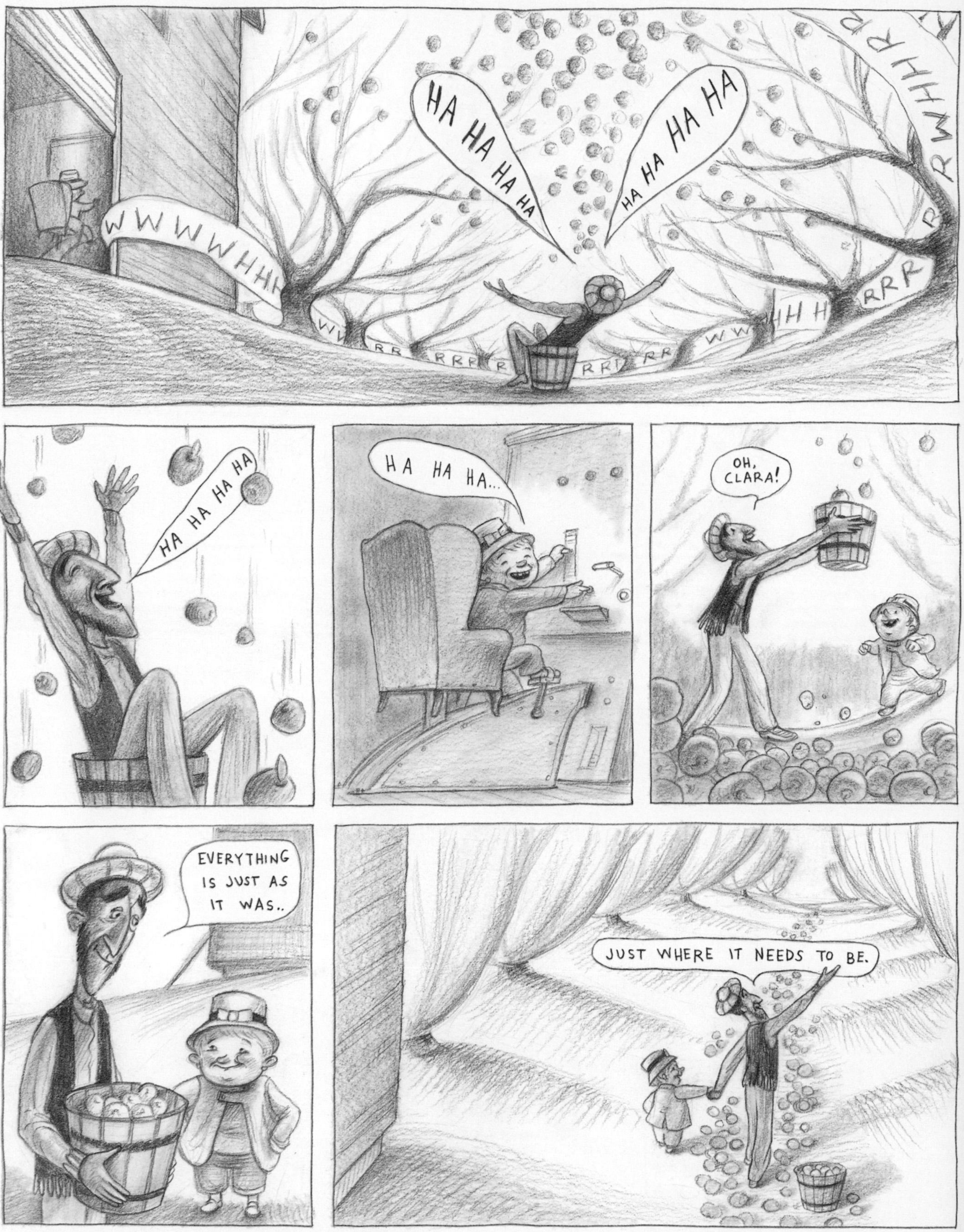
WWWWWHHH
RRR
HA HA HA HA
HA HA HA HA
RRR
WHHH
RRR
RWHHRP
HA HA HA HA
HA HA HA...
OH, CLARA!
EVERYTHING IS JUST AS IT WAS..
JUST WHERE IT NEEDS TO BE.

SHE'LL KNOW THIS, TOO..
MY LITTLE GRANDCHILD.
YOU AND I, CLARA..
..WE'LL SHOW HER HOW A TRUE SMILE IS MADE.

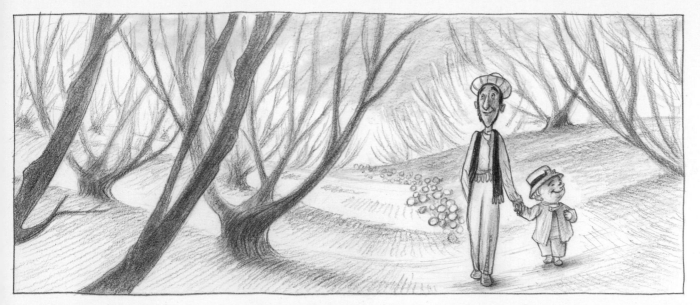

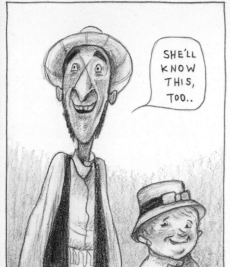

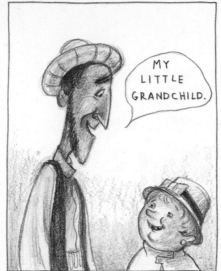

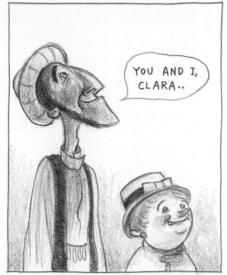

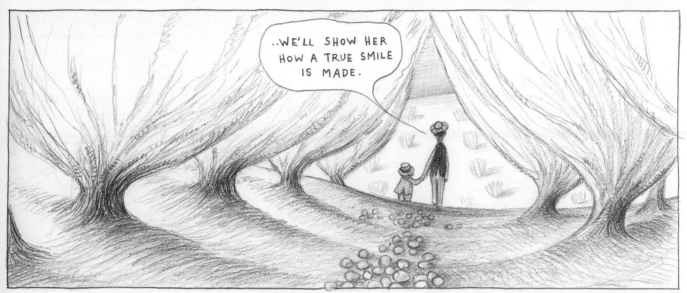

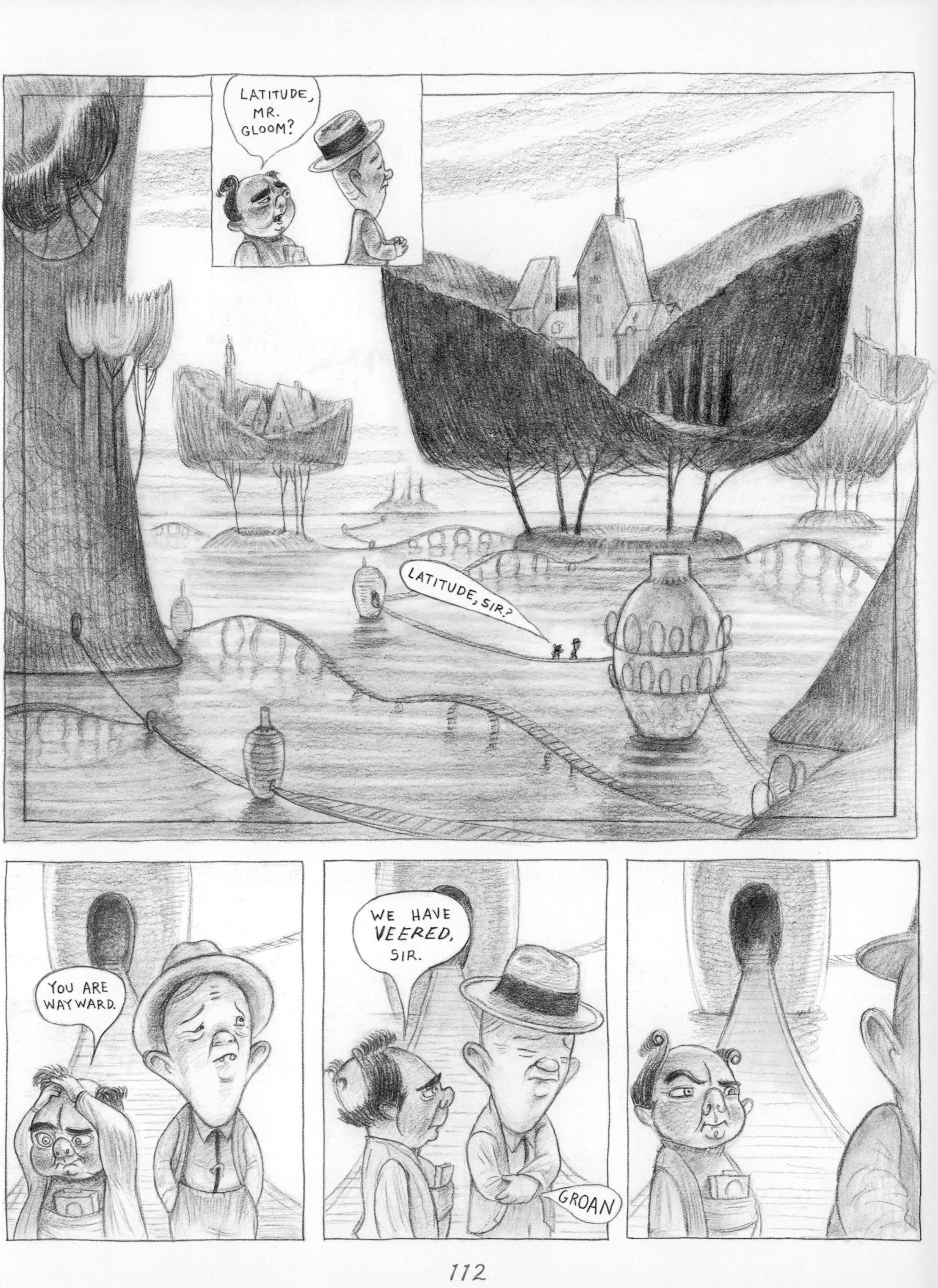
LATITUDE, MR. GLOOM?
LATITUDE, SIR?
YOU ARE WAYWARD.
WE HAVE VEERED, SIR.
GROAN

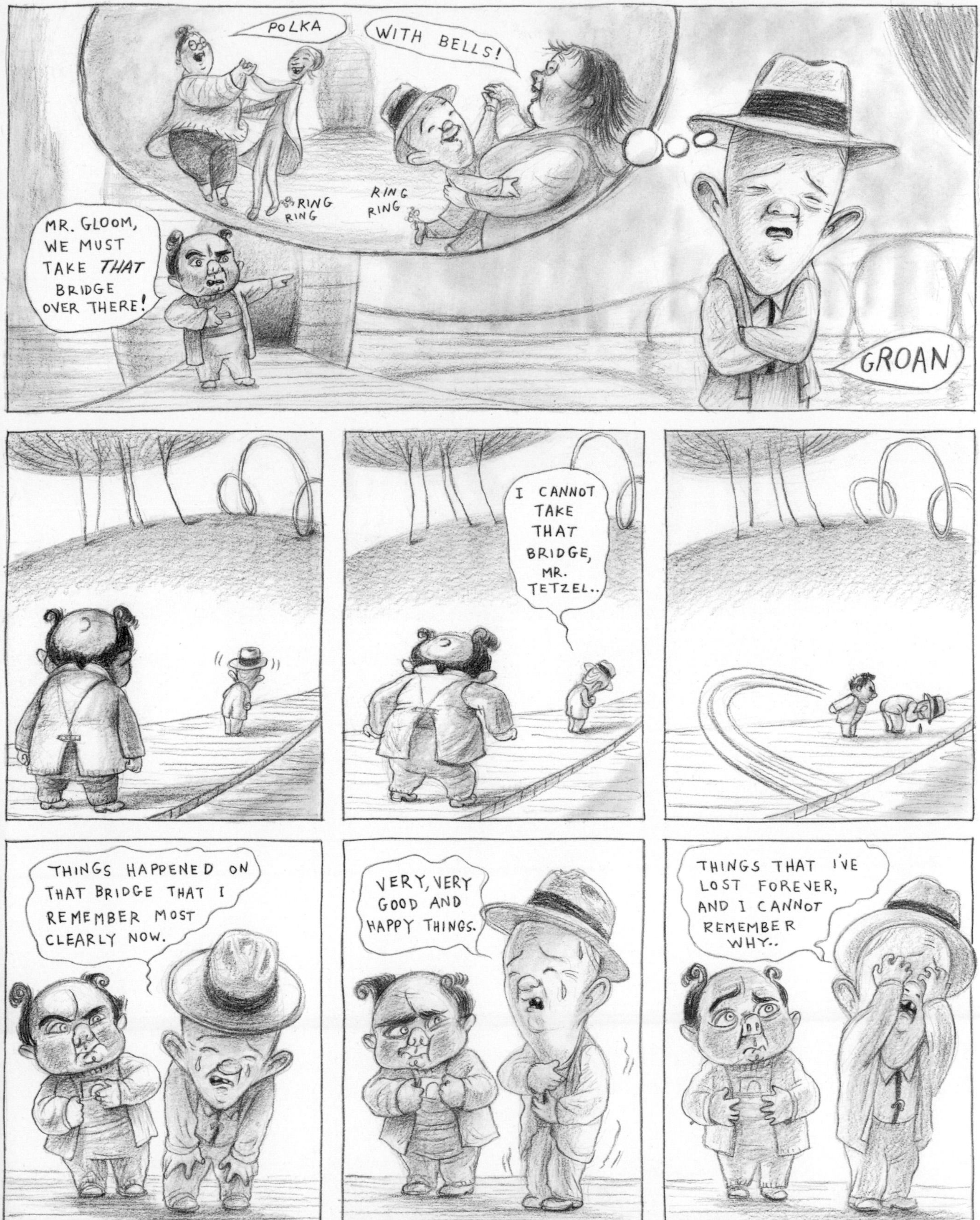
POLKA
WITH BELLS!
RING RING
RING RING
MR. GLOOM, WE MUST TAKE THAT BRIDGE OVER THERE!
GROAN
I CANNOT TAKE THAT BRIDGE, MR. TETZEL..
THINGS HAPPENED ON THAT BRIDGE THAT I REMEMBER MOST CLEARLY NOW.
VERY, VERY GOOD AND HAPPY THINGS.
THINGS THAT I'VE LOST FOREVER, AND I CANNOT REMEMBER WHY..

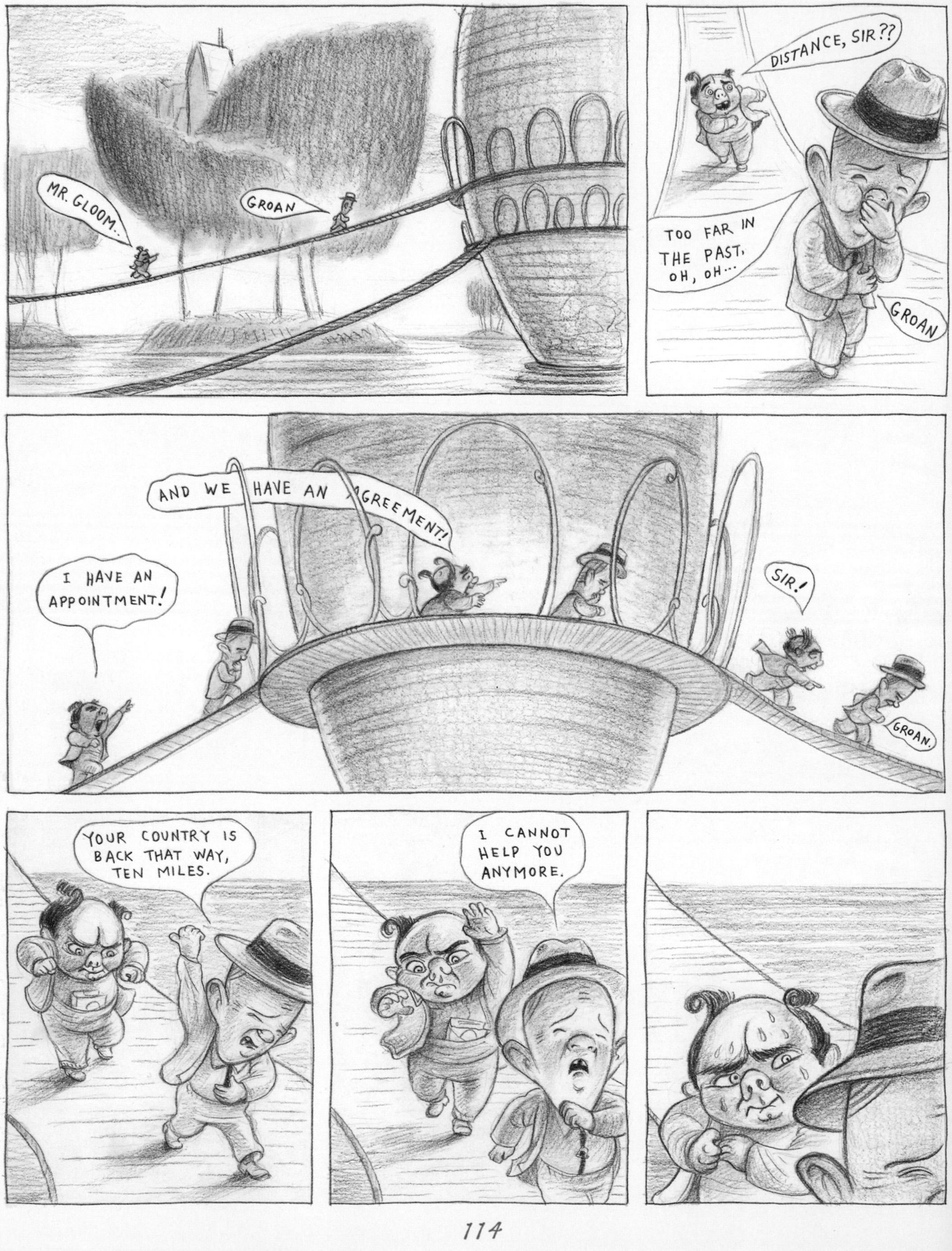
MR. GLOOM..
GROAN
DISTANCE, SIR??
TOO FAR IN THE PAST, OH, OH...
GROAN
AND WE HAVE AN AGREEMENT!
I HAVE AN APPOINTMENT!
SIR!
GROAN.
YOUR COUNTRY IS BACK THAT WAY, TEN MILES.
I CANNOT HELP YOU ANYMORE.

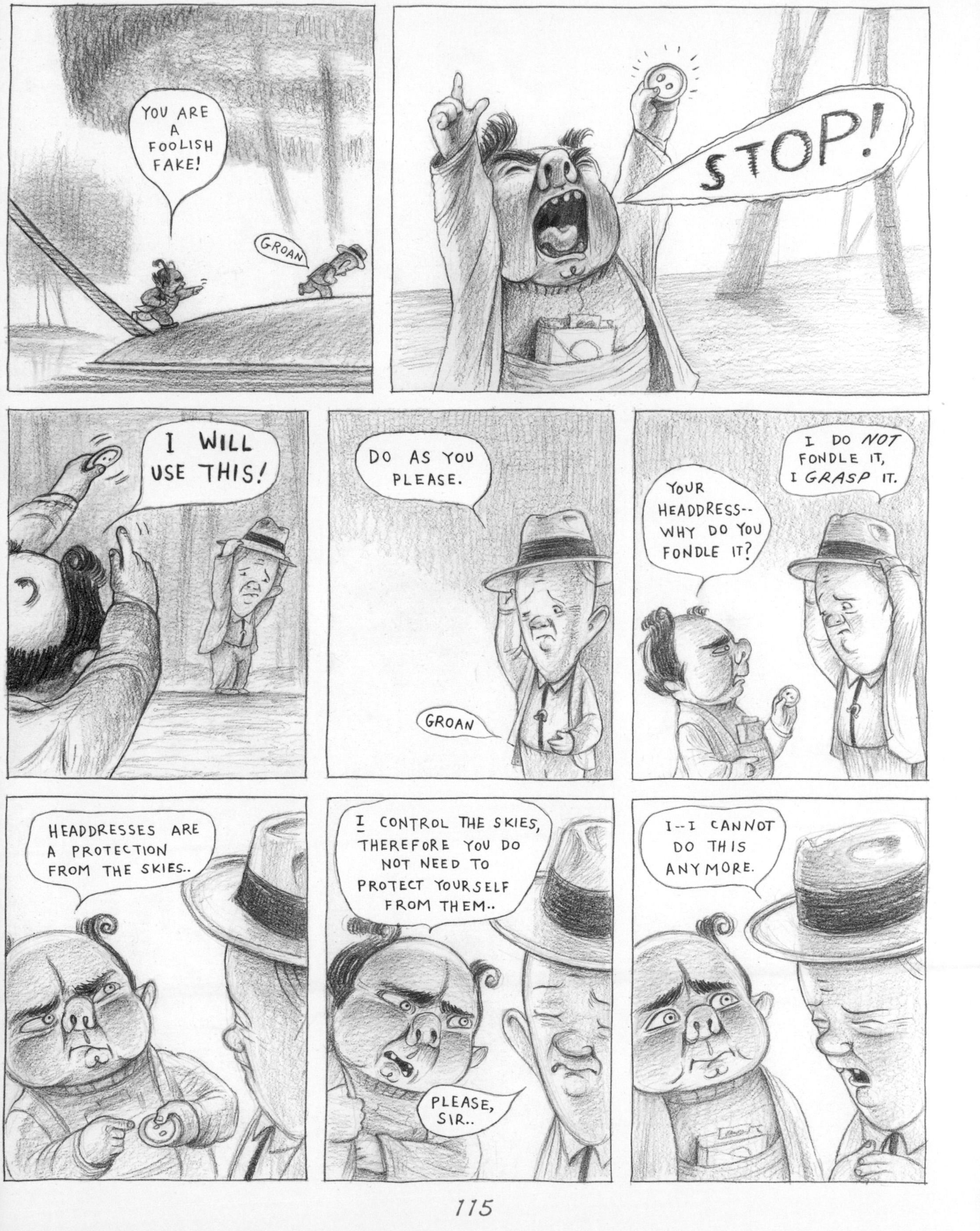
YOU ARE A FOOLISH FAKE!
GROAN
STOP!
I WILL USE THIS!
DO AS YOU PLEASE.
GROAN
YOUR HEADDRESS-- WHY DO YOU FONDLE IT?
I DO *NOT* FONDLE IT, I *GRASP* IT.
HEADDRESSES ARE A PROTECTION FROM THE SKIES..
I CONTROL THE SKIES, THEREFORE YOU DO NOT NEED TO PROTECT YOURSELF FROM THEM..
PLEASE, SIR..
I--I CANNOT DO THIS ANYMORE.

SIR! IF YOU HAD NOT INVADED MY COUNTRY WITH YOUR BUMBLING, BARBAROUS MEDIOCRITY . . . . .
I WAS ONLY PASSING THROUGH.
.. THEN I WOULD NOT BE HERE . . . .
SIR-- YOUR COUNTRY IS A
. . THEN I WOULD BE THERE, KEEPING MY APPOINTMENT!
SIR! YOU LIVE INSIDE A WALL!
OF COURSE I DO! A COUNTRY MUST HAVE ITS FORTIFICATIONS, YOU, YOU YOU LAZY-EYED GOOF!
AND YOU DO NOT UNDERSTAND MEASUREMENTS OF ANY SORT!
FOOL OF FOOLS! I UNDERSTAND ALL.
MY COUNTRY IS ALL!
DOTH YOU HAVE A COUNTRY? DOTH YOU HAVE A BOOK?? YOU DOTH NOT!
JOATZLE

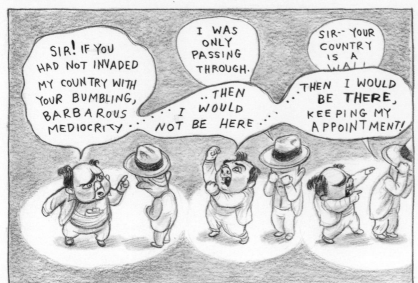

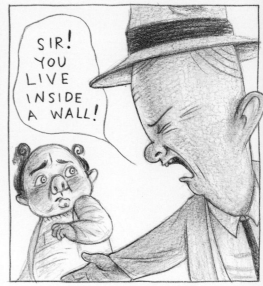

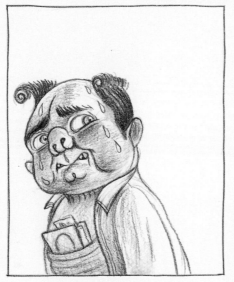

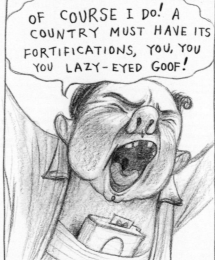

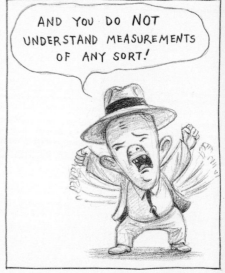

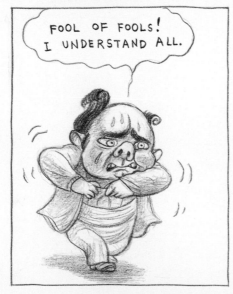

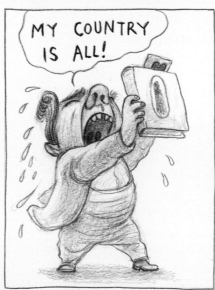

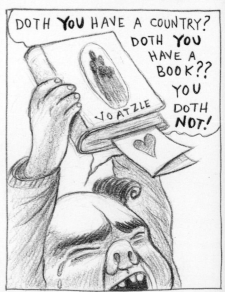

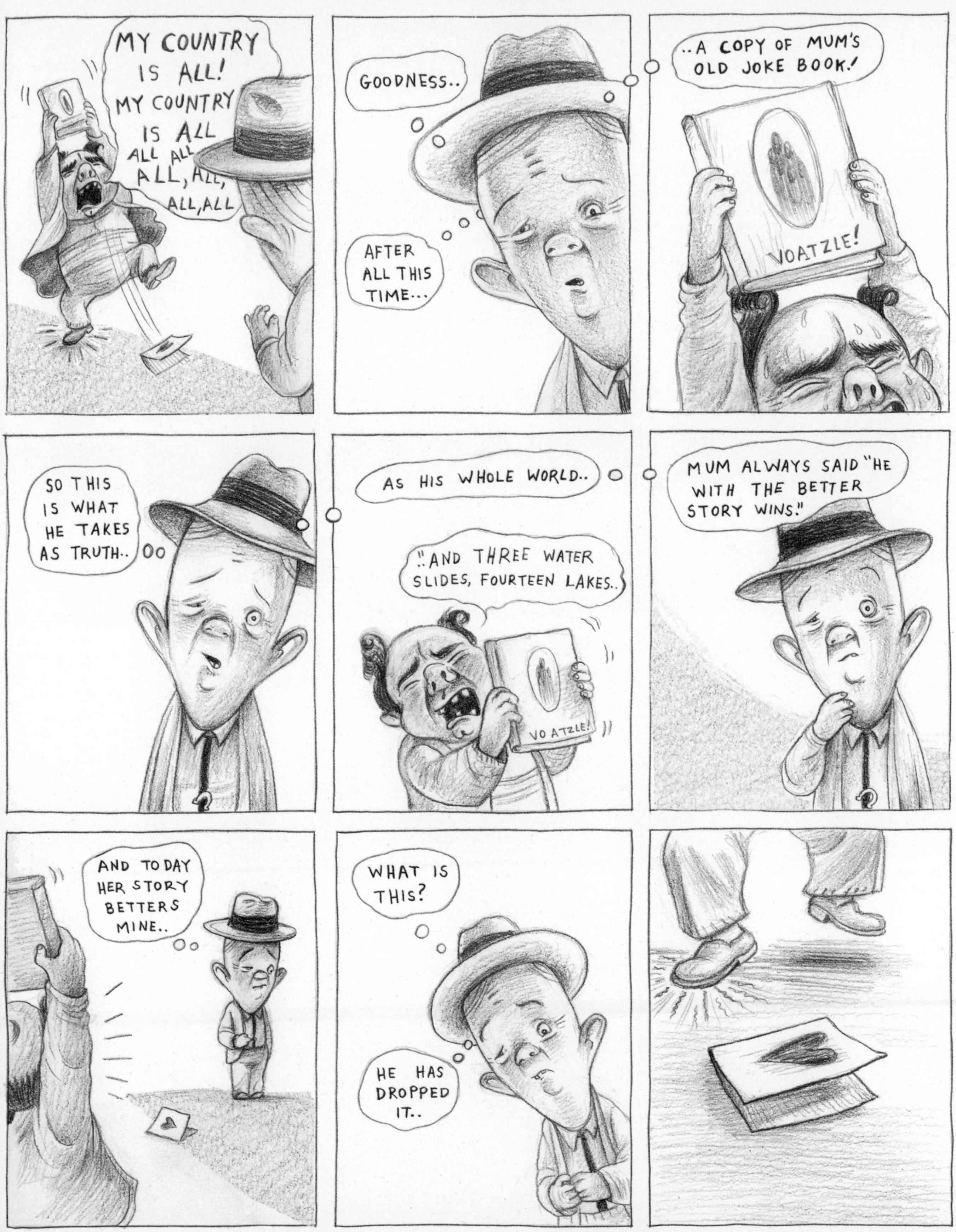
MY COUNTRY IS ALL! MY COUNTRY IS ALL ALL ALL ALL, ALL, ALL, ALL
GOODNESS..
AFTER ALL THIS TIME...
..A COPY OF MUM'S OLD JOKE BOOK!
VOATZLE!
SO THIS IS WHAT HE TAKES AS TRUTH..
AS HIS WHOLE WORLD..
"..AND THREE WATER SLIDES, FOURTEEN LAKES..
VOATZLE!
MUM ALWAYS SAID "HE WITH THE BETTER STORY WINS."
AND TODAY HER STORY BETTERS MINE..
WHAT IS THIS?
HE HAS DROPPED IT..

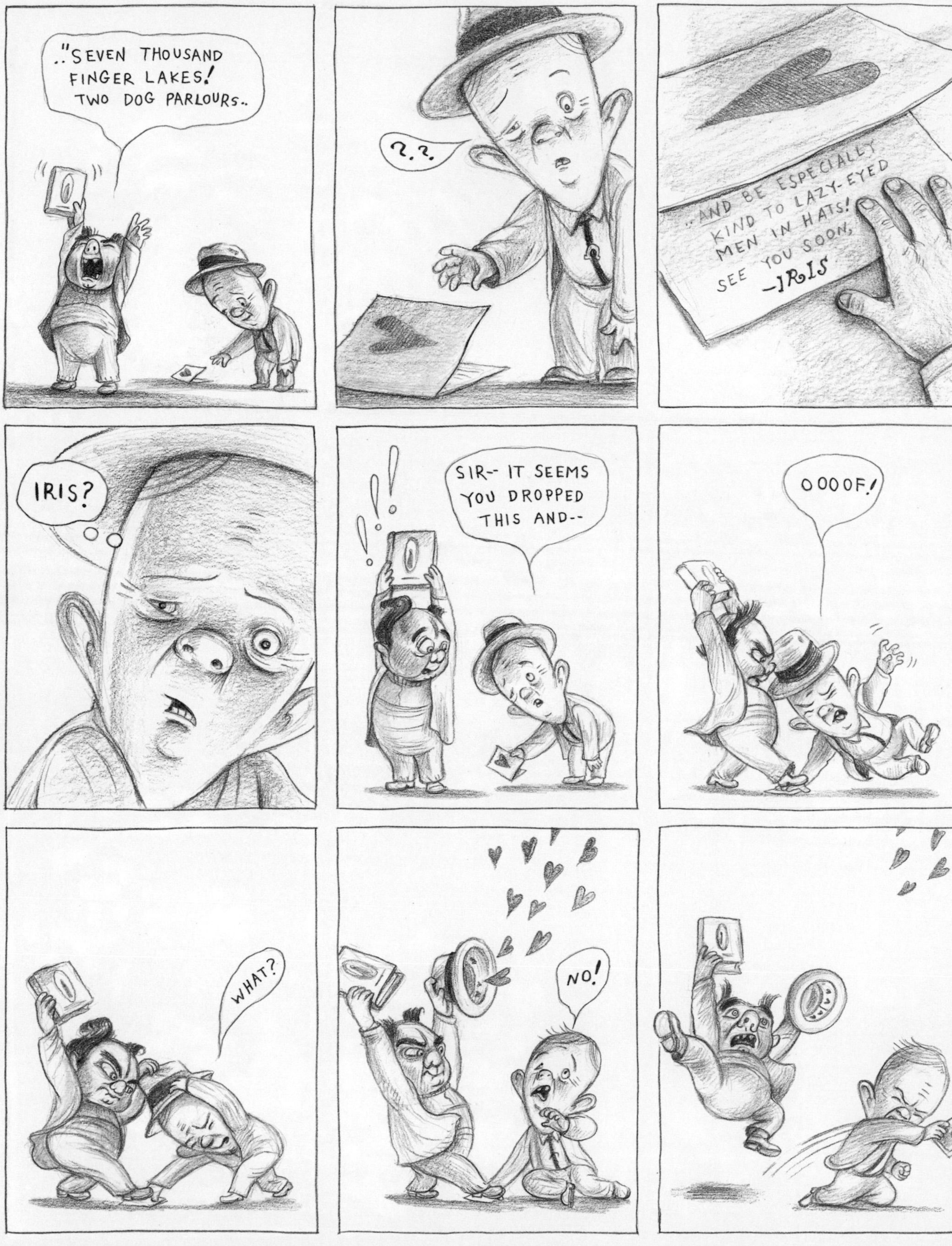

.."SEVEN THOUSAND FINGER LAKES! TWO DOG PARLOURS..
?.?.
..AND BE ESPECIALLY KIND TO LAZY-EYED MEN IN HATS! SEE YOU SOON, -IRIS
IRIS?
SIR-- IT SEEMS YOU DROPPED THIS AND--
OOOOF!
WHAT?
NO!

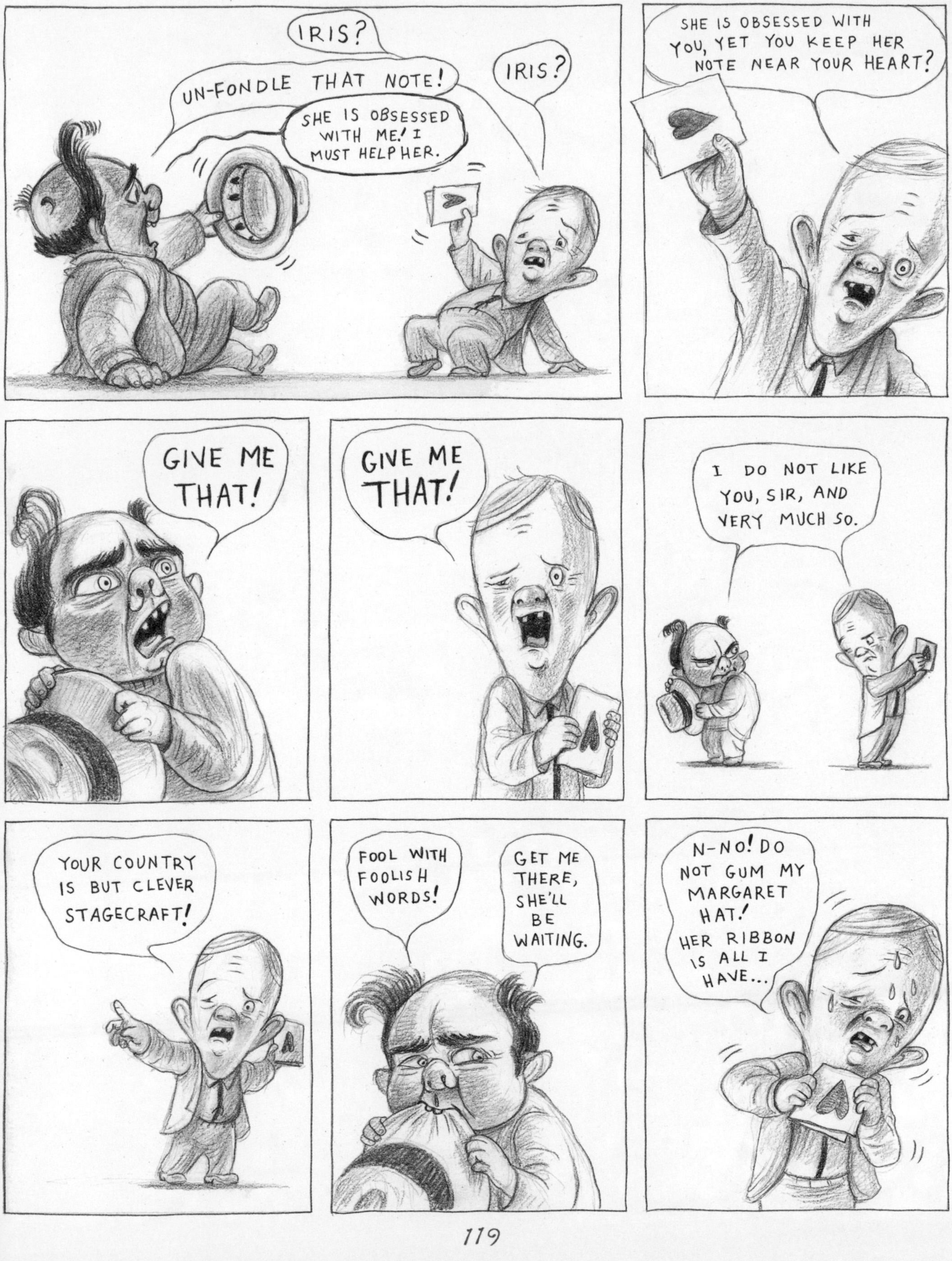
IRIS?
UN-FONDLE THAT NOTE!
SHE IS OBSESSED WITH ME! I MUST HELP HER.
IRIS?
SHE IS OBSESSED WITH YOU, YET YOU KEEP HER NOTE NEAR YOUR HEART?
GIVE ME THAT!
GIVE ME THAT!
I DO NOT LIKE YOU, SIR, AND VERY MUCH SO.
YOUR COUNTRY IS BUT CLEVER STAGECRAFT!
FOOL WITH FOOLISH WORDS!
GET ME THERE, SHE'LL BE WAITING.
N-NO! DO NOT GUM MY MARGARET HAT!
HER RIBBON IS ALL I HAVE...

"RIBBON"? YOU SPEAK GIBBERISH.
AND I DO NOT HAVE TO HELP YOU, BECAUSE YOU ARE HATLESS NOW.
?
NO! KEEP YOUR EYES AWAY!!
DEAR TETZEL, - THERE IS MORE THAN ONE WAY BACK! - DON'T BELIEVE EVERYTHING YOU READ! - BE KIND TO LAZY-EYED MEN IN HATS. SEE YOU SOON, - IRIS
HOW CAN THIS BE?
SHE SPEAKS LIKE THE IRIS I KNEW BUT LONG AGO..
WHEN DID YOU RECEIVE THIS NOTE?
BEFORE BREAKFAST.
THIS HAT STINKS. I SHALL RID IT FROM MY HEAD AND THROW IT INTO THE SEA..
NO, SIR!!!!!
!

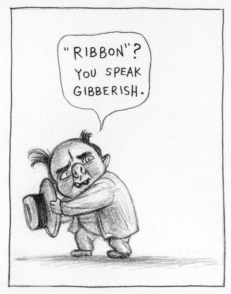

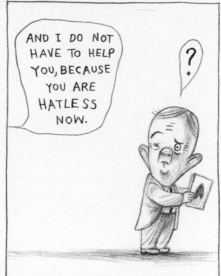

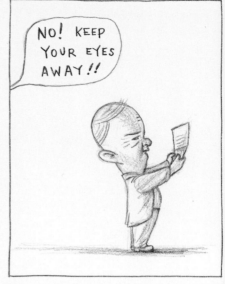

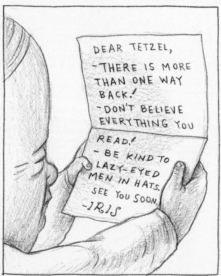

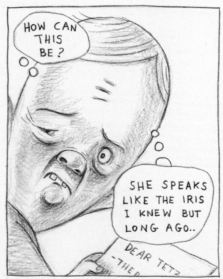

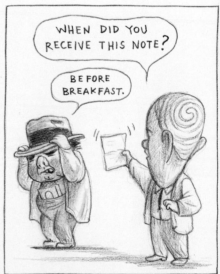

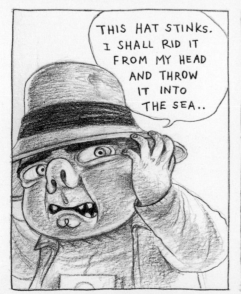

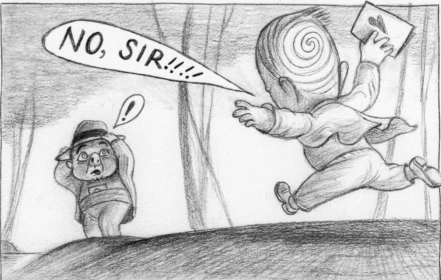

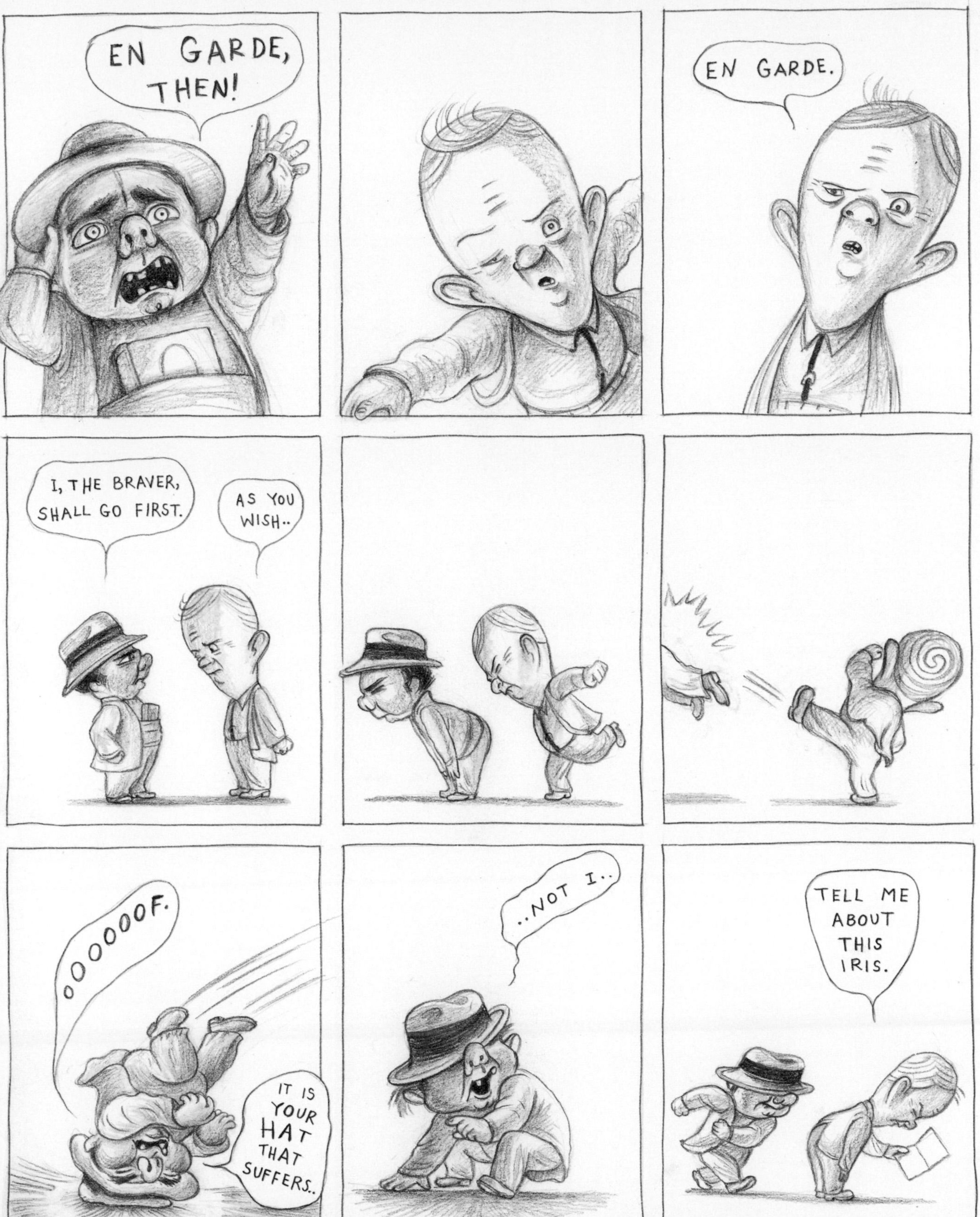
EN GARDE, THEN!
EN GARDE.
I, THE BRAVER, SHALL GO FIRST.
AS YOU WISH..
OOOOOOF.
IT IS YOUR HAT THAT SUFFERS..
..NOT I..
TELL ME ABOUT THIS IRIS.

I'LL TELL YOU A THING OR TWO..

OOOOOF

SHE VISITED MY FAIR LAND, TOOK NOTE OF MY SWARTHY GOOD LOOKS..

.. AND WAS.. VERY APPRECIATIVE OF..

.. MY.. POWER TO CONTROL THE SKIES...

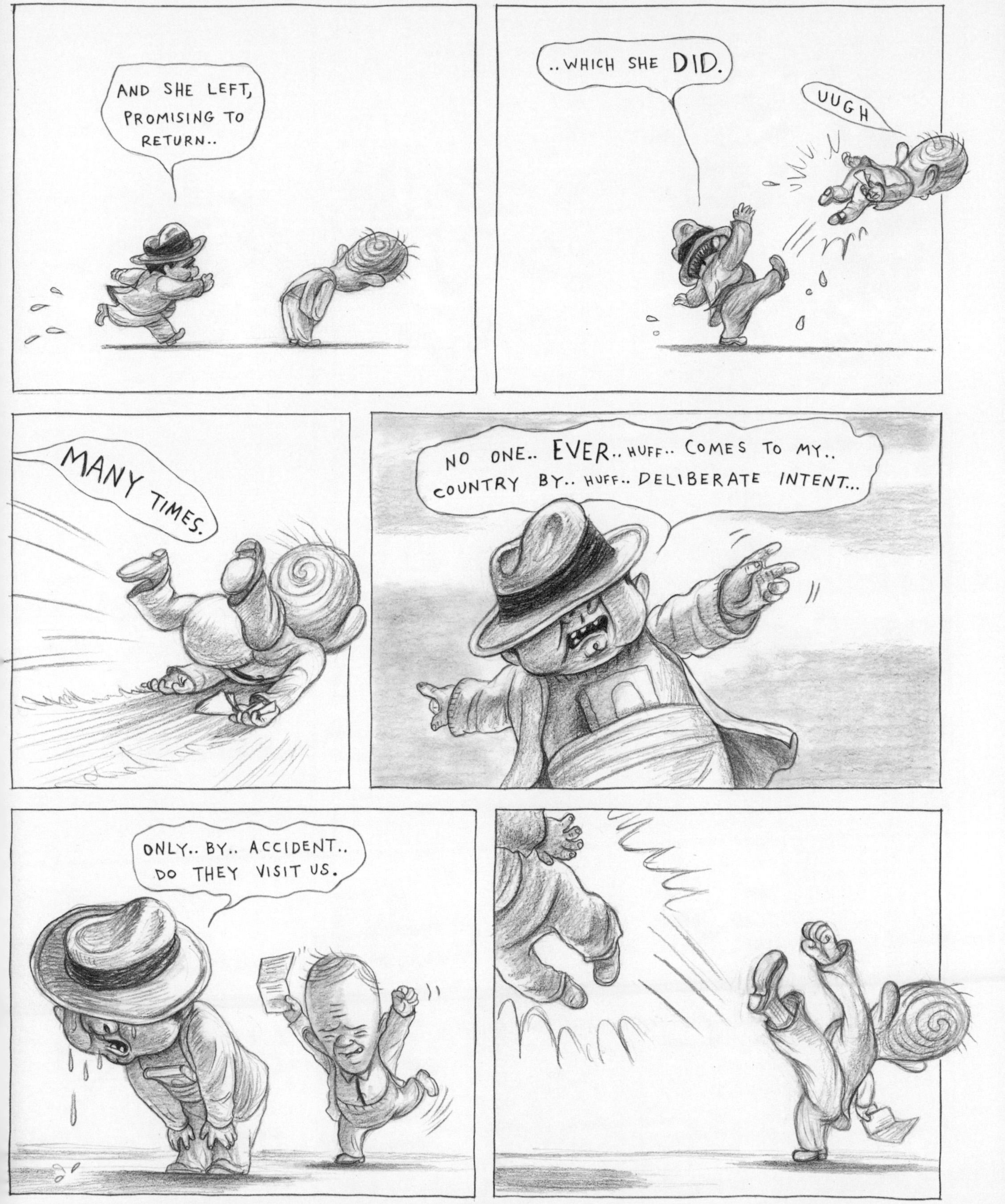
AND SHE LEFT, PROMISING TO RETURN..
..WHICH SHE DID.
UUGH
MANY TIMES.
NO ONE.. EVER.. HUFF.. COMES TO MY.. COUNTRY BY.. HUFF.. DELIBERATE INTENT...
ONLY.. BY.. ACCIDENT.. DO THEY VISIT US.

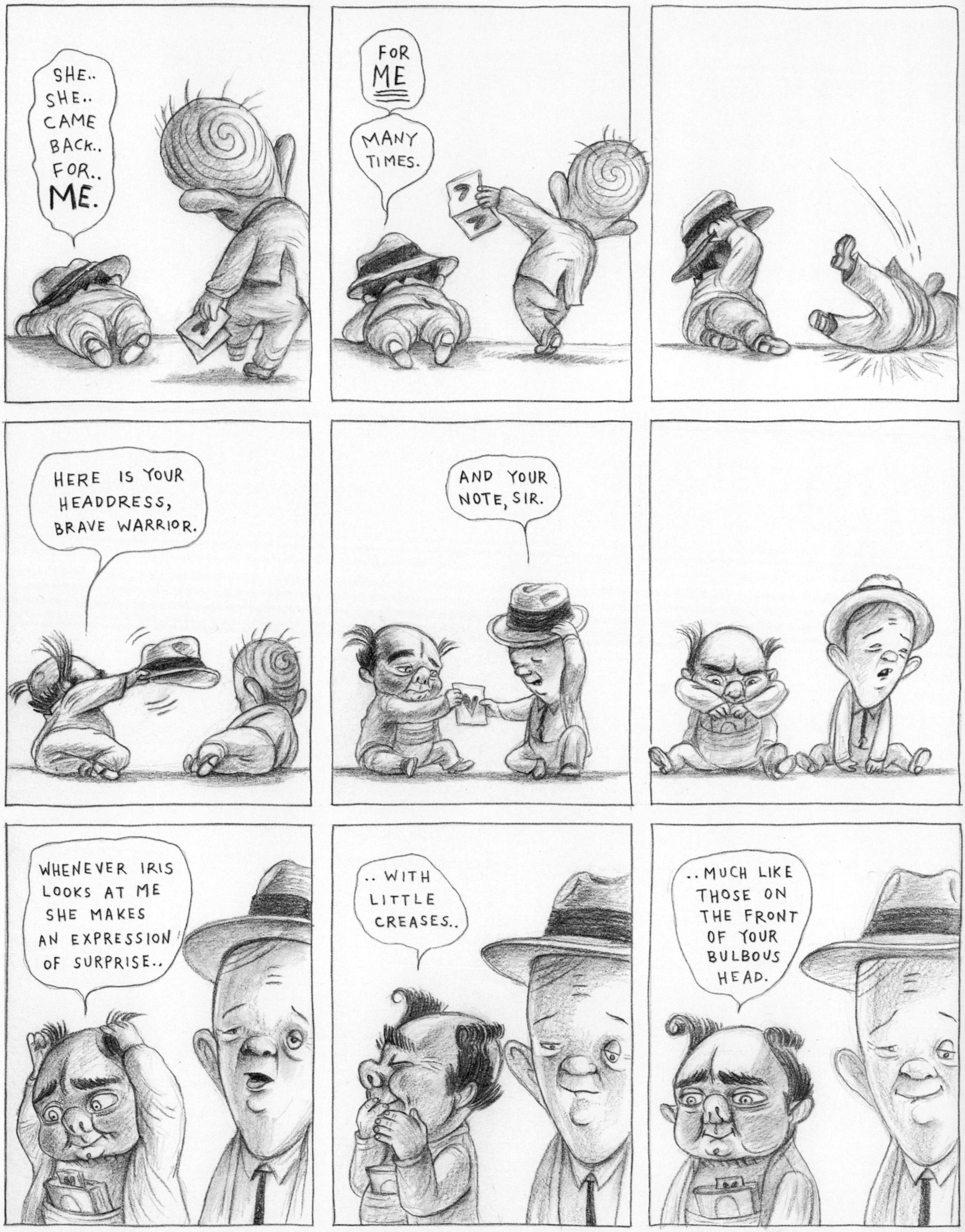
SHE.. SHE.. CAME BACK.. FOR.. ME.
FOR ME
MANY TIMES.
HERE IS YOUR HEADDRESS, BRAVE WARRIOR.
AND YOUR NOTE, SIR.
WHENEVER IRIS LOOKS AT ME SHE MAKES AN EXPRESSION OF SURPRISE..
.. WITH LITTLE CREASES..
.. MUCH LIKE THOSE ON THE FRONT OF YOUR BULBOUS HEAD.

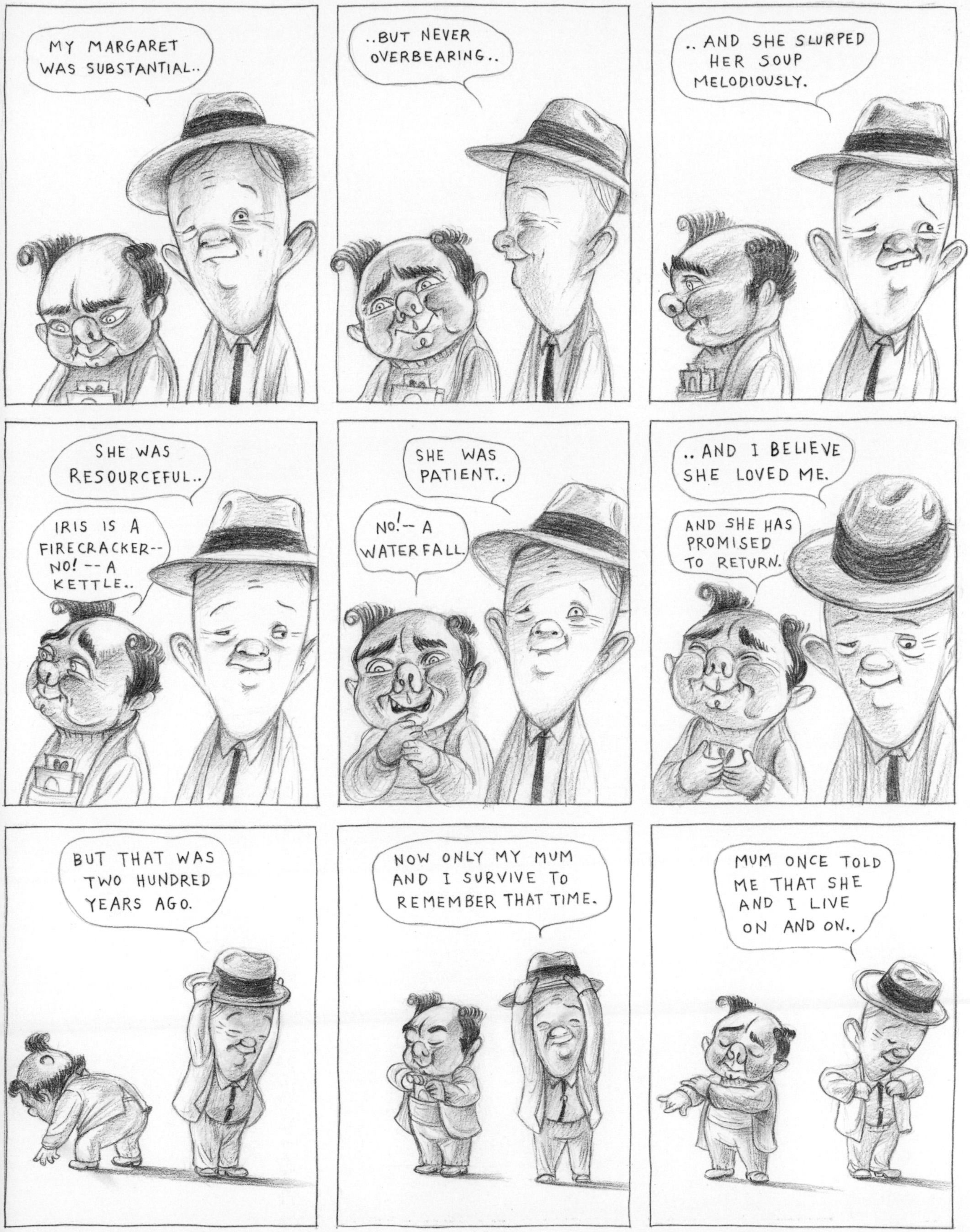
MY MARGARET WAS SUBSTANTIAL..
..BUT NEVER OVERBEARING..
.. AND SHE SLURPED HER SOUP MELODIOUSLY.
SHE WAS RESOURCEFUL..
IRIS IS A FIRECRACKER-- NO! -- A KETTLE..
SHE WAS PATIENT..
NO!-- A WATERFALL.
.. AND I BELIEVE SHE LOVED ME.
AND SHE HAS PROMISED TO RETURN.
BUT THAT WAS TWO HUNDRED YEARS AGO.
NOW ONLY MY MUM AND I SURVIVE TO REMEMBER THAT TIME.
MUM ONCE TOLD ME THAT SHE AND I LIVE ON AND ON..

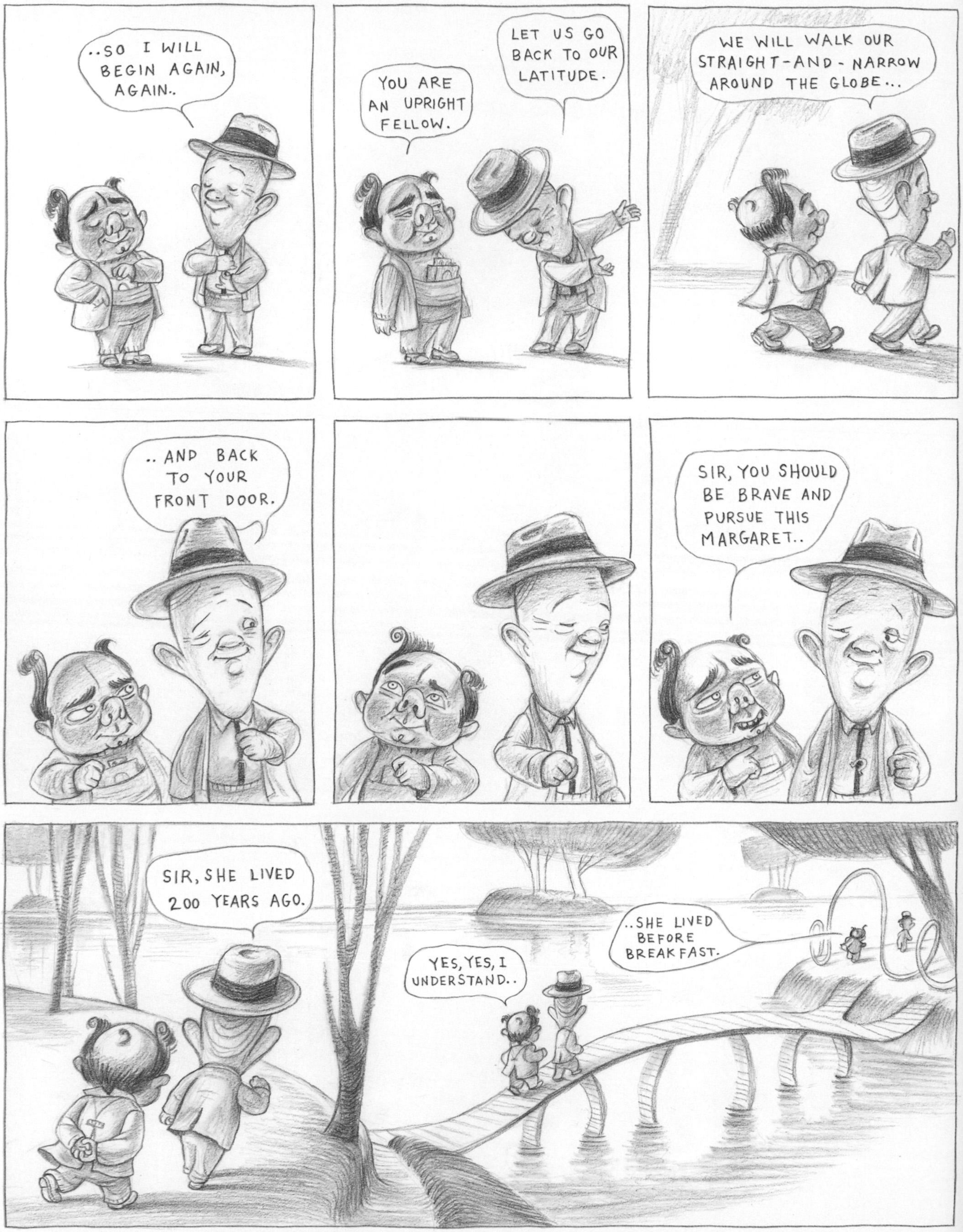
..SO I WILL BEGIN AGAIN, AGAIN..
YOU ARE AN UPRIGHT FELLOW.
LET US GO BACK TO OUR LATITUDE.
WE WILL WALK OUR STRAIGHT-AND-NARROW AROUND THE GLOBE...
..AND BACK TO YOUR FRONT DOOR.
SIR, YOU SHOULD BE BRAVE AND PURSUE THIS MARGARET..
SIR, SHE LIVED 200 YEARS AGO.
YES, YES, I UNDERSTAND..
..SHE LIVED BEFORE BREAKFAST.

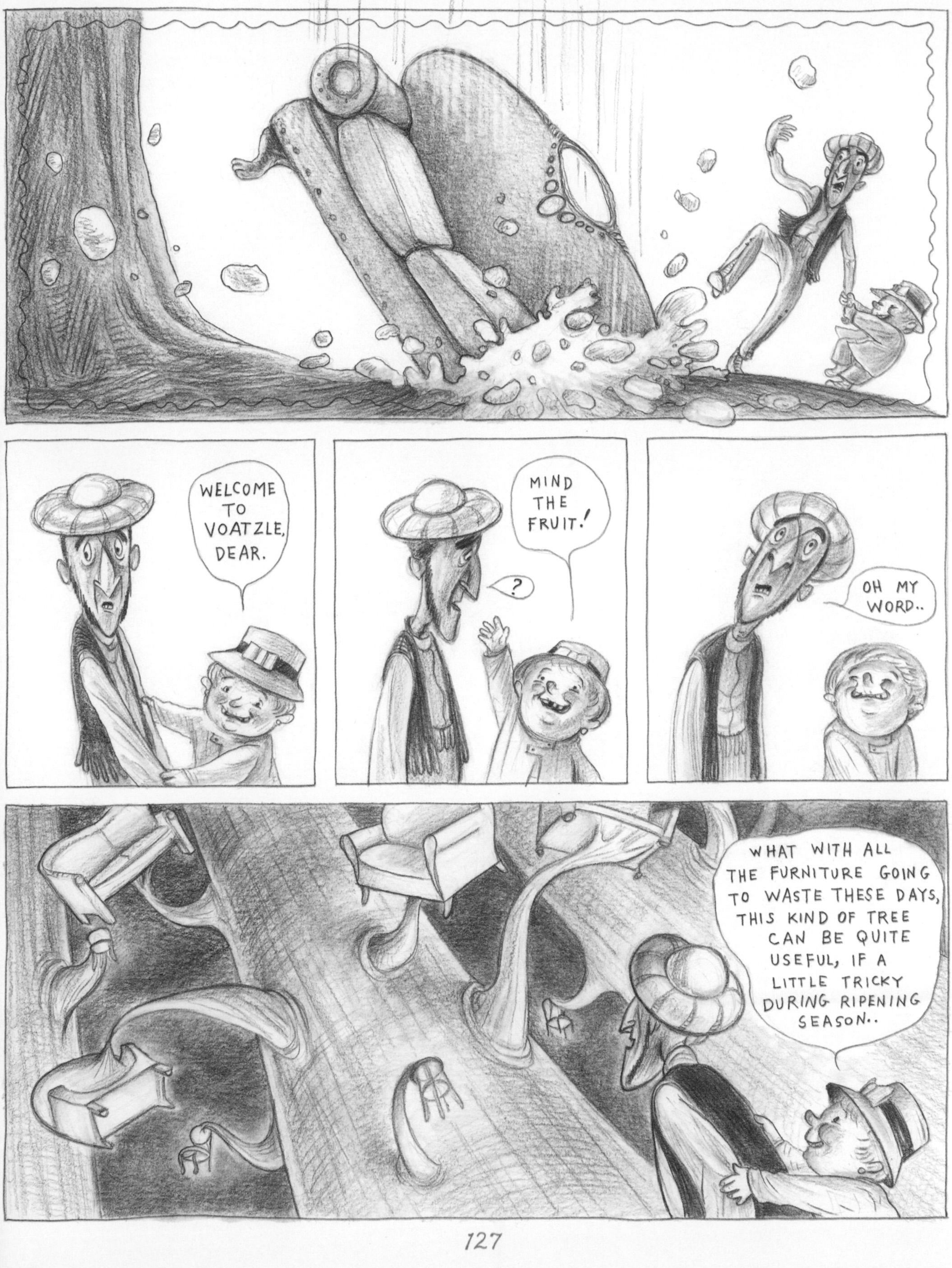
WELCOME TO VOATZLE, DEAR.
MIND THE FRUIT!
?
OH MY WORD..
WHAT WITH ALL THE FURNITURE GOING TO WASTE THESE DAYS, THIS KIND OF TREE CAN BE QUITE USEFUL, IF A LITTLE TRICKY DURING RIPENING SEASON..

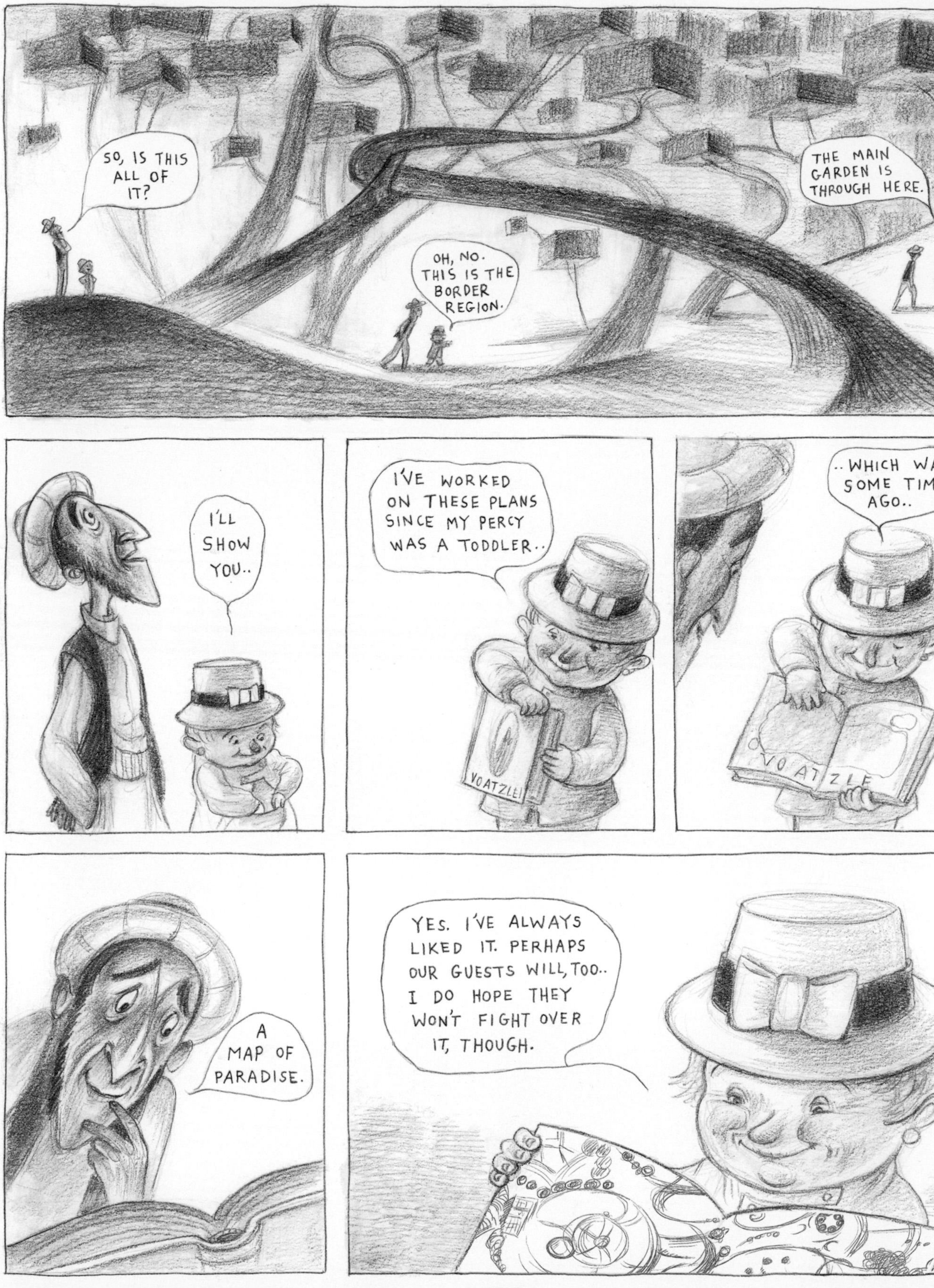
SO, IS THIS ALL OF IT?
OH, NO. THIS IS THE BORDER REGION.
THE MAIN GARDEN IS THROUGH HERE.
I'LL SHOW YOU..
I'VE WORKED ON THESE PLANS SINCE MY PERCY WAS A TODDLER..
VOATZLE
..WHICH WAS SOME TIME AGO..
VOATZLE
A MAP OF PARADISE.
YES. I'VE ALWAYS LIKED IT. PERHAPS OUR GUESTS WILL, TOO.. I DO HOPE THEY WON'T FIGHT OVER IT, THOUGH.

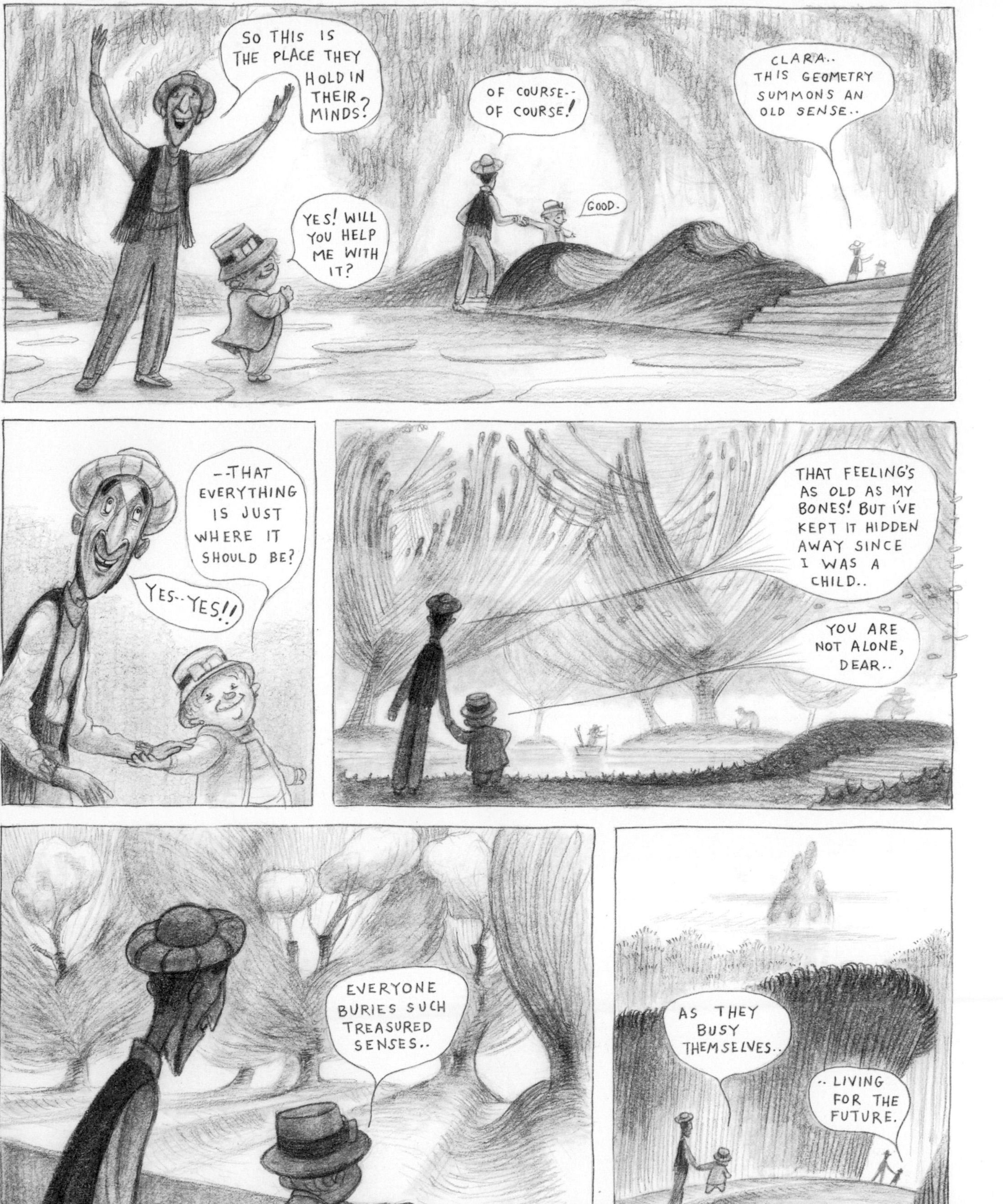
SO THIS IS THE PLACE THEY HOLD IN THEIR MINDS?
YES! WILL YOU HELP ME WITH IT?
OF COURSE-- OF COURSE!
GOOD.
CLARA.. THIS GEOMETRY SUMMONS AN OLD SENSE..
--THAT EVERYTHING IS JUST WHERE IT SHOULD BE?
YES--YES!!
THAT FEELING'S AS OLD AS MY BONES! BUT I'VE KEPT IT HIDDEN AWAY SINCE I WAS A CHILD..
YOU ARE NOT ALONE, DEAR..
EVERYONE BURIES SUCH TREASURED SENSES..
AS THEY BUSY THEMSELVES..
.. LIVING FOR THE FUTURE.

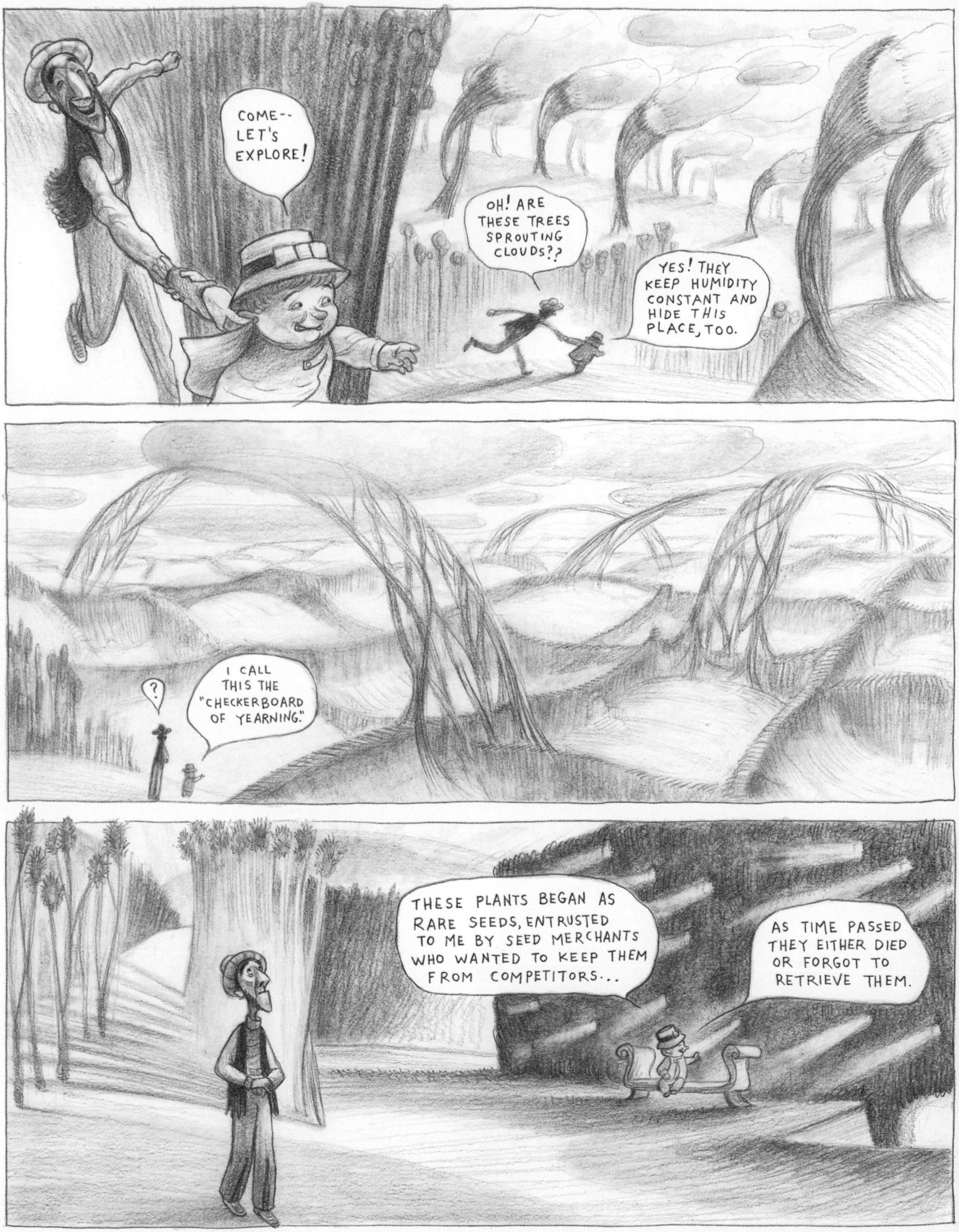
COME-- LET'S EXPLORE!
OH! ARE THESE TREES SPROUTING CLOUDS??
YES! THEY KEEP HUMIDITY CONSTANT AND HIDE THIS PLACE, TOO.
?
I CALL THIS THE "CHECKERBOARD OF YEARNING."
THESE PLANTS BEGAN AS RARE SEEDS, ENTRUSTED TO ME BY SEED MERCHANTS WHO WANTED TO KEEP THEM FROM COMPETITORS...
AS TIME PASSED THEY EITHER DIED OR FORGOT TO RETRIEVE THEM.

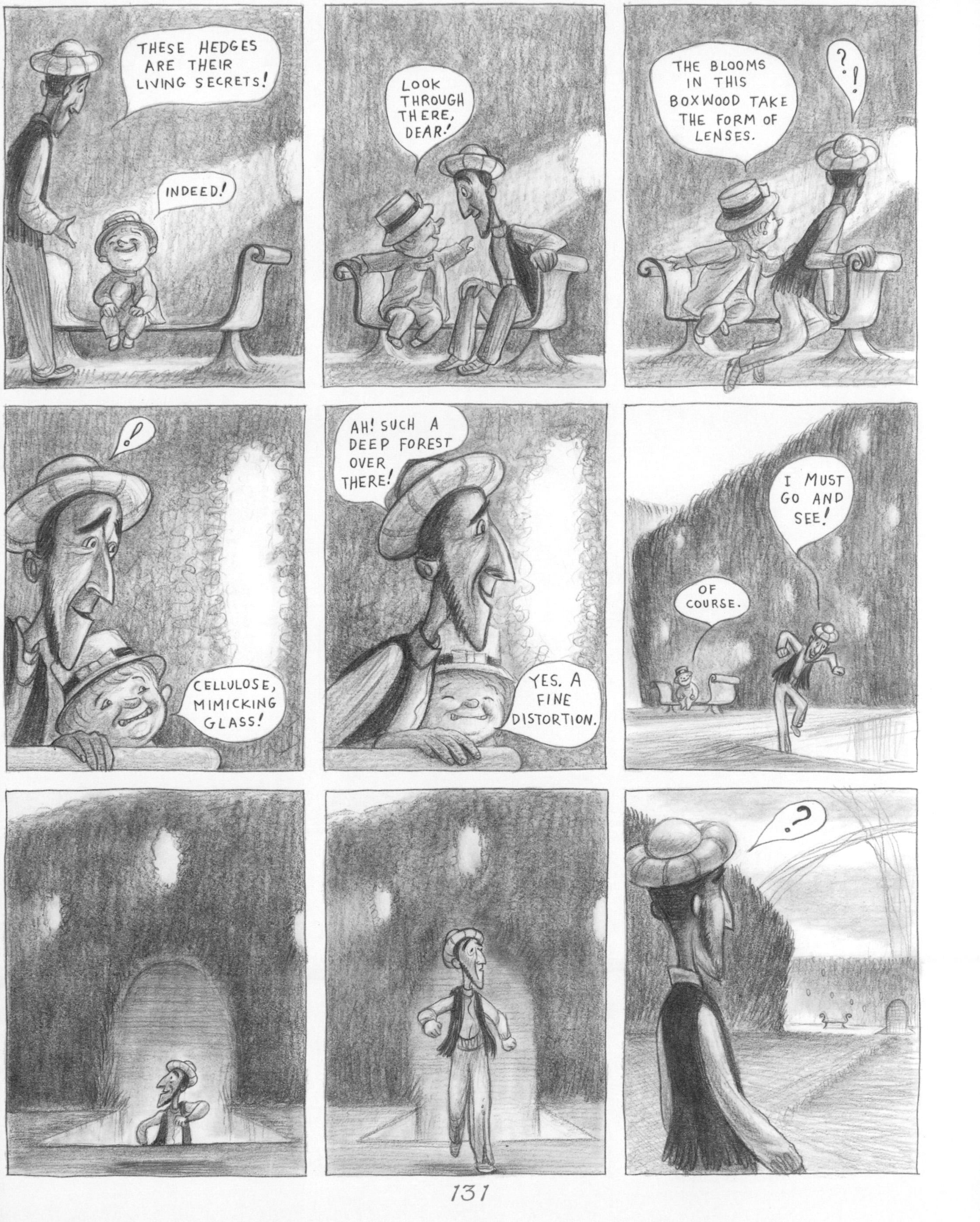
THESE HEDGES ARE THEIR LIVING SECRETS!
INDEED!
LOOK THROUGH THERE, DEAR!
THE BLOOMS IN THIS BOXWOOD TAKE THE FORM OF LENSES.
?!
!
CELLULOSE, MIMICKING GLASS!
AH! SUCH A DEEP FOREST OVER THERE!
YES. A FINE DISTORTION.
I MUST GO AND SEE!
OF COURSE.
?

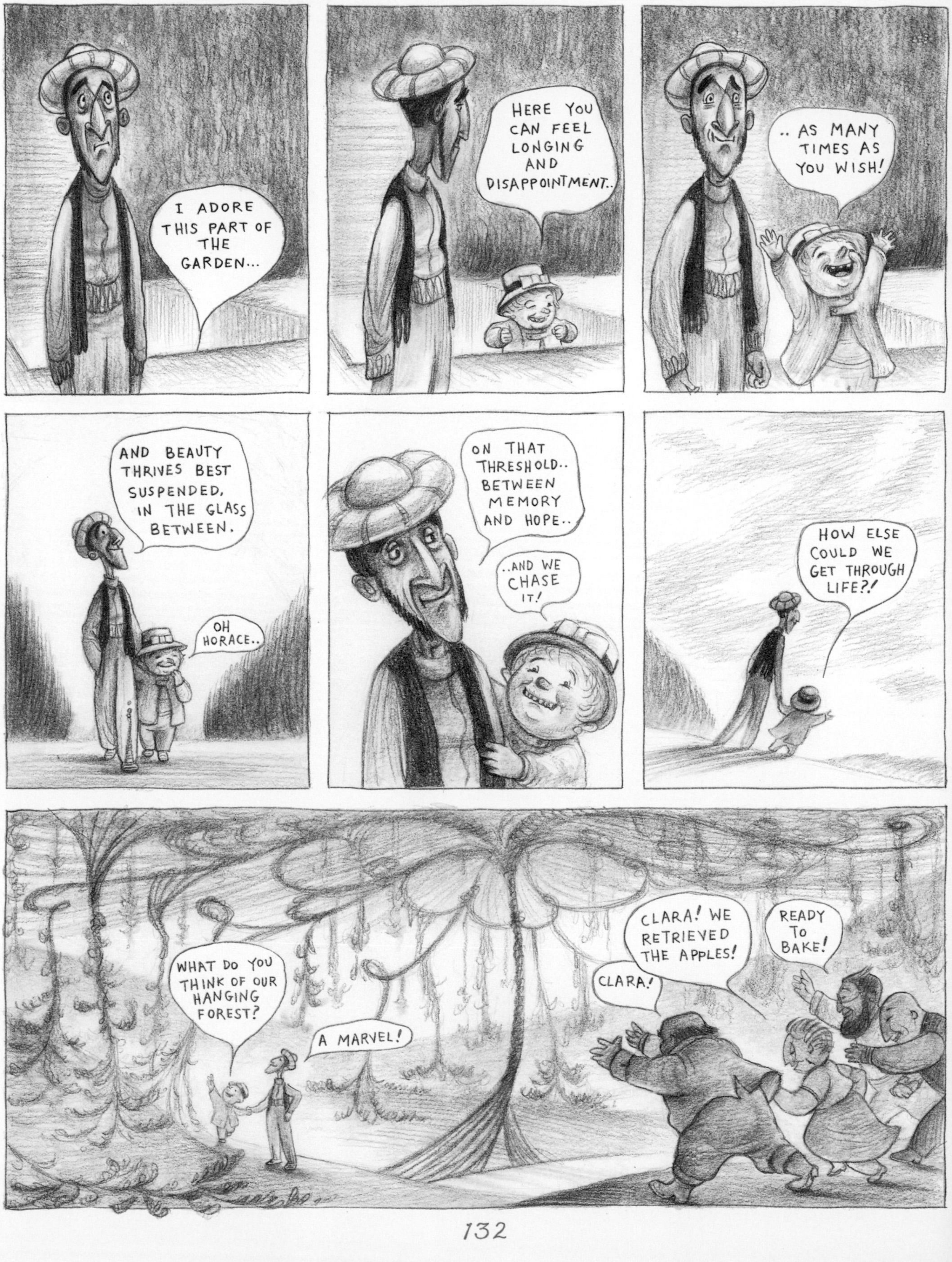

I ADORE THIS PART OF THE GARDEN...
HERE YOU CAN FEEL LONGING AND DISAPPOINTMENT..
.. AS MANY TIMES AS YOU WISH!
AND BEAUTY THRIVES BEST SUSPENDED, IN THE GLASS BETWEEN.
OH HORACE..
ON THAT THRESHOLD.. BETWEEN MEMORY AND HOPE..
..AND WE CHASE IT!
HOW ELSE COULD WE GET THROUGH LIFE?!
WHAT DO YOU THINK OF OUR HANGING FOREST?
A MARVEL!
CLARA!
CLARA! WE RETRIEVED THE APPLES!
READY TO BAKE!

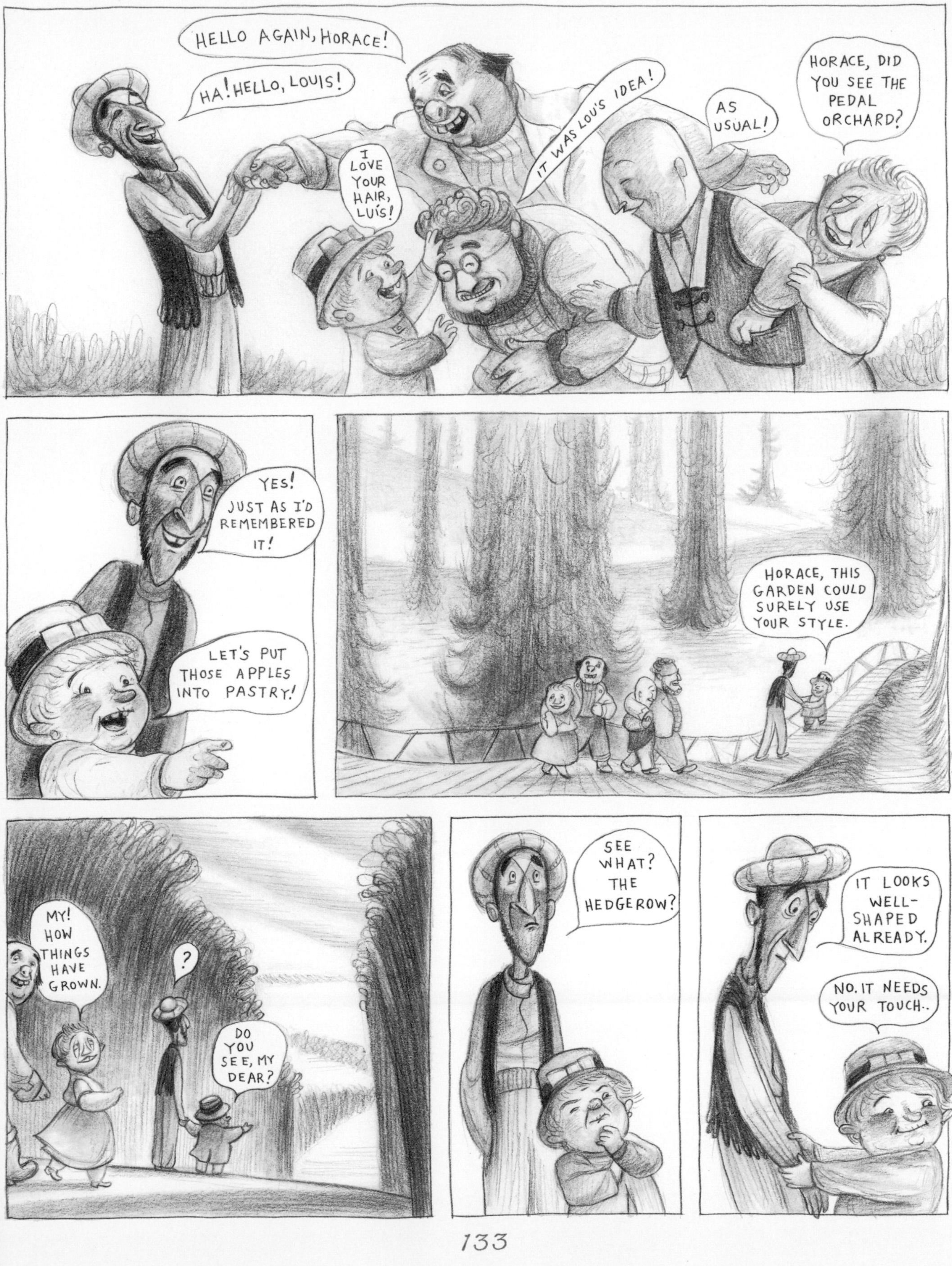
HELLO AGAIN, HORACE!
HA! HELLO, LOUIS!
I LOVE YOUR HAIR, LUÍS!
IT WAS LOU'S IDEA!
AS USUAL!
HORACE, DID YOU SEE THE PEDAL ORCHARD?
YES! JUST AS I'D REMEMBERED IT!
LET'S PUT THOSE APPLES INTO PASTRY!
HORACE, THIS GARDEN COULD SURELY USE YOUR STYLE.
MY! HOW THINGS HAVE GROWN.
?
DO YOU SEE, MY DEAR?
SEE WHAT? THE HEDGEROW?
IT LOOKS WELL-SHAPED ALREADY.
NO. IT NEEDS YOUR TOUCH..

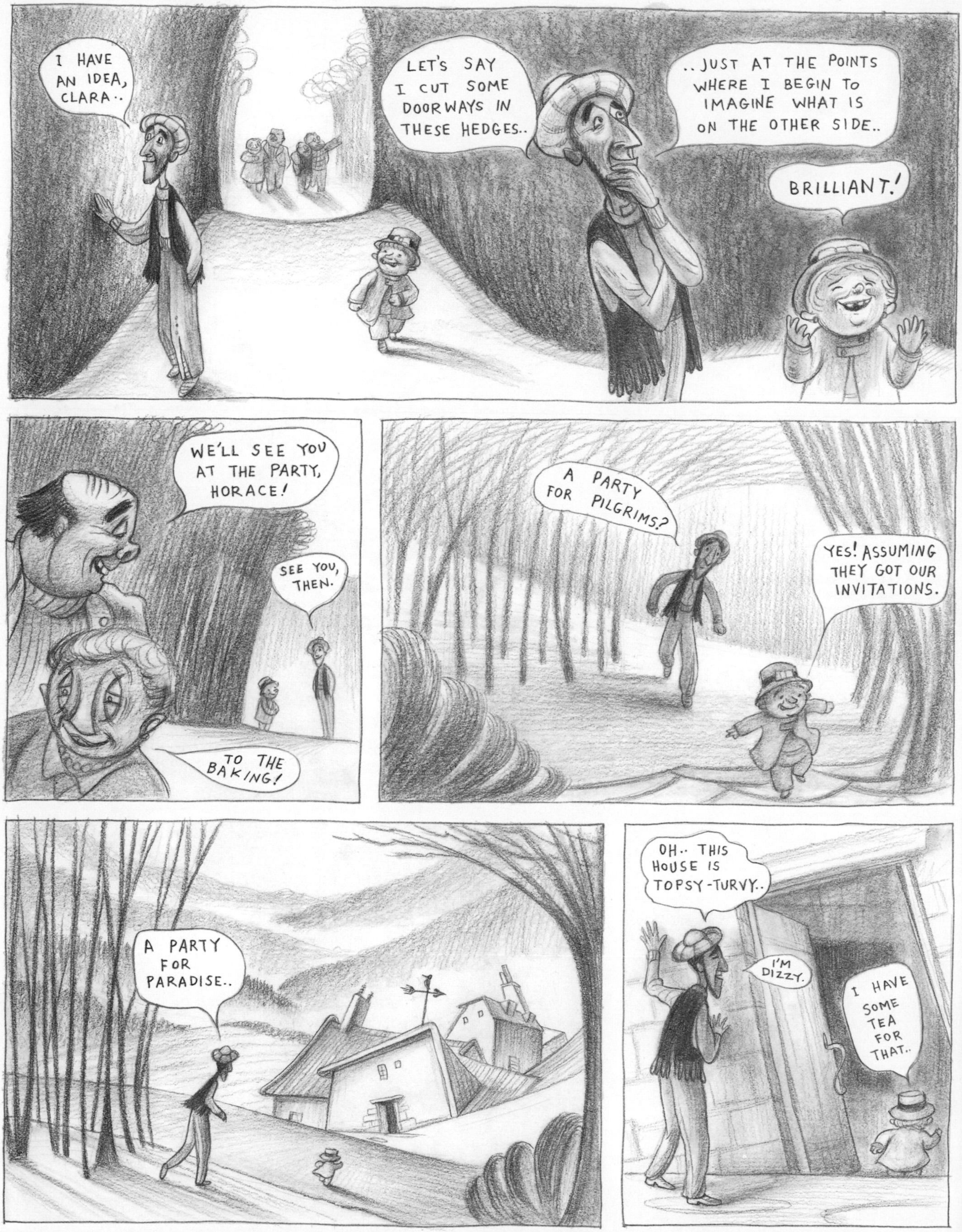
I HAVE AN IDEA, CLARA..
LET'S SAY I CUT SOME DOORWAYS IN THESE HEDGES..
..JUST AT THE POINTS WHERE I BEGIN TO IMAGINE WHAT IS ON THE OTHER SIDE..
BRILLIANT!
WE'LL SEE YOU AT THE PARTY, HORACE!
SEE YOU, THEN.
TO THE BAKING!
A PARTY FOR PILGRIMS?
YES! ASSUMING THEY GOT OUR INVITATIONS.
A PARTY FOR PARADISE..
OH.. THIS HOUSE IS TOPSY-TURVY..
I'M DIZZY.
I HAVE SOME TEA FOR THAT..

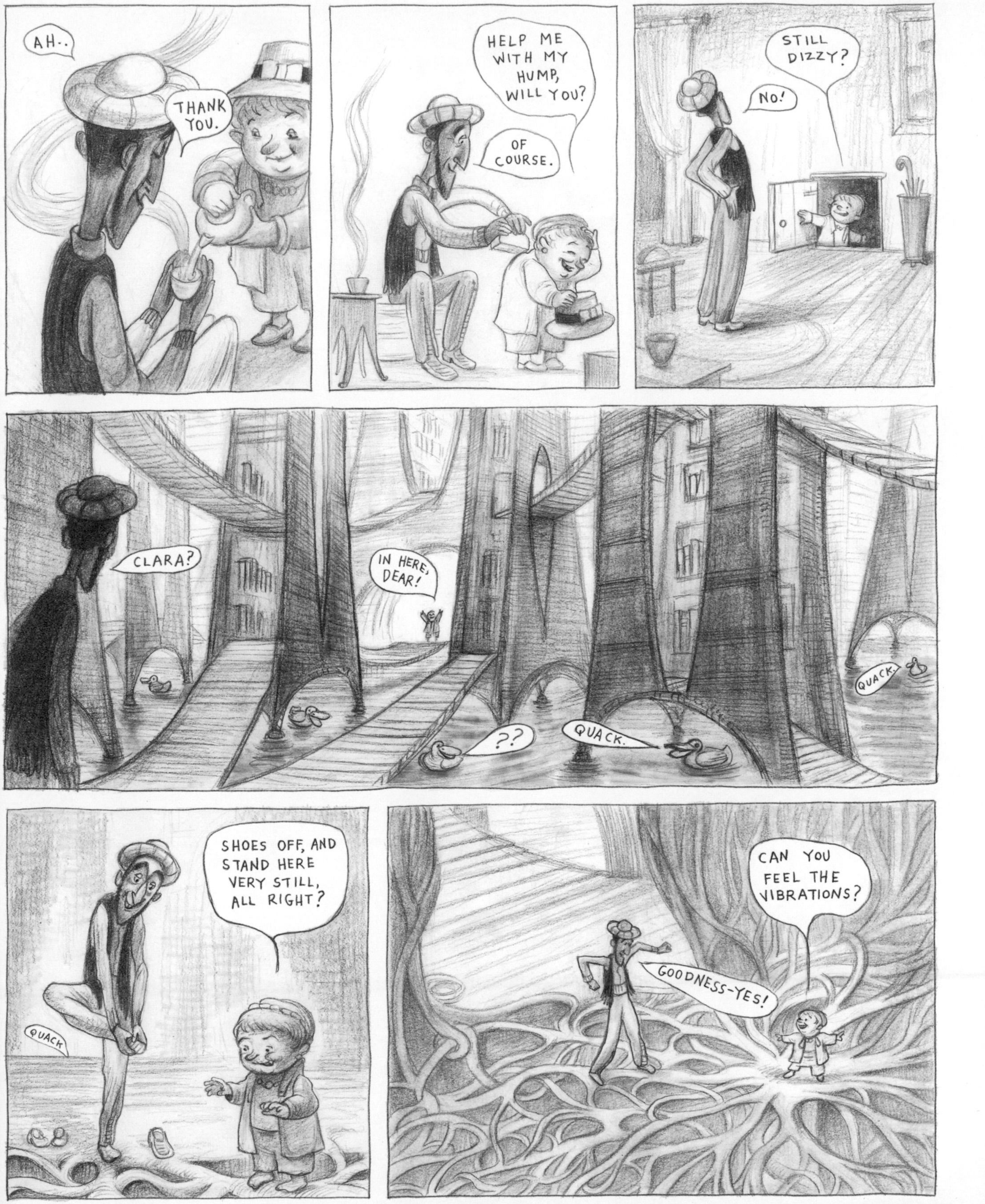
AH..
THANK YOU.
HELP ME WITH MY HUMP, WILL YOU?
OF COURSE.
STILL DIZZY?
NO!
CLARA?
IN HERE, DEAR!
QUACK.
??
QUACK.
SHOES OFF, AND STAND HERE VERY STILL, ALL RIGHT?
QUACK
CAN YOU FEEL THE VIBRATIONS?
GOODNESS-YES!

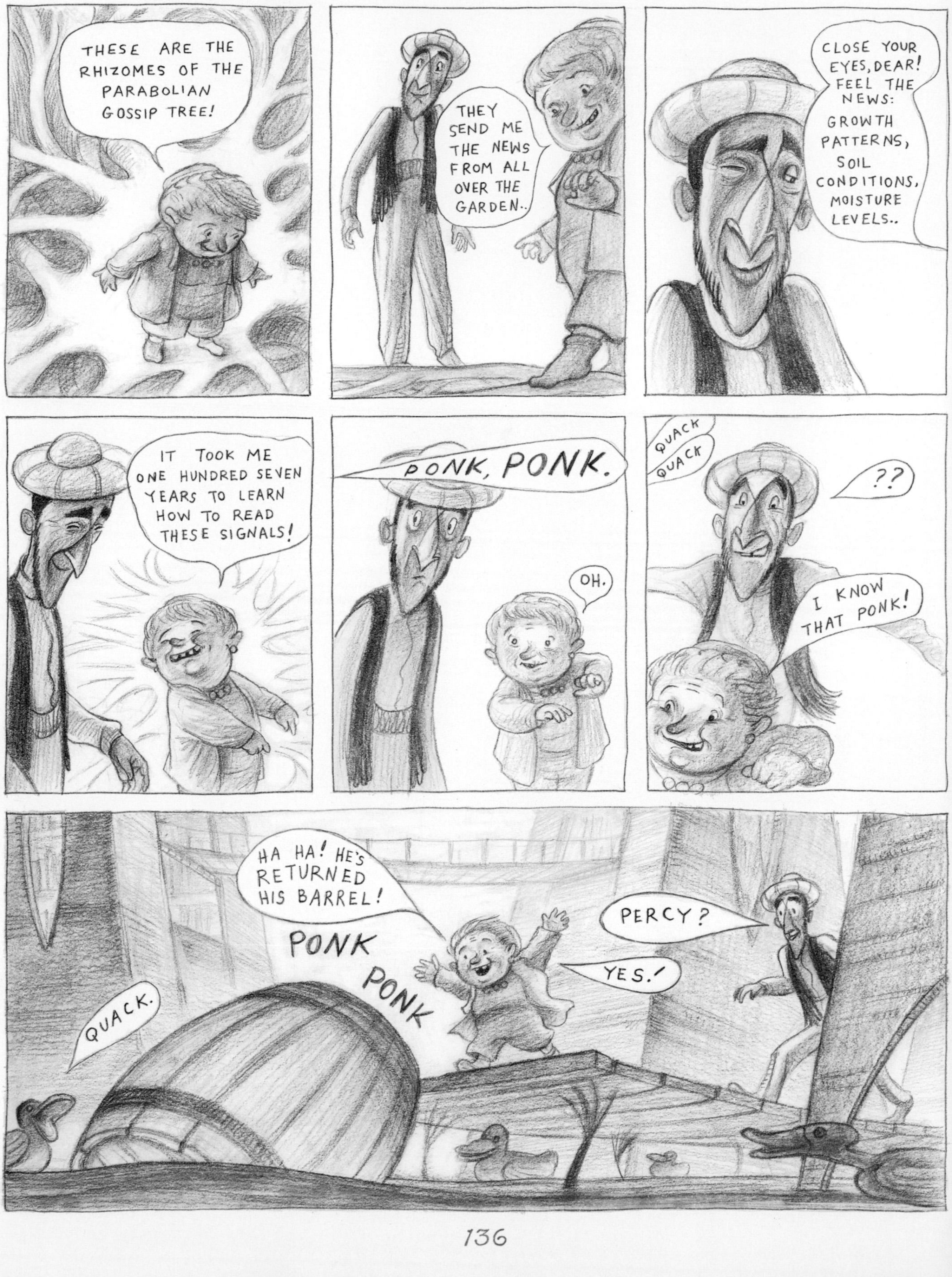
THESE ARE THE RHIZOMES OF THE PARABOLIAN GOSSIP TREE!
THEY SEND ME THE NEWS FROM ALL OVER THE GARDEN..
CLOSE YOUR EYES, DEAR! FEEL THE NEWS: GROWTH PATTERNS, SOIL CONDITIONS, MOISTURE LEVELS..
IT TOOK ME ONE HUNDRED SEVEN YEARS TO LEARN HOW TO READ THESE SIGNALS!
PONK, PONK.
OH.
QUACK
QUACK
??
I KNOW THAT PONK!
HA HA! HE'S RETURNED HIS BARREL!
PONK
PONK
PERCY?
YES.!
QUACK.

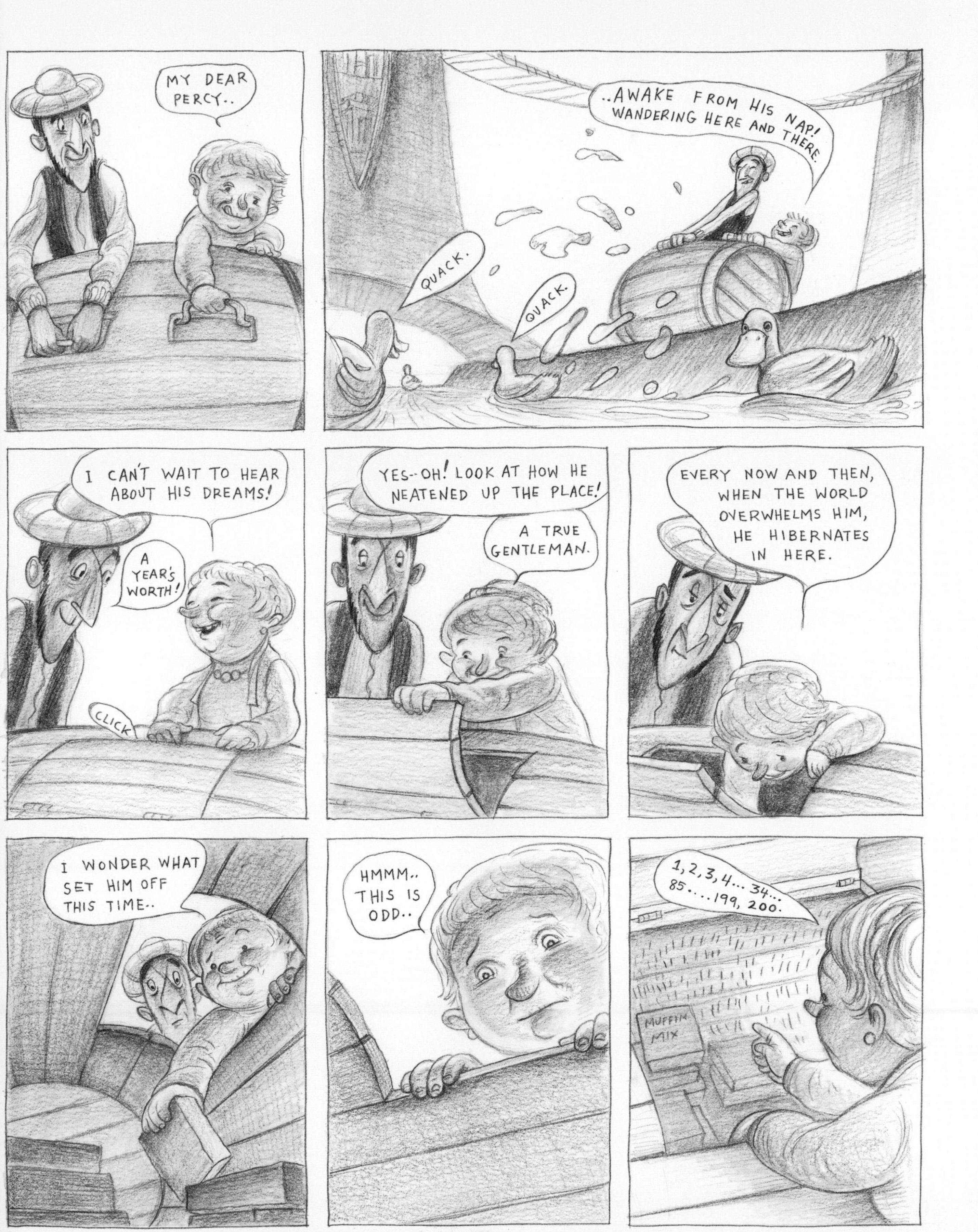
MY DEAR PERCY..
..AWAKE FROM HIS NAP! WANDERING HERE AND THERE.
QUACK.
QUACK.
I CAN'T WAIT TO HEAR ABOUT HIS DREAMS!
A YEAR'S WORTH!
CLICK
YES--OH! LOOK AT HOW HE NEATENED UP THE PLACE!
A TRUE GENTLEMAN.
EVERY NOW AND THEN, WHEN THE WORLD OVERWHELMS HIM, HE HIBERNATES IN HERE.
I WONDER WHAT SET HIM OFF THIS TIME..
HMMM.. THIS IS ODD..
1, 2, 3, 4... 34... 85....199, 200.
MUFFIN MIX

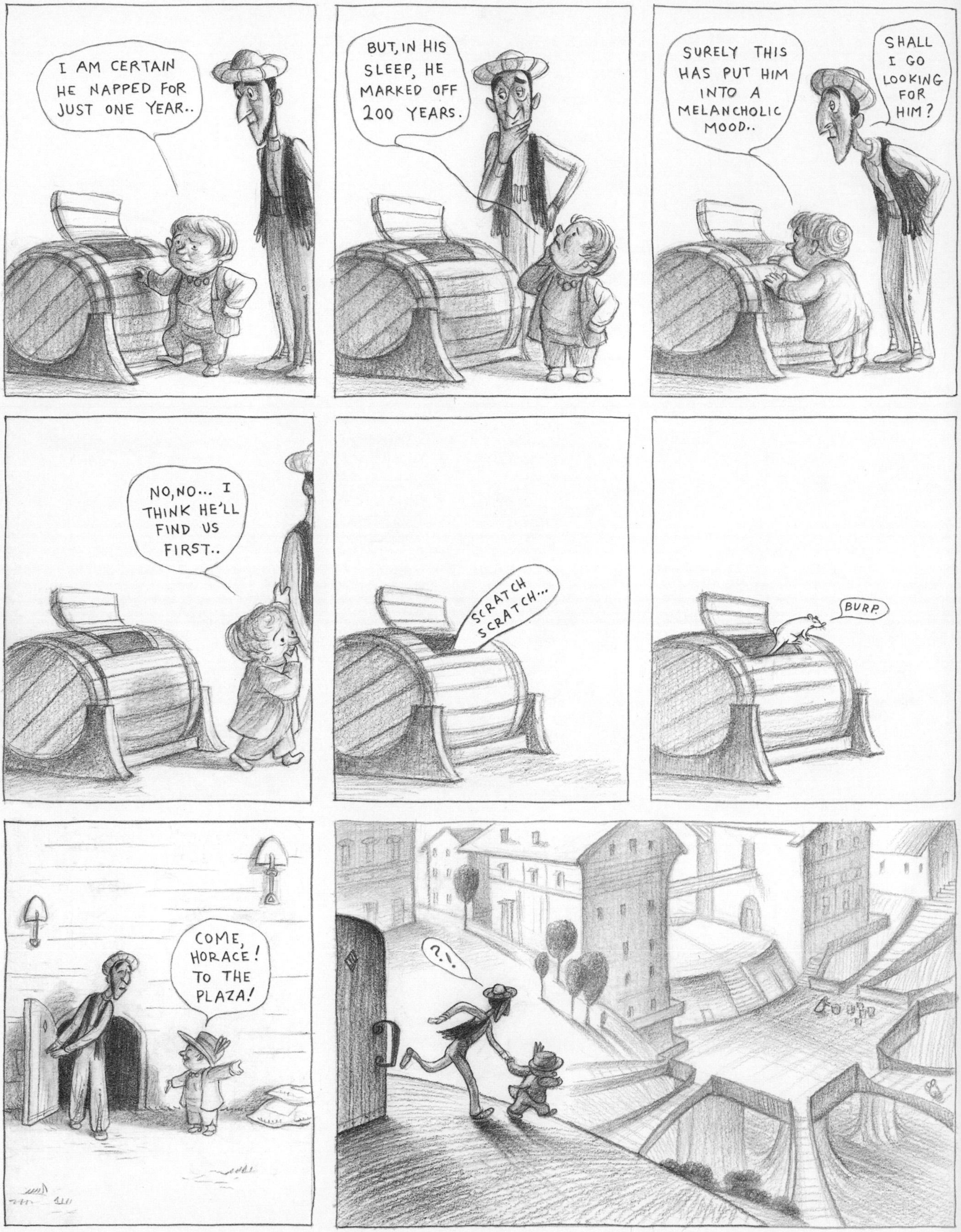
I AM CERTAIN HE NAPPED FOR JUST ONE YEAR..
BUT, IN HIS SLEEP, HE MARKED OFF 200 YEARS.
SURELY THIS HAS PUT HIM INTO A MELANCHOLIC MOOD..
SHALL I GO LOOKING FOR HIM?
NO, NO... I THINK HE'LL FIND US FIRST..
SCRATCH SCRATCH...
BURP.
COME, HORACE! TO THE PLAZA!
?!

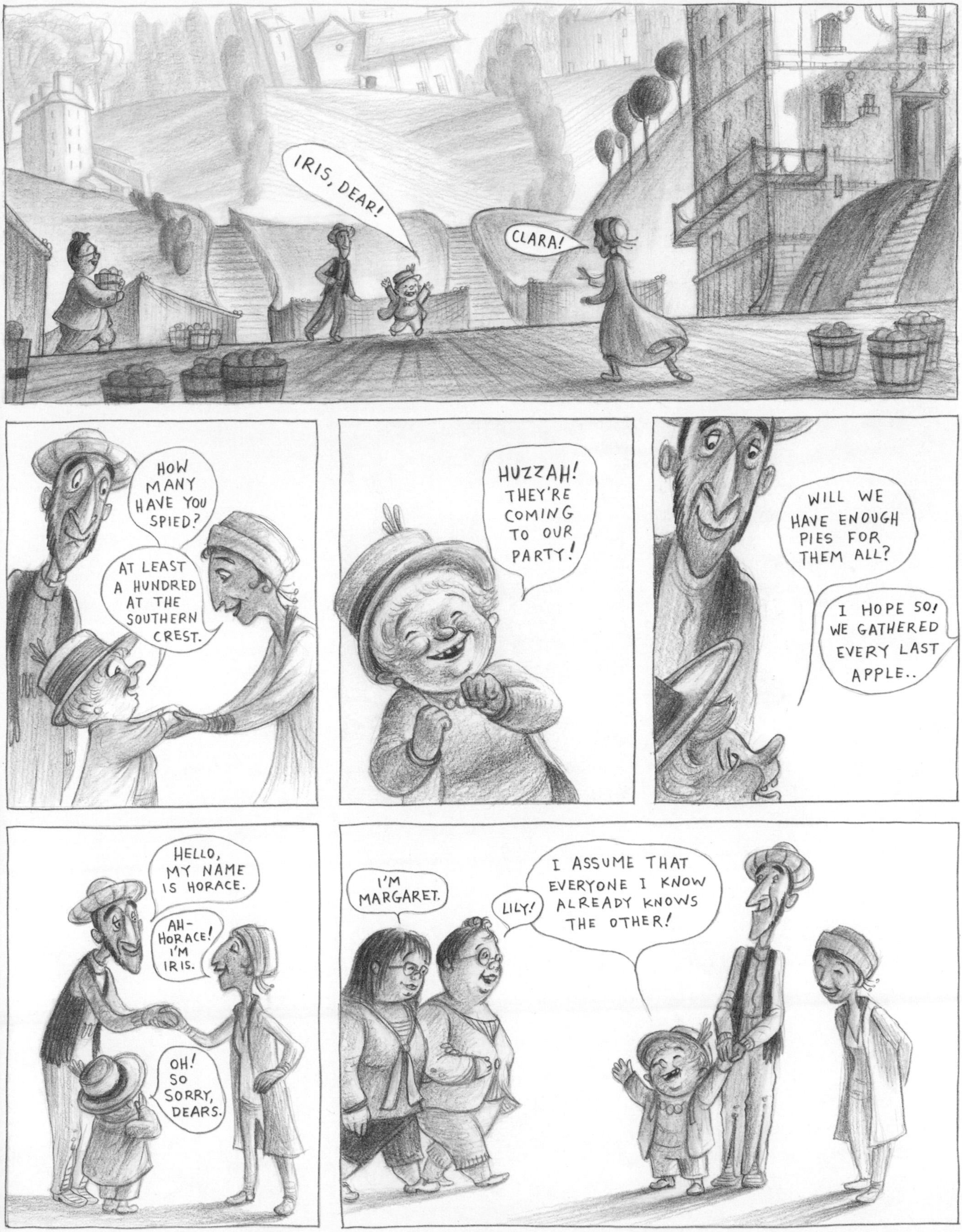

IRIS, DEAR!
CLARA!
HOW MANY HAVE YOU SPIED?
AT LEAST A HUNDRED AT THE SOUTHERN CREST.
HUZZAH! THEY'RE COMING TO OUR PARTY!
WILL WE HAVE ENOUGH PIES FOR THEM ALL?
I HOPE SO! WE GATHERED EVERY LAST APPLE..
HELLO, MY NAME IS HORACE.
AH- HORACE! I'M IRIS.
OH! SO SORRY, DEARS.
I'M MARGARET.
LILY!
I ASSUME THAT EVERYONE I KNOW ALREADY KNOWS THE OTHER!

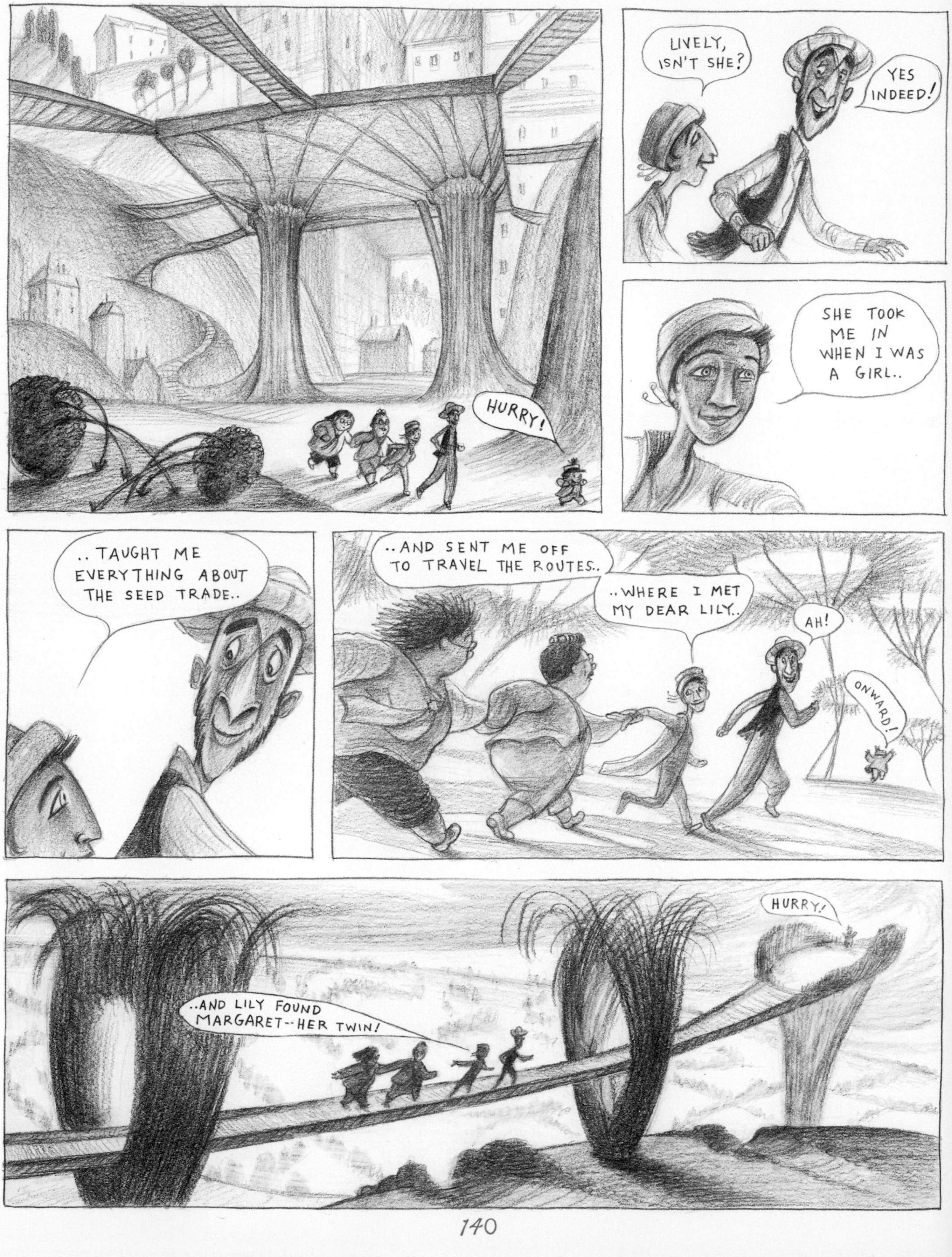
HURRY!
LIVELY, ISN'T SHE?
YES INDEED!
SHE TOOK ME IN WHEN I WAS A GIRL..
..TAUGHT ME EVERYTHING ABOUT THE SEED TRADE..
..AND SENT ME OFF TO TRAVEL THE ROUTES..
..WHERE I MET MY DEAR LILY..
AH!
ONWARD!
HURRY!
..AND LILY FOUND MARGARET--HER TWIN!

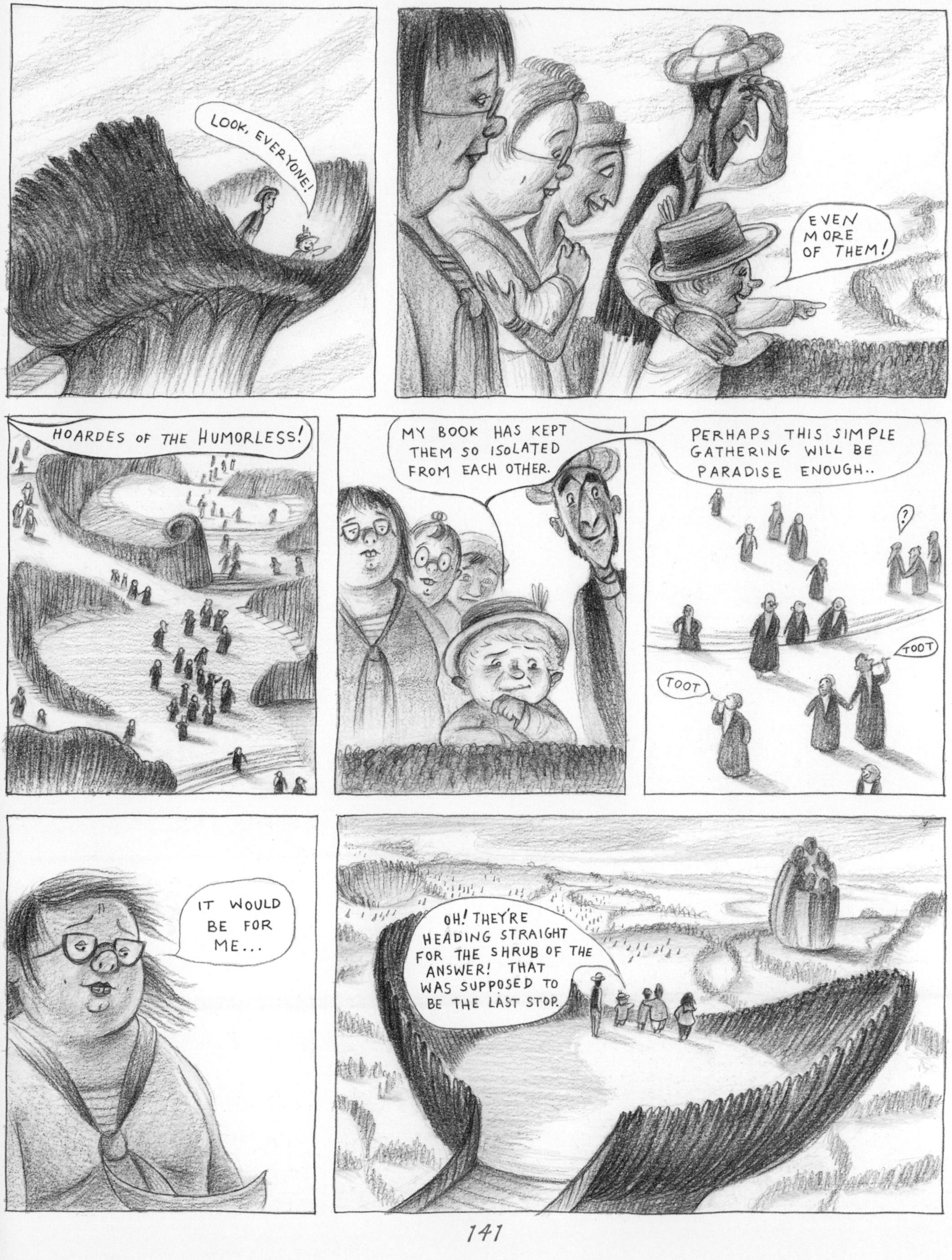
LOOK, EVERYONE!
EVEN MORE OF THEM!
HOARDES OF THE HUMORLESS!
MY BOOK HAS KEPT THEM SO ISOLATED FROM EACH OTHER.
PERHAPS THIS SIMPLE GATHERING WILL BE PARADISE ENOUGH..
?
TOOT
TOOT
IT WOULD BE FOR ME...
OH! THEY'RE HEADING STRAIGHT FOR THE SHRUB OF THE ANSWER! THAT WAS SUPPOSED TO BE THE LAST STOP.

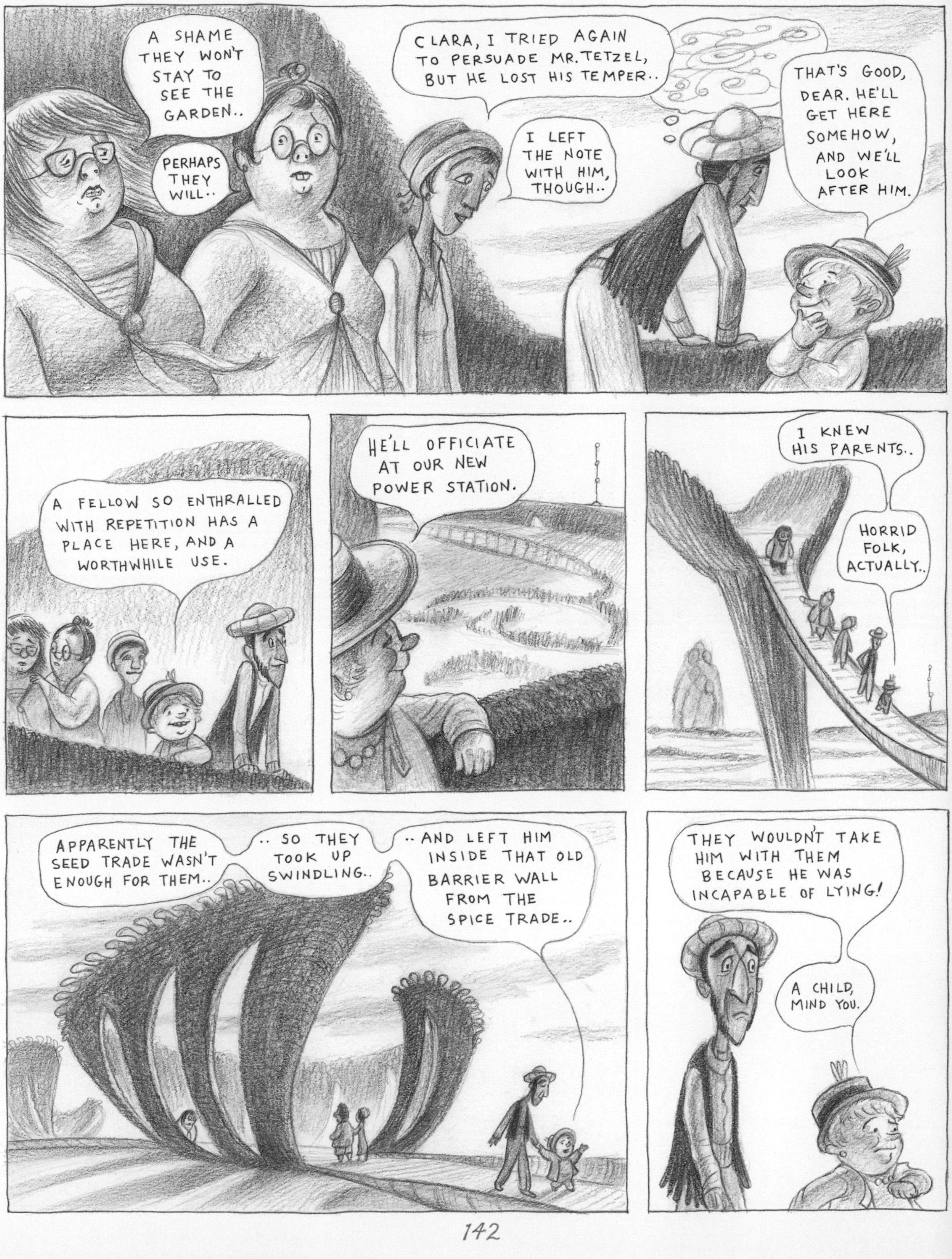
A SHAME THEY WON'T STAY TO SEE THE GARDEN..
PERHAPS THEY WILL..
CLARA, I TRIED AGAIN TO PERSUADE MR. TETZEL, BUT HE LOST HIS TEMPER..
I LEFT THE NOTE WITH HIM, THOUGH..
THAT'S GOOD, DEAR. HE'LL GET HERE SOMEHOW, AND WE'LL LOOK AFTER HIM.
A FELLOW SO ENTHRALLED WITH REPETITION HAS A PLACE HERE, AND A WORTHWHILE USE.
HE'LL OFFICIATE AT OUR NEW POWER STATION.
I KNEW HIS PARENTS..
HORRID FOLK, ACTUALLY..
APPARENTLY THE SEED TRADE WASN'T ENOUGH FOR THEM..
.. SO THEY TOOK UP SWINDLING..
.. AND LEFT HIM INSIDE THAT OLD BARRIER WALL FROM THE SPICE TRADE..
THEY WOULDN'T TAKE HIM WITH THEM BECAUSE HE WAS INCAPABLE OF LYING!
A CHILD, MIND YOU.

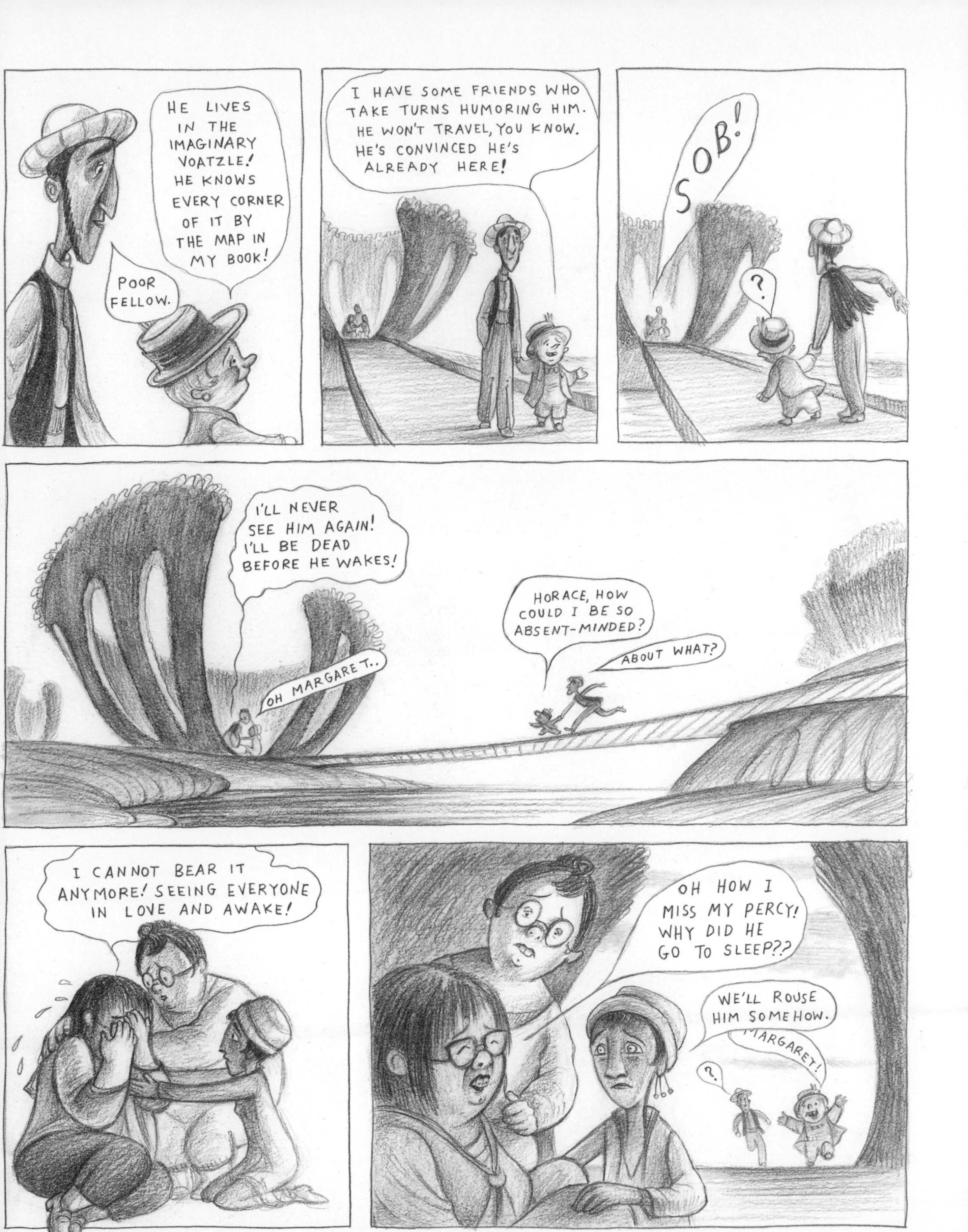
HE LIVES IN THE IMAGINARY VOATZLE! HE KNOWS EVERY CORNER OF IT BY THE MAP IN MY BOOK!
POOR FELLOW.
I HAVE SOME FRIENDS WHO TAKE TURNS HUMORING HIM. HE WON'T TRAVEL, YOU KNOW. HE'S CONVINCED HE'S ALREADY HERE!
SOB!
?
I'LL NEVER SEE HIM AGAIN! I'LL BE DEAD BEFORE HE WAKES!
OH MARGARET..
HORACE, HOW COULD I BE SO ABSENT-MINDED?
ABOUT WHAT?
I CANNOT BEAR IT ANYMORE! SEEING EVERYONE IN LOVE AND AWAKE!
OH HOW I MISS MY PERCY! WHY DID HE GO TO SLEEP??
WE'LL ROUSE HIM SOMEHOW.
MARGARET!
?

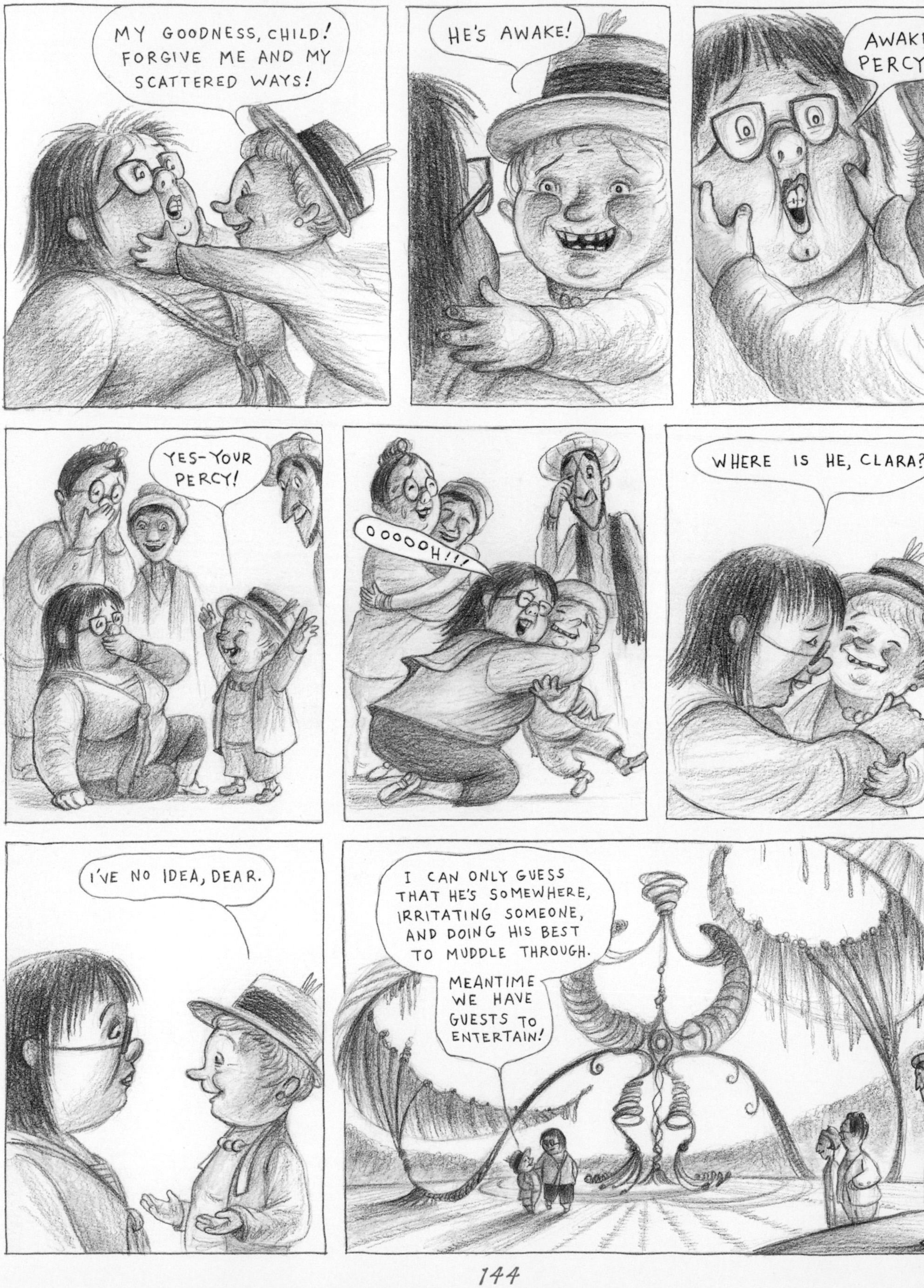
MY GOODNESS, CHILD! FORGIVE ME AND MY SCATTERED WAYS!
HE'S AWAKE!
AWAKE? PERCY??
YES-YOUR PERCY!
OOOOOH!!!
WHERE IS HE, CLARA?
I'VE NO IDEA, DEAR.
I CAN ONLY GUESS THAT HE'S SOMEWHERE, IRRITATING SOMEONE, AND DOING HIS BEST TO MUDDLE THROUGH.
MEANTIME WE HAVE GUESTS TO ENTERTAIN!

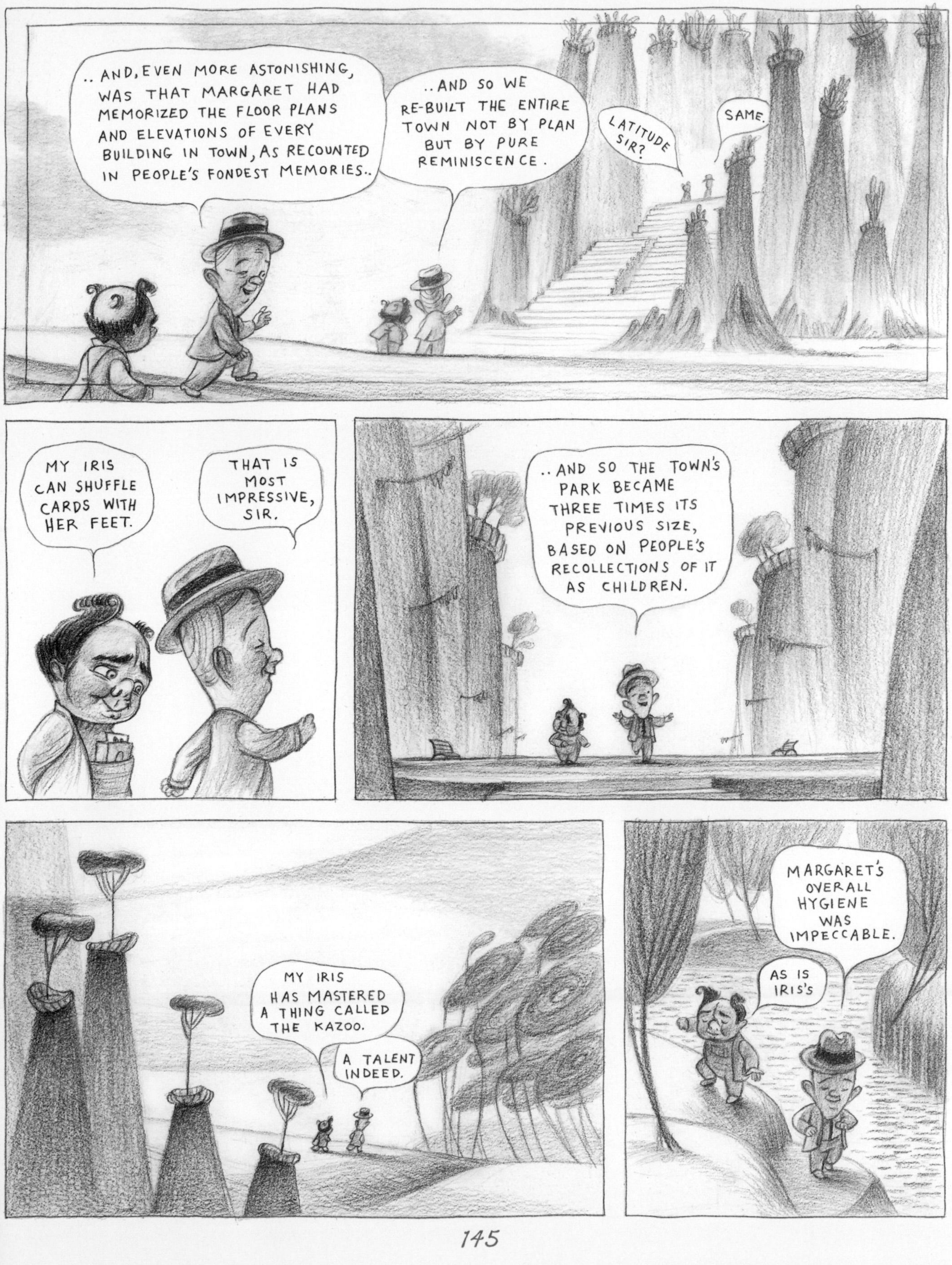
..AND, EVEN MORE ASTONISHING, WAS THAT MARGARET HAD MEMORIZED THE FLOOR PLANS AND ELEVATIONS OF EVERY BUILDING IN TOWN, AS RECOUNTED IN PEOPLE'S FONDEST MEMORIES..
..AND SO WE RE-BUILT THE ENTIRE TOWN NOT BY PLAN BUT BY PURE REMINISCENCE.
LATITUDE SIR?
SAME.
MY IRIS CAN SHUFFLE CARDS WITH HER FEET.
THAT IS MOST IMPRESSIVE, SIR.
..AND SO THE TOWN'S PARK BECAME THREE TIMES ITS PREVIOUS SIZE, BASED ON PEOPLE'S RECOLLECTIONS OF IT AS CHILDREN.
MY IRIS HAS MASTERED A THING CALLED THE KAZOO.
A TALENT INDEED.
MARGARET'S OVERALL HYGIENE WAS IMPECCABLE.
AS IS IRIS'S

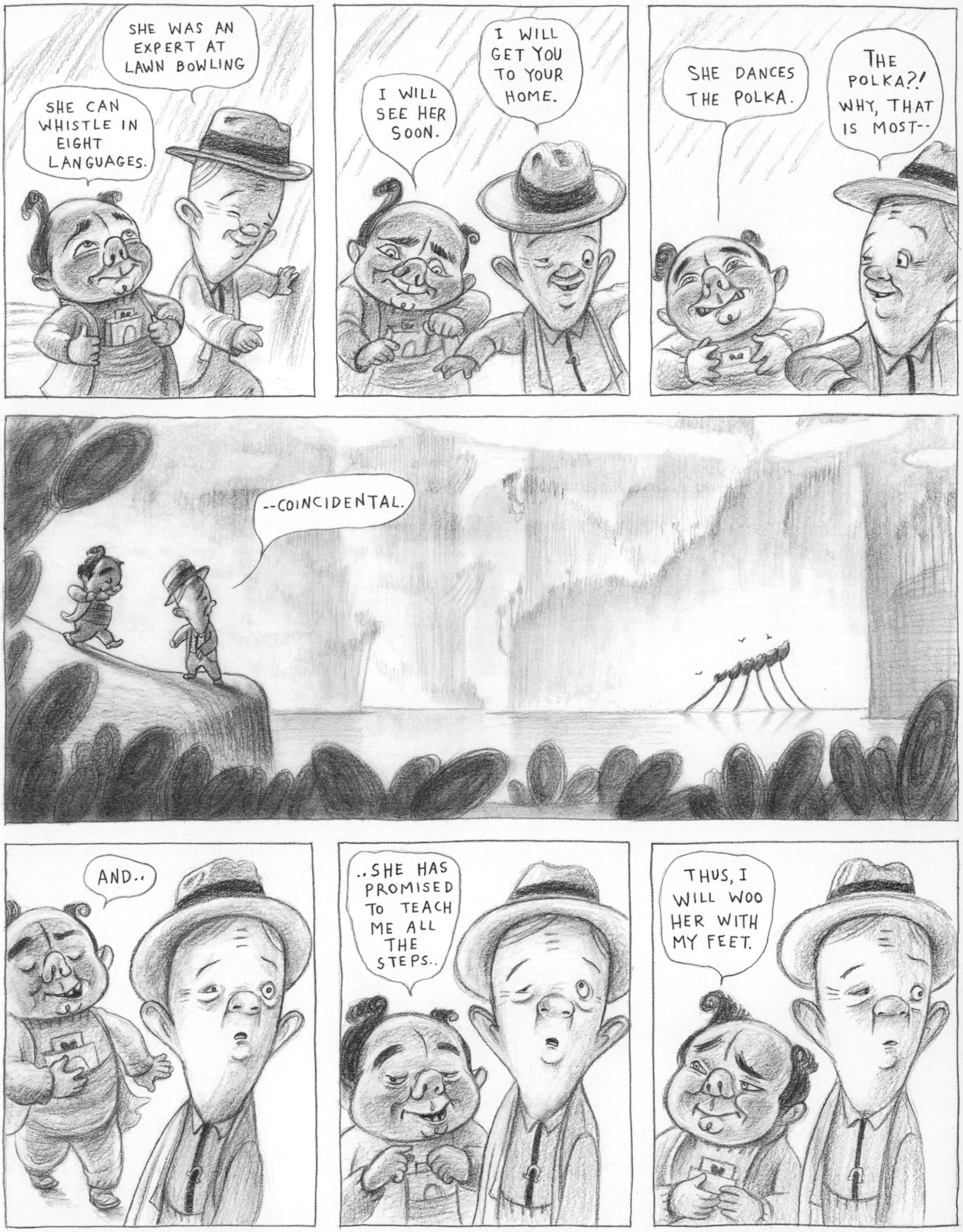
SHE WAS AN EXPERT AT LAWN BOWLING
SHE CAN WHISTLE IN EIGHT LANGUAGES.
I WILL GET YOU TO YOUR HOME.
I WILL SEE HER SOON.
SHE DANCES THE POLKA.
THE POLKA?! WHY, THAT IS MOST--
--COINCIDENTAL.
AND..
..SHE HAS PROMISED TO TEACH ME ALL THE STEPS..
THUS, I WILL WOO HER WITH MY FEET.

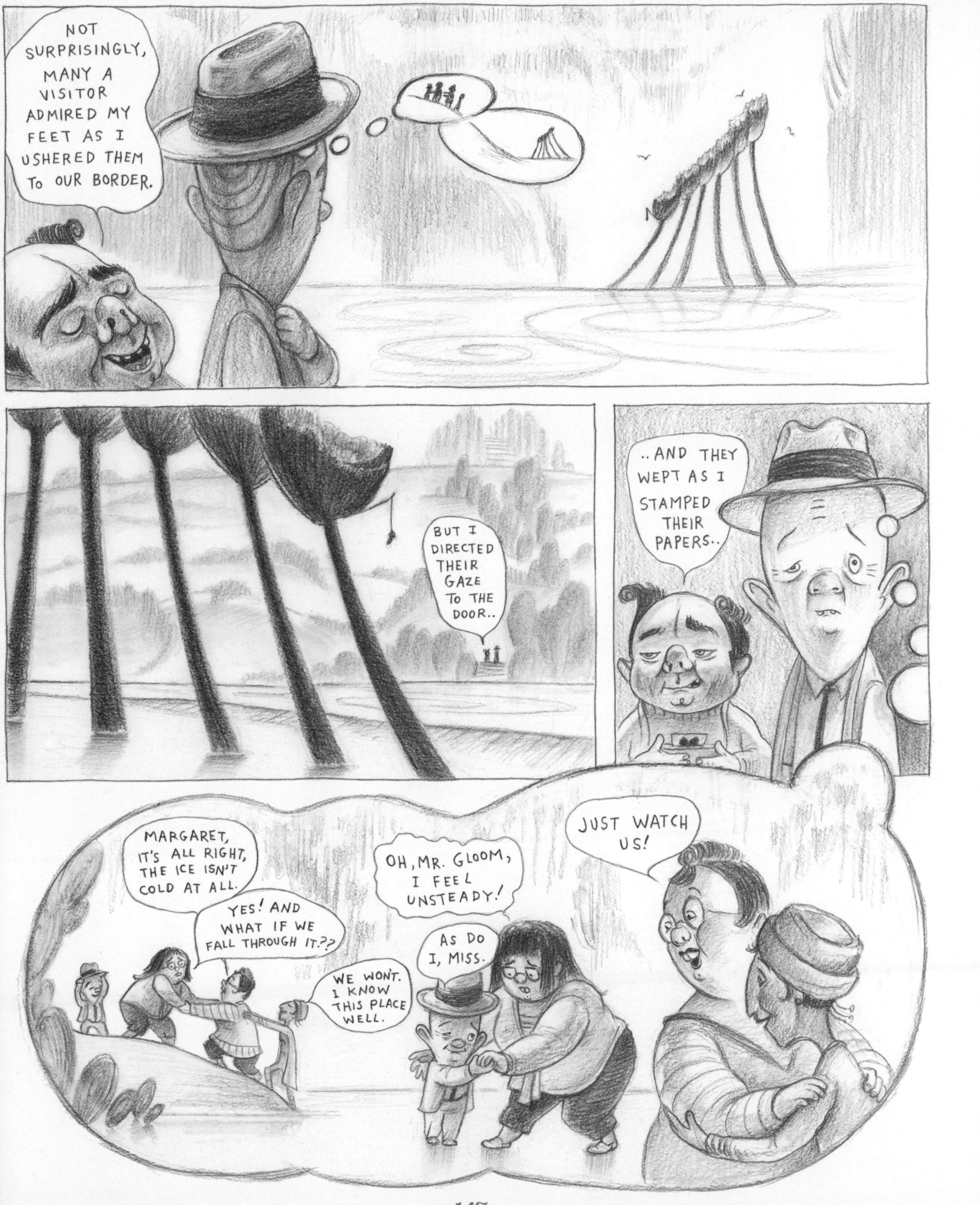
NOT SURPRISINGLY, MANY A VISITOR ADMIRED MY FEET AS I USHERED THEM TO OUR BORDER.
BUT I DIRECTED THEIR GAZE TO THE DOOR..
..AND THEY WEPT AS I STAMPED THEIR PAPERS..
MARGARET, IT'S ALL RIGHT, THE ICE ISN'T COLD AT ALL.
YES! AND WHAT IF WE FALL THROUGH IT.??
WE WON'T. I KNOW THIS PLACE WELL.
OH, MR. GLOOM, I FEEL UNSTEADY!
AS DO I, MISS.
JUST WATCH US!

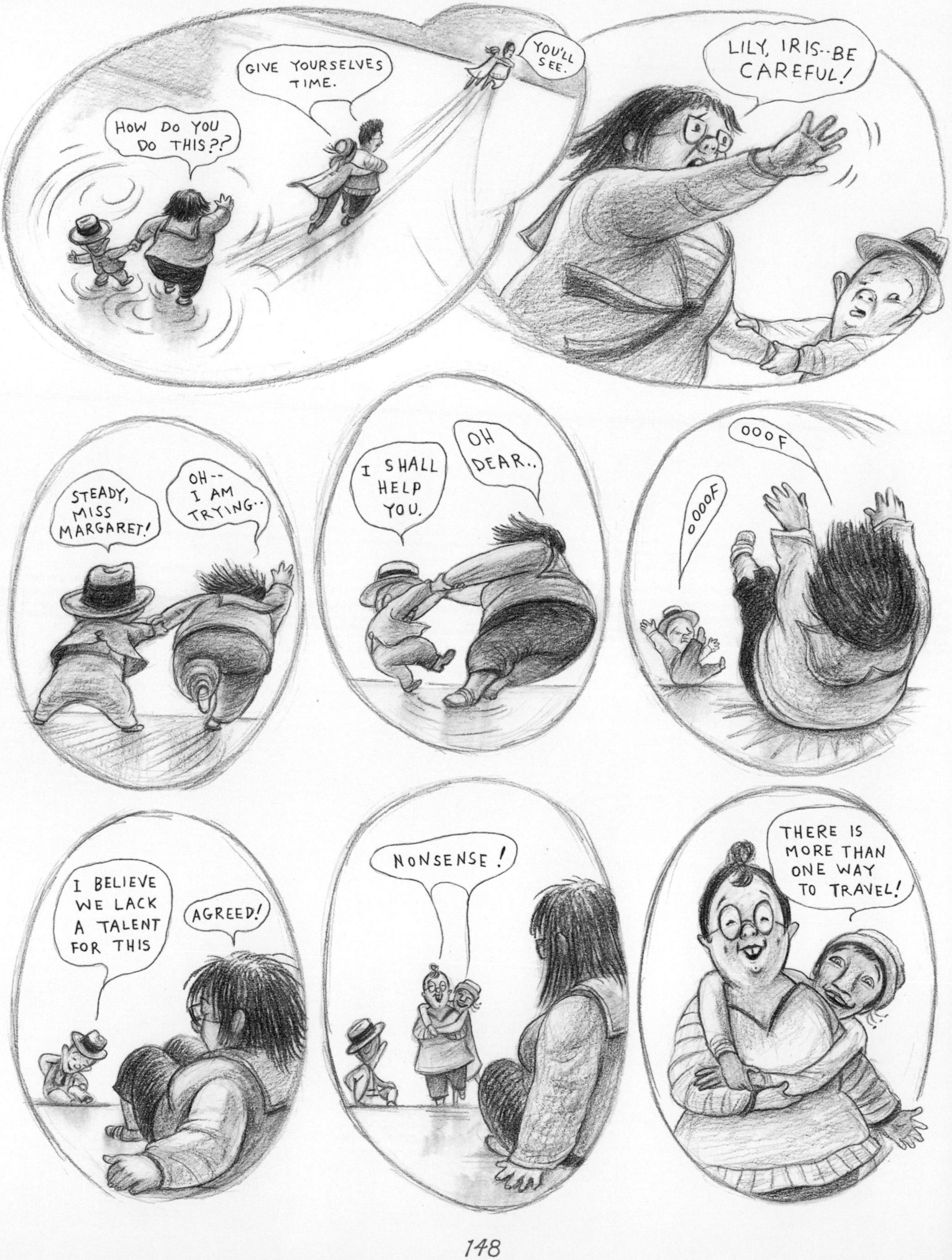
HOW DO YOU DO THIS??
GIVE YOURSELVES TIME.
YOU'LL SEE.
LILY, IRIS--BE CAREFUL!
STEADY, MISS MARGARET!
OH-- I AM TRYING..
I SHALL HELP YOU.
OH DEAR..
OOOF
OOOOF
I BELIEVE WE LACK A TALENT FOR THIS
AGREED!
NONSENSE!
THERE IS MORE THAN ONE WAY TO TRAVEL!

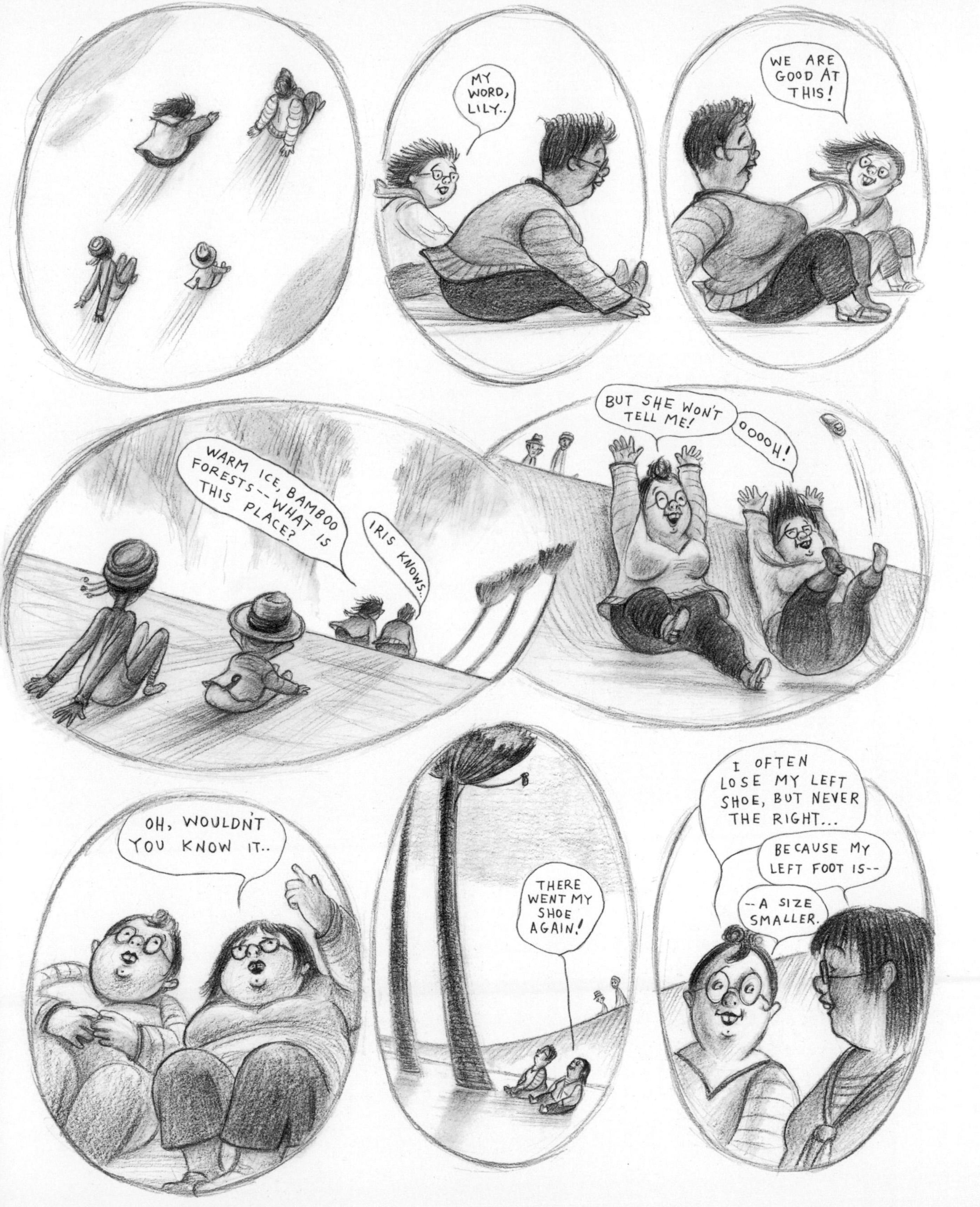
MY WORD, LILY..
WE ARE GOOD AT THIS!
WARM ICE, BAMBOO FORESTS--WHAT IS THIS PLACE?
IRIS KNOWS.
BUT SHE WON'T TELL ME!
OOOOH!
OH, WOULDN'T YOU KNOW IT..
THERE WENT MY SHOE AGAIN!
I OFTEN LOSE MY LEFT SHOE, BUT NEVER THE RIGHT...
BECAUSE MY LEFT FOOT IS--
--A SIZE SMALLER.

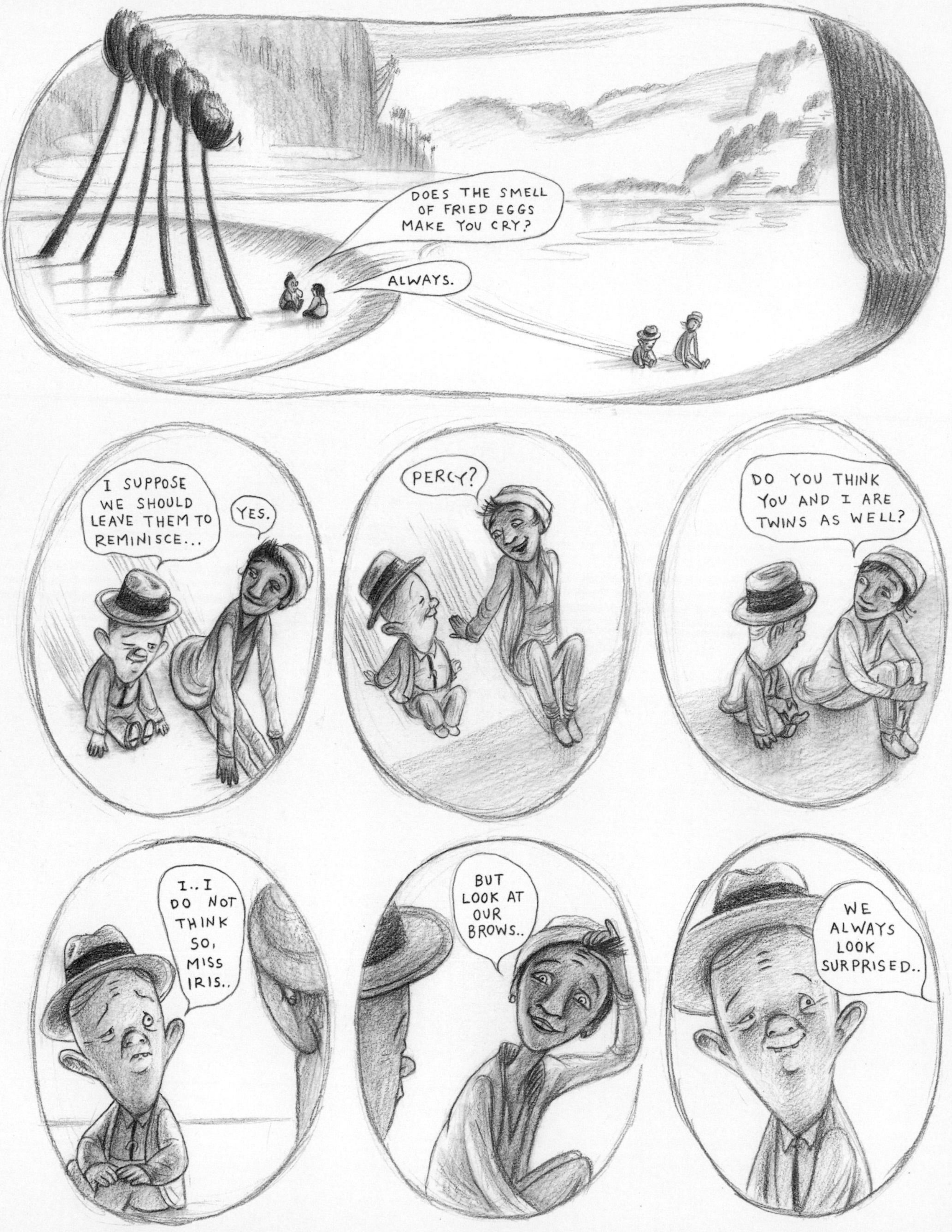
DOES THE SMELL OF FRIED EGGS MAKE YOU CRY?
ALWAYS.
I SUPPOSE WE SHOULD LEAVE THEM TO REMINISCE...
YES.
PERCY?
DO YOU THINK YOU AND I ARE TWINS AS WELL?
I.. I DO NOT THINK SO, MISS IRIS..
BUT LOOK AT OUR BROWS..
WE ALWAYS LOOK SURPRISED..

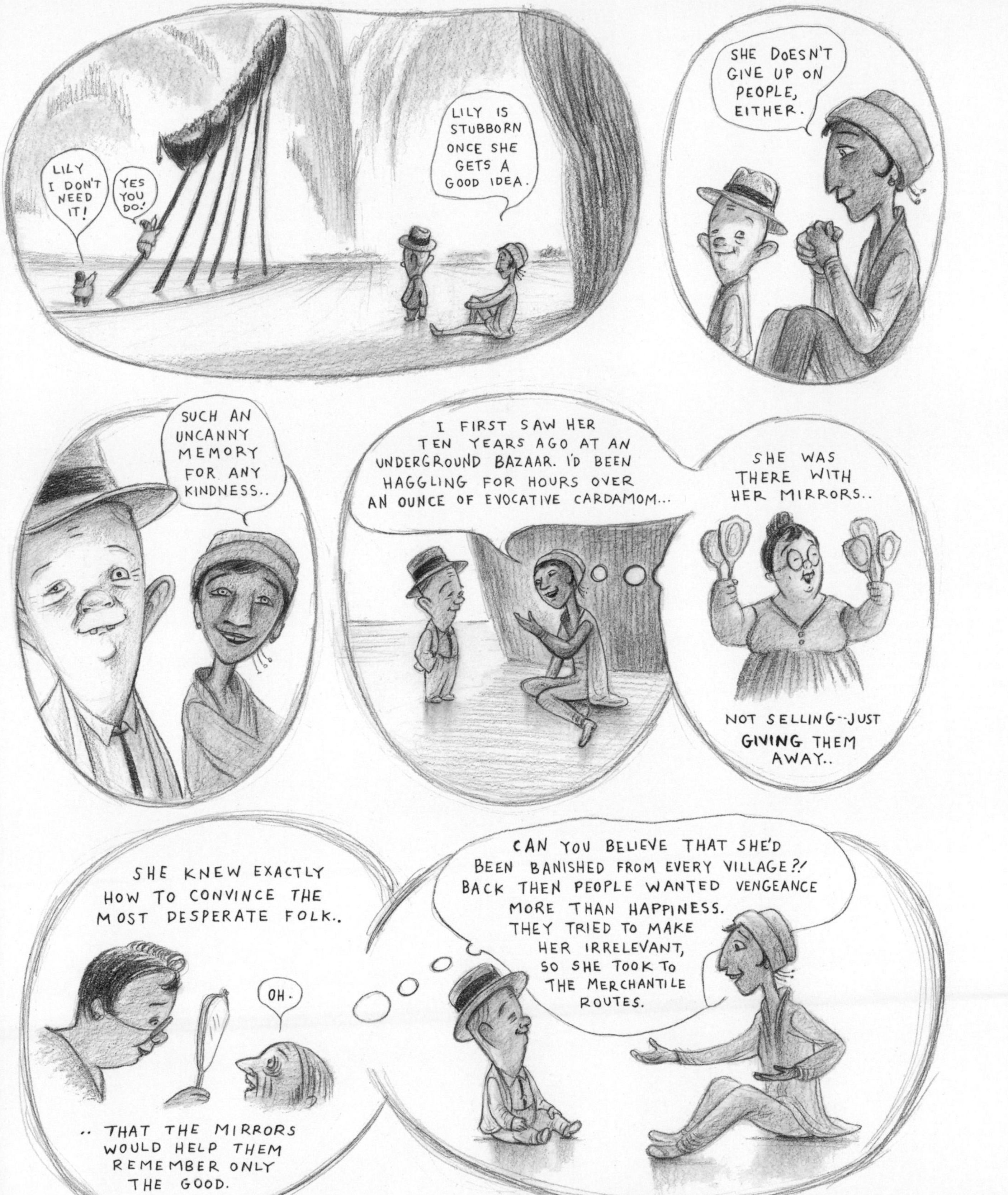
LILY I DON'T NEED IT!
YES YOU DO!
LILY IS STUBBORN ONCE SHE GETS A GOOD IDEA.
SHE DOESN'T GIVE UP ON PEOPLE, EITHER.
SUCH AN UNCANNY MEMORY FOR ANY KINDNESS..
I FIRST SAW HER TEN YEARS AGO AT AN UNDERGROUND BAZAAR. I'D BEEN HAGGLING FOR HOURS OVER AN OUNCE OF EVOCATIVE CARDAMOM...
SHE WAS THERE WITH HER MIRRORS..
NOT SELLING--JUST **GIVING** THEM AWAY..
SHE KNEW EXACTLY HOW TO CONVINCE THE MOST DESPERATE FOLK..
OH.
.. THAT THE MIRRORS WOULD HELP THEM REMEMBER ONLY THE GOOD.
CAN YOU BELIEVE THAT SHE'D BEEN BANISHED FROM EVERY VILLAGE?! BACK THEN PEOPLE WANTED VENGEANCE MORE THAN HAPPINESS. THEY TRIED TO MAKE HER IRRELEVANT, SO SHE TOOK TO THE MERCHANTILE ROUTES.

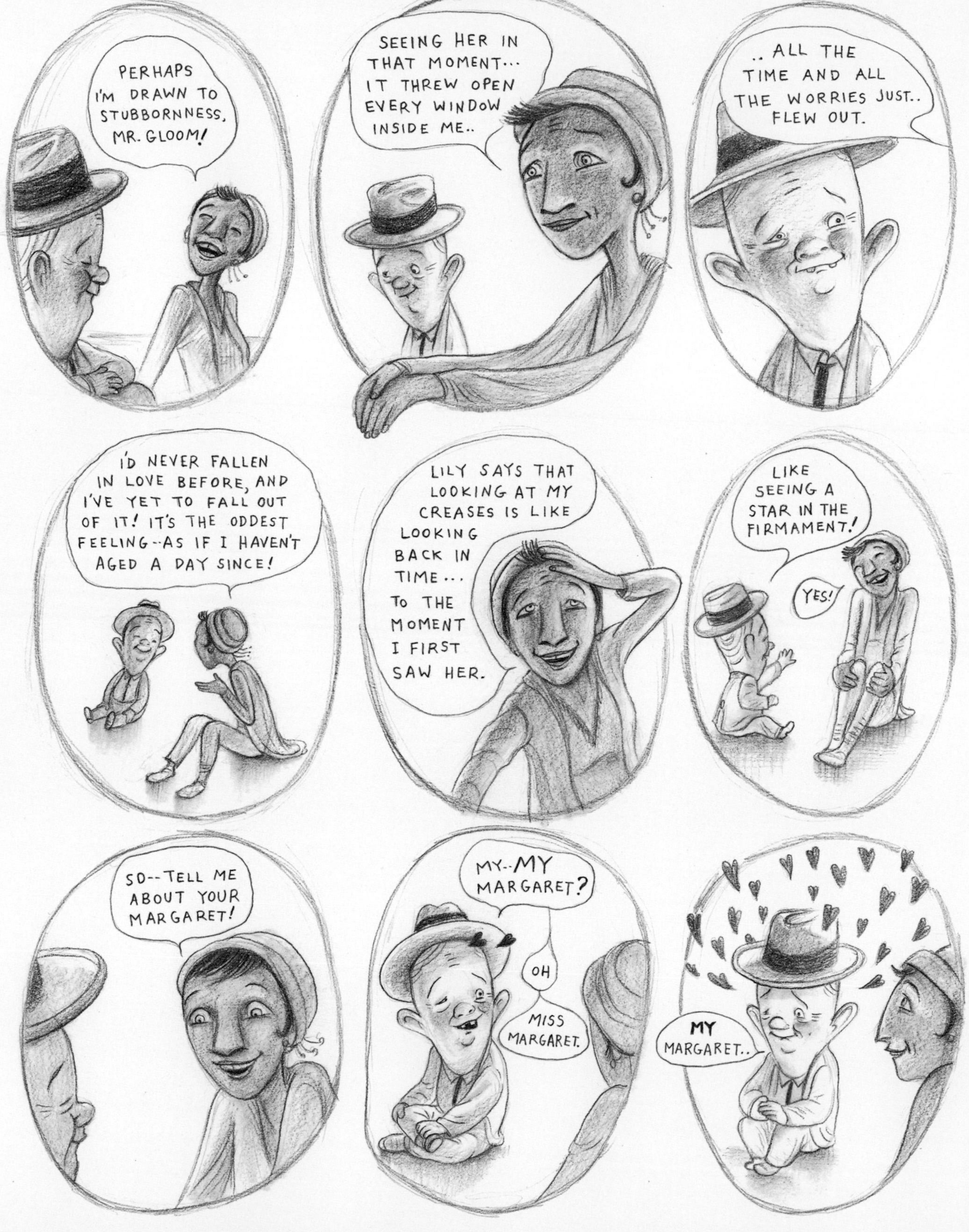
PERHAPS I'M DRAWN TO STUBBORNNESS, MR. GLOOM!
SEEING HER IN THAT MOMENT... IT THREW OPEN EVERY WINDOW INSIDE ME..
.. ALL THE TIME AND ALL THE WORRIES JUST.. FLEW OUT.
I'D NEVER FALLEN IN LOVE BEFORE, AND I'VE YET TO FALL OUT OF IT! IT'S THE ODDEST FEELING--AS IF I HAVEN'T AGED A DAY SINCE!
LILY SAYS THAT LOOKING AT MY CREASES IS LIKE LOOKING BACK IN TIME... TO THE MOMENT I FIRST SAW HER.
LIKE SEEING A STAR IN THE FIRMAMENT!
YES!
SO--TELL ME ABOUT YOUR MARGARET!
MY--MY MARGARET?
OH
MISS MARGARET.
MY MARGARET..

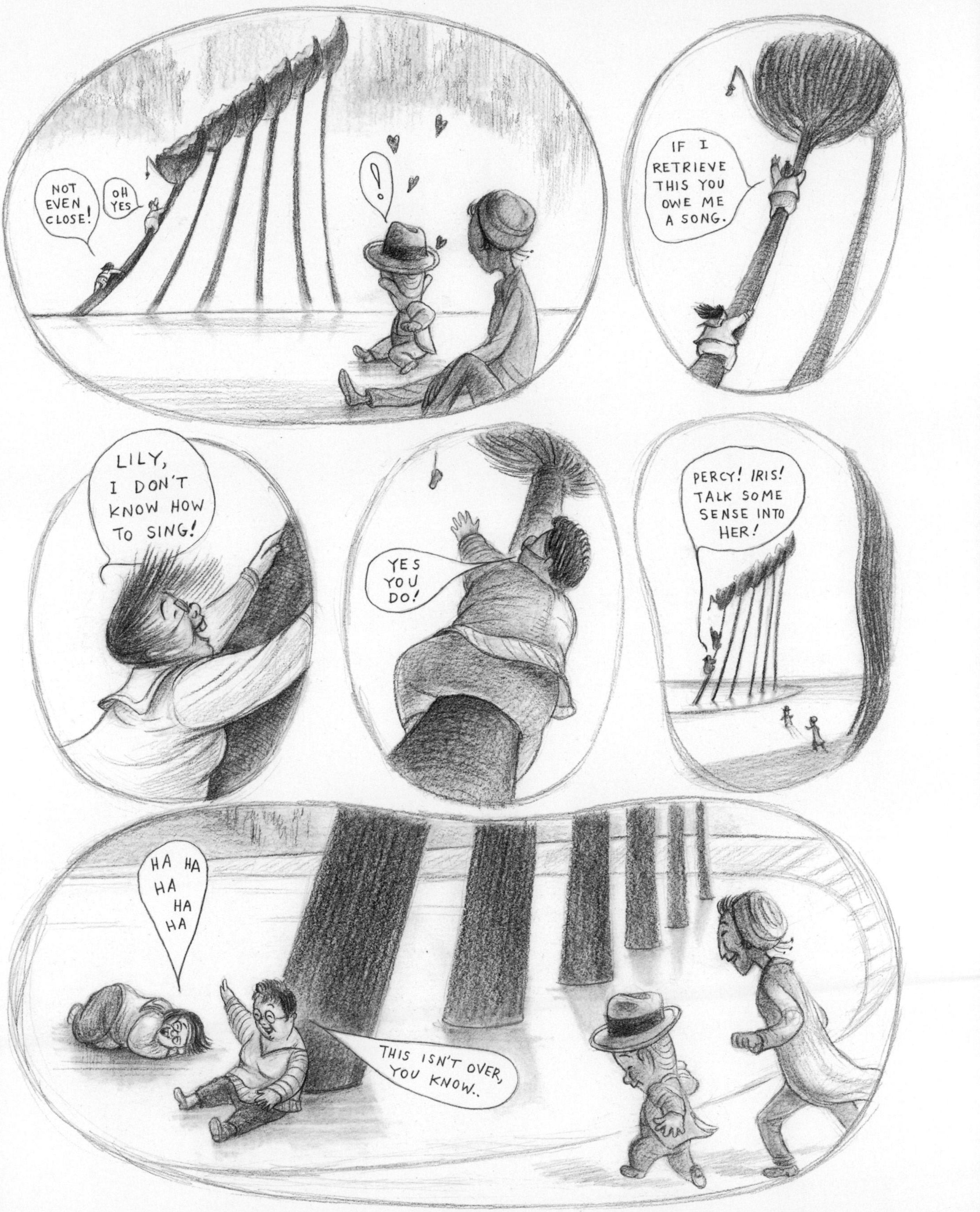
NOT EVEN CLOSE!
OH YES
!
IF I RETRIEVE THIS YOU OWE ME A SONG.
LILY, I DON'T KNOW HOW TO SING!
YES YOU DO!
PERCY! IRIS! TALK SOME SENSE INTO HER!
HA HA HA HA HA
THIS ISN'T OVER, YOU KNOW..

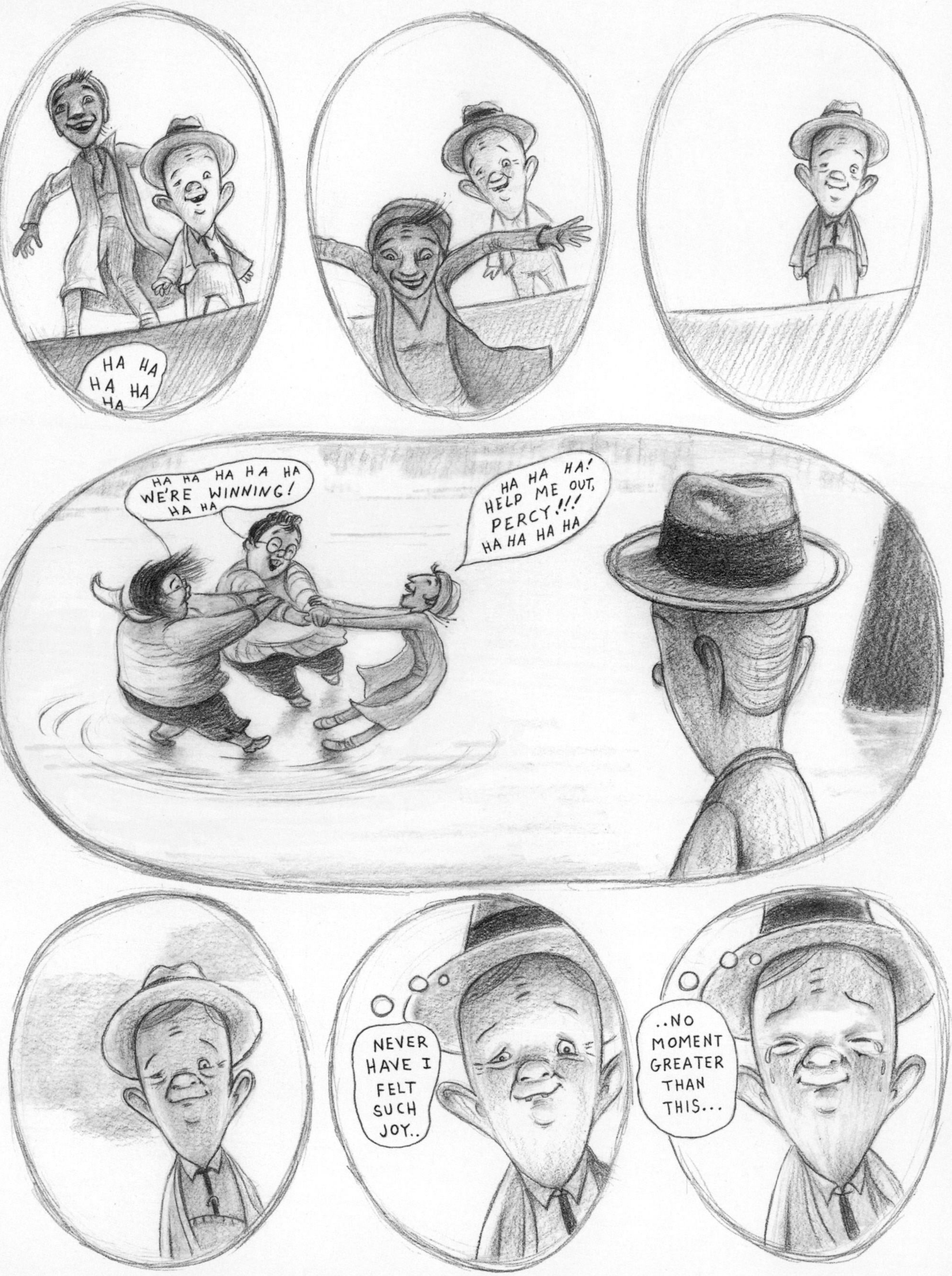
HA HA
HA HA
HA
HA HA HA HA HA
WE'RE WINNING!
HA HA
HA HA HA!
HELP ME OUT,
PERCY!!!
HA HA HA HA
NEVER HAVE I FELT SUCH JOY..
..NO MOMENT GREATER THAN THIS...

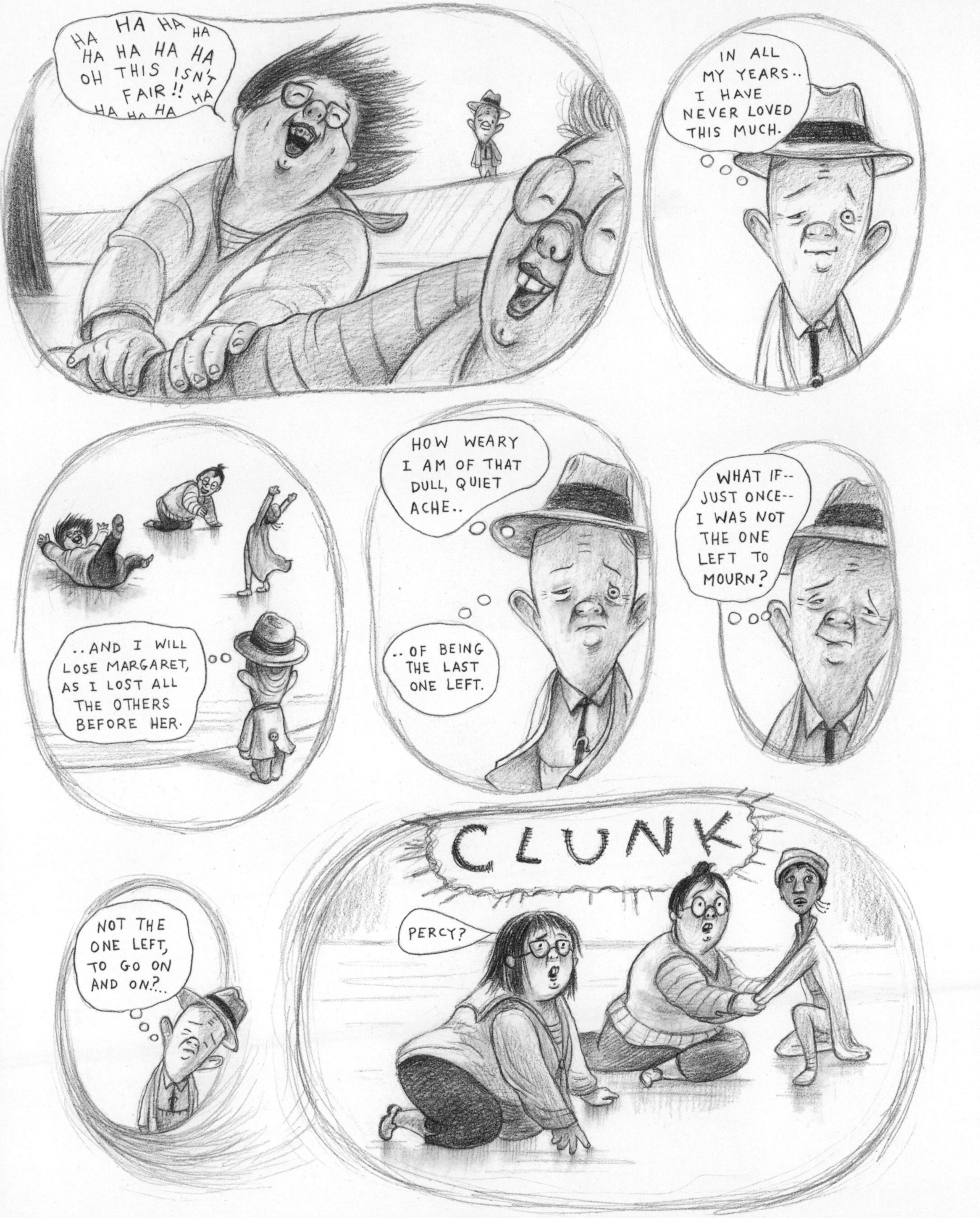
HA HA HA HA HA HA HA HA OH THIS ISN'T FAIR!! HA HA HA HA
IN ALL MY YEARS.. I HAVE NEVER LOVED THIS MUCH.
..AND I WILL LOSE MARGARET, AS I LOST ALL THE OTHERS BEFORE HER.
HOW WEARY I AM OF THAT DULL, QUIET ACHE..
..OF BEING THE LAST ONE LEFT.
WHAT IF-- JUST ONCE-- I WAS NOT THE ONE LEFT TO MOURN?
NOT THE ONE LEFT, TO GO ON AND ON?...
CLUNK
PERCY?

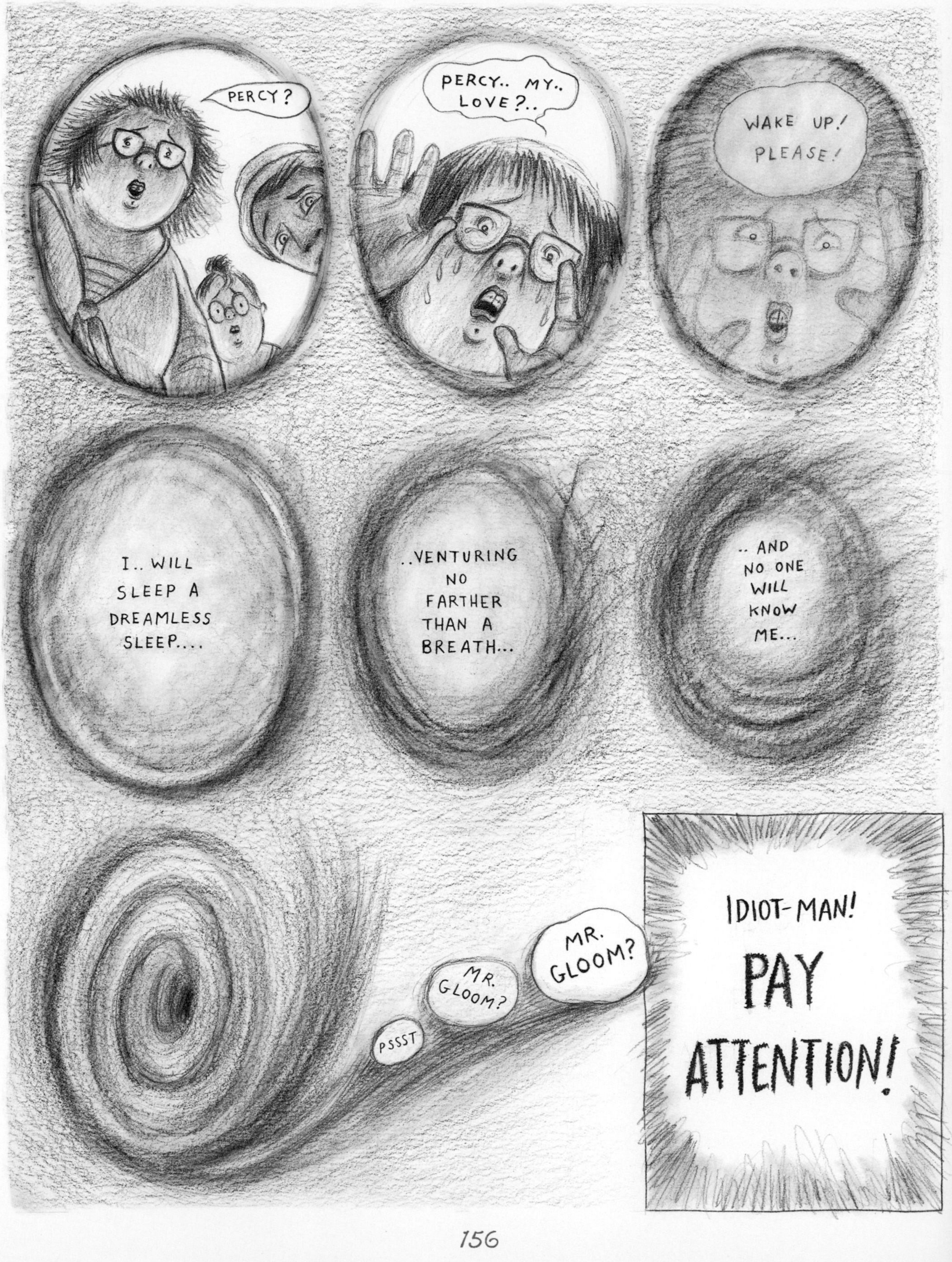
PERCY?
PERCY.. MY.. LOVE?..
WAKE UP! PLEASE!
I.. WILL SLEEP A DREAMLESS SLEEP....
..VENTURING NO FARTHER THAN A BREATH...
.. AND NO ONE WILL KNOW ME...
PSSST
MR. GLOOM?
MR. GLOOM?
IDIOT-MAN! PAY ATTENTION!

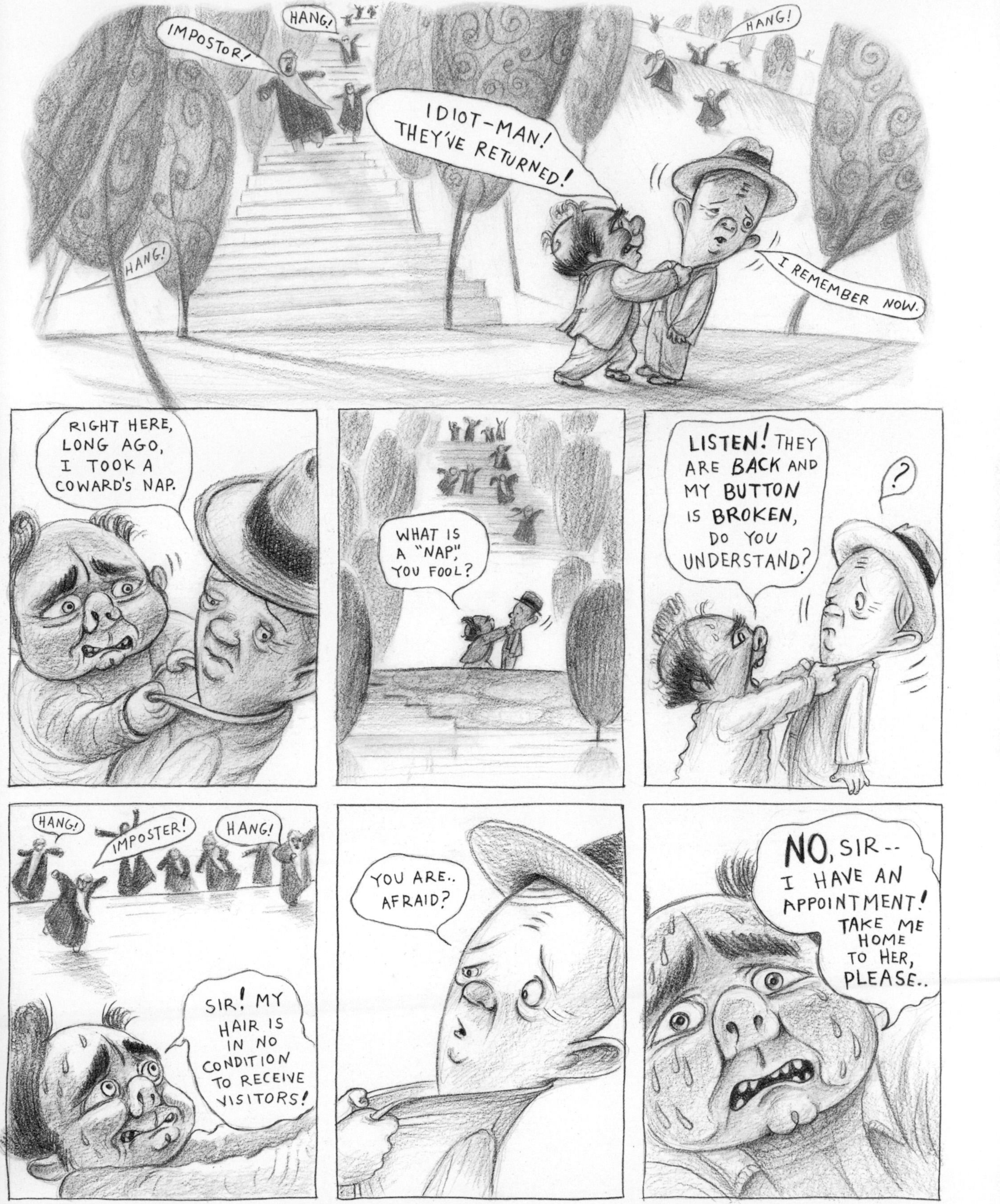
HANG!
IMPOSTOR!
HANG!
HANG!
IDIOT-MAN! THEY'VE RETURNED!
I REMEMBER NOW.
RIGHT HERE, LONG AGO, I TOOK A COWARD'S NAP.
WHAT IS A "NAP," YOU FOOL?
LISTEN! THEY ARE BACK AND MY BUTTON IS BROKEN, DO YOU UNDERSTAND?
?
HANG!
IMPOSTER!
HANG!
SIR! MY HAIR IS IN NO CONDITION TO RECEIVE VISITORS!
YOU ARE.. AFRAID?
NO, SIR -- I HAVE AN APPOINTMENT! TAKE ME HOME TO HER, PLEASE..

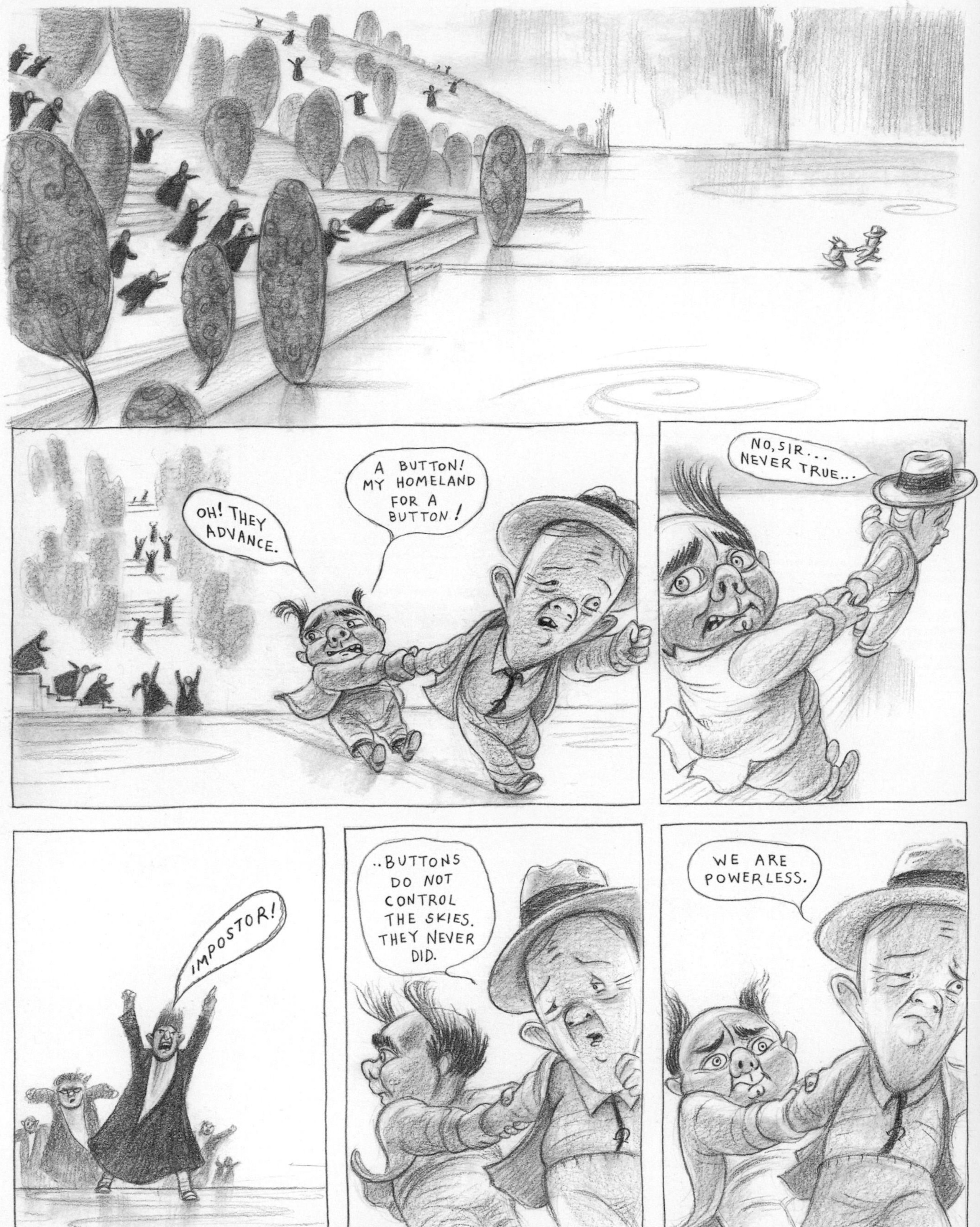
OH! THEY ADVANCE.
A BUTTON! MY HOMELAND FOR A BUTTON!
NO, SIR... NEVER TRUE...
IMPOSTOR!
..BUTTONS DO NOT CONTROL THE SKIES. THEY NEVER DID.
WE ARE POWERLESS.

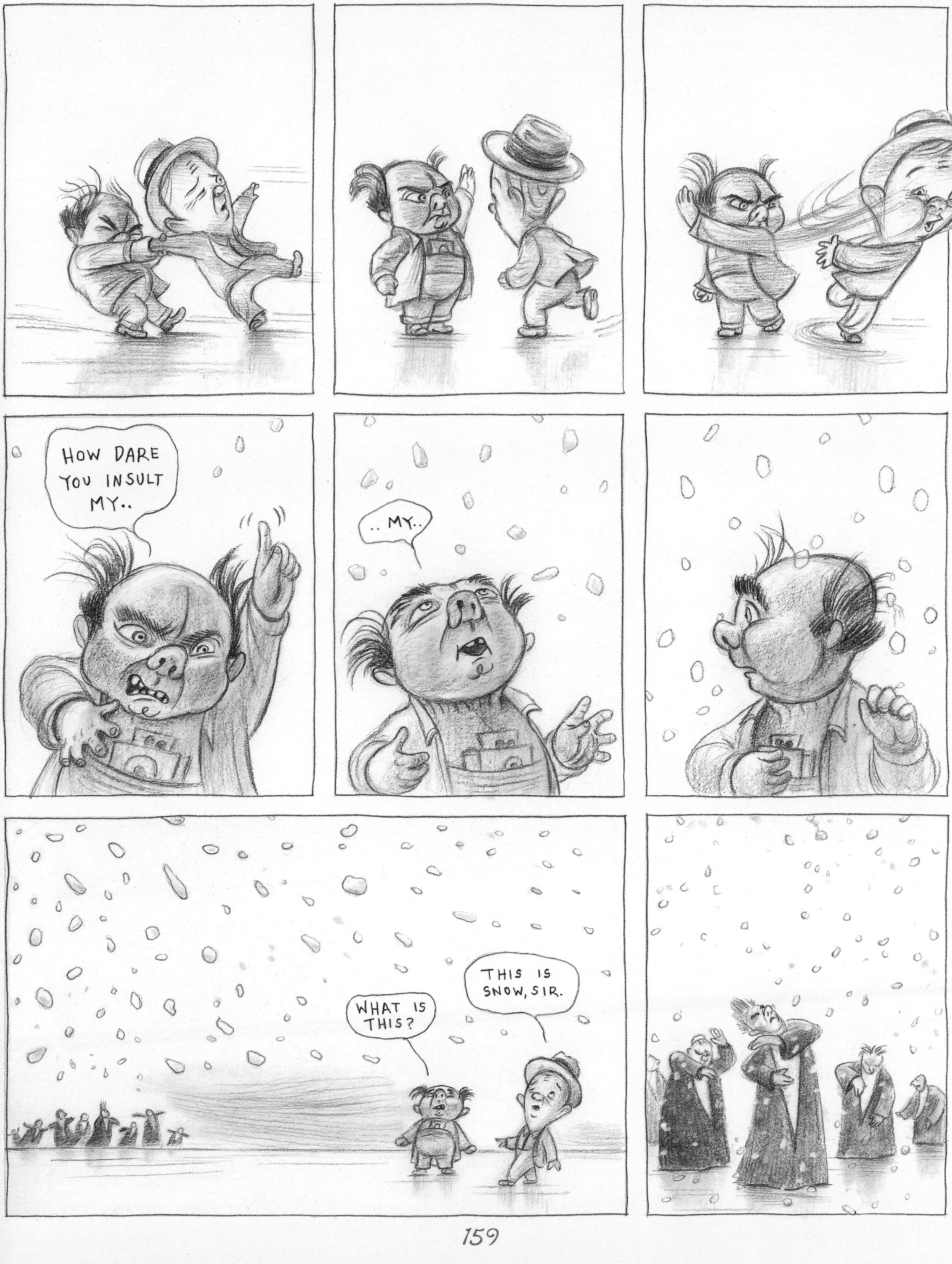
HOW DARE YOU INSULT MY..
.. MY..
WHAT IS THIS?
THIS IS SNOW, SIR.

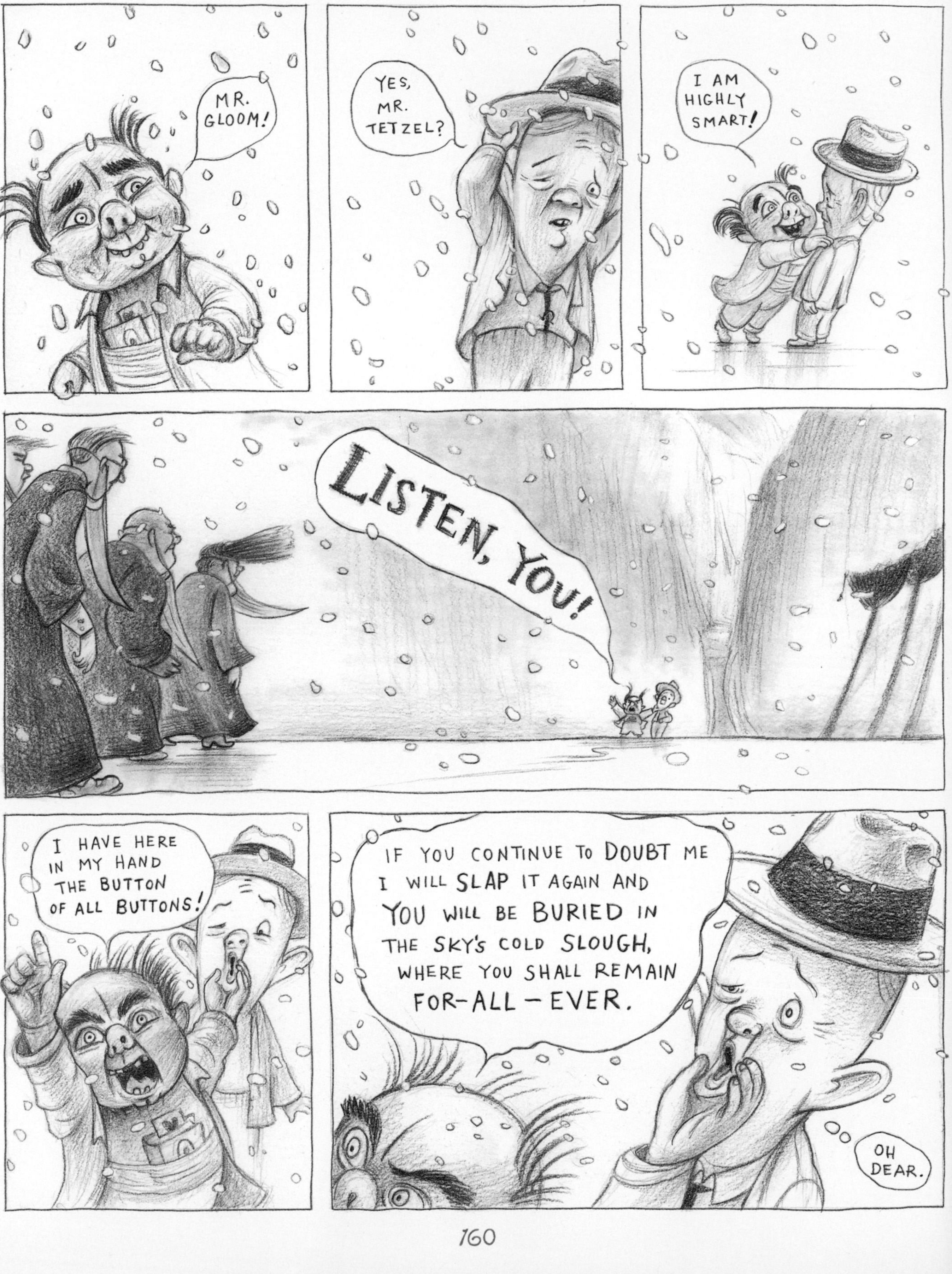
MR. GLOOM!
YES, MR. TETZEL?
I AM HIGHLY SMART!
LISTEN, YOU!
I HAVE HERE IN MY HAND THE BUTTON OF ALL BUTTONS!
IF YOU CONTINUE TO DOUBT ME I WILL SLAP IT AGAIN AND YOU WILL BE BURIED IN THE SKY'S COLD SLOUGH, WHERE YOU SHALL REMAIN FOR-ALL-EVER.
OH DEAR.

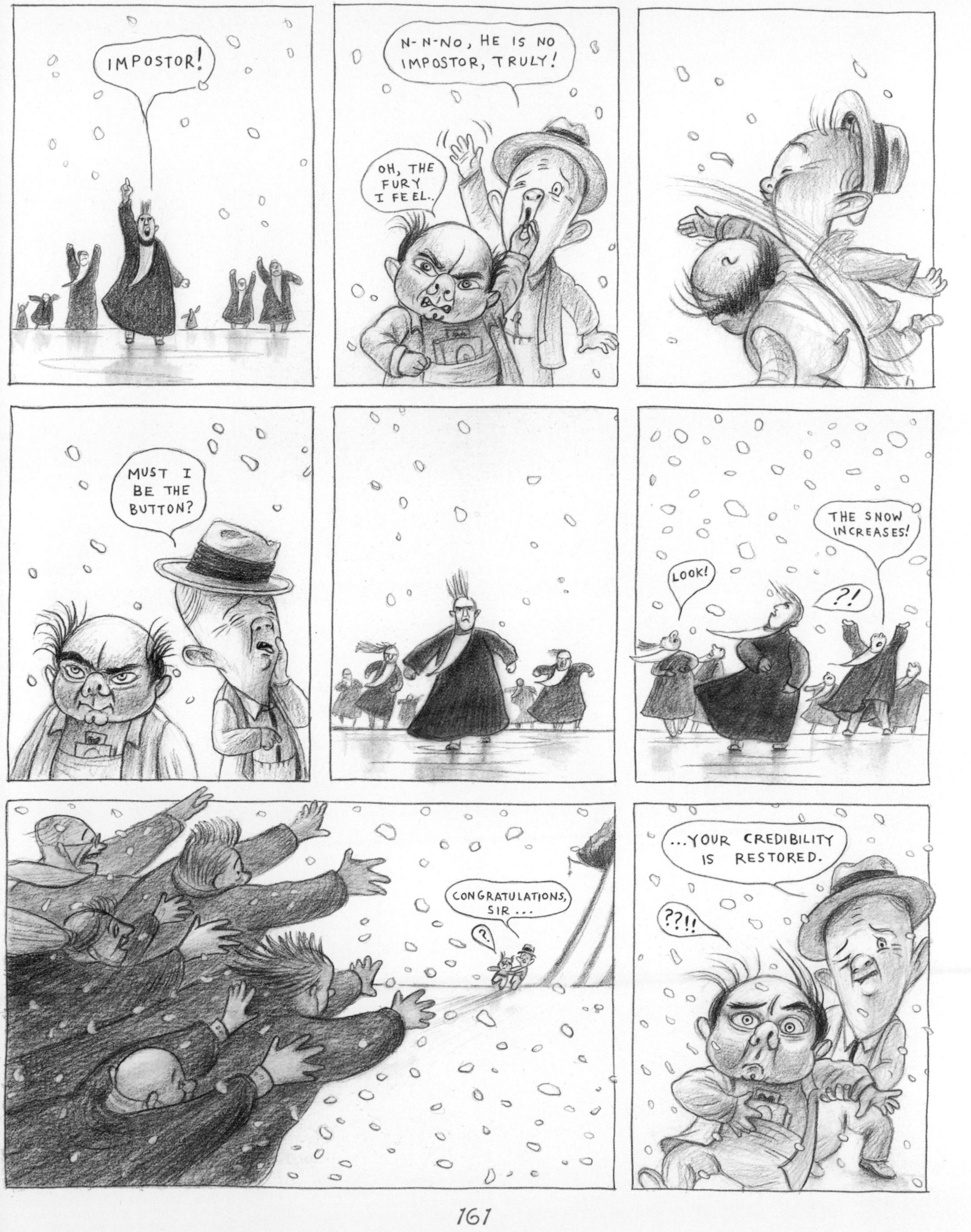
IMPOSTOR!
N-N-NO, HE IS NO IMPOSTOR, TRULY!
OH, THE FURY I FEEL..
MUST I BE THE BUTTON?
LOOK!
THE SNOW INCREASES!
?!
CONGRATULATIONS, SIR...
?
...YOUR CREDIBILITY IS RESTORED.
??!!

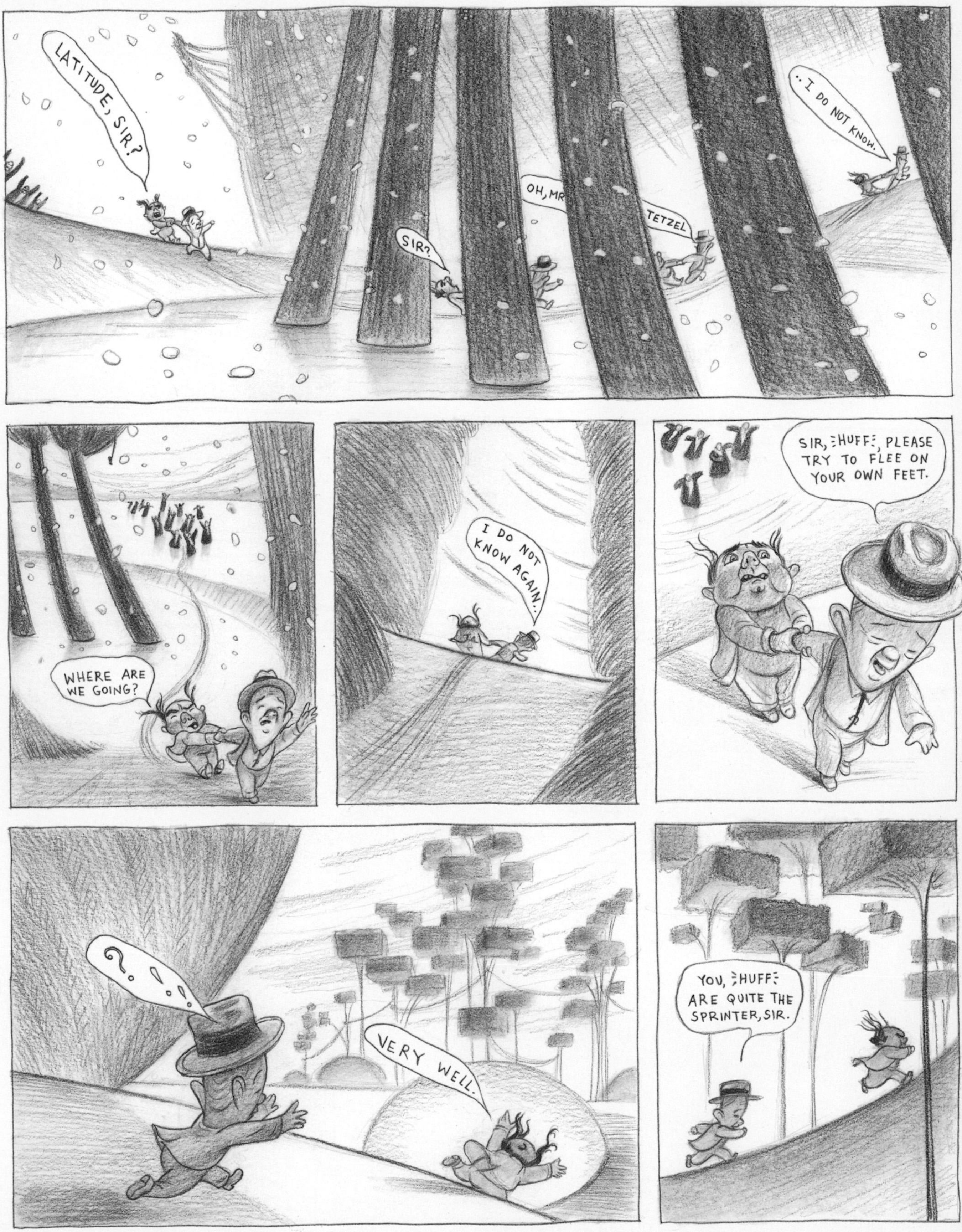
LATITUDE, SIR?
OH, MR
SIR?
TETZEL
.. I DO NOT KNOW.
WHERE ARE WE GOING?
I DO NOT KNOW AGAIN...
SIR, HUFF, PLEASE TRY TO FLEE ON YOUR OWN FEET.
?.!.!
VERY WELL.
YOU, HUFF ARE QUITE THE SPRINTER, SIR.

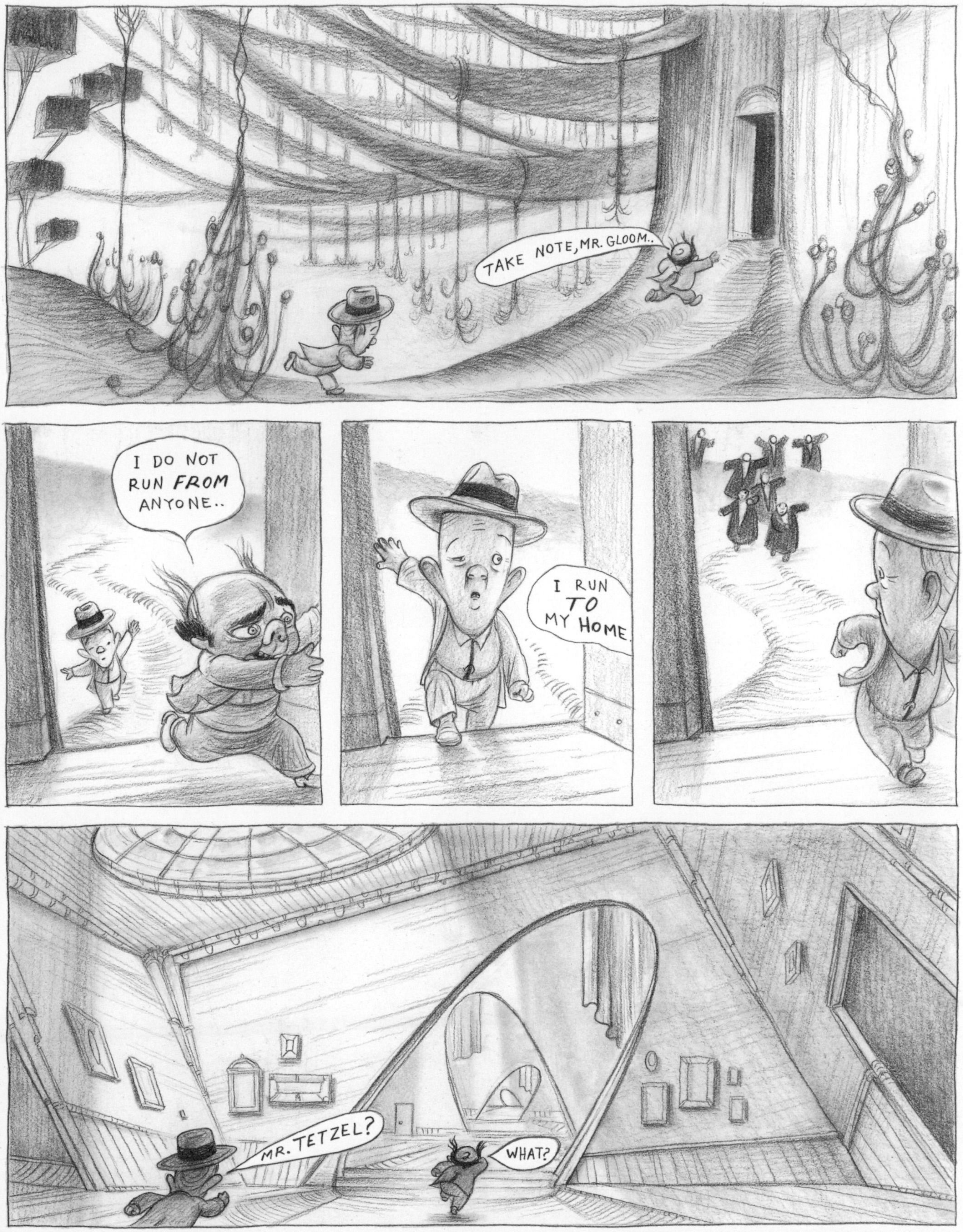
TAKE NOTE, MR. GLOOM..
I DO NOT RUN FROM ANYONE..
I RUN TO MY HOME.
MR. TETZEL?
WHAT?

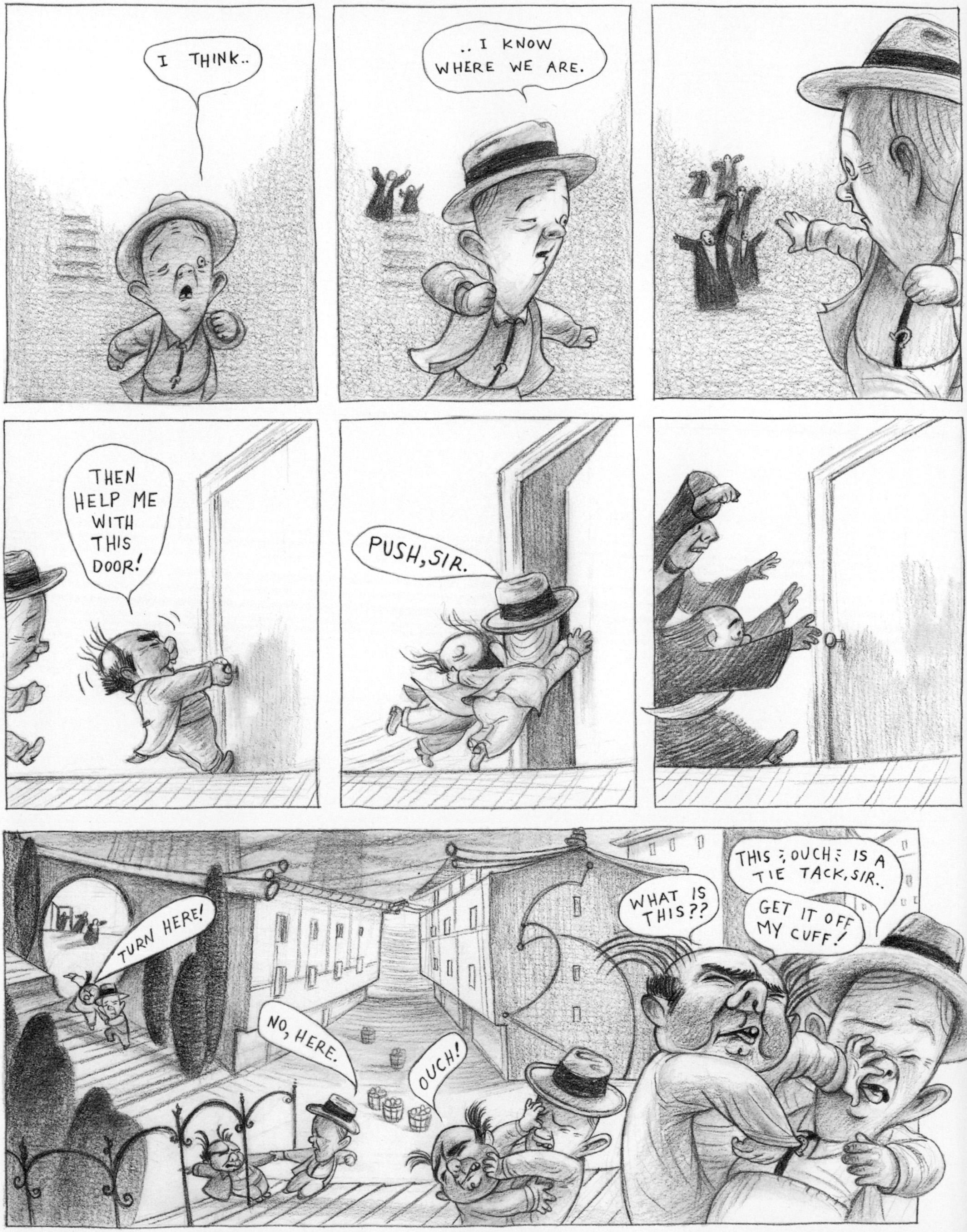
I THINK..
..I KNOW WHERE WE ARE.
THEN HELP ME WITH THIS DOOR!
PUSH, SIR.
TURN HERE!
NO, HERE.
OUCH!
WHAT IS THIS??
THIS ;OUCH; IS A TIE TACK, SIR..
GET IT OFF MY CUFF!

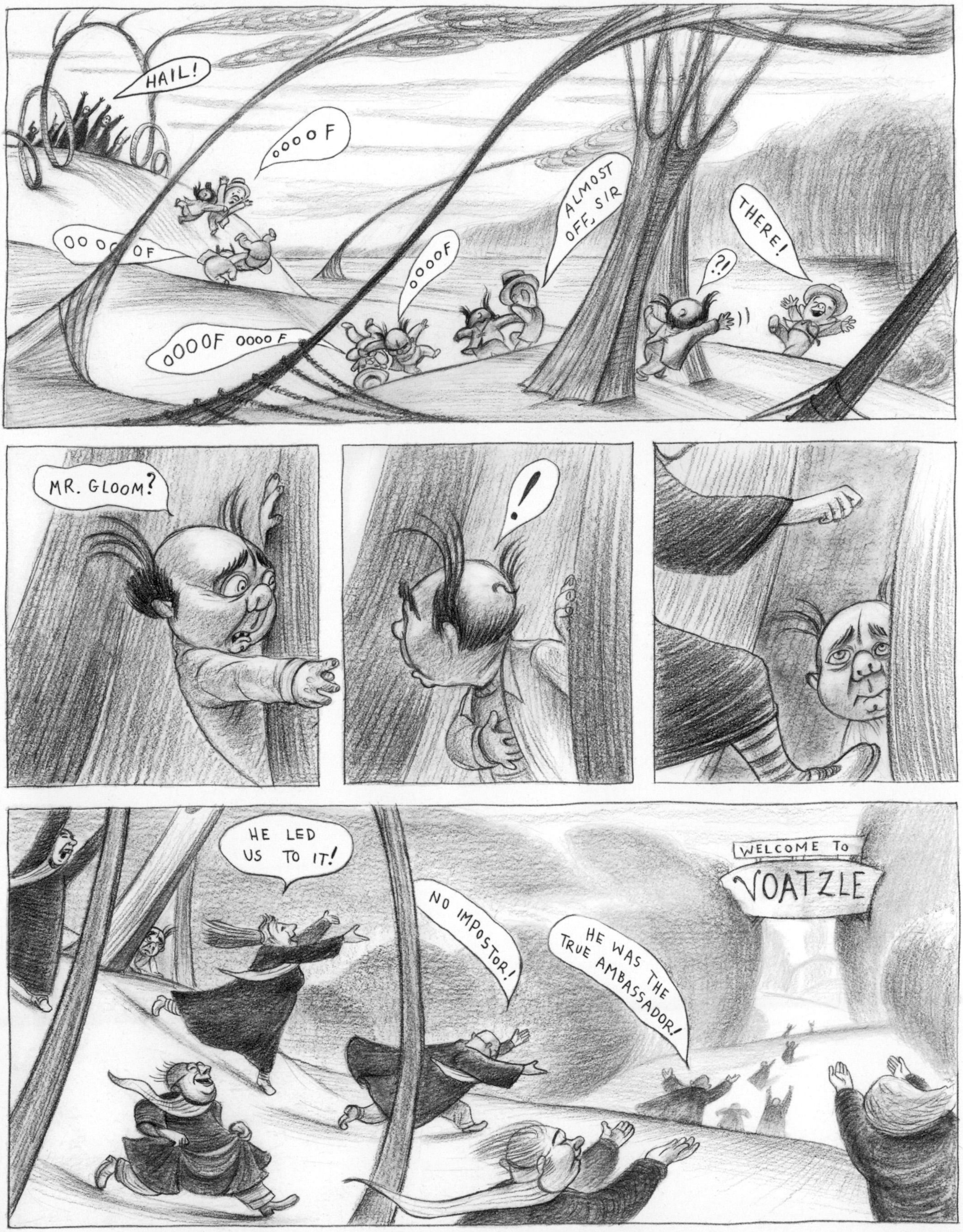
HAIL!
OOOOF
OO OOOOF
OOOOF OOOOF
OOOOF
ALMOST OFF, SIR
?!
THERE!
MR. GLOOM?
!
HE LED US TO IT!
NO IMPOSTOR!
HE WAS THE TRUE AMBASSADOR!
WELCOME TO
VOATZLE

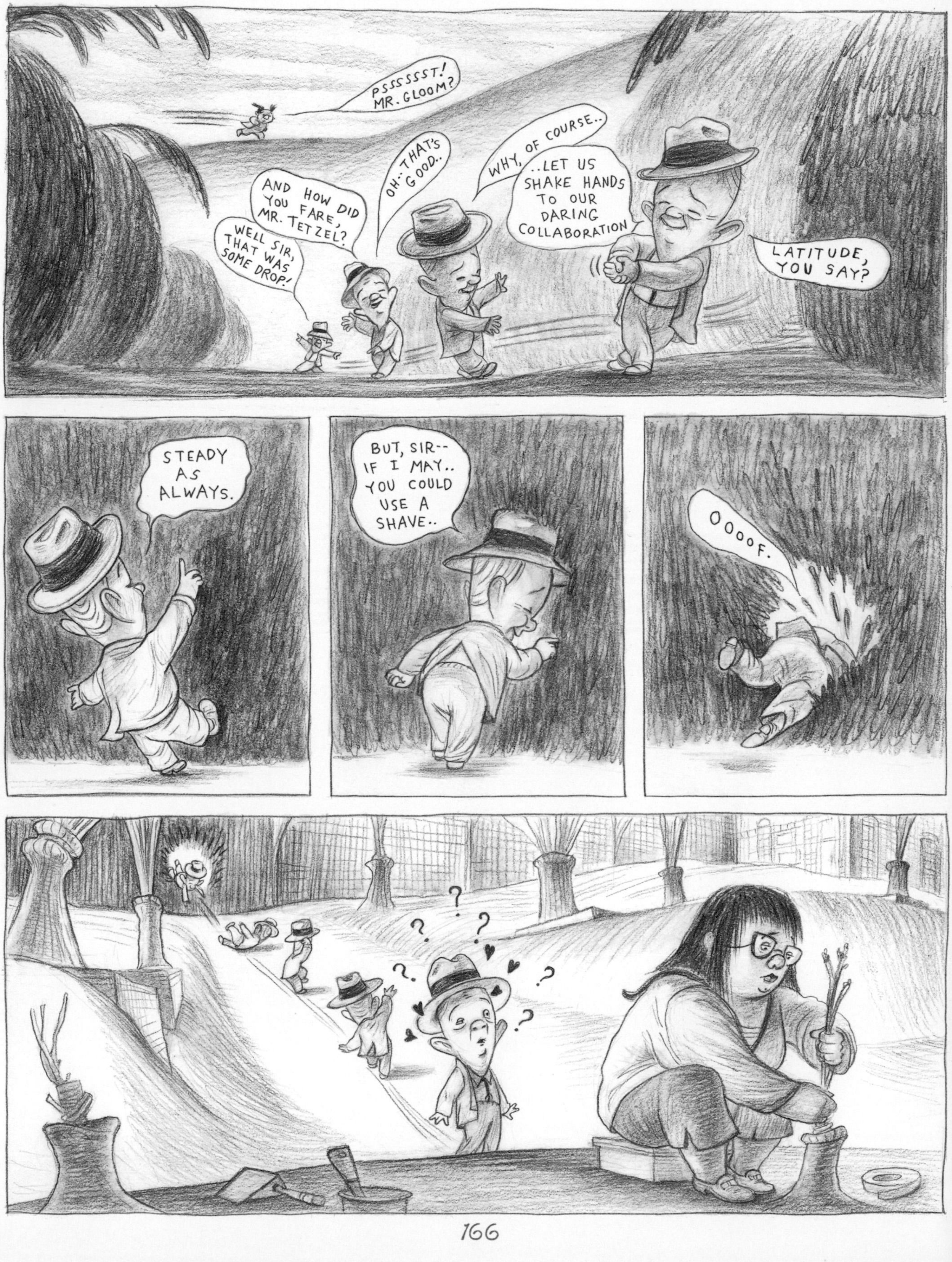
PSSSSSST! MR. GLOOM?
AND HOW DID YOU FARE, MR. TETZEL?
WELL SIR, THAT WAS SOME DROP!
OH.. THAT'S GOOD..
WHY, OF COURSE..
..LET US SHAKE HANDS TO OUR DARING COLLABORATION
LATITUDE, YOU SAY?
STEADY AS ALWAYS.
BUT, SIR-- IF I MAY.. YOU COULD USE A SHAVE..
OOOOF.

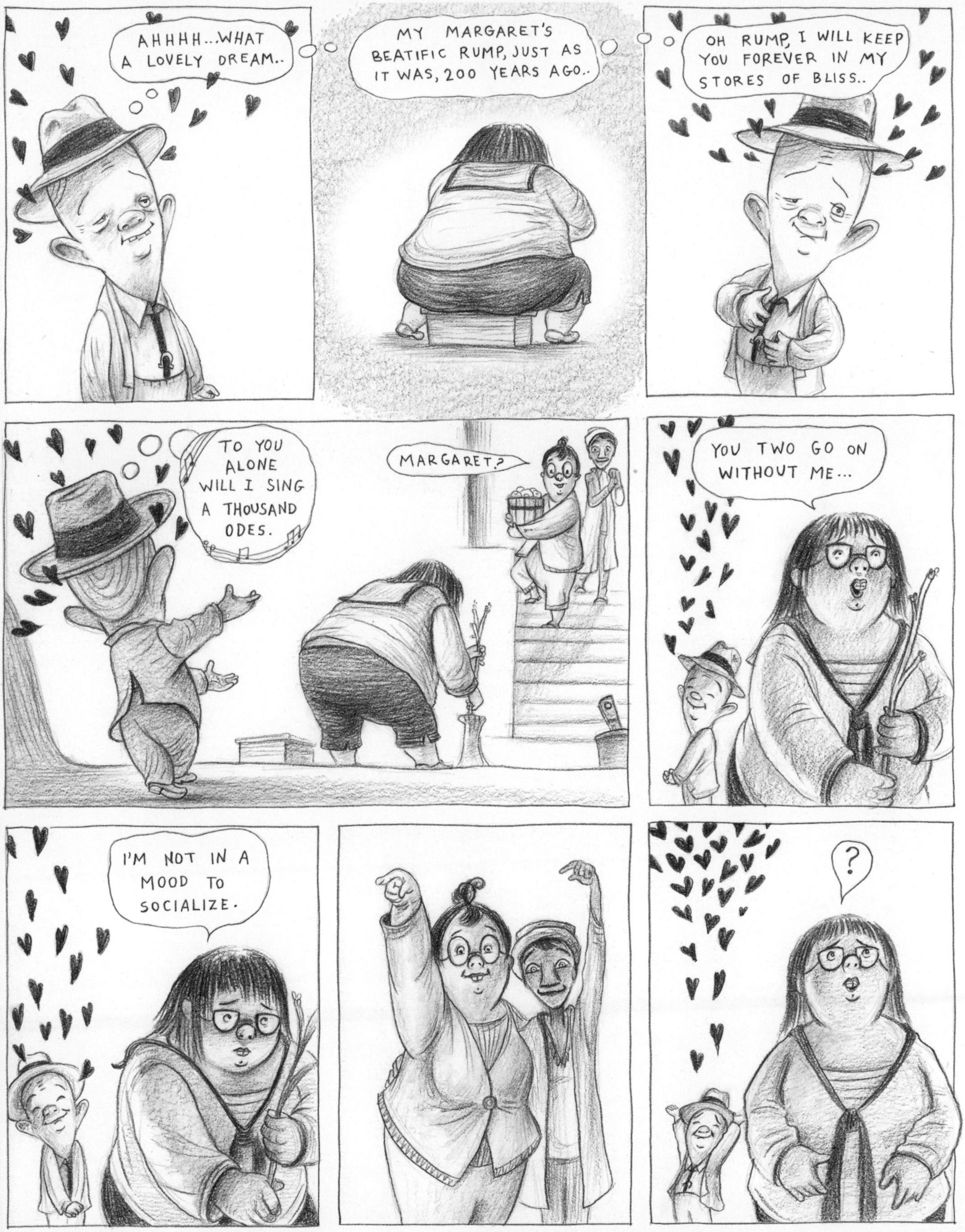
AHHHH...WHAT A LOVELY DREAM..
MY MARGARET'S BEATIFIC RUMP, JUST AS IT WAS, 200 YEARS AGO..
OH RUMP, I WILL KEEP YOU FOREVER IN MY STORES OF BLISS..
TO YOU ALONE WILL I SING A THOUSAND ODES.
MARGARET?
YOU TWO GO ON WITHOUT ME...
I'M NOT IN A MOOD TO SOCIALIZE.
?

PERCY??
PERCY!!
THE DREAM SPEAKS?
M--MARGARET?
AM--AM I AWAKE??
YES! AND DON'T EVER SLEEP AGAIN!
OH, OH..
WHAT AN UNBEARABLE YEAR IT'S BEEN!
A YEAR?
PERCY!!!
AH!

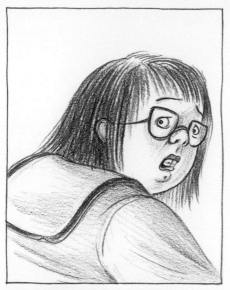

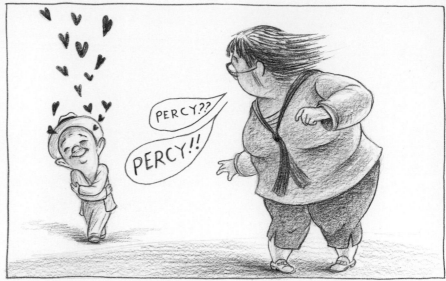

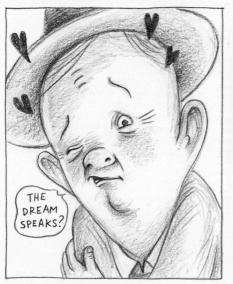

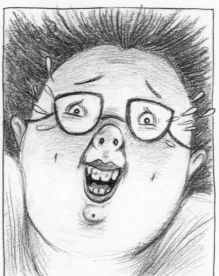

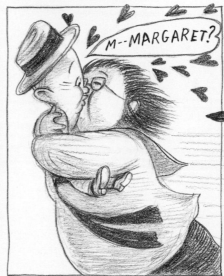

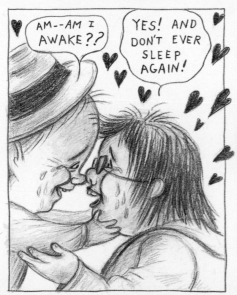

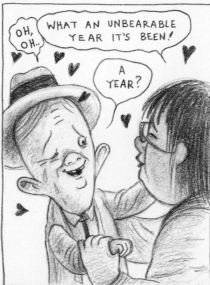

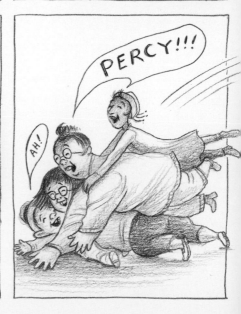

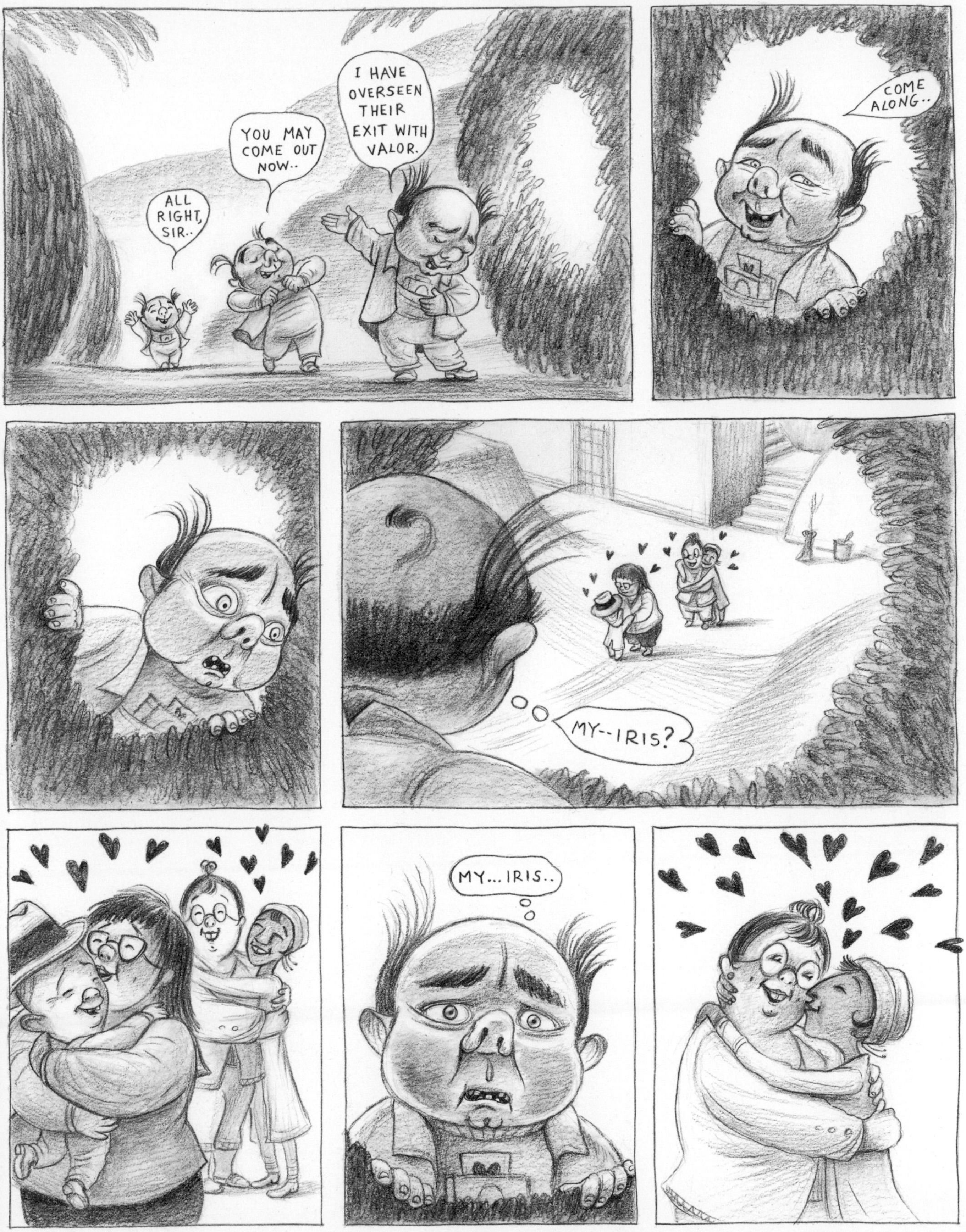
I HAVE OVERSEEN THEIR EXIT WITH VALOR.
YOU MAY COME OUT NOW..
ALL RIGHT, SIR..
COME ALONG..
MY--IRIS?
MY... IRIS..

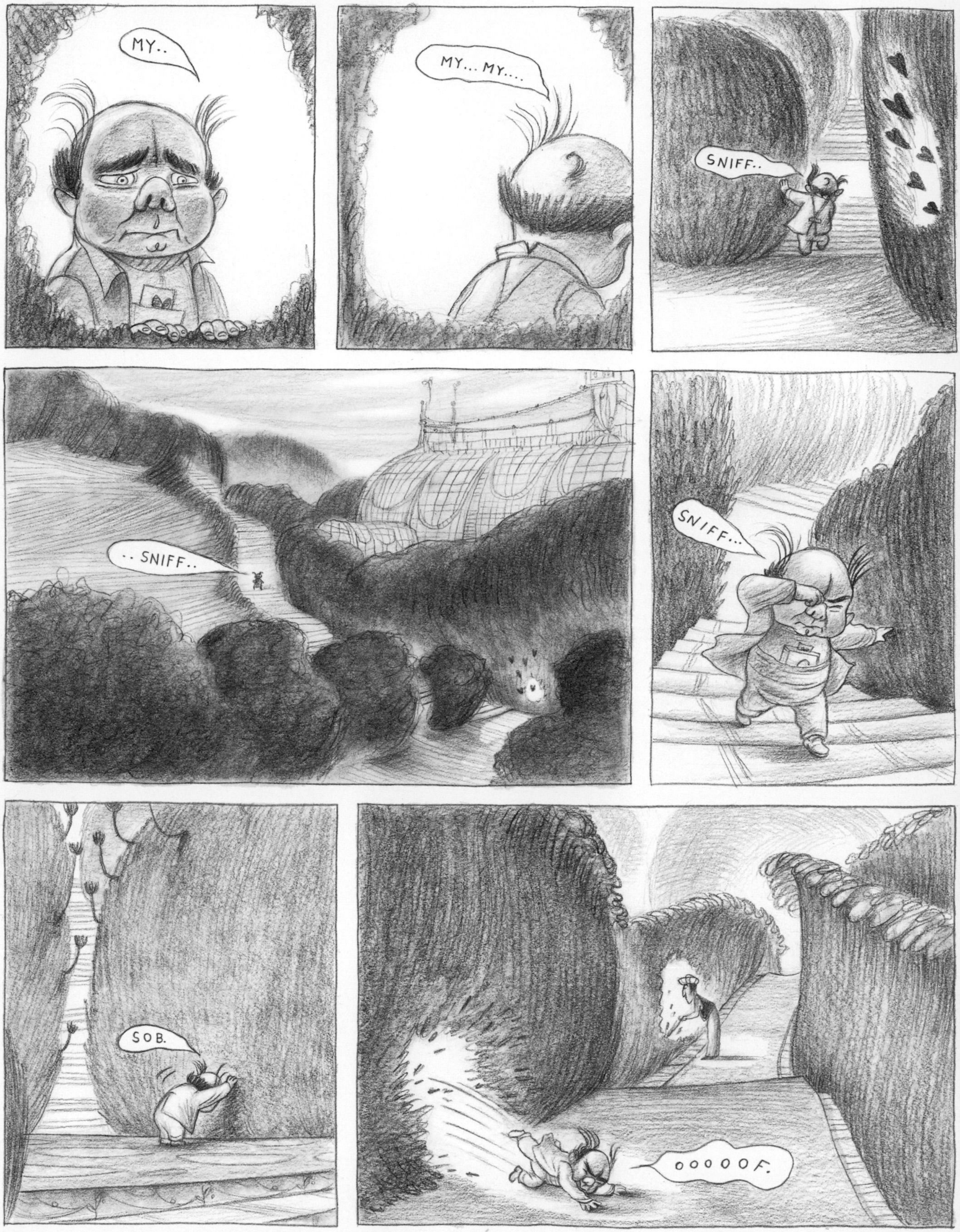
MY..
MY... MY....
SNIFF..
.. SNIFF..
SNIFF...
SOB.
OOOOOF.

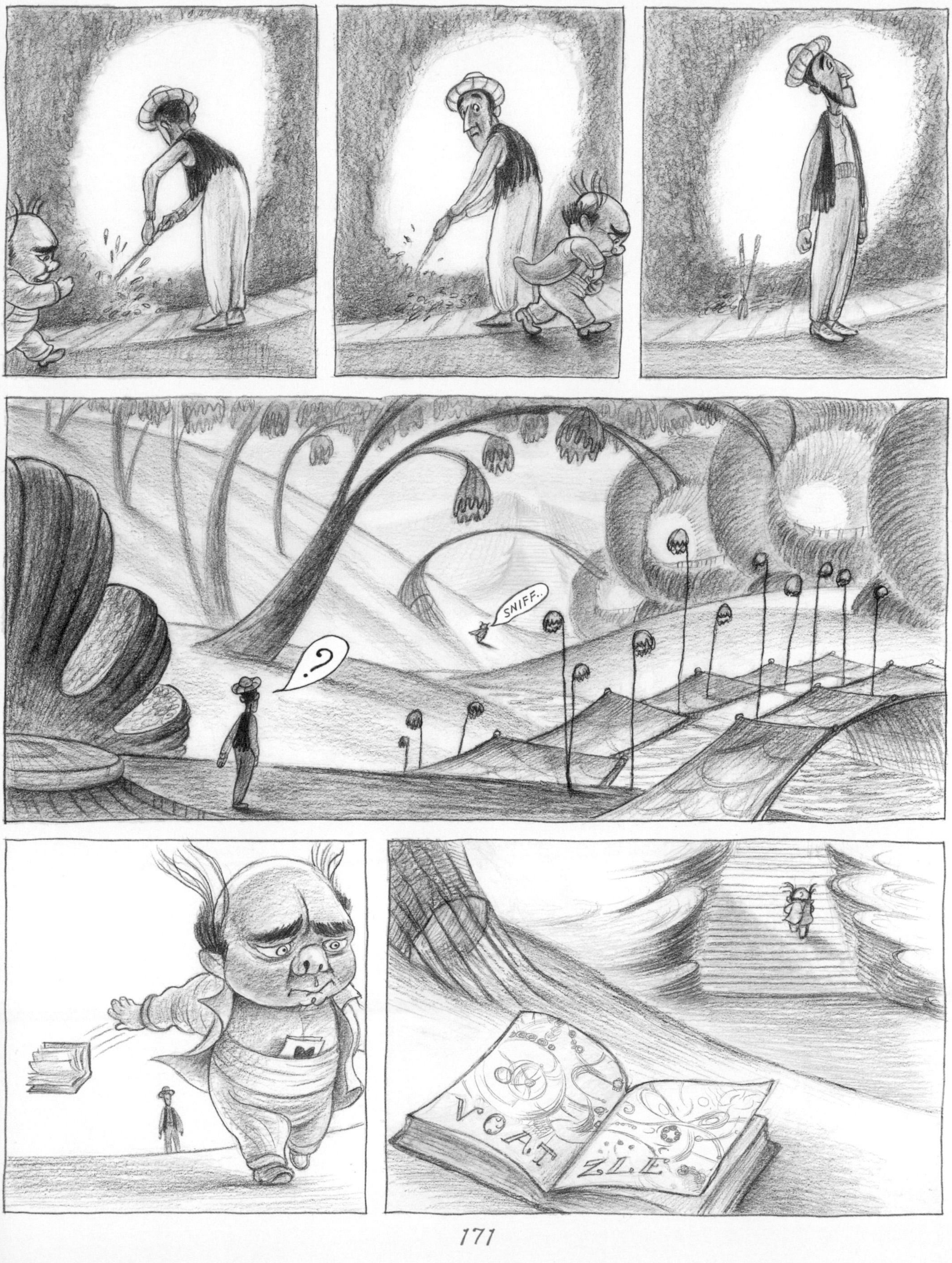
SNIFF..
?
VCAT
ZLE

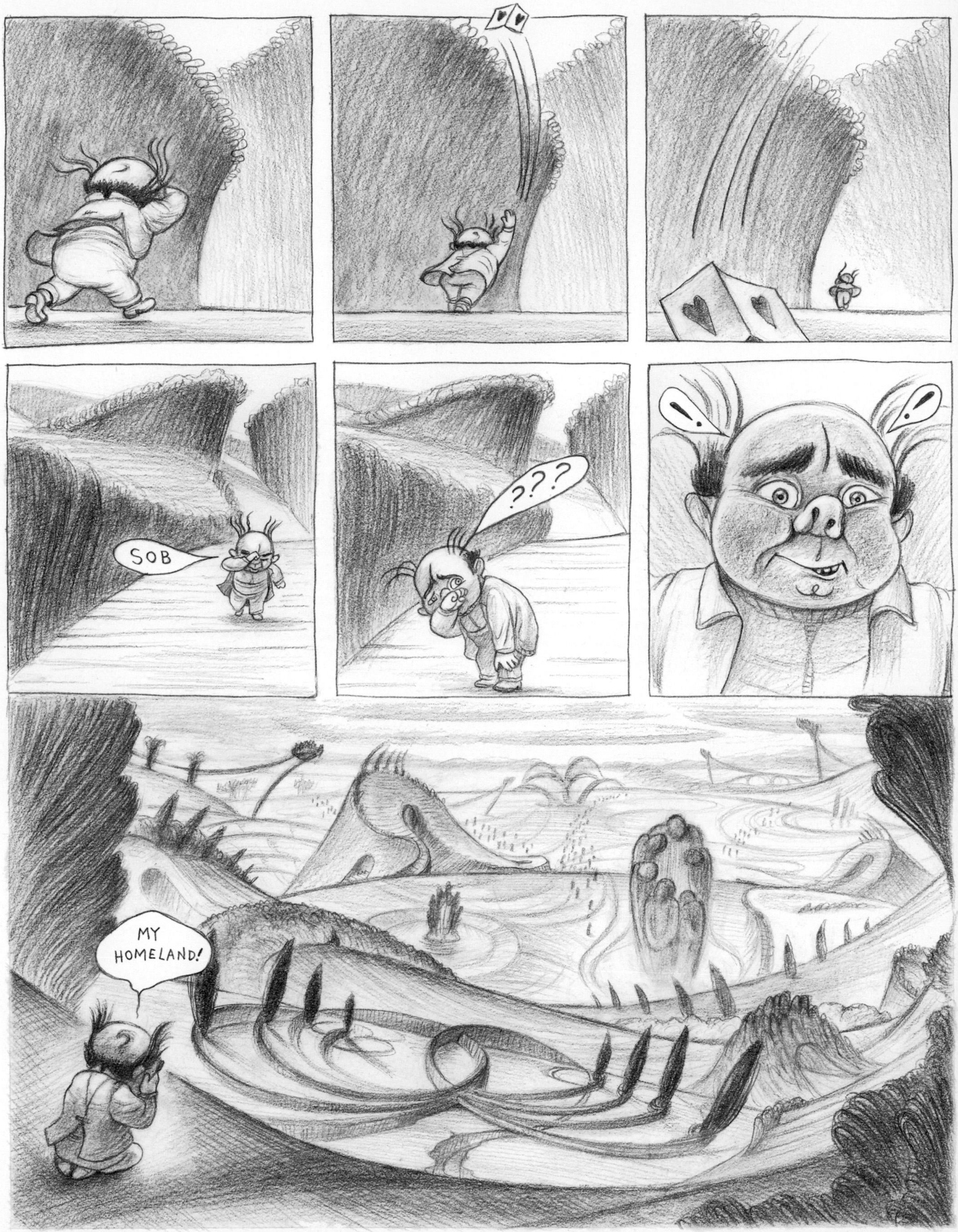
SOB
???
!
!
MY HOMELAND!

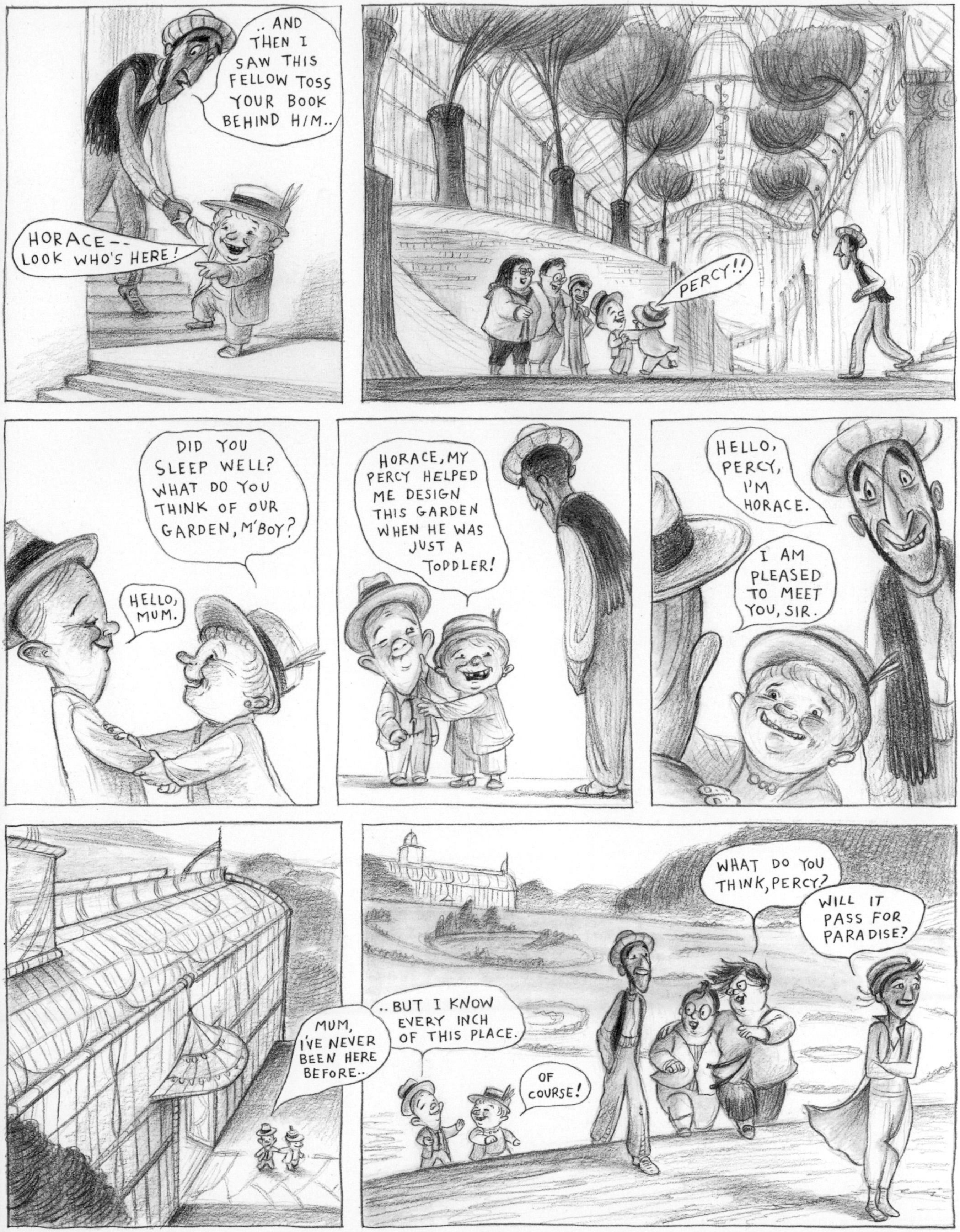
.. AND THEN I SAW THIS FELLOW TOSS YOUR BOOK BEHIND HIM..
HORACE-- LOOK WHO'S HERE!
PERCY!!
DID YOU SLEEP WELL? WHAT DO YOU THINK OF OUR GARDEN, M'BOY?
HELLO, MUM.
HORACE, MY PERCY HELPED ME DESIGN THIS GARDEN WHEN HE WAS JUST A TODDLER!
HELLO, PERCY, I'M HORACE.
I AM PLEASED TO MEET YOU, SIR.
MUM, I'VE NEVER BEEN HERE BEFORE..
.. BUT I KNOW EVERY INCH OF THIS PLACE.
OF COURSE!
WHAT DO YOU THINK, PERCY?
WILL IT PASS FOR PARADISE?

IS THIS SUPPOSED TO BE--

YES.

REMEMBER THAT BOOK YOU USED TO SCRIBBLE ON WHEN YOU WERE THREE?

OH-- THIS IS THE MAP I USED TO COLOR!

INDEED!

HARD TO BELIEVE THE BOOK IS STILL POPULAR, FOR SUCH DIFFERENT REASONS. SO-- HERE IS THEIR "VOATZLE".

AND TODAY, BY THE BOOK'S CALCULATIONS, IS WHEN IT IS SUPPOSED TO APPEAR.

MMM HMM.

I FELT OBLIGED TO GIVE THEM WHAT THEY HOPED FOR.

STILL, MUM, THEY'LL ASK QUESTIONS..

..AND DEMAND ANSWERS..

..BECAUSE THAT IS WHAT PEOPLE DO.

I'VE HAD QUITE A DAY, MUM, BUT NOW IT ALL MAKES SENSE.

CLARA! THE PIES ARE ALL BAKED!

HA! OOOH!

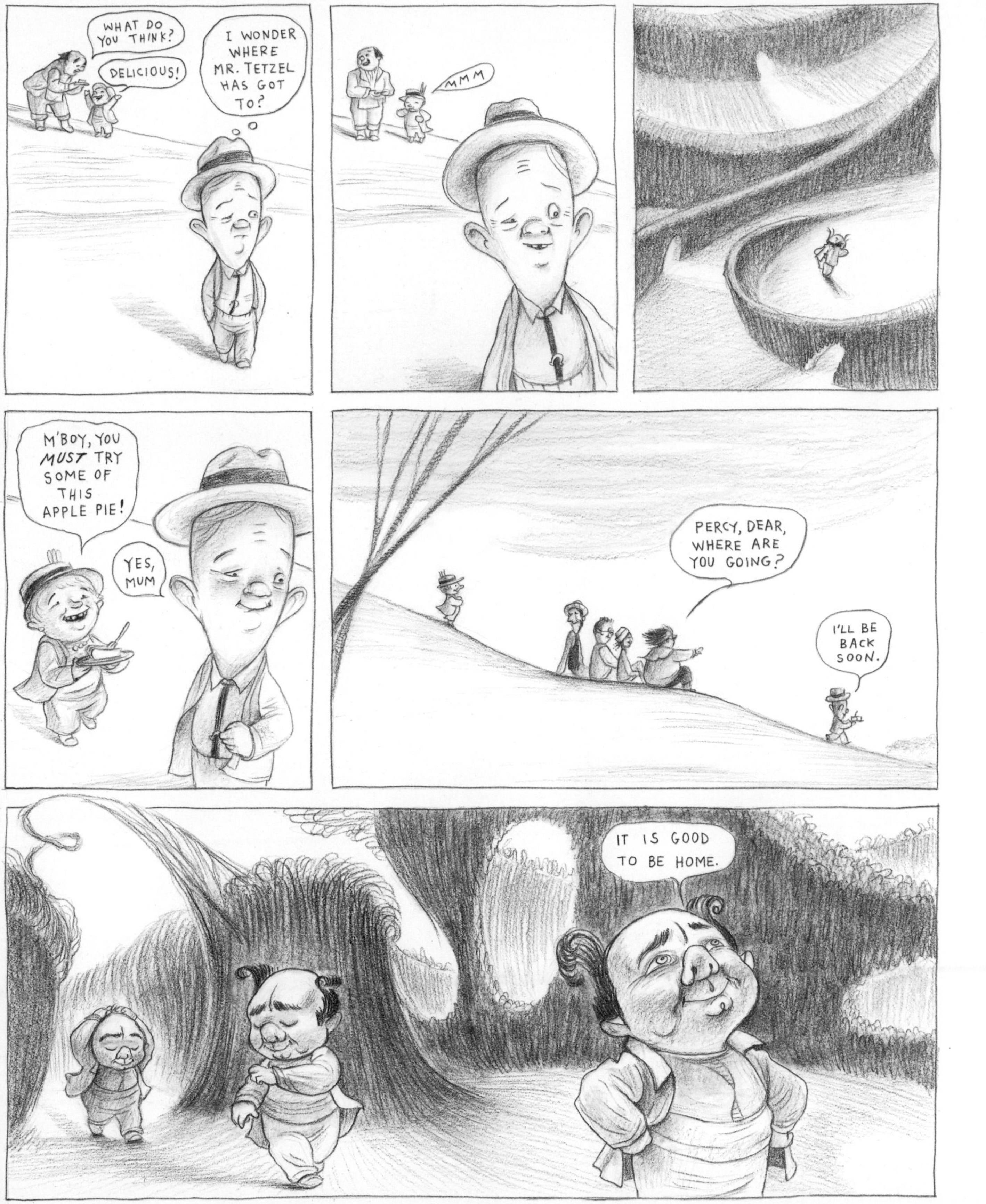
WHAT DO YOU THINK?
DELICIOUS!
I WONDER WHERE MR. TETZEL HAS GOT TO?
MMM
M'BOY, YOU *MUST* TRY SOME OF THIS APPLE PIE!
YES, MUM
PERCY, DEAR, WHERE ARE YOU GOING?
I'LL BE BACK SOON.
IT IS GOOD TO BE HOME.

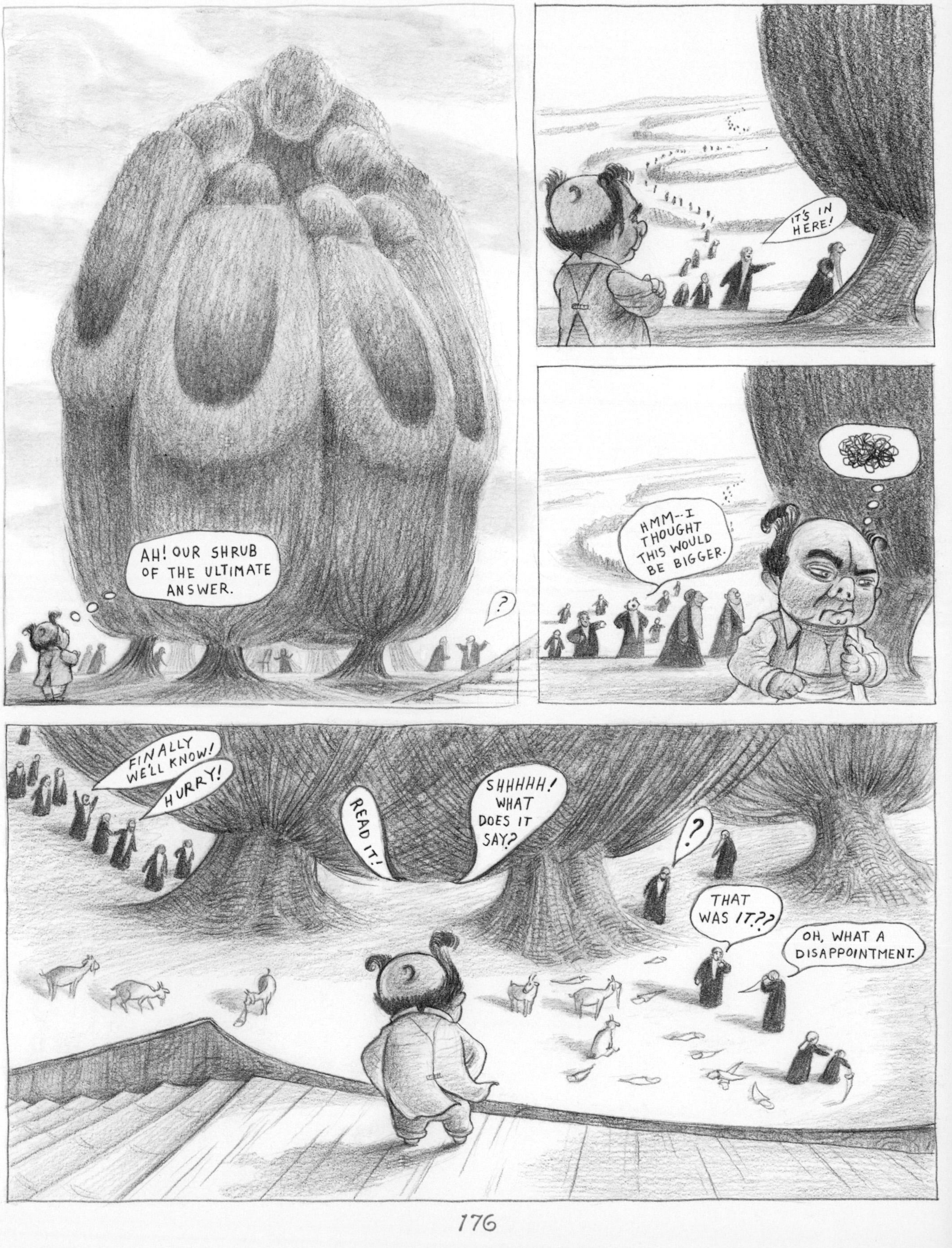
AH! OUR SHRUB OF THE ULTIMATE ANSWER.
?
IT'S IN HERE!
HMM--I THOUGHT THIS WOULD BE BIGGER.
FINALLY WE'LL KNOW!
HURRY!
READ IT!
SHHHHH! WHAT DOES IT SAY?
?
THAT WAS IT???
OH, WHAT A DISAPPOINTMENT.

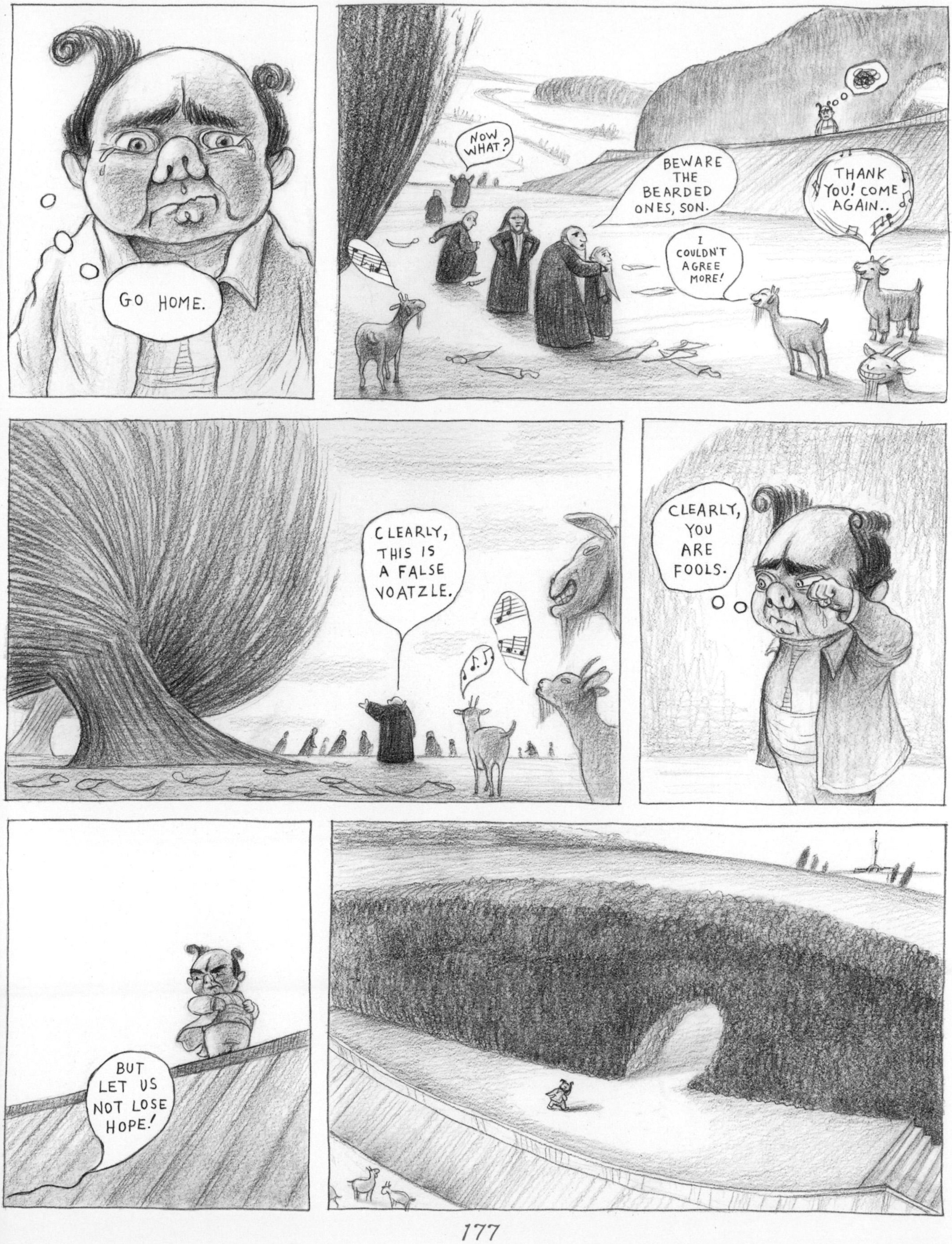
GO HOME.
NOW WHAT?
BEWARE THE BEARDED ONES, SON.
I COULDN'T AGREE MORE!
THANK YOU! COME AGAIN..
CLEARLY, THIS IS A FALSE VOATZLE.
CLEARLY, YOU ARE FOOLS.
BUT LET US NOT LOSE HOPE!

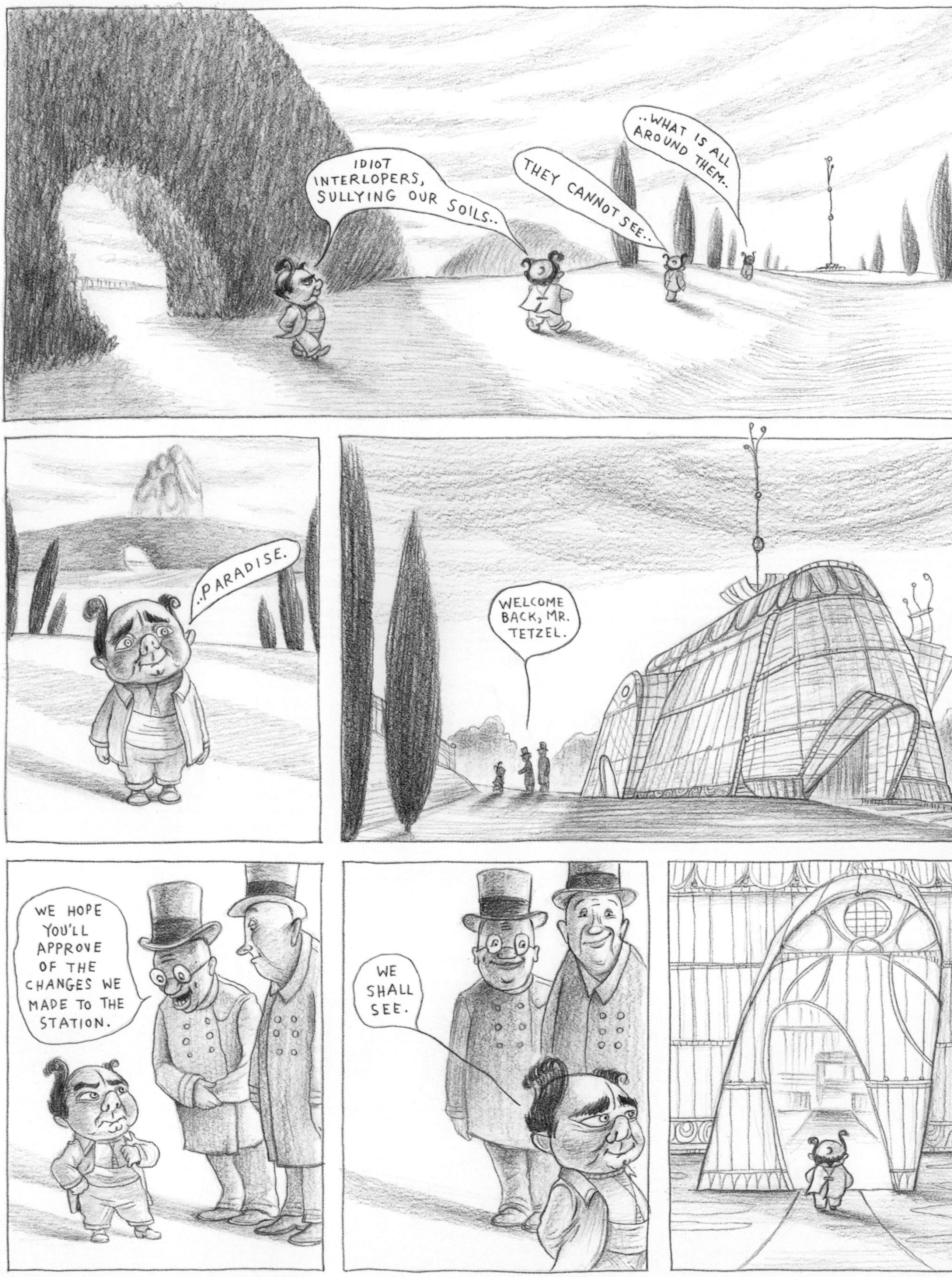
IDIOT INTERLOPERS, SULLYING OUR SOILS..
THEY CANNOT SEE..
..WHAT IS ALL AROUND THEM..
..PARADISE.
WELCOME BACK, MR. TETZEL.
WE HOPE YOU'LL APPROVE OF THE CHANGES WE MADE TO THE STATION.
WE SHALL SEE.

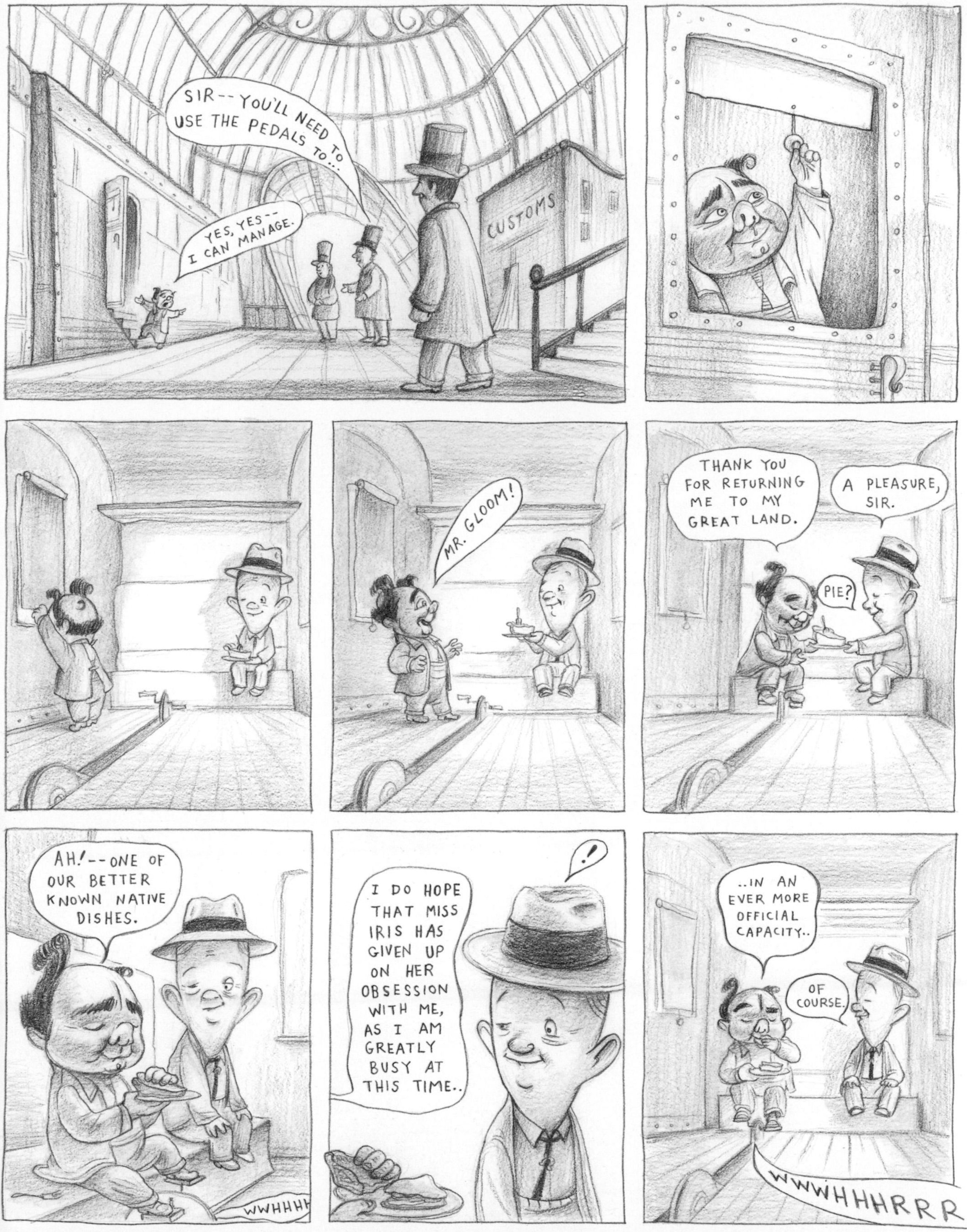
SIR--YOU'LL NEED TO USE THE PEDALS TO...
YES, YES--I CAN MANAGE.
CUSTOMS
MR. GLOOM!
THANK YOU FOR RETURNING ME TO MY GREAT LAND.
A PLEASURE, SIR.
PIE?
AH!--ONE OF OUR BETTER KNOWN NATIVE DISHES.
WWHHHH
!
I DO HOPE THAT MISS IRIS HAS GIVEN UP ON HER OBSESSION WITH ME, AS I AM GREATLY BUSY AT THIS TIME..
..IN AN EVER MORE OFFICIAL CAPACITY..
OF COURSE.
WWWHHHRRR

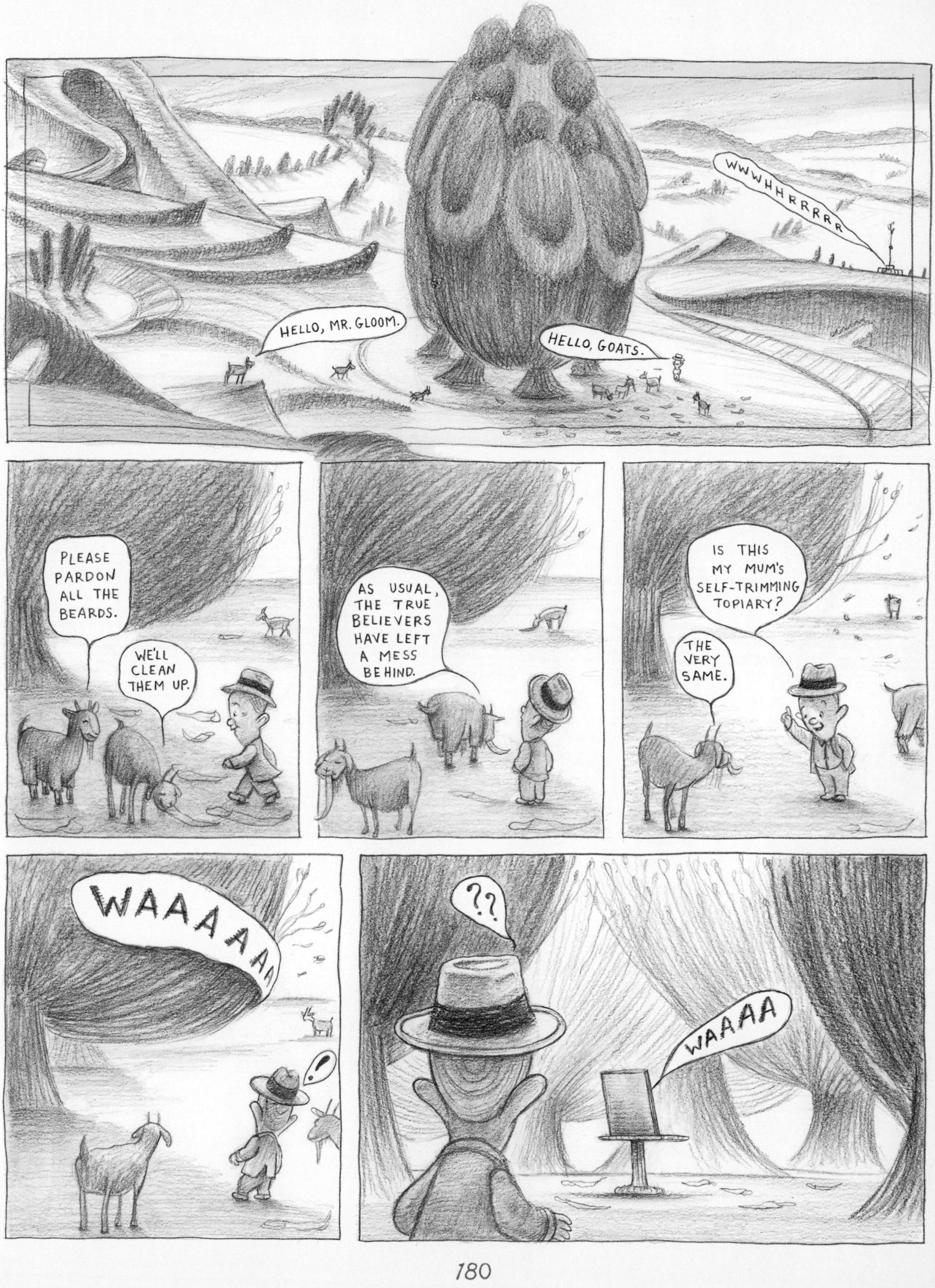
WWWHHRRRRRR
HELLO, MR. GLOOM.
HELLO, GOATS.
PLEASE PARDON ALL THE BEARDS.
WE'LL CLEAN THEM UP.
AS USUAL, THE TRUE BELIEVERS HAVE LEFT A MESS BEHIND.
IS THIS MY MUM'S SELF-TRIMMING TOPIARY?
THE VERY SAME.
WAAAAAA
!
??
WAAAA

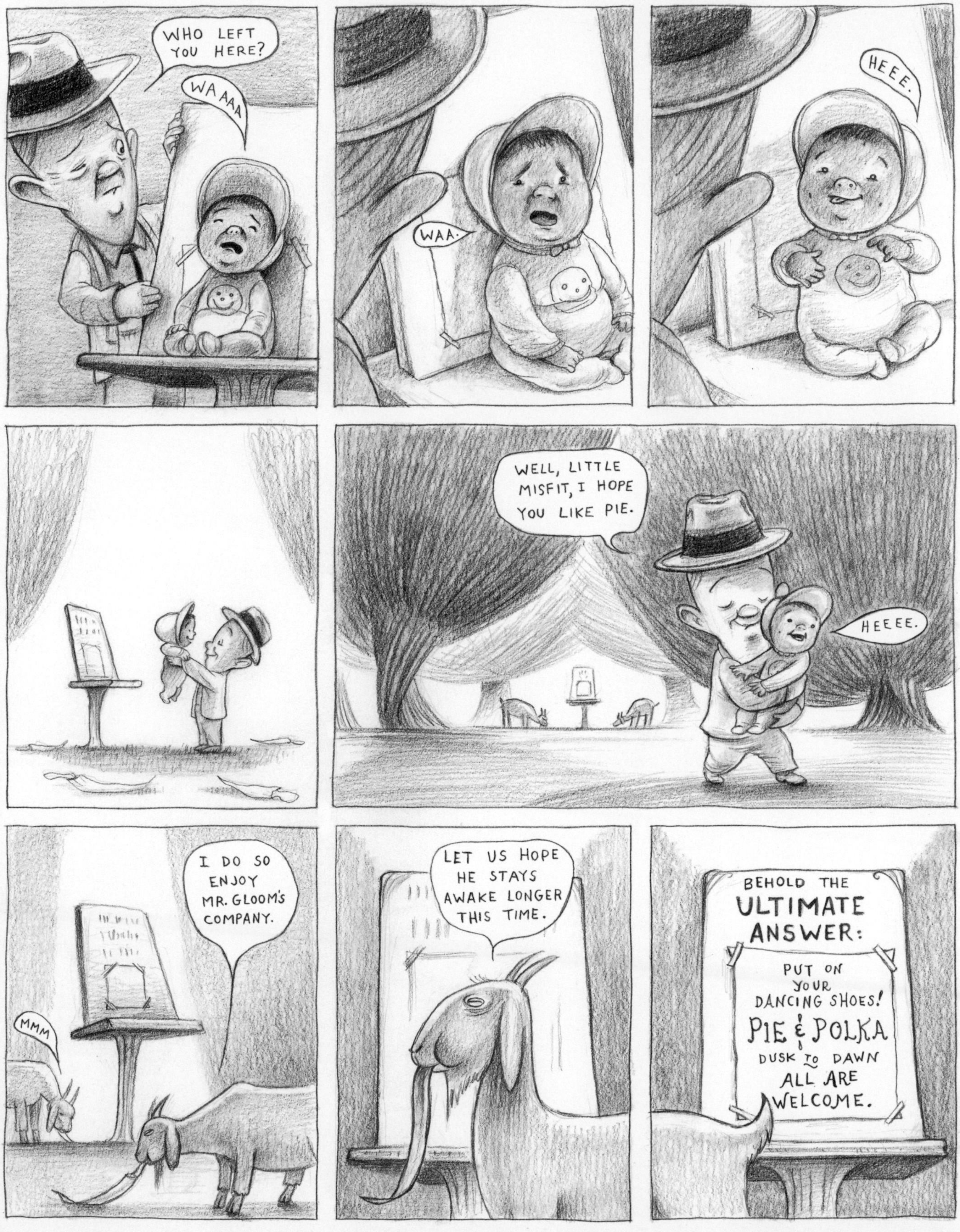
WHO LEFT YOU HERE?
WA AAA
WAA.
HEEE.
WELL, LITTLE MISFIT, I HOPE YOU LIKE PIE.
HEEEE.
MMM
I DO SO ENJOY MR. GLOOM'S COMPANY.
LET US HOPE HE STAYS AWAKE LONGER THIS TIME.
BEHOLD THE ULTIMATE ANSWER:
PUT ON YOUR DANCING SHOES!
PIE & POLKA
DUSK TO DAWN
ALL ARE WELCOME.

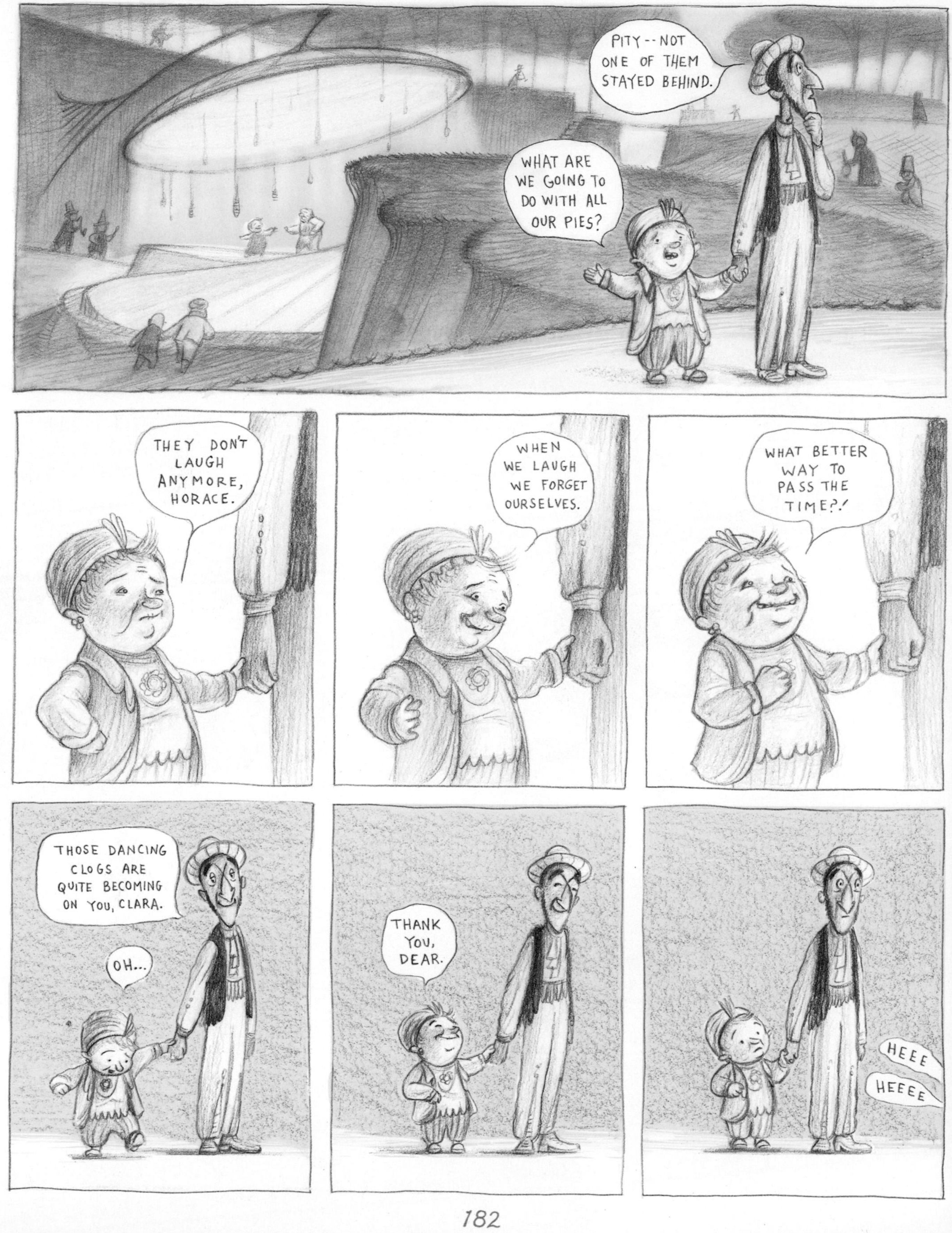
PITY -- NOT ONE OF THEM STAYED BEHIND.
WHAT ARE WE GOING TO DO WITH ALL OUR PIES?
THEY DON'T LAUGH ANYMORE, HORACE.
WHEN WE LAUGH WE FORGET OURSELVES.
WHAT BETTER WAY TO PASS THE TIME?!
THOSE DANCING CLOGS ARE QUITE BECOMING ON YOU, CLARA.
OH...
THANK YOU, DEAR.
HEEE
HEEEE